BY THE EDITORS OF

CONSUMER GUIDE®

The Ultimate Baby Name Book

Consultant:
Cleveland Kent Evans, Ph.D.
American Name Society

Table of Contents

Consultant and Contributing Writer: Dr. Cleveland Kent Evans annually conducts one of the most comprehensive surveys on name usage in the United States. His current work in given names involves personality, social psychology, anthropology, and popular culture. He has written many articles for popular and scholarly publications and has appeared on both radio and television programs. Dr. Evans is currently associate professor of psychology at Bellevue College. He is a member of the American Name Society.

Contributing Writer: Kelsey Harder

NAMES FOR BOYS

NAMES FOR GIRLS

Introduction

What Will We Name Our Baby?

Some parents know exactly what they'll name their baby long before the child is born. They have a favorite name that they're sure will be just right for their child, or there's a family name that they want to pass on to the next generation. But most parents are not very sure about their baby's name. They know that the choice of a name is the first of many important decisions they'll make for their child, and they want to make the best choice, because their child will probably use this name for his or her entire life.

The Ultimate Baby Name Book is designed to help you make this important decision and to find the best name for your baby. The first step in this exciting process is to consider as many names as you can. In this book, you'll find thousands of names. Many of these names have a brief but interesting write-up about the name's origin and history, along with a list of famous people with the name, nicknames, other spellings, and variations. Reading about the names that appeal to you will help you pick a name that says exactly what you want your baby's name to say. You'll be especially interested in the name's origin if you want to choose a name that reflects your ethnic background. You'll be interested in the name's history whether you're looking for a name that is popular today or one that is more nostalgic. You'll want to know about famous people or well-known characters from movies and literature who have had the name, because this is part of the heritage you pass on to your child with the name. If you want your baby to have an unusual name, you may want to choose one of the many you can find in this book.

Expert Advice

Although you're free to give your baby any name you choose, deciding what to call your baby shouldn't be put off until the last minute. Parents are known to behave irrationally at the time of a baby's birth, and they should remember that their spur-of-the-moment inspiration for their baby's name will affect that child for a lifetime. Before you choose a name, take time to ask yourself a few questions:

Is the name easy to spell and to pronounce?
Is it easy to remember?

What nicknames can be derived from it?

Do the initials form a word? If so, is that word likely to prove embarrassing in any way?

Does the name fit the gender of the child?

We also recommend that you give your child a full name rather than a diminutive form of the name. A name that's cute for a baby may not age well. Katherine Louise is preferable to Katie Lou. You can always give a child a nickname, and the traditional form will remain his or her legal name.

Use care in naming your child after a well-known, living person, such as a politician or entertainer. You cannot predict the future of anyone's career, and your child might be stuck with a name that has a negative connotation.

Consider your last name, especially if it's hyphenated. Does the first name you've selected flow easily with the middle and last name? Also, avoid using first names that, in conjunction with your last name, are too cute, such as Barbie Doll, Crystal Glass, Candy Barr, Phil Fuller, or Sandy Rhodes.

Both parents should agree on the baby's name well in advance of the due date. Once you've decided on a name, you should try to stick with it and avoid last-minute changes. Read this book with your family, make lists of your favorite names, and discuss your reactions. Your child will appreciate your thoughtfulness.

What's in a Name?

Is it better to have a name common to your age group, one that everyone has heard, or an unusual name, one that may cause comment when people first hear it? Psychologists and sociologists who have studied this question for years still cannot agree on the answer.

On one hand, a great deal of evidence shows that when people hear a particular name, they have strong and specific stereotypes about what sort of person bears that name. For example, most Americans expect a woman named Courtney to be attractive and successful but one named Bertha to be obese and loud. Research has found that teachers may give a higher grade to a school paper by a student named Michael than to one by Hubert, even though the papers are identical. And photographs of attractive young women called Jennifer or Christine are more likely to win a beauty contest than equally attractive pictures labeled Ethel or Gertrude. Much of this research has found a strong correlation between the frequency of a name in our culture and its rated desirability, especially when names for boys are concerned.

On the other hand, research that compares *actual people* with common first names to those with unusual names often shows the latter having an advantage. People with unusual first names are more likely to be listed in *Who's Who* and are more successful as psychologists. College women with uncommon first names score higher on scales of sociability and self-acceptance; they are also more likely to have a positive sense of individuality, which helps them to resist peer pressure.

Why do these different studies seem contradictory? Part of the answer is that the first set of studies forced people to form impressions based on the name alone. In contrast, recent research shows that including information about an actual person compensates for most of the negative effects of stereotypes and creates a different context in which to view a name. For example, if told we were going to meet a man named Igor, we might conjure up the image of an ugly, stupid, and evil character like Frankenstein's henchman. But if Igor turned out to be a handsome and intelligent young man who explained that his parents had admired the composer Igor Stravinsky, we would probably find his name to be intriguing and sophisticated.

Another reason for the conflicting results from this research is that uncommon names and names with negative images are not necessarily the same. Boys called Derry or Nash and girls called Calista or Meadow will have a chance to create their own first impressions, free from established stereotypes. They can develop a positive, individual self-concept unhampered by the negative images that go along with names such as Adolph, Eunice, Minnie, or Elmer.

In the final analysis, of course, your choice of a common or unusual name depends on what you believe is best for your child. After all, there are many occasions in life, such as submitting a job application or seeking admission to college, where a name does have a chance to create a positive image on its own. Having a popular name such as Ashley or Nicholas at such times might be an advantage. If, on the other hand, individuality and creativity are especially important to you, a more unusual name might be better.

But whichever line of thought you follow, remember that a name is more than just a neutral label. The names you give your children will become lasting and very important parts of their self-image. Of course, merely selecting a desirable name for your child does not guarantee happiness and success, but boys called Cobra, Deemon, Lavoris, Notorrious, Rogue, or Taynt and girls called Bilge, Muff, Passion, Sprout, Surreal, or Twinkle will clearly have a hard time overcoming the belligerent or ridiculous images names such as these evoke. (All these names were given to real children born in the United States in 1991!)

After this discussion, if you feel that you would like to ensure that your child either does or does not have a very popular name, review the following list of the 40 most common names given to boys and girls born in the United States in 1991.

Popular Names for Girls		
Ashley	Chelsea	Tiffany
Brittany, Brittney	Elizabeth	Kristen, Kristin
Jessica	Jennifer	Heather
Sarah, Sara	Lauren	Shelby
Amanda	Nicole	Hannah
Megan	Courtney	Erica, Erika
Samantha	Amber	Melissa
Caitlin, Katelyn	Rebecca	Michelle
Kayla	Kelsey	Kelly
Katherine, Catherine	Christina	Taylor
Emily	Danielle	Brianna
Stephanie	Jasmine	Victoria
Rachel	Lindsey, Lindsay	Alyssa
Crystal		

Popular Names for Boys		
Michael	Justin	Brian, Bryan
Christopher	Daniel	Jordan
Joshua	Steven, Stephen	Alexander
Matthew, Mathew	Zachary	Kevin
James	Jonathan	Thomas
Andrew	Robert	Dylan, Dillon
Brandon	Jacob	Corey, Cory
Nicholas	William	Aaron
John, Jon	Anthony	Timothy
Tyler	Kyle	Benjamin
David	Cody	Jeffrey, Jeffery
Joseph	Eric, Erik	Adam
Ryan	Sean, Shawn, Shaun	Richard
Charles		

Today, many parents in the United States want the name that they choose for their baby to reflect their ethnic heritage. Although the names they pick may be unusual in this country, these parents are interested in choosing names that are popular in the country where their ancestors lived. Of course, names in other parts of the world go through fads and fashions just as they do in the United States. The names in the following lists have been recently popular in other parts of the world.

Girls' Names	Boys' Names
Arabic Popular Names	
A'isha	Abdullah
Aminah	Ali
Fatima	Dawud
Khadija	Hasan
Latifah	Jamal
Na'ila	Khalid
Rana	Salih
Sabah	Sayyid
Um-Kalthum	Tawfiq
Zaynab	Yusuf
French Popular Names	
Audrey	Cedric
Aurelie	Guillaume
Celine	Jerome
Elodie	Julien
Emilie	Mathieu
Julie	Mickael
Laetitia	Nicolas
Melanie	Romain
Stephanie	Sebastien
Virginie	Vincent
German Popular Names	
Andrea	Andreas
Anja	Christian
Birgit	Frank
Christiane	Jurgen
Claudia	Markus
Kirsten	Michael
Martina	Peter
Petra	Ralf
Sabine	Stefan
Sandra	Thomas
Susanne	Uwe

Irish Popular Names

Aoife	Brendan
Ciara	Brian
Cliona	Colm
Dearbhail	Conor
Deirdre	Diarmaid
Emer	Donal
Fiona	Finnbar
Niamh	Kevin
Orlaith	Kieran
Sinead	Niall

Israeli Popular Names

Gali	Ariel
Limor	Asaf
Liron	Dan
Nili	Gal
Ofra	Noam
Rotem	Ofer
Ruth	Ron
Tali	Tomer
Vered	Uri
Yardena	Yonatan

Italian Popular Names

Anna	Francesco
Annunziata	Gerardo
Donatella	Giacomo
Elena	Giovanni
Eleonora	Girolamo
Francesca	Giuseppe
Giovanna	Leone
Lucia	Leopoldo
Maria	Lorenzo
Paola	Mario
Rosina	Paolo

Japanese Popular Names

Hiroko	Akira
Junko	Hiroshi
Keiko	Kenji
Machiko	Masao

Mariko	Satoru
Masami	Tadashi
Reiko	Takashi
Sachiko	Takeshi
Toshiko	Yoshiaki
Yoko	Yuji

Russian Popular Names

Amelija	Aleksandr
Anastasija	Anton
Ivanna	Feodor
Katerina	Grigorij
Luiza	Igor
Melanija	Ivan
Nadezda	Leon
Olga	Mikhail
Raisa	Rotislav
Svetlana	Vladimir

Swahili Popular Names

Aisha	Azizi
Aziza	Bakari
Halima	Hamisi
Jamila	Jabari
Kamaria	Kitwana
Layla	Mwinyi
Mwanajuma	Sadiki
Sanura	Salehe
Waseme	Shomari
Zahra	Suberi

Swedish Popular Names

Anna	Anders
Carina	Bjorn
Elisabet	Erik
Eva	Gustaf
Gunilla	Hans
Ingrid	Jorgen
Kristina	Krister
Lena	Mikael
Maria	Per
Monica	Stefan
Ulla	Ulf

Baby Names and Customs

As long as there has been language, there have been names. Naming is the first task of speech through which we differentiate one person or thing from all others. Every society has a naming system, and all these systems have certain common elements. Throughout the world, each child is assigned a sound or series of sounds that will be his or her name. Because that name is a part of the language of the child's parents, it immediately identifies the child as belonging to a particular society. So our names identify us both as individuals and as members of a group.

Throughout Africa, a child's naming day is a festive occasion that usually occurs a week or so after the birth. Girls are named sooner than boys, but only by a day or two. An older person bestows the name, first by whispering it to the baby, because a newborn should know his or her name before anyone else does, then by announcing the name to everyone attending the ceremony.

Many Native Americans developed naming systems in which a person's individual name included the name of his or her clan. For example, all the members of a clan that has the bear as its totem animal have names relating to bears, such as Black-Bear Tracks and Black-Bear Flashing Eyes. In some groups, children are given secret names that are not revealed until the child reaches puberty or another important stage of life. In other Native American nations, an event at a child's birth may become the child's name. Today, a person living on a reservation may have one name at home but a different name when he or she is off the reservation.

In China, all given names are created out of words in the Chinese language and have an obvious, immediate meaning. Names are believed to reflect the character of the person, and great care is taken in selecting a child's name. Usually about a month after the child is born the parents attempt to create an original name. Many girls are given names that signify beauty, such as Sweet Willow or Morning Star. Boys are given names that reflect strength and good health. In rural areas, most Chinese names still include a "generation name," a word or syllable that is the same for all children born in a family in the same generation. Three sisters, for example, might be named Yuan-Chun, Ying-Chun, and Xi-Chun, which mean "First Spring," "Welcome Spring," and "Cherish Spring." With China's one-child policy, this custom is fading in urban areas, but some Americans of Chinese descent continue this tradition by giving all their children names containing the same syllable. Mr. and Mrs. Marson Ma of Detroit, Michigan, for example, have 15 children whose names are Marlene, Marson, Marshall, Martha, Marvin, Marco, Marsha,

Marcus, Margit, Mario, Marlowe, Marla, Marek, Marvel, and Marisa. As shown by this example, most Chinese-Americans give their children American-style first names, although often giving a Chinese-language name as the middle name, as in Brittany Ngon Lee.

Europe has many traditional naming customs. In Iceland, the father's first name is passed on to his child with the addition of "-son" (son of) or "-dottir" (daughter of). This means that last names change with every generation: Einar Jonsson's children will be Stefan Einarsson and Kristin Einarsdottir. In Russia, children have a family name, a given name, and a middle name that is their father's given name. All the children in a family have the same middle name.

In some families, names are influenced by religious customs. Many Roman Catholics name their children after saints. A calendar of saints lists at least one saint for each day of the year, so a child may simply be given the name of the saint on whose day he or she is born. For example, a boy born on July 12 might be named Jason; a girl born on June 19, Elizabeth. Traditional belief holds that this saint is the patron of the child and watches over him or her.

Jewish names are some of the oldest names still in use today. A Jewish boy is named officially when he is circumcised on the eighth day after his birth. A girl is named as soon as possible after her birth. Traditionally, an Ashkenazic Jewish child is not named for a living person for fear that the Angel of Death will mistake the child for the older person if their names are the same.

African-American Names

Since the 1960s, some African-Americans have begun to give their children names from many different African cultures. Some adults have also changed their names to African or Muslim names. Because slaves were often assigned the surnames of their owners and given common first names, choosing African names is a way for African-Americans to acknowledge their heritage before slavery. However, only a few genuine African names, such as Ayana, Kwame, and Sade, have become widely popular in the African-American community. Muslim names from the Arabic language such as Iesha, Jamal, Kareem, and Shakira have actually been more successful recently, even with African-American families who have not adopted the Islamic religion.

African-Americans also commonly create new names for their children by combining their own set of fashionable sounds and syllables. Names for girls formed in this way are called Lakeisha names after one of the prime examples. Lakeisha names are created by linking a fashionable prefix, such as "Sha-," "La-," "Ka-," "Shan-," or "Ty-," with a fashionable suffix, such as "-isha," "-ika," "-onda," "-ae," or "-ice." The resulting names are always accented on the second syllable. Several of these innovative creations, such as Kanisha, Lashonda, Quanisha, Shameka, Shanae, and Shaniqua, have achieved wide popularity in the African-American community, and a few of them, such as Lashay and Latasha, are beginning to be used by people from other ethnic backgrounds. Names for boys that have been created similarly include DeJuan, Deonte, Jamar, Ladarius, and Quantavious.

As this last list of examples shows, African-Americans commonly give sons as well as daughters names that are accented on the second syllable. Other Americans avoid this, and so any boy's name with that sound pattern in American English, such as Bernard, Demetrius, Maurice, or Tyrone, becomes predominantly African-American no matter what its cultural origin. A final factor that makes African-American naming patterns different from those of other groups is that while black parents often name their children after white celebrities, fictional or real, most white parents do not name their children after blacks. This means that most children named after African-American characters such as Jaleesa on *A Different World,* played by Dawnn Lewis, or famous persons such as the singers Sade and Shanice are themselves African-American. The one exception to this is Whitney Houston, whose popularity has inspired many Americans from all ethnic backgrounds to name their daughters Whitney.

Hispanic-American Names

Traditionally, Hispanic-American babies may be given the names of several saints, and both male and female saints are considered appropriate for both boys and girls. Hispanic-Americans often choose names that seem more religious than the names preferred by many other Americans. Boys are often named Jesus, Angel, and Salvador. Girls are often named in honor of the Virgin Mary, using words from her devotional titles such as Araceli, Rocio, Consuelo, Dolores, and Mercedes. Other traditional Spanish names popular in the Hispanic-American community include Carlos, Enrique, Fernando, Francisco, Jaime, Javier, Jorge, Jose, Juan, Julio, Luis, Marcos, and Miguel for boys and Adriana, Beatriz, Carolina, Daniela, Gabriela, Isabel, Maria, and Raquel for girls.

However, not all the names popular with Hispanic-Americans today are traditionally Spanish names. Hector, Oscar, and Rene have long been popular names for boys in Latin America, and non-

Spanish immigrants to Central and South America, as well as the modern media, have introduced many new names just as in the United States and Canada. In particular, Spanish-language television programs called *telenovelas,* most of them produced in Mexico, have popularized the names of their stars and characters wherever they are shown, including in the United States. For example, Vanessa, a very British name invented by English author Jonathan Swift, is now extremely popular in the Hispanic-American community because it was the name of the title character in a television program starring Lucia Mendez, one of Mexico's favorite actresses. Other non-Spanish names now more popular with Latinos than Anglos in the United States include Bianca, Cynthia, Daisy, Evelyn, Karina, Lissette, Tatiana, and Yvette for girls and Christian, Edgar, Edwin, George, Giovanni, Ivan, and Omar for boys. The name Ariel is rapidly becoming popular both for Hispanic-American boys and for girls of other ethnic groups.

Media Influences on Naming

The popularity of Ariel as a name for girls can be traced to the Disney movie *The Little Mermaid,* showing that Hispanic parents are certainly not the only ones affected by modern media when it comes to finding new names for their offspring. Indeed, most names that suddenly become popular are inspired by figures in entertainment or sports, whether they are real actors or athletes such as Ryan O'Neal or Dominique Wilkins or fictional characters such as Jenna Wade on the television program *Dallas.*

Of course, modern parents are not the only ones affected by the media of their day. Thelma, for example, suddenly became a popular name for English and American girls after British author Marie Corelli invented it for the beautiful heroine of her best-selling novel *Thelma,* published in 1887. But since the 1950s, television has been the most effective medium at creating new name fashions. Bailey and Mallory, for example, previously male names, became popular for girls when female characters called Bailey and Mallory appeared on *WKRP in Cincinnati* and *Family Ties,* respectively, in the 1980s. Although a few American parents had named sons Dylan after Welsh poet Dylan Thomas or perhaps musician Bob Dylan in the 1960s, the name exploded in popularity in the 1990s only after the character Dylan McKay appeared on *Beverly Hills 90210.* As another example, Hayden was a rare name until actor Craig T. Nelson's character Hayden Fox on *Coach* inspired many parents to choose this name.

Daytime soap operas also affect what Americans name their children. Kayla, now one of the top ten names for girls in the United

States, barely existed before Kayla Brady appeared on *Days of Our Lives* in 1982. More recently, Macy has become fashionable for girls since Macy Spectra Forrester began going through her fictional crises on *The Bold and the Beautiful*. Caleb, Seth, Angel, Lily, and Sierra owe part of their popularity to *As the World Turns*, and although it did not stay on the air, *Santa Barbara* managed to establish Eden and Laken as names for American girls before it was canceled.

Popular music is another part of the entertainment industry that affects what Americans name their children. Rock ballads by the groups Lookingglass and Fleetwood Mac inspired many girls to be named Brandy and Rhiannon. Mariah Carey has recently joined Whitney Houston as a pop singer with many namesakes, and though Elvis has never really caught on as a name for boys, there are signs that Presley may be about to take off as a name for girls! Some parents even name their daughters after rock music groups, as exemplified by the Chantels in the 1950s and Tesla in the 1990s.

People Who Name Themselves

All new parents hope to come up with a name that their child will use and enjoy throughout his or her life, but for various reasons many people choose to change their names. Here are the names of some well-known people and their original names:

Famous Names	Original Names
Muhammad Ali	Cassius Marcellus Clay, Jr.
Woody Allen	Allen Stewart Konigsberg
Lauren Bacall	Betty Joan Perski
Anne Bancroft	Annemarie Italiano
Brigitte Bardot	Camille Javal
Jack Benny	Benjamin Kubelsky
George Burns	Nathan Birnbaum
Richard Burton	Richard Walter Jenkins
Red Buttons	Aaron Chwatt
Michael Caine	Maurice Joseph Micklewhite
Chubby Checker	Ernest Evans
Cher	Cherilyn Sarkisian
Alice Cooper	Vincent Damon Furnier
Joan Crawford	Lucille Le Sueur
Rodney Dangerfield	Jacob Cohen
Bobby Darin	Walden Robert Cassotto
Kirk Douglas	Issur Danielovitch Demsky

Bob Dylan	Robert Allen Zimmerman
Douglas Fairbanks	Julius Ullman
W.C. Fields	William Claude Dukenfield
Judy Garland	Frances Gumm
Cary Grant	Alexander Archibald Leach
Harry Houdini	Ehrich Weiss
Elton John	Reginald Kenneth Dwight
Boris Karloff	William Henry Pratt
Marilyn Monroe	Norma Jean Baker
Mike Nichols	Michael Igor Peschowsky
Roy Rogers	Leonard Slye
Mickey Rooney	Joe Yule, Jr.
Jane Seymour	Joyce Frankenberg
Danny Thomas	Amos Jacobs
Tina Turner	Annie Mae Bullock
John Wayne	Marion Michael Morrison
Stevie Wonder	Steveland Morris Hardaway

Naming Your Baby

The choice of your baby's name is a very important decision, and this book is designed to help you choose a name that both you and your child will enjoy for a lifetime. *The Ultimate Baby Name Book* presents a comprehensive selection of names from around the world and gives you information about each name. You and your family should take time to look through the whole book and make a list of the names you like. Then spend some time reading about these names. The origin and history of some names may surprise you; other names will prove to be just what you're looking for. When you find that a name is a nickname, variation, or form of another name, be sure to look up the original name (printed in boldface type) to learn more about the name you're considering. As you read this book and talk with your family about names that you like, your list of possible names will grow shorter, and a name that you feel is the very best name for your baby boy or girl will begin to stand out.

A This one-letter name could be interpreted as meaning "excellent" or "the best." It is still very rare but is now being chosen by a few parents inspired by actor A Martinez of television's *L.A. Law*. His original first name was Adolfo, which he drastically shortened to avoid the present negative connotations of the name **Adolf.**

Aarao (see **Aaron**)

Aaro (see **Aaron**)

Aaron Hebrew *Aharon*, perhaps "enlightened" or "shining." Aaron was the older brother of Moses. Because Aaron was born during the Israelite bondage in Egypt, his name may also be derived from an Egyptian word meaning "mountain," referring to an exalted religious leader. In the 1980s, this biblical name suddenly became more popular than it had been in years.

Famous names: Aaron Burr (3rd U.S. vice-president)
               Aaron Copland (composer)

Nicknames: **Ari, Ronnie, Ronny**

Other spelling: **Arron**

Variations: **Aarao** (Portuguese), **Aaro** (Finnish), **Aaronas** (Latvian), **Aronne** (Italian), **Aron** (Rumanian), **Haroun** (Arabic)

Aaronas (see **Aaron**)

Abbot, Abbott Aramaic *abba,* "father." *Abba* was a title of respect in Aramaic, the language that Jesus and the disciples used. In the sense of "father," it was used by Christians as a title for the head, or supervisor, of a monastery. Although seldom used now as a given name, Abbot occurred sporadically during the 17th and 18th centuries.

Famous name: Abbot Thayer (American painter)

Nicknames: **Ab, Abb**

Ab (see **Abbot, Abner**)

Abb (see **Abbot, Abner**)

Abe (see **Abraham**)

Abel Hebrew *hebel,* "breath" or "evanescent"; also, possibly connected with Assyrian *ablu,* "son." Abel was the second son of Adam and Eve. He was killed by his brother Cain in the first murder, as recorded in the Book of Genesis.

Famous name: Abel Green (magazine editor)

Abie (see **Abraham**)

Abner Hebrew "father of light." In the Bible, Abner was the uncle of King Saul and commander of his army. He supported Ishbosheth against David, the king of Israel. After slaying Joab's brother, Abner was attempting to work out a compromise with David when Joab killed him. Al Capp used the name for the title character of his long-running comic strip, *Li'l Abner.*

Famous name: Abner Doubleday (legendary inventor of baseball)

Nicknames: **Ab, Abb**

Variation: **Avner** (Hebrew)

Abraham Hebrew "father of many." In the Book of Genesis, the founder of the Hebrew people was originally named Abram, but his name was changed at God's command: "Neither shall thy name any more be called Abram, but thy name shall be Abraham; for a father of many nations I have made thee." Like most Old Testament names, this name was not widely used until the time of the Protestant Reformation in the 16th century.

Famous name: Abraham Lincoln (16th U.S. president)

Nicknames: **Abe, Abie, Bram**

Variations: **Abramo** (Italian), **Ibrahim** (Arabic)

Abramo (see **Abraham**)

Ace Latin "unit"; metaphorically, "the best." Ace is usually a nickname, but it can also be a given name. During World War

I, pilots who destroyed a certain number of enemy planes, usually three, were given the honorary title Ace.

Famous name: James "Ace" Wilson (baseball player)

Variations: **Acey, Acie**

Acey (see **Ace**)

Achill (see **Achilles**)

Achille (see **Achilles**)

Achilles Greek, meaning unknown. Achilles was a legendary warrior and the chief of the Myrmidons. He is the main character in Homer's *Iliad,* where he represents the Greek character and is a symbol for Greek nationalism. Achilles killed Hector, the great Trojan, but was himself slain by Paris, whose abduction of Helen caused the Trojan War. Achilles died when the arrow shot by Paris entered his heel, the only vulnerable spot on his body. This is the origin of the term "Achilles' heel," which connotes any small weakness that can cause physical trouble. The name is not often used in the United States, but was formerly well known in Europe.

Famous name: Achilles Tatius (Greek rhetorician)

Nicknames: **Quina, Quito**

Variations: **Achill** (Hungarian), **Achille** (Italian), **Achilleus** (Greek), **Ahil** (Bulgarian), **Akhylliy** (Ukrainian), **Akilles** (Norwegian), **Aquiles** (Portuguese and Spanish)

Achilleus (see **Achilles**)

Acie (see **Ace**)

Acton Old English *actun,* "town by the oaks." In medieval times, place names often became the nicknames of people who came from that place. These nicknames later became hereditary surnames. Acton is a surname, but it can be used as a first name.

Ad (see **Adam, Adlai**)

Adair Scottish form of **Edgar.** This name has a long Scottish tradition. Adventurous Scots took it with them to England, India, and the Americas. James Adair was an English trader with the Chickasaw and Cherokee Indians; he wrote a history of them in which he claimed that they descended from the

Hebrews. Some children were named in his honor, introducing this surname as a first name.

Adam Hebrew *adama,* "earth, clay." As the first masculine name in the Bible, it is one of the oldest recorded names. Because of Adam's fall from grace, the name was seldom used by Jewish families until the 20th century. As a Christian name, it was well used in England and Scotland during the Middle Ages and until the 18th century. It's become popular since the 1970s.

Famous names: Adam Clayton Powell (clergyman and member of Congress)
Adam Smith (economist)

Nicknames: **Ad, Ade, Addy**

Variations: **Adamo** (Italian), **Adan** (Spanish), **Adao** (Portuguese), **Adhamh** (Irish and Scottish)

Adamo (see **Adam**)

Adan (see **Adam**)

Adao (see **Adam**)

Addy (see **Adam, Adlai**)

Ade (see **Adam, Adrian**)

Adelbert (see **Albert**)

Adhamh (see **Adam**)

Adlai Hebrew "Yahweh is justice." The name occurs only once in the Bible; it's noted as the name of the father of Shaphat, the shepherd for King David. But it has become well known through the Stevenson family, in which members of three generations have had this unusual name: Adlai Ewing Stevenson (U.S. vice-president), Adlai Ewing Stevenson, Jr. (statesman, diplomat, ambassador, and twice a candidate for president of the United States), and Adlai Ewing Stevenson III (U.S. senator).

Nicknames: **Ad, Addy**
Variation: **Adley**

Adler Old German "eagle." This name is usually a surname, but it is sometimes used as a given name.

Adley (see Adlai)

Adolf (see Adolph)

Adolfo (see Adolph)

Adolph Old German "noble wolf" from *athal* [noble] + *wolfa* [wolf].
Adolph was once a favorite German name, but since World
War II, few parents have chosen this name because of its
association with Adolf Hitler. However, Adolph has an ancient
and honorable tradition as a name of noble leaders and saints.
The German Bishop Adolphus was granted sainthood for his
work among the poor, and Adolphus has also been a common
name in the royal family of Sweden.
   Famous names: Adolph Coors (businessman)
                    Adolf Krebs (biochemist)
                    Adolphe Menjou (actor)
   Nicknames: **Dolf, Dolfie, Dolph**
   Variations: **Adolf** (German), **Adolfo** (Spanish), **Adolphe**
        (French), **Adolpho** (Spanish), **Adolphus** (Latin)

Adolphe (see Adolph)

Adolpho (see Adolph)

Adolphus (see Adolph)

Adrian Latin *Hadrianus,* "from the Adriatic." To the Roman, this
name indicated that a person was from Adria, or Atri, on the
Adriatic Sea. The famous Roman emperor Hadrian, a military
genius, built a wall of defense in the Roman province of Britain
between Solway Firth and the mouth of the Tyne. Six popes
have taken the name, including Adrian IV, the only English
pope. Currently, Adrian is becoming more popular in the
United States.
   Famous name: Adrian Bolt (conductor)
   Nicknames: **Ade, Adry, Hadrian**
   Variations: **Adriano** (Italian), **Adrien** (French), **Andreian**
        (Russian), **Arrian** (Scandinavian)

Adriano (see Adrian)

Adrien (see Adrian)

Adry (see Adrian)

Afonso (see **Alfonso**)

Agostinho (see **Augustus**)

Agostino (see **Augustus**)

Agustin (see **Augustus**)

Ahil (see **Achilles**)

Aidan Gaelic *Aedan,* form of *Aed,* "fire." Aidan is the name of an Irish-born monk sent from Iona to Scotland to convert the then-heathen English to Christianity.
    Famous name: Aidan Quinn (actor)

Akeem Probably a Nigerian form of **Hakeem.** This name continues to be quite popular with African-Americans, even though the man who made it famous, Nigerian-born basketball player Akeem Olajuwon, now prefers to be known by the more proper Muslim form **Hakeem.**

Akhylliy (see **Achilles**)

Akilles (see **Achilles**)

Akoni (see **Anthony**)

Aksel (see **Axel**)

Al (see **Alan, Alastair, Albert, Alexander, Alfonso, Alfred, Alton, Alvin**)

Alain (see **Alan**)

Alan Celtic, meaning uncertain, perhaps "rock." The name was introduced into England in 1066 by the Norman leader Alain, earl of Brittany. After it entered Britain, it also became popular in Scotland and Wales. The name also became standard in English ballads. Alan-a-Dale was a companion of Robin Hood in some of the ballads of the English outlaw hero.
    Famous names: Alan Jay Lerner (dramatist)
                  Alan B. Shepard, Jr. (astronaut)
                  Alan Thicke (television host and actor)
    Nicknames: **Al, Allie**
    Other spellings: **Allan, Allen, Alyn**
    Variations: **Alain** (French), **Alano** (Spanish), **Alanus** (Latin)

Alano (see **Alan**)

Alanus (see **Alan**)

Alasdair (see **Alastair**)

Alastair, Alistair Gaelic form of **Alexander.** Most American
parents who name their babies Alastair are not thinking about
a connection to the name Alexander, which is currently very
popular. Percy Bysshe Shelley used the name in "Alastor, or
the Spirit of Solitude," a semiautobiographical poem.

Famous name: Alistair Cooke (journalist)

Nicknames: **Al, Alec**

Other spelling: **Alasdair**

Variations: **Alaster** (English and Scottish), **Alastor**

Alaster (see **Alastair**)

Alastor (see **Alastair**)

Albert Old German *Adalbert,* "noble and bright," from *athal* [noble]
+ *berhta* [bright]. There are several saints with this name,
including St. Albert the Great, a 13th-century monk known for
his study of the natural sciences, which earned him the
nickname "Universal Doctor" but also caused him to be
suspected of using magic. The name became extremely popular
after Albert Francis Augustus Charles Emmanuel married
Queen Victoria of England in 1840. It is much less popular
today.

Famous name: Albert Einstein (physicist)

Nicknames: **Al, Bert, Bertie, Beto, Tito**

Variations: **Adelbert** (Dutch), **Albertko** (Slovakian), **Alberto**
(Portuguese, Spanish, and Italian), **Albertok** (Polish),
Albertukas (Latvian), **Albrecht, Alpo** (Finnish), **Alvertos**
(Greek), **Aubert** (French), **Bechtel** (German), **Delbert**

Albertko (see **Albert**)

Alberto Spanish, Italian, and Portuguese form of **Albert.** This
name continues to be common in the U.S. Hispanic
community.

Famous names: Alberto Salazar (marathoner)
                        Alberto Tomba (Olympic skier)

Albertok (see **Albert**)

Albertukas (see **Albert**)

Albrecht (see **Albert**)

Aldis (see **Aldous**)

Aldo (see **Aldous**)

Aldon (see **Alton**)

Aldos (see **Aldous**)

Aldous Variation of *Aldo,* German "old" or "wise." The name was
found in England as early as the 13th century and may date
back to the Norman Conquest. The Aldine editions are early
printed volumes of Greek and Latin authors, which were
named for the Venetian printer Aldus Manutius. He was also
the inventor of italic type.
Famous name: Aldous Huxley (novelist)
Variations: **Aldis, Aldo, Aldos, Aldus** (modern Latin), **Eldon**

Aldus (see **Aldous**)

Alec Scottish form of **Alexander.** This name is rapidly increasing in
use, with some parents undoubtedly being inspired by the
recent fame of actor Alec Baldwin. Most modern parents don't
seem to mind that "smart aleck" has been a common term for a
know-it-all since the 1870s.
Famous name: Sir Alec Guinness (actor)
Other spelling: **Aleck**

Aleck (see **Alec**)

Alejandro Spanish form of **Alexander,** commonly used by Hispanic
parents in the United States.
Famous names: Alejandro Pena (baseball player)
Alejandro Portes (sociologist)
Other spelling: **Alexandro**

Alek (see **Alexander**)

Aleksander (see **Alexander**)

Alessandro (see **Alexander**)

Alex This short form of **Alexander** is now also popular as a first name in its own right, partly because of Alex Keaton, the character played by Michael J. Fox on the television series *Family Ties.*

Variation: **Alika** (Hawaiian)

Alexander Greek "defender of men." In the *Iliad,* Homer sometimes calls Paris, the son of Priam, Alexandros. It's also another name for the goddess Hera. Alexander the Great was a Greek general who conquered vast amounts of territory around the Mediterranean and established an empire. The name has been especially popular in Scotland for over 700 years, and it is enjoying a strong revival in the United States, where it is now one of the 50 most popular names for boys, and in England.

Famous names: Alexander Graham Bell (inventor of the telephone)
Alexander Fleming (discoverer of penicillin)
Alexander Pope (poet)

Nicknames: **Al, Alec, Alek, Alex, Sandy**

Variations: **Alastair** (Gaelic), **Alejandro** (Spanish), **Aleksander** (Polish), **Alessandro** (Italian), **Alexandr** (Czech), **Alexandre** (French), **Sandor** (Hungarian)

Alexandr (see **Alexander**)

Alexandre (see **Alexander**)

Alexandro (see **Alejandro**)

Alexis Greek "defender, helper." Like **Angel** and **Ariel,** this was originally a male name and is still often used for boys by Hispanics, but now is almost exclusively a name for girls in other American communities. Alexis de Tocqueville was an early 19th-century French author whose books about his travels in the United States are still prized for the insights they give into American character and values.

Alf (see **Alfred, Alfonso**)

Alfa (see **Alfonso**)

Alfie (see **Alfred, Alfonso**)

Alfonsin (see **Alfonso**)

Alfonso Old German *Adolfuns,* "noble and eager," from *athal* [noble] + *funsa* [ready]. This Spanish royal name was brought to Spain by the Visigoths, and there have been several kings of Spain and Portugal of this name. Alfonso X of Spain, known as Alfonso the Wise, was a noted astronomer; a crater on the moon was named in his honor.

Famous names: Alphonse Daudet (novelist)
                     Alphonsus Rodriguez (saint)
                     Alphonso Smith (basketball player)

Nicknames: **Al, Alf, Alfie, Foncho, Fonz, Fonzie, Fonzo, Poncho, Ponso**

Variations: **Afonso** (Portuguese), **Alfa** (Czech), **Alfonsin** (Spanish), **Alfonz** (Slovakian), **Alifonzo, Alonso, Alonzo, Alphons** (German), **Alphonse, Alphonsus** (Latin)

Alfonz (see **Alfonso**)

Alfred Old English *Aelfred* from *aelf* [elf] + *raed* [counsel]. In the mythology and traditions of Germanic and English countries, elves are considered to be wise and good counselors. This belief is reflected in the name of Alfred the Great, last major king of England before the Norman Conquest. Other English kings before Alfred had also carried the name. It was in common use until the 16th century and came back into fashion in the 18th century when Old English names became popular. However, it is not often given to American boys today.

Famous names: Alfred, Lord Tennyson (poet)
                     Alfred Hitchcock (movie director)
                     Alfred Nobel (inventor and initiator of the Nobel Prize)
                     Alfred Emanuel Smith (governor of New York)

Nicknames: **Al, Alf, Alfie, Alfy, Fito, Fred, Freddie, Fredo**

Variations: **Alfredas** (Lithuanian), **Alfredo** (Spanish and Italian), **Alfredos** (Greek), **Avery, Elfred, Lafredo**

Alfredas (see **Alfred**)

Alfredo Spanish, Italian, and Portuguese form of **Alfred.** The name is still fairly popular with Hispanic-Americans.

Nicknames: **Feyo, Fito, Fredo**

Variation: **Lafredo**

Alfredos (see **Alfred**)

Alfy (see **Alfred**)

Ali Arabic and Swahili "placed on the highest." Many African names are of Muslim origin, especially in the countries of North and East Africa. Ali is occasionally used among African-Americans today.
Famous name: Muhammad Ali (boxer)

Alifonzo (see **Alfonso**)

Alika (see **Alex**)

Allan Variation of **Alan.**
Famous name: Allan Pinkerton (detective)

Allen (see **Alan**)

Allie (see **Alan, Alton**)

Alois (see **Louis**)

Aloisius (see **Louis**)

Alonso, Alonzo Spanish short forms of **Alfonso.** For unknown reasons, this was a fairly popular name with Anglo-Americans in the United States during the 19th century. It is mostly being used in the African-American community today.
Famous name: Alonzo G. Decker (cofounder, Black & Decker Co.)
Nicknames: **Lon, Lonnie, Lonny**

Aloys (see **Louis**)

Aloysius (see **Louis**)

Alphons (see **Alfonso**)

Alphonse (see **Alfonso**)

Alphonsus (see **Alfonso**)

Alpo (see **Albert**)

Alten (see **Alton**)

Alton Old English *ald-tun,* "old town," or *aewiell-tun,* "town at head of the stream." Several towns in the United States are named Alton (Illinois, Missouri, and New Hampshire). They were named for early settlers, reversing the tradition of people taking their names from the place they live. Alton, Illinois, for example, was named for Alton Easton, the son of the town's founder.
Famous name: Alton Lennon (member of Congress)
Nicknames: **Al, Allie**
Variations: **Aldon, Alten**

Aluin (see **Alvin**)

Aluino (see **Alvin**)

Alv (see **Alvin**)

Alvertos (see **Albert**)

Alvin Old English *Aethelwine,* "noble friend," from *aethel* [noble] + *wine* [friend]; or *Aelfwine* from *aelf* [elf] + *wine* [friend]. An Old English compound name, Alvin has never been very popular. In the early 20th century in the southern part of the United States, many boys were named Alvin because of the heroism of Sergeant Alvin Cullum York in World War I. Modern Americans are likely to associate the name with the mischievous cartoon character Alvin the Chipmunk. The name is now more popular with African-Americans than with other ethnic groups.
Famous name: Alvin Ailey (choreographer)
Nicknames: **Al, Alv, Alvy**
Variations: **Aluin** (French), **Aluino, Alvino** (Italian and Spanish), **Alwin** (German), **Alwyn, Aylwin, Elvin, Elwin**

Alvino (see **Alvin**)

Alvy (see **Alvin**)

Alwin, Alwyn (see **Alvin**)

Alyn (see **Alan**)

Amadee (see **Amadeus**)

Amadeo (see **Amadeus**)

Amadeus Latin "lover of God." Several saints have been named Amadeus, including Amadeus of Lausanne and Amadeus of Portugal, who reformed the Franciscan Order. Amadeus IX of Saxony was beatified in 1677. Amadis of Gaul was a legendary medieval knight whose exploits form the center of a cycle of romances. The name received considerable publicity in the 1980s through the movie *Amadeus,* which is a fictional version of the life of Wolfgang Amadeus Mozart.

   Variations: **Amadee** (French), **Amadeo** (Italian), **Amadis** (Spanish), **Amias, Amyas, Amyot**

Amadis (see **Amadeus**)

Amar (see **Omar**)

Amblaoibh (see **Olaf**)

Ameer (see **Amir**)

Amias (see **Amadeus**)

Amir Arabic "local ruler, prince." This is now one of the more common Muslim names in the African-American community.

   Famous name: Amir Naderi (film director)

   Other spelling: **Ameer**

Ammon In the Old Testament, Ammon is the name of a country northeast of the Dead Sea. The city of Amman, Jordan, is built on the site of Ammon's ancient capital. The Ammonites were bitter enemies of the Israelites, but in the Book of Mormon, Ammon is the name of two different admirable characters. The name Ammon has been regularly used in Utah since the 1980s.

Amos Hebrew "burden" or "burden carrier." Amos was a shepherd, and when he listened to the Lord, he became a prophet.

   Famous names: Amos Bronson Alcott (writer)

   Amos Oz (novelist)

Amyas (see **Amadeus**)

Amyot (see **Amadeus**)

Andel (see **Angelo**)

Anders (see **Andrew**)

Anderson English and Scandinavian "son of **Andrew.**" Although Anderson is one of the ten most common last names in the United States, it is only rarely used as an American first name. However, for unknown reasons it has recently become extremely popular as a first name for boys in Brazil.

Andie (see **Andrew**)

Andonios (see **Anthony**)

Andor (see **Andrew**)

Andre French form of **Andrew.** The name has become a popular given name for African-Americans.
    Famous names: Andre Agassi (tennis player)
                  Andre Gide (author)
                  Andre Maginot (politician)
                  Andre Malraux (writer)
    Nickname: **Andy**

Andrea (see **Andrew**)

Andreas (see **Andrew**)

Andrei (see **Andrew**)

Andreian (see **Adrian**)

Andrejc (see **Andrew**)

Andrejko (see **Andrew**)

Andres Spanish form of **Andrew.** This name continues to be popular with Hispanic-Americans.
    Famous name: Andres Segovia (classical guitarist)

Andrew Greek *andreas* or *andreios,* "man, manly, strong." This is one of the top ten names for boys in the United States. St. Andrew was the first disciple of Jesus and the brother of St. Simon Peter. St. Andrew is the patron saint of Scotland. He is also the patron saint of Russia, and an unsubstantiated tradition claims that he preached there. During the Middle Ages, the saint was so popular in England that several hundred churches were named for him.
    Famous names: Andrew Carnegie (industrialist)

Andrew Jackson (7th U.S. president)
Andrew Johnson (17th U.S. president)

Nicknames: **Andie, Andy, Dandie, Dandy, Necho, Tandy, Tito**

Variations: **Anders** (Scandinavian), **Andor** (Hungarian), **Andre** (French), **Andrea** (Italian), **Andreas** (Greek), **Andrei** (Russian and Ukrainian), **Andrejc** (Slovenian), **Andrejko** (Slovakian), **Andres** (Spanish), **Andrius** (Lithuanian), **Andrzej** (Polish), **Andzs** (Latvian), **Antti** (Finnish), **Drew**, **Ondrej** (Czech)

Andrique (see **Henry**)

Andrius (see **Andrew**)

Andrzej (see **Andrew**)

Andy Form of **Andre** or **Andrew**. This nickname is sometimes used as an official given name, especially in the American South.

Famous name: Andy Warhol (artist)

Andzs (see **Andrew**)

Angel Spanish form of **Angelo**. In previous centuries, this was also a male name in England, especially in Cornwall. Angel Clare is the most prominent male in Thomas Hardy's novel *Tess of the D'Urbervilles*. Angel is still quite a popular male name with Hispanic-Americans, but other groups now use it only as a name for girls.

Famous name: Angel Cordero, Jr. (jockey)

Angelo Italian form of Greek *Angelos*, "a messenger"; originally from Hebrew "a messenger of God." Italians brought the name Angelo to the United States, and it is popular among Italian-Americans. It is also popular with Hispanic-Americans, although they like Angel even more.

Famous name: Angelo Roncalli (Pope John XXIII)

Nicknames: **Angie, Gelo, Lito**

Variations: **Angel** (Spanish and Cornish), **Andel** (Czech), **Angelyar** (Russian), **Angyal** (Hungarian), **Aniol** (Polish), **Anzhel** (Russian)

Angelyar (see **Angelo**)

Angie (see **Angelo**)

Angyal (see Angelo)

Anibal (see Hannibal)

Aniol (see Angelo)

Ansel A short form of **Anselm,** Old German *ans* [divine] + *helm* [helmet]. Ansel is given on rare occasions to American boys today, perhaps in honor of Ansel Adams (1902–1984), a great American photographer of the 20th century. In 1985, a peak in Yosemite National Park was named Mt. Ansel Adams in his memory.

Anselm (see Ansel)

Anson English surname, "Agnes" or "Ann's son." Like **Nelson** and **Rodney,** the use of Anson as a first name originally honored a British naval hero: in this case George, Lord Anson (1697–1762), an admiral who had famous victories over both the Spanish and French fleets in the 1740s. Anson was established as a first name in North America by 1770, and although it reached its peak of popularity around 1810, it has never died out. Between 1974 and 1984 it was kept in the public eye by actor Anson Williams, featured as Potsie on the television series *Happy Days.*

Antal (see Anthony)

Antek (see Anthony)

Anthony Latin *Antonius,* a family name of no specific meaning but sometimes translated as "inestimable, priceless one." This name has long been popular in Western Europe and in the Americas because of St. Anthony, the ascetic and founder of Christian monasticism. Shakespeare's plays *Julius Caesar* and *Antony and Cleopatra,* in which Mark Antony is a major character, have helped increase the popularity of this Roman family name. In the United States, the name is usually spelled with an "h," changing the pronunciation from its traditional one. The older pronunciation is reflected in the nickname Tony. Anthony has remained among the 30 most popular names for many years.

Famous names: Sir Anthony Hopkins (actor)
Anthony Kennedy (U.S. Supreme Court justice)
Anthony Trollope (English novelist)

Nicknames: **Nico, Toncho, Tonek, Toni, Tonico, Tonio, Tony**

Variations: **Akoni** (Hawaiian), **Andonios** (Greek), **Antal** (Hungarian), **Antek** (Polish), **Antoine** (French), **Anton** (Bulgarian, Czech, German, Norwegian, Rumanian, Russian, Serbian, Slovenian, Swedish, and Ukrainian), **Antonio** (Spanish and Italian)

Antjuan (see Antoine)

Antoine French form of **Anthony.** Like **Andre,** this French name has been very popular in the 20th century with African-American parents. **Antwan** is actually a more popular spelling in the United States today than the original French form. Antoine de Saint-Exupery was the French aviator who wrote the classic children's story *The Little Prince.* Ironically, Antoine is presently falling out of fashion in France, and the French are using the English form **Anthony** to name their sons.

Other spellings: **Antjuan, Antwan, Antwon**

Anton Slavic and Germanic form of **Anthony.**

Famous name: Anton Chekhov (writer)

Antonio Spanish and Italian form of **Anthony.** This form is now extremely popular in the United States with both Hispanic-Americans and African-Americans and is among the 100 most often used names for boys. Antonio is the merchant in Shakespeare's *The Merchant of Venice.*

Famous name: Antonio Vivaldi (composer)

Antti (see Andrew)

Antwan, Antwon (see Antoine)

Anzhel (see Angelo)

Aodh (see Hugh)

Aoidh (see Hugh)

Aquiles (see Achilles)

Ar (see Armand)

Arcy (see Darcy)

Arel (see **Ariel**)

Ari (see **Aaron, Aristo**)

Ariel Hebrew "lion of God." In the Book of Ezra, Ariel is listed as one of Ezra's chiefs and is sent to Iddo to obtain ministers for the house of God. The name is also in the Book of Isaiah, where it's used as another name for Jerusalem. Shakespeare made Ariel the witty, light, and graceful spirit in *The Tempest.* Milton used the name in *Paradise Lost* for one of the rebel angels. Percy Bysshe Shelley referred to himself as Ariel, and one of his biographers, Andre Maurois, entitled his book on Shelley *Ariel.* As a name for boys, Ariel is growing in popularity with Hispanic-Americans, but other Americans now generally only use the name for girls. It is quite popular as a name for boys in modern Israel because of the fame of Ariel Sharon, a politician and former general.
Variations: **Arel, Arik** (Israeli)

Arik (see **Ariel**)

Aristelo (see **Aristo**)

Aristeo, Aristio (see **Aristo**)

Aristo Greek *aristos,* "best"; also, form of Aristophanes or Aristotle. Originally, this name was a prefix that showed that the person named was of the highest quality, or the best. Aristophanes was a Greek writer of comedy. Aristotle was one of the great philosophers among the ancient Greeks, a student of Plato, and a teacher of Alexander the Great.
Nickname: **Ari**
Variations: **Aristeo, Aristio, Aristelo**

Arley (see **Harley**)

Arlow (see **Harlow**)

Arm (see **Armand**)

Armand French form of **Herman.** Armand is still much rarer than **Armando** in the United States, in spite of the recent fame of actor Armand Assante.
Nicknames: **Ar, Arm**

Armando Spanish form of **Herman.** Its enduring popularity with parents of Hispanic descent makes this by far the most common derivative of **Herman** in the modern United States.

Famous name: Armando Acosta (film director)

Armant (see **Herman**)

Armin Form of **Herman.** This is actually a short form of *Arminius,* the Latin form of **Herman.** The original Arminius was a leader of the ancient Germanic tribes that defeated the Roman armies in A.D. 9 and thus prevented the Roman empire from extending east of the Rhine. Armin Shimerman is the actor who plays Quark, the Ferengi businessman on the television series *Star Trek: Deep Space Nine.*

Arminio (see **Herman**)

Armond (see **Herman**)

Arn (see **Arnold**)

Arnaldo (see **Arnold**)

Arnaud (see **Arnold**)

Arne, Arnie (see **Arnold**)

Arnold Old German *Arenvald* from *arn* [eagle] + *wald* [ruler]. Arnold became a very popular name in the 12th and 13th centuries in England. The version of the name brought to England by the Normans was Arnaut. From the 17th to the 19th centuries, the name dropped from use, only to be revived in the late 19th century. It does not appeal to many parents today, but this may change in the future when the children who have grown up knowing Arnold Schwarzenegger as a macho hero have sons of their own.

Famous names: Arnold Bennett (writer)
　　　　　　　　Arnold Palmer (golfer)
　　　　　　　　Arnold Schoenberg (composer)
　　　　　　　　Arnold Toynbee (historian)

Nicknames: **Arn, Arnie, Noldy**

Variations: **Arnaldo** (Italian), **Arnaud** (French), **Arne** (Czech), **Arnoldo** (Spanish), **Arnolds** (Latvian), **Arnot** (Hungarian)

Arnoldo (see **Arnold**)

Arnolds (see Arnold)

Arnot (see Arnold)

Aron (see Aaron)

Aronne (see Aaron)

Arrian (see Adrian)

Arrigo (see Harry)

Arron (see Aaron)

Art (see Arthur)

Artair (see Arthur)

Artek (see Arthur)

Arthur Probably Latin *Artorius,* a family name; also, possibly Celtic *artos,* "a bear," or Irish *art,* "a stone." Long associated with the name of one of the earliest kings in Britain, King Arthur of the Round Table, the name first occurs in a short Latin chronicle written by a Breton monk, Nennius. The legend is believed to have originated in the Celtic region of what are now Wales and Cornwall, England. The romance of Arthur began to develop piecemeal, a poem here and another there, until a composite of Arthur and the Knights of the Round Table was formed into an integrated whole, *Morte d'Arthur* by Sir Thomas Malory, in 1485. The legend became a symbol of the spirit of England, and many poets have been attracted to it. Edmund Spenser's *The Faerie Queene* uses the legend as the framework. Alfred, Lord Tennyson, published his *Idylls of the King* in 1859. Matthew Arnold, William Morris, Samuel Clemens (Mark Twain), and Edwin Arlington Robinson also wrote about the Arthurian legend. Thus King Arthur became a popular symbol of manliness and chivalry for Victorian parents, and his name was extremely popular for American boys born between 1875 and 1930. Since then its popularity has continued to fall, and it's now not among the 200 most popular names for boys.

Famous names: Arthur Ashe (tennis player)

Arthur Meier Schlesinger (historian)

Nicknames: **Art, Artek, Artie, Arty, Turi, Tuto**

Variations: **Artair** (Scottish Gaelic), **Arthuro, Artur** (Bulgarian, Czech, German, Hungarian, Swedish, and Portuguese), **Arturo** (Italian and Spanish), **Artus** (French)

Arthuro (see **Arthur**)

Artie, Arty (see **Arthur**)

Artur (see **Arthur**)

Arturo (see **Arthur**)

Artus (see **Arthur**)

Asa Hebrew "healer." Asa was the king of Judah and son of Abijah, who was the son of David. He attempted to reform his people by destroying images of false gods.

Ash (see **Ashley**)

Ashleigh (see **Ashley**)

Ashley Old English "ash tree meadow" from *aesc* [ash tree] + *leah* [field]; a surname often used as a first name. This name is almost exclusively given to girls in the United States. Before 1960, it was a name for boys in the United States, and it still is a popular name for boys in the 1990s in England and Australia. In those countries, the spelling of the name is related to gender, with Ashley being a male name and Ashleigh a female form.
Famous name: Ashley Montagu (author)
Nicknames: **Ash, Lee**
Other spellings: **Ashleigh, Ashlie**

Ashlie (see **Ashley**)

Ashton English place name and surname, "ash tree farm."
Although now commonly a name for girls as **Ashley,** Ashton is still fairly often given to boys in the United States, especially by African-American parents.
Famous name: Ashton Phelps, Jr. (newspaper publisher)

Asti (see **Augustus**)

Aubert (see **Albert**)

Augie (see **Augustus**)

Auguste (see **Augustus**)

Augustyn (see **Augustus**)

Augustus Latin "venerable." The name was introduced into
England directly from Germany when the House of Hanover
became the royal family. Augustine, the diminutive of
Augustus, had been common in England during the Middle
Ages because of the adulation of St. Augustine, the author of
The Confessions and *The City of God.* But it has dropped from
use and now occurs only rarely.
Famous name: Auguste Rodin (sculptor)
Nicknames: **Augie, Chucho, Gus, Gussy**
Variations: **Agostinho** (Portuguese), **Agostino** (Italian), **Agustin**
(Spanish), **Asti** (Swedish), **Auguste** (French), **Augustyn**
(Polish)

Austen (see **Austin**)

Austin Form of Latin *Augustus.* This became a surname in medieval
England and later was taken up again as a first name.
Formerly, it was used most often in Texas in honor of Stephen
F. Austin, a leader in the Texas war for independence from
Mexico and for whom the city of Austin, Texas, was named.
Recently, however, the name has become very fashionable all
across the United States as parents search for alternatives to
the previously faddish **Justin** and **Dustin.** In 1991, Austin
became one of the 50 most popular names for American boys.
Other spelling: **Austen**

Ave (see **Averill**)

Averell (see **Averill**)

Averil (see **Averill**)

Averill Old English *Everild,* "boar warrior," from *eofor* [boar] + *hild*
[battle].
Famous name: Averell Harriman (diplomat)
Nicknames: **Ave, Avie**
Other spelling: **Averil**
Variation: **Averell** (English)

Avery Norman French form of **Alfred.** Avery has an excellent chance of becoming more popular now that it has been used as the baby's name on the hit television series *Murphy Brown*.

Famous names: Avery Brooks (actor)
Avery Schreiber (comedian)

Avner (see **Abner**)

Avie (see **Averill**)

Axel Danish form of **Absalom,** a biblical Hebrew name meaning "father of peace." That meaning is somewhat ironic because Absalom was the son of King David who started a civil war against his father and whose death caused David great anguish. Because of that history, Absalom has never been a popular name in English-speaking countries, but Axel was extremely popular in both Denmark and Sweden in the early 20th century. A few American parents are starting to name their sons Axel in the 1990s, perhaps because of the fame of Axl Rose of the rock music group Guns N' Roses.

Other spellings: **Aksel, Axl**

Axl (see **Axel**)

Aylwin (see **Alvin**)

Bailey Old English *beg-leah,* "wood or clearing where berries grow"; also, English *bailiff,* which comes from Latin *baiulus,* "porter." But in Middle English, *baile* meant "outside the castle wall," so it's impossible to determine the exact derivation of the name. Most Scots who are named Bailey claim the place-name derivation, while the English seem to prefer the occupational name. Bailey is now only rarely used for boys, but it is an increasingly popular name for girls. Geoffrey Chaucer gave the name Baillie to the innkeeper in *The Canterbury Tales.*
   Variations: **Baillie** (English and Scottish), **Baily, Bayley**

Baillie, Baily (see **Bailey**)

Balto (see **Walter**)

Bard (see **Barden**)

Barden Old English "barley valley." This name is usually a surname, but it is sometimes given to a son as a way of keeping a family name in use. It was originally an interlanguage compound formed from Old English *barrig,* "barley," and Scottish *denne,* "small valley."
   Nickname: **Bard**
   Variation: **Bardon**

Bardon (see **Barden**)

Barn (see **Barnaby, Bernard**)

Barna (see **Barnaby**)

Barnaba (see **Barnaby**)

Barnabe (see **Barnaby**)

Barnaby Greek from Aramaic *Barnabas,* "son of consolation." The prefix "bar-" means "son of" in Aramaic. Barnabas was a companion and aid to St. Paul in his missionary work. The name has been used in England since the Middle Ages. Charles Dickens used the name for the title character of *Barnaby Rudge,* and *Barnaby Jones* was the name of a long-running television series.

Nicknames: **Barn, Barney**

Variations: **Barna** (Hungarian), **Barnaba** (Italian and Polish), **Barnabe** (French, Portuguese, and Spanish), **Bernabe** (Spanish), **Varnava** (Russian)

Barnard (see **Bernard**)

Barney Form of **Barnaby** or **Bernard.** This name immediately brings to mind the happy purple dinosaur on the popular public television program for preschoolers.

Famous name: Barney Frank (member of Congress)

Other spelling: **Barnie**

Barnie (see **Barney**)

Baron (see **Barron**)

Barrie (see **Barry**)

Barron Old German "a free man." Spelled *baron,* this name became a royal title.

Famous name: James Barron Adler (publisher)

Variation: **Baron**

Barry Irish *bearach,* "spear." This name was exclusively Irish until the 20th century when it became popular in England and the United States. The large number of Irish immigrants to those two countries probably influenced the spread of the name.

Famous name: Barry Goldwater (politician)

Variation: **Barrie**

Bart Form of **Bartholomew** or **Barton.** This name is now identified with the television cartoon character Bart Simpson. His creator, Matt Groening, named him Bart because it's an anagram for "brat."

Famous name: Bart Starr (football player)

Bartal (see **Bartholomew**)

Barth (see **Bartholomew**)

Barthelemy (see **Bartholomew**)

Bartholomaus (see **Bartholomew**)

Bartholomew Hebrew "son of Talmai" from Aramaic *telem,* "furrow." This name contains the prefix "bar-," which means "son of." Little is known of St. Bartholomew; the only reference to him is in the Gospel of Mark, where he is listed as one of the apostles. He is supposed to have preached in India and in Armenia, where he is said to have been skinned alive and then crucified head down. The Gospel of Bartholomew was deemed apocryphal and was condemned. The name became popular in England after the 12th century, with almost 200 churches dedicated to the saint, but it is rarely given as a name for boys in any English-speaking country today. Ben Jonson's play *Bartholomew Fair* pictures the famous August fair at Smithfield.

Nicknames: **Bart, Barth, Bartie, Bartle, Bat, Tola, Toli**

Variations: **Bartal** (Hungarian), **Barthelemy** (French), **Bartholomaus** (German), **Bartollo, Bartolo** (Italian and Spanish), **Bartolome** (Spanish), **Bartolomej** (Czech), **Bartolomeu** (Portuguese), **Bartos** (Czech), **Bertalan** (Hungarian), **Vartolomej** (Bulgarian), **Vartolomeu** (Rumanian)

Bartie (see **Bartholomew**)

Bartle (see **Bartholomew**)

Bartollo, Bartolo (see **Bartholomew**)

Bartolome (see **Bartholomew**)

Bartolomej (see **Bartholomew**)

Bartolomeu (see **Bartholomew**)

Barton Old English *Beretun* from *bere* [barley or corn] + *tun* [farm]. Barton is better known as a surname than as a first name, with several famous—or infamous—people carrying the name, including Clara Barton, who organized the American Red Cross and worked to reform women's prisons. Elizabeth Barton was known as "the Maid of Kent." She prophesied against the marriage of Henry VIII and Anne Boleyn. After the marriage she claimed that Henry was no longer a king favored by God. For this "treasonable act," she was executed at Tyburn.

Famous name: Barton MacLane (actor)

Nickname: **Bart**

Bartos (see **Bartholomew**)

Bartram (see **Bertram**)

Bas (see **Basil**)

Basil Greek *basileios,* "royal." Several saints had this name, including St. Basil the Great, founder of the Eastern Orthodox Church. His father was St. Basil; his mother, St. Emmelia.

Famous names: Vassily Cateforis (mathematician)
            Basil Rathbone (actor)

Nicknames: **Bas, Vas**

Variations: **Basileus** (Dutch), **Basilio** (Spanish, Portuguese, and Italian), **Basilius** (Swedish), **Bazyli** (Polish), **Vasili, Vasilios** (Greek), **Vasska** (Russian), **Vazul** (Hungarian)

Basileus (see **Basil**)

Basilio (see **Basil**)

Basilius (see **Basil**)

Baste (see **Sebastian**)

Bastien (see **Sebastian**)

Basto (see **Sebastian**)

Bat (see **Bartholomew**)

Bayley (see **Bailey**)

Bazyli (see **Basil**)

Beau French "handsome." Originally a nickname for a good-looking or well-dressed young man, this name is associated with

the American South because it was the short form of
Beauregard, a French surname meaning "handsome-look." This
was used as a first name in honor of Pierre Beauregard, the
Confederate general who ordered the shelling of Fort Sumter,
South Carolina, that began the Civil War. Today, however,
Beau is used nearly equally by parents in all parts of the United
States and was the 231st most popular name for boys in 1991.

Famous names: Beau Bridges (actor)

Other spelling: **Bo**

Beauregard (see **Beau**)

Bechtel (see **Albert, Bertram**)

Beltran (see **Bertram**)

Ben Usually a form of **Benedict, Benjamin, Bennett, Bentley,** or
Bernard; also, from Scots *beann,* "peak," or Hebrew *ben,* "son
of." It sometimes appears as a separate name.

Famous names: Ben Jonson (dramatist)
Ben Shahn (painter)

Bendek (see **Benedict**)

Benedetto (see **Benedict**)

Benedict Latin *benedictus,* "blessed." Several saints and 15 popes
have been named Benedict. The name connotes holiness and
austerity. Benedict of Nursia, the father of Western
monasticism and founder of the Benedictine Order, made such
strict rules and insisted on such a high level of asceticism while
he was an abbot that his monks tried to poison him. The name
does not occur in England before the Norman Conquest.
Benedict used to be a humorous name for a newly married man
who formerly had been a confirmed bachelor.

Famous name: Benedict Arnold (American Revolutionary
traitor)

Nicknames: **Ben, Benito, Benny, Betto, Dick**

Variations: **Bendek** (Polish), **Benedetto** (Italian), **Benediktas**
(Latvian), **Benedicto** (Spanish), **Benedikt** (Bulgarian,
Czech, and German), **Bengt** (Swedish), **Benoit** (French),
Pentti (Finnish), **Venediktos** (Greek)

Benedicto (see **Benedict**)

Benedikt (see **Benedict**)

Benediktas (see **Benedict**)

Bengt (see **Benedict**)

Beniamin (see **Benjamin**)

Beniamino (see **Benjamin**)

Beniek (see **Benjamin**)

Benito (see **Benedict**)

Benjamin Hebrew "son of the south" or "son of the right hand."
This name can be found in three places in the Bible. In Genesis,
Benjamin is the youngest son of Jacob, who was originally
named Benoni, "son of my sorrow," because of the pain he
caused his mother as she was dying giving birth to him. Jacob
renamed him. In Chronicles, the sons of Benjamin are listed,
and a grandson Benjamin is noted. A Benjamin also appears as
the son of Hiram in the Book of Ezra. The name became
common in England during the 17th century and remained
popular until the late 19th century when the use of biblical
names began to decline. Recently, the name has made a strong
recovery, and it ranks among the 40 most used names for
American boys. Some of its recent popularity may be traced to
baby boomers remembering the character of Ben Cartwright in
the 1960s television series *Bonanza.*

Famous names: Benjamin Britten (composer)
                     Benjamin Franklin (statesman and inventor)
                     Benjamin Spock (pediatrician)

Nicknames: **Ben, Benjy, Bennie, Benny, Mincho**

Variations: **Beniamin** (Polish), **Beniamino** (Italian), **Binyamin**
(Hebrew), **Benjaminas** (Lithuanian), **Beniek** (Polish),
Veniamin, Venya, Venyamin (Russian)

Benjaminas (see **Benjamin**)

Benjy (see **Benjamin, Benny**)

Bennett Variation of **Benedict.** This name appears most often as a
surname, as in Jane Austen's *Pride and Prejudice,* which
describes the attempt to marry off the five daughters of the
Bennet family.

Nickname: **Ben**

Bennie (see **Benjamin**)

Benny Form of **Benedict, Benjamin,** or **Bernard.** The name has been used in literature for mentally handicapped characters, such as Benjy in William Faulkner's *The Sound and the Fury,* Benny in John Steinbeck's *Of Mice and Men,* and Benny on the television series *L.A. Law.*

Variation: **Benjy**

Benoit (see **Benedict**)

Bent (see **Bentley**)

Bentley Old English *beonet-leah,* "bent-grass meadow." Americans over age 40 may remember this name from the television series *Bachelor Father,* which originally aired from 1957 to 1962. In this comedy, John Forsythe played Bentley Gregg, a playboy attorney who became guardian for his orphaned teenage niece.

Nicknames: **Ben, Bent, Lee**

Other spelling: **Bently**

Bently (see **Bentley**)

Bernabe (see **Barnaby**)

Bernal (see **Bernard**)

Bernaldino (see **Bernard**)

Bernard Old German *Berinhard,* "brave as a bear," from *berin* [a bear] + *hard* [firm]. This name came to England at the time of the Norman Conquest and has been popular since the 12th century. In the United States, it is usually accented on the second syllable, but in Britain it's pronounced "BURR-nerd." Several saints have had this name. St. Bernard of Montjoux, the patron saint of mountaineers, did missionary work in the Alps, where two passes, as well as a breed of life-saving dogs, are named for him. St. Bernard of Clairvaux reformed the Cistercian monasteries and was noted for his great wisdom and his skill as a mediator.

Famous names: Bernard M. Baruch (economist)
Bernard Malamud (novelist)

Nicknames: **Barn, Barney, Ben, Benny, Bernie, Berny, Dino, Nado, Nayo**

Variations: **Barnard, Bernal, Bernaldino, Bernardin** (French), **Bernardino** (Italian, Spanish, and Portuguese), **Bernardo, Bernat** (Hungarian), **Vernaldo, Vernardino** (Spanish), **Vernardinos** (Greek)

Bernardin (see **Bernard**)

Bernardino (see **Bernard**)

Bernardo (see **Bernard**)

Bernat (see **Bernard**)

Bernie (see **Bernard**)

Berny (see **Bernard**)

Bert Form of **Albert, Bertram, Burton, Delbert, Egbert, Herbert, Hubert, Norbert,** or **Robert;** from Old German *berhta,* "bright."
Famous name: Bert Lahr (actor)

Bertalan (see **Bartholomew**)

Bertie (see **Albert, Bertram, Egbert, Herbert, Norbert**)

Berton (see **Burton**)

Bertram Old German *Berahtraben* from *berhta* [bright] + *hraben* [raven]. This name came into England at the time of the Norman Conquest. It was regularly used in the 19th century, but it's unusual today. Shakespeare used the name for the Count of Rousillon in *All's Well That Ends Well,* and Sir Walter Scott used it in *Castle Dangerous.*
Famous name: Bertrand Russell (philosopher)
Nicknames: **Bert, Bertie**
Variations: **Bartram** (English), **Bechtel** (German), **Beltran** (Spanish), **Bertrand** (French), **Bertrando** (Italian), **Bertrao** (Portuguese)

Bertrand (see **Bertram**)

Bertrando (see **Bertram**)

Bertrao (see **Bertram**)

Berty (see **Burton**)

Beto (see **Albert, Robert**)

Betto (see **Benedict**)

Bhaltair (see **Walter**)

Bictar (see **Victor**)

Bili (see **Billy**)

Bill Form of **William.**
> Famous names: Bill Clinton (42nd U.S. President)
> Bill Cosby (actor)
> Bill Moyers (journalist)

Billie (see **Billy**)

Billy Form of **William.** Sometimes this name is chosen by entertainers or used by men in occupations in which a nickname seems more appropriate than a formal name. As a separate given name, it ranks in the top 200 most popular names for boys in the United States. Like most pet forms of masculine names, it is more often given as an official form by parents in the South than in other parts of the United States.
> Famous names: William Franklin "Billy" Graham (evangelist)
> Alfred Manuel "Billy" Martin (baseball manager)
> Billy Crystal (comedian)

Other spelling: **Billie**
Variations: **Bili** (Rumanian), **Vila** (Czech), **Vili** (Hungarian)

Binyamin (see **Benjamin**)

Biron (see **Byron**)

Bjarne (see **Bjorn**)

Bjorn Swedish, from Old Norse "bear."
> Famous name: Bjorn Borg (tennis player)
Other spelling: **Bjorne**
Variation: **Bjarne** (Danish and Norwegian)

Bjorne (see **Bjorn**)

Blaan (see **Blaine**)

Blain (see **Blaine**)

Blaine Scots Gaelic *Blaan,* "yellow." This surname has begun to
appear as a given name, especially in the United States where
Celtic names for children are in vogue. The only saint of this
name was St. Blane of Scotland, who is also known as St.
Blaan.
Famous name: Blaine Peterson (hockey player)
Other spellings: **Blane, Blain**
Variation: **Blaan**

Blair Gaelic *blar,* "plain, battlefield." Although still given to some
boys, this surname is now more commonly given as a first name
to girls in the United States.
Famous names: Blair Kiel (football player)
Blair Underwood (actor)

Blake Old English *blac,* "pale," "loss of color," or "shining white";
also, Old English *blaec,* "black" or "dark." Confusion between
these two similar-sounding Old English words means that this
name can be said to mean its own opposite. Until the 20th
century, this was almost always a surname. As a given name, it
is gaining popularity and now ranks among the 100 most
common names for American boys. Blake Carrington, the
wealthy oil baron played by John Forsythe in the 1980s
television series *Dynasty,* probably helped increase parents'
awareness of the name as a possible choice for their sons. It
also fits in with the current vogue for short names starting with
"B," including **Brad, Braden, Brett, Brent, Brock,** and **Bryce.**
Famous name: Blake Edwards (movie director)

Blane (see **Blaine**)

Bo In Sweden and Denmark, this is a popular name derived from
Old Norse *bua,* "householder"; in the United States, it's usually
considered a respelling of **Beau.**
Famous names: Bo Goldman (screenwriter)
Bo Jackson (athlete)

Bob Form of **Robert.** Bob is actually quite rare as an official form
on birth certificates, but many famous Roberts prefer to be
known as Bob.

Famous names: Bob Dylan (singer)
Bob Hope (comedian)
Bob Newhart (comedian)

Boba (see **Boris**)

Bobbie (see **Robert**)

Bobby Form of **Robert.** This nickname is often combined with another name, such as Bobby Joe and Bobby Lee. Like **Billy,** Bobby is still frequently used as an official name in the southern part of the United States, and it ranks among the 200 most commonly used names for American boys. Bobby is also a popular nickname for politicians, entertainers, and athletes.
Famous name: Bobby Darin (singer and actor)
Bobby Fischer (chess champion)

Bodog Hungarian "happy"; used in Hungary as a "translation" of **Felix.**

Bomani Ngoni (Malawi) "warrior." This name is occasionally used by African-Americans who want to give their children an African first name.

Borenka (see **Boris**)

Boris Tartar *Bogoris,* "small"; later associated in Russia with the Slavic word *bor,* "battle." The ninth-century King Boris of Bulgaria was the first Slavic ruler to accept Christianity. The 11th-century Ukrainian St. Boris was murdered by his brother after Boris refused to raise his sword against him. Following Boris's burial in St. Basil's Church, miracles were said to occur at his grave. He is the patron saint of Moscow. Recently, Boris has become a popular name for German boys because of the fame of tennis player Boris Becker.
Famous names: Boris Godunov (tsar of Russia)
Boris Karloff (actor)
Nicknames: **Boba, Borenka, Borisik, Borka, Borya**
Variations: **Borys** (Polish), **Borysko** (Ukrainian)

Borisik (see **Boris**)

Borka (see **Boris**)

Borya (see **Boris**)

Borys (see **Boris**)

Borysko (see **Boris**)

Brad Old English *brad*, "broad"; also, shortened form of **Bradley** or **Bradford.** Many Americans born in the 1950s and 1960s will associate this name with the "overly normal" character played by Barry Bostwick in the cult film *The Rocky Horror Picture Show.* Although still usually a nickname, Brad is now being used as an independent first name enough to rank just below the top 300 names given to American boys.

Famous name: Brad Davis (actor)

Braden Irish Gaelic *Bradain*, "salmon." Rare as a first name until recently, Braden is growing in popularity with parents who like the sound of names such as **Brandon** or **Brian** but want something a bit less common for their own sons.

Other spellings: **Brayden, Braydon**

Bradford Old English "broad ford." This place name developed first into a surname, but now it's often used as a first name. Such use probably originally honored William Bradford (1590–1657), the first governor of Plymouth Colony in Massachusetts.

Nickname: **Brad**

Bradie (see **Brady**)

Bradlee (see **Bradley**)

Bradley Old English "broad meadow." This place name that became a surname is now common as a first name. Its popularity may have been influenced by the fame of Omar Bradley, a World War II general. Bradley was especially popular in the late 1970s and was still among the top 70 names in 1991.

Famous name: Bradley Smith (author)

Nicknames: **Brad, Lee**

Other spellings: **Bradlee, Bradly**

Bradly (see **Bradley**)

Brady Irish Gaelic *Bradaigh*, perhaps from *bradach*, "spirited"; also, Old English *brad eage*, "broad or wide-set eyes," or *brad eg*, "broad island." This surname is still another name for boys starting with "Br-" that is fashionable today. It's hard for many younger baby boomers not to think of the television series *The Brady Bunch* when they hear this name; obviously, parents whose last name is Bunche or something similar should avoid calling their sons Brady.

Famous name: Brady Anderson (baseball player)

Other spelling: **Bradie**

Brage Old Norse *bragr,* "most excellent." Brage was the Norse god of poetry.

Famous name: Brage Golding (university president)

Bram (see **Abraham**)

Brandon English place name, "hill covered with broom," although in Ireland sometimes a form of **Brendan.** This aristocratic British surname first gained notice in 1953 when Brandon DeWilde played the young boy in the classic Western film *Shane.* The name really took off, however, when another child actor, Brandon Cruz, played Eddie on television's *The Courtship of Eddie's Father* in the late 1960s to early 1970s. By 1985, Brandon was second only to Michael as a name for African-American boys and was hovering just below the top ten list for whites. The name's popularity was also helped by Brandon Tartikoff, head of programming at NBC during the 1980s. Tartikoff was one of the few TV executives to become a celebrity in his own right. There were signs that the name was just beginning to fade when it suddenly surged back into the top ten for boys of all races in 1991. This was undoubtedly caused by Brandon Walsh, the high-school heartthrob played by Jason Priestley on *Beverly Hills, 90210;* the same show has generated a flood of babies named **Dylan.** All in all, Brandon provides a classic example of how television affects the choice of names by American parents.

Brayden, Braydon (see **Braden**)

Brendan Irish Gaelic *Breanainn,* itself a form of Welsh *breenhin,* "prince." This name is revered in Ireland because of St. Brendan the Navigator, a sixth-century monk whose extensive travels gave rise to the legend that he discovered the New World years before Christopher Columbus. Long popular in Ireland, Brendan is gaining renewed interest from American parents because of the great popularity of **Brandon.** In 1991, the name was holding a place just below the top 100 names given boys in the United States.

Famous names: Brendan Behan (playwright)
Brendan Shanahan (hockey player)

Brennan, Brennen Irish Gaelic *Braonain,* "moisture, drop of water, tear." This Irish surname is being used as a modern first name as some parents search for alternatives to **Brandon** or **Brendan.** Although examples of famous persons with Brennan as a first name aren't easy to find, some parents who give the name to their sons might think of it as honoring Supreme Court Justice William J. Brennan, Jr.

Brent Celtic "high"; or Old English "burnt," as in a burned place or field. Brent recently became popular in the United States after **Brett** had paved the way, and in turn it has led to the even more recent popularity of such similar names as Brant and Brenton. Brent Spiner is the actor who plays Lt. Commander Data on the popular television series *Star Trek: The Next Generation.*

Famous name: Brent Musberger (sports announcer)

Bret, Brett Celtic *Breton* from Old French *Briton,* "a person from Brittany." Brett has become popular in the United States and now ranks about 70th among the most often used names. It was brought to the attention of Americans by the hit television series *Maverick,* which originally ran from 1957 to 1962. Its gambler hero Bret Maverick made actor James Garner famous, and he briefly revived the character in 1982 in a series called *Bret Maverick.* Later, the popularity of baseball player George Howard Brett may have also contributed to the name's success.

Famous name: Bret Harte (author)

Brian Probably from Celtic *Brigonos,* "high, noble." This name is popular in Ireland because of the legendary Irish hero King Brian Boroimhe, who lived in the tenth century. The name Brian was introduced to England with the Norman Conquest by Breton vassals of William the Conqueror. It dropped from use as a given name outside of Ireland during the 18th and 19th centuries, but it made a strong return and ranked among the top ten names in the United States during the 1970s and 1980s. Its popularity is now beginning to recede somewhat, but it was still among the top 30 American names in 1991.

Famous names: Brian Boitano (figure skater)
Brian Dennehy (actor)
Brian Keith (actor)

Variations: **Briano** (Italian), **Bryant**

Briano (see **Brian**)

Brice (see **Bryce**)

Brock Old English *brocc,* "badger," or *broc,* "brook." This may
have originally been a nickname for someone who was accused
of "badgering" or pestering his neighbors. Brock was 230th on
the list of names given American boys in 1991.
Famous name: Brock Peters (actor)

Bronson Middle English *Brunson,* "son of the brown man." For
unknown reasons, this was a fairly popular name in Hawaii
during the 1980s. Some parents who give this name may be
thinking of actor Charles Bronson, star of action movies such
as *Death Wish.* His original last name was Buchinski.
Famous name: Bronson Pinchot (actor and comedian)

Brooks English "dweller by the brook."
Famous names: Brooks Atkinson (drama critic)
Brooks Reed (lawyer)

Bru (see **Bruno**)

Bruce French *Braose,* a place name, possibly meaning "muddy" or
"from the brush thicket." The Bruces of Scotland were
originally Normans and came from Bruys, France, during the
Norman Conquest. The most famous member of the family,
Robert "the Bruce," was king of Scotland in the 14th century.
Bruce was rare as a first name outside Scotland until the 1930s,
but it was extremely fashionable in the United States from 1940
until 1970. Its popularity is now receding, and it was the 225th
most common name for American boys born in 1991.
Famous names: Bruce Jenner (track athlete)
Bruce Morton (TV announcer)
Bruce Springsteen (singer)
Nickname: **Brucie**
Variations: **Bruhs, Bruis** (French), **Bruys** (Scottish)

Brucie (see **Bruce**)

Bruhs (see **Bruce**)

Bruis (see **Bruce**)

Bruni, Bruny (see **Bruno**)

Bruno Old German *brun,* "brown," usually associated with bears. This name is not as popular in the United States as it is in Germany, where it is associated with the 11th-century St. Bruno of Cologne. After a brilliant career as a professor of theology and philosophy, he founded the Carthusian Order at Grenoble. He was made a saint in 1623, and his day is October 6. In the 1960s, Bruno was a popular name in France, and it is also used in Italy and Poland.
    Nicknames: **Bru, Bruni, Bruny**
    Variations: **Brunonas** (Lithuanian)

Brunonas (see **Bruno**)

Bruys (see **Bruce**)

Bryant Form of **Brian.** This name is especially popular with African-Americans due to the fame of television newscaster Bryant Gumbel; it is also regularly used by white parents.

Bryce Form of **Brice,** Celtic name of unknown meaning. The original Brice was a monk who became bishop of Tours, France, in 397 and was venerated as a saint after he was unjustly accused of adultery. The name is fairly popular today, being part of the fashion for names for boys starting with "Br-." Parents in the Western United States are choosing it more often than Easterners, perhaps being influenced by Utah's spectacular Bryce Canyon National Park.
    Famous name: Brice Marden (artist)
    Other spelling: **Brice**

Burl (see **Burleigh**)

Burleigh Old English *Burgelea* from *burg* [fort] + *leah* [meadow]. William Cecil, baron of Burleigh, was the chief minister to Elizabeth I of England.
    Famous name: Burleigh Arland "Stubblebeard" Grimes
                     (baseball player)
    Nickname: **Burl**
    Variation: **Burley**

Burley (see **Burleigh**)

Burt Short form of **Burton.**
    Famous name: Burt Reynolds (actor)

Burton Old English *burhton,* "farmstead near a fortress," from *burh* [fortified place] + *tun* [town]. In earlier times, people often took the name of the place where they lived. These names start out as surnames but later spin off given names.

Nicknames: **Bert, Berty, Burt**

Other spelling: **Berton**

Byron Old English *byrum,* "at the cattle sheds." This homely name was originally given to "the person who lives in the cow barn." It was first used as a given name in honor of one of the great English poets, George Noel Gordon, Lord Byron, author of *Don Juan* and *Childe Harold's Pilgrimage.*

Famous name: Byron Raymond White (football player, U.S. Supreme Court justice)

Variation: **Biron**

Cain (see **Kane**)

Cal (see **Calvin**)

Cale (see **Caleb**)

Caleb Hebrew *kalebh,* "dog." In the Bible, Caleb is one of the 12 spies sent by Moses to scout the land of Canaan before the Israelites enter it. Because he and Joshua are the only ones of the 12 who urge the people to have faith in God's promises that they will overcome the Canaanites, Caleb and his family are given the city of Hebron when the Israelites conquer it years later. Caleb became a popular name with the Puritans in colonial New England, and unlike many other obscure biblical names that they brought into use, it never completely died out. Since the 1970s it has been enjoying a revival, and Caleb was the 63rd most common name given to American boys in 1991. Some of its recent popularity may be linked to the character Caleb Snyder on the television soap opera *As the World Turns.*
Nickname: **Cale**

Calicho (see **Carlos**)

Calo (see **Carlos**)

Calv (see **Calvin**)

Calvin Latin *calvinus,* "bald." This French surname was turned into a first name in honor of John Calvin, a Protestant reformer and theologian and the founder of the Calvinist movement. During the presidency of John Calvin Coolidge, many parents named their baby boys Calvin. Today, the name is more popular with

African-Americans than with other parents in the United States, but the comic strip *Calvin and Hobbes* may encourage parents from all ethnic backgrounds to choose this name.

Famous name: Calvin Coolidge Julius Caesar Tuskahoma
"Buster" McLish (baseball pitcher)

Nicknames: **Cal, Calv**

Variation: **Calvino** (Spanish and Italian)

Calvino (see **Calvin**)

Cam (see **Cameron**)

Cameron Scots Gaelic *camsron,* "bent nose," or *cambrun,* "bent hill." This name is very popular in Scotland, where it's the name of a great clan. Two great Scottish theologians, John Cameron and Richard Cameron, are commemorated when Scottish boys are given this name. Recently, Cameron also became more popular as a first name in the United States, reaching 55th place among boys born in 1991.

Famous name: Cameron Mitchell (actor)

Nickname: **Cam**

Canute (see **Knut**)

Carey (see **Cary**)

Carl Form of German **Karl,** itself a variation of **Charles.** Carl was brought to the United States by German immigrants in the 19th century and had become one of the top 50 names for American boys from all ethnic backgrounds by 1900. The name remained popular until about 1950, but its use has since fallen steadily. Ironically, since 1960, after the name started to go out of fashion in America, Carl has become a very common name in England and Wales.

Famous names: Carl Gustav Jung (psychoanalyst)
Carl Lewis (Olympic track athlete)
Carl Sandburg (poet)

Variation: **Karl** (German, Russian, Serbian, Swedish, and Norwegian)

Carleton (see **Carlton**)

Carlino (see **Carlos**)

Carlo (see **Charles**)

Carlos Spanish form of **Charles**. This is still an extremely popular name with Hispanic parents in the United States, and it has sometimes been used by non-Hispanic-Americans, especially in Appalachia.
Variations: **Calicho, Calo, Carlino, Carlucho**

Carlton, Carleton Variation of **Charlton**. Although these two names have the same origin, Carlton is a great deal more popular than Charlton as a first name in the United States.
Famous name: Carlton Fisk (baseball player)

Carlucho (see **Carlos**)

Carmen Spanish and Italian form of Hebrew "the garden." This name is usually given to girls in Spanish-speaking countries, but in Italy it is more often a masculine name.
Famous name: Carmen Fanzone (baseball player)

Carol (see **Charles**)

Carroll (see **Charles**)

Carter Norman French *cartier,* "cart-driver." This name is inching up in popularity today. Perhaps this is related to the improvement in the reputation of former President Jimmy Carter as his work with Habitat for Humanity and other charitable organizations becomes better known. Carter Dickson is the pseudonym of John Dickson Carr, a well-known writer of detective stories.

Cary Middle English *Kari,* perhaps "pleasant stream"; or Irish Gaelic *O Ciardha,* "son of the dark one." Actor Cary Grant (born Archibald Leach) was solely responsible for the name's popularity.
Other spelling: **Carey**

Cas (see **Casper**)

Casey Irish Gaelic *Cathasach,* "watchful." As a name for boys, this immediately brings to mind J. L. "Casey" Jones, the train engineer whose sacrifice of his own life to save those of his passengers in a 1900 wreck near Monroe, Virginia, is immortalized in the famous ballad. He received his nickname because he was born in Cayce, Kentucky. In 1991, this was the 71st most common first name given to American boys, but it is now even more popular for girls.

Casper Danish and English variation of **Jasper,** possibly from a Persian word meaning "treasurer." Traditionally, Casper was one of the three kings who came to Bethlehem to worship the baby Jesus, but there is no biblical mention of the name. Its association with the friendly cartoon ghost has kept the name from gaining much popularity in the United States.

Famous name: Casper Weinberger (statesman)

Nicknames: **Cas, Jas**

Variations: **Gaspar** (Spain), **Gaspare** (Italian), **Jasper** (English), **Kaspar** (German)

Cass (see **Cassius**)

Cassius Latin family name, perhaps from Latin *cassus,* "hollow." This name came into use after Shakespeare used it in *Julius Caesar* as the name of one of the conspirators with Marcus Junius Brutus to assassinate Julius Caesar. The name also appears in *Antony and Cleopatra,* where it is used for a minor character.

Famous names: Cassius Marcellus Clay (abolitionist)
　　　　　　　　Cassius Jackson Keyser (mathematician)

Nickname: **Cass**

Cece (see **Cecil**)

Cecil Latin *Caecilius,* a Roman family name from *caecus,* "blind." This name probably began as a Roman nickname and developed into a surname. It has been used as a forename for a long time, but it has never been very popular and is now not even one of the 500 names most often given to boys in the United States. Because there have been several famous female saints named **Cecilia,** the feminine version of the name has become more popular than Cecil.

Famous names: Cecil Beaton (photographer)
　　　　　　　　Cecil B. DeMille (movie producer)
　　　　　　　　Cecil John Rhodes (financier)

Nicknames: **Cece, Ces**

Variations: **Cecilio** (Italian and Spanish), **Cecilius** (Dutch), **Celio** (Portuguese), **Sessylt** (Welsh)

Cecilio (see **Cecil**)

Cecilius (see **Cecil**)

Ced (see **Cedric**)

Cedric This name first appeared in *Ivanhoe* by Sir Walter Scott, who may have mistaken it for *Cerdic,* the mythical founder of West Saxony; *Cerdic* may derive from Welsh *Caradawg,* "amiable." The origin of Cedric is uncertain, but it became popular after Sir Walter Scott published *Ivanhoe,* in which Cedric is the father of the heroine Rowena. The central character in Frances Hodgson Burnett's *Little Lord Fauntleroy,* published in 1886, also has this name. Surprisingly, this very English name made the top ten in France during the 1970s. In the United States, the name is now primarily used by African-Americans.

Famous name: Sir Cedric Hardwicke (actor)

Nicknames: **Ced, Rick, Rickie, Ricky**

Variation: **Cerdic**

Celio (see **Cecil**)

Cerdic (see **Cedric**)

Ces (see **Cecil**)

Chabalito (see **Salvador**)

Chad Old English *Ceadda,* perhaps based on Welsh *cad,* "battle." St. Chad was a seventh-century bishop of Lichfield, England, who was noted for being extraordinarily humble and devout. Chad was a rare name, used mostly by Roman Catholics in England, until it was brought to the attention of Americans by singer Chad Mitchell in the 1960s and given more impetus by actor Chad Everett when he appeared as Dr. Joe Gannon on the television series *Medical Center* in the early 1970s. Chad was among the top 50 names for American boys from 1975 through 1984; by 1991, it had slipped back to 88th place.

Famous names: Chad Klein (fashion model)
Chad Lowe (actor)

Chal (see **Chalmers**)

Chalmers Scottish form of Old French *chaumbre,* "bedchamber" or "private servant."
Famous name: Chalmers P. Wylie (member of Congress)
Nickname: **Chal**

Charles Old German *carl,* "a man," through Latin *Carolus.* Charles has remained a consistently popular name from the time of Charlemagne (Charles the Great), the king of the Franks and emperor of the West. The name came to England with the Norman Conquest, but did not become popular until the royal Stuart family began to use the name Charles. Its popularity continues today, with Charles, prince of Wales, the heir apparent to the throne of England. In the United States, it was one of the top ten names for boys between 1830 and 1950 and still ranked 40th in 1991, although it is more popular east than west of the Mississippi.
Famous names: Charles Darwin (naturalist)
Charles de Gaulle (World War II French general, later president of France)
Charles Dickens (novelist)
Charles Kuralt (newscaster)
Charles Augustus Lindbergh (aviator)
Nicknames: **Charley, Charlie, Charly, Chick, Chuck, Chucky, Lito**
Variations: **Carl, Carlo** (Italian), **Carlos** (Portuguese and Spanish), **Carol** (Rumanian), **Carroll** (English), **Karl** (German and Russian), **Karel** (Czech), **Karlis** (Latvian), **Karol** (Polish), **Karolek** (Polish), **Karolis** (Lithuanian), **Karoly** (Hungarian)

Charley, Charlie, Charly (see **Charles, Charlton**)

Charlton Old English *Ceorlatun,* "town of freemen," from *ceorl* [freeman] + *tun* [town]. Parents who choose the name Charlton are fans of Charlton Heston or want to preserve a family name.
Nicknames: **Charley, Charlie, Charly**
Variations: **Carleton, Carlton**

Chase Old French *chaceur,* "hunter." This surname became a popular American first name in the 1980s when Robert Foxworth played the character Chase Gioberti on the television drama *Falcon Crest.* It may have been helped by its similarity in sound to **Jason.** The name is holding its own near the bottom of the most popular 100 names for boys in the early 1990s.

Famous name: Chase Twichell (poet)

Chavo (see **Salvador**)

Chento (see **Vincent**)

Ches (see **Chester**)

Chester Old English *ceaster,* "walled town" or "fortress." As a place name, Chester dates to the Roman occupation of England, when it referred to people who lived in the *castra,* or camp.

Famous names: Chester A. Arthur (21st U.S. president)
Chet Huntley (TV news announcer)

Nicknames: **Ches, Chet**

Chet (see **Chester**)

Chick (see **Charles**)

Chico (see **Francisco**)

Chimone (see **Simon**)

Chioke Ibo (Nigeria) "gift of God." African children are prized and treated as welcome gifts for their parents. Chioke reflects this belief, as do names from other cultures, including the Hebrew name Jonathan, "gift of the Lord (God)."

Chombo (see **Jerome**)

Chomo (see **Jerome**)

Chretien (see **Christian**)

Chris Shortened form of **Christian** or **Christopher.** Although Chris qualifies as a nickname, it appears independently often enough to be among the top 500 names for boys. When Chris is used as a nickname in the United States, it is usually a shortened form of Christopher.

Christ (see **Christian, Christopher**)

Christian Greek *kristos,* "anointed one," through Latin

Christianus, "Christian." Although this name is especially popular with Hispanic-Americans, it is now often being chosen by other American parents as well. In England, Christian was at the height of its historic popularity in the late 17th century because it is the name of the central allegorical character in John Bunyan's *Pilgrim's Progress.* The name continued to be popular throughout the 18th century, but its use began to decline in the 19th century. Basketball player Christian Laettner and actor Christian Slater are two famous Americans who are helping revive interest in this name.

Famous names: Christiaan Neethling Barnard (surgeon)
Christian Dior (fashion designer)

Nicknames: **Chris, Christ, Christy, Kit, Kris, Krys**

Variations: **Chretien** (French), **Christino, Crisciano** (Portuguese), **Cristian** (Spanish and Rumanian), **Cristiano** (Italian), **Hristo** (Bulgarian), **Keresztely** (Hungarian), **Khristian, Kristian, Kristjanis** (Latvian), **Krizas** (Lithuanian), **Krystian** (Polish)

Christino (see **Christian**)

Christoforus (see **Christopher**)

Christoph, Christophe (see **Christopher**)

Christopher Greek *Kristophoros,* "Christ bearing" (one who carries Christ in his heart), through Latin *Christopherus.* The name comes from a legend of a huge, ugly, strong man who offered to carry a small boy across a river. The child grew heavier and heavier until Christopher thought he would drown. As he was beginning to despair, the child revealed himself to be the Christ Child who was carrying the world on his shoulders. No historic saint by this name exists, only the allegorical legend. Christopher is the patron of travelers and car drivers, and his day is July 25. The name has been used throughout the centuries. In the United States, it has been the second or third most common name for boys since about 1970.

Famous names: Christopher Columbus (navigator)
Christopher Marlowe (Elizabethan dramatist)
Christopher Reeve (actor)

Nicknames: **Chris, Christ, Christy, Kester, Kit, Kris, Kriss, Stoffel, Tobal, Tobalito**

Variations: **Christoforus** (Dutch), **Christoph** (German),

Christophe (French), **Cristobal** (Spanish), **Cristoforo** (Italian), **Cristovao** (Portuguese), **Hristofor** (Macedonian), **Kristaps** (Latvian), **Kristof** (Slovakian and Hungarian), **Kristoffer** (Swedish)

Christy (see **Christian, Christopher**)

Chucho (see **Augustus**)

Chuck Pet form of **Charles.** Chuck is primarily a nickname, but it's occasionally used as a given name.
Famous names: Chuck Berry (singer)
Chuck Connors (actor)

Chucky (see **Charles**)

Cirilio (see **Cyril**)

Cirill (see **Cyril**)

Cirillo (see **Cyril**)

Cirilo (see **Cyril**)

Ciro (see **Cyrus**)

Cisco (see **Francisco**)

Clair, Clare (see **Clarence**)

Clarence English, from the title of the duke of Clarence, itself from Clare, a place name in Suffolk, England, from Celtic "bright or warm stream." In Shakespeare's *Richard III,* George, duke of Clarence, is executed by his brother Edward IV and the duke of Gloucester, later Richard III. The play was often performed in the United States during the 19th century. *Clarence* was also the title of a novel by American author Catharine Maria Sedgwick published in 1830, which became one of the first bestsellers written by a woman. As a result, Clarence became a popular first name in America and was among the top 20 names for American men born between 1870 and 1910. Clarence maintained its popularity with African-Americans years after it had gone out of fashion with other parents, but it's rapidly going out of style with them as well.
Famous names: Clarence Darrow (lawyer)
Clarence Thomas (U.S. Supreme Court justice)
Nicknames: **Clair, Clare**

Clark Greek *kleros* and Latin *clericus,* "religious person, clergyman," through English *clerk,* "scholar" or "a man of learning." When this occupational name is spelled Clark, it reflects the British pronunciation of the word "clerk." Over the centuries, the word has changed its meaning from "religious scholar" to "an employee in a shop or store." The former meaning is still retained in the word "cleric."
Famous name: Clark Gable (actor)
Variation: **Clarke**

Clarke (see **Clark**)

Claud, Claude Latin *claudus,* "lame." This Roman family name originally described a handicap. Claud was a popular name in late 19th-century America, but it's been almost completely out of fashion since, possibly because it's too close in sound to the word *clod.* Robert Graves's novels *I, Claudius* and *Claudius the God,* which became a PBS television series, have recently made the name familiar to many Americans.
Famous names: Emperor Claudius (Roman ruler possibly named for the handicap)
Claude Debussy (composer)
Claude Monet (painter)
Claude Rains (actor)
Nicknames: **Claudy, Cloyo**
Variations: **Claudicio, Claudino, Claudio** (Portuguese, Spanish, and Italian), **Claudiu** (Rumanian), **Claudius** (Dutch and English), **Klaudiusz** (Polish), **Klavdii** (Russian), **Kolos** (Hungarian)

Claudicio (see **Claud**)

Claudino (see **Claud**)

Claudio (see **Claud**)

Claudiu (see **Claud**)

Claudius (see **Claud**)

Claudy (see **Claud**)

Claus (see **Nicholas**)

Clay Old English *claeg,* "clay." This surname was initially used as a first name to honor Henry Clay, a 19th-century American statesman who was the chief designer of the Missouri Compromise of 1850.

Clayton English place name, "farm on clayey ground." This surname has been regularly used as a first name in the United States since the 1850s and is still often used today, remaining in the top 150 names for American boys.

Famous name: Clayton Yeutter (Republican Party official)

Cleante (see **Cleanth**)

Cleantes (see **Cleanth**)

Cleanth Probably from the Greek proper name *Cleanthes.* Cleanthes was a stoic philosopher and the successor to Zeno. In John Dryden's tragedy *Cleomenes,* Cleanthes is the captain who befriends Cleomenes. In *The Old Law,* a play by Philip Massinger, Thomas Middleton, and Will Rowley, Cleanthes is the son of Leonides and the model of fatherly devotion. A character of the name also appears in four of Moliere's plays. The name is rarely used today.

Famous name: Cleanth Brooks (literary critic)

Variations: **Cleante, Cleantes**

Cleaveland (see **Cleveland**)

Clem (see **Clement**)

Clemencio (see **Clement**)

Clement Latin *clemens,* "kind, gentle, mild, merciful." Clement was a disciple of St. Paul, and according to tradition, he was baptized by St. Peter. Clement was the third pope after Peter and Cletus, and he was martyred by the Emperor Trajan for preaching to mine workers. Condemned to death, Clement was drowned with an anchor tied to his neck. His day is November 23, and he is the patron saint of sailors. The name is very rare in the United States but is gaining popularity in France.

Famous name: Clement Attlee (prime minister of Great Britain)

Nicknames: **Clem, Clemmie, Menz, Te, Tente**

Variations: **Clemencio** (Spanish), **Clemente** (Italian, Spanish, and Portuguese), **Kelemen** (Hungarian), **Klemens** (German, Latvian, and Polish), **Klemensas** (Lithuanian),

Klement (Czech and Slovakian), **Klementos** (Greek), **Kliment** (Bulgarian and Russian), **Klymentiy** (Ukrainian)

Clemente (see **Clement**)

Clemmie (see **Clement**)

Cleve Form of **Cleveland** or **Clive**. In the United States, Cleve is almost always short for **Cleveland;** that is certainly the case for both Cleve Jones, founder of the NAMES AIDS Memorial Quilt, and Cleve Francis, the African-American physician who has a successful career as a country and western singer.

Cleveland Old English "cliff land." This surname became an American first name in honor of Grover Cleveland, the 22nd and 24th president of the United States.
Famous name: Cleveland Amory (animal rights activist)
Nickname: **Cleve**
Variation: **Cleaveland**

Cliff (see **Clifford**)

Clifford Old English "a stream-crossing near a cliff." Clifford became a popular name in the latter part of the 19th century. It currently ranks near the bottom of the 300 most popular names for boys.
Famous names: Clifford Philip Case (U.S. senator)
Clifford Odets (playwright)
Cliff Robertson (actor)
Nicknames: **Cliff, Cliffy**

Cliffy (see **Clifford**)

Clint Short form of **Clinton,** now frequently given as an official name due to the fame of actor and director Clint Eastwood.
Famous name: Clint Black (country singer)

Clinton English place name, "hill town," from Old Norse *klettr* [hill] + Old English *tun* [town]. This name was given to people who lived in a town on a hill.
Nickname: **Clint**

Clive Old English *clif,* "cliff." After Robert Clive conquered India, this surname became a given name in England, but it has never caught on in the United States.

Famous name: Clive Barnes (critic)

Variations: **Cleve, Clyve**

Clodoveo (see **Louis**)

Clovis (see **Louis**)

Cloyo (see **Claud**)

Clyde Celtic "river" or Welsh "heard from far away"; also, "cleansing," in reference to *Clota,* a river goddess. Water names are the oldest names in existence and seem able to survive well through the years, even though their forms change so much that positive identification of their etymology becomes difficult. There is a River Clyde in Scotland, and the Firth of Clyde is an estuary formed by that river. The Clydesdale breed of horses originated in the Clyde valley. In North Wales, a small river is named Clwyd. The cluster of these names indicates that they may all refer to a river goddess. As a surname, Clyde occurs often in Scotland and Northern Ireland, and it was carried by the Scots as they moved to new lands. The place name occurs in New York, Ohio, and Vermont. In the United States, Clyde was quite popular as a first name in the late 19th century while the similar-sounding **Claud** was even more popular, but it is only rarely used today. However, it has recently been a common name among blacks of West Indian descent living in England.

Famous names: Clyde Cessna (airplane manufacturer)

Clyde Edward McCollough (baseball catcher)

Clyve (see **Clive**)

Cnut (see **Knut**)

Cody Irish surname either from Gaelic *Cuidightheach,* "helpful person," or *Mac Oda,* "son of Otto." Cody became a first name in the American West in honor of Buffalo Bill Cody, the famous Western showman. It has been fashionable west of the Mississippi since the early 1980s and has rapidly spread eastward since television talk show host Kathie Lee Gifford gave birth to her son Cody in 1990 and made him a main topic of conversation on *Live with Regis and Kathie Lee.* Cody is now among the top 25 names for American boys, and some girls are also now being given the name.

Famous name: Cody Custer (rodeo bull-riding champion)
Other spellings: **Kodie, Kody**

Col (see **Colin**)

Colacho (see **Colin, Nicholas**)

Colan (see **Colin**)

Colby Old Norse "Koli's farm," English place name. Koli was an Old Norse nickname for a swarthy person. This last name is now being used as a first name quite often, probably because it sounds so similar to the previous fads **Cody** and **Colton.** It was already 130th on the popularity list for American boys in 1991 and still rising.

Cole Old English *col*, "coal-black"; or a form of **Nicholas.** Like **Colby,** this name is now rapidly increasing in use as American parents have begun to search for alternatives to similar popular names such as **Kyle** and **Cody.**
Famous name: Cole Porter (musician and composer)

Colin Scottish from Gaelic *cailean*, "youth" or "cadet"; also, a medieval shortened form of **Nicholas.** A variation of this name yields Old King Cole, a mythical king of Britain. The origin of Colin, however, is in France, where it was a form of **Nicol.** It came to England either during or just after the Norman Invasion, and it's had steady use ever since. Edmund Spenser's *Colin Clout's Come Home Again* indicates that the name was used among rural people, and Spenser himself used Colin as a pseudonym. The name of the collie originated in a real Middle English dog's name: Colle. This is another indication that the name was commonly used by country people, who often give their animals popular names for people.
Famous names: Colly Cibber (actor and comic playwright)
Colin Powell (U.S. Army general)
Variations: **Col, Colacho, Colan, Collie, Collin**

Collie (see **Colin**)

Collin (see **Colin**)

Colt (see **Colton**)

Colton Old English *colt-tun,* "town where colts are bred"; also,

"Cola's or Koli's town." Colton has become surprisingly popular during the last few years and is now among the 100 most common names for American boys. Some parents may see it as a more formal version of **Colt,** a name that received much of exposure during the 1980s when Lee Majors played stuntman Colt Seavers on the television series *The Fall Guy.*

Nickname: **Colt**

Con, Conny (see **Konrad**)

Conor, Connor Irish Gaelic *Conchobar,* "wolf-lover." This has been a popular name in Ireland since the Middle Ages and was borne by several early Irish kings. Conor's popularity is soaring in the United States; it rose from 191st to 101st as a name for American boys between 1989 and 1991, but the reasons for this are obscure. Eric Clapton's hugely popular song "Tears in Heaven" is a memorial to his son Conor who died at the age of four, but the song came out in 1992 and so couldn't have caused the increased use of the name.

Famous name: Conor Cruise O'Brien (Irish statesman and author)

Conrad (see **Konrad**)

Corey, Cory Old Norse *Kori* or Irish Gaelic *Comhraide,* both of unknown meaning. Corey became common as a first name for African-American boys in the late 1960s because of Corey Baker (played by Marc Copage), the title character's son on *Julia,* and probably the first African-American child featured on an American television series. In 1991, Corey was 33rd on the list of names given to American boys.

Famous names: Corey Feldman (actor)
Corey Pavin (golfer)

Other spellings: **Korey, Kory**

Courtney Middle English *de Curtenay* from *Courtenay,* Norman French place name, "short one's manor." Although Courtney is now an extremely popular name for girls, it is also regularly given to boys in the African-American community. In 1991, it was 130th on the list of names given to nonwhite boys in the United States.

Cragg (see **Craig**)

Craig Celtic *creag*, "crag." This Scottish surname became popular as a given name during the 1950s. It remained quite popular through the 1970s, but is now rapidly going out of style.

Famous names: Craig Morton (football player)
Craig Stevens (actor)

Variation: **Cragg**

Crisciano (see **Christian**)

Cristian (see **Christian**)

Cristiano (see **Christian**)

Cristobal (see **Christopher**)

Cristoforo (see **Christopher**)

Cristovao (see **Christopher**)

Curt (see **Curtis, Kurt**)

Curtis Old French *corteis*, "courteous." Introduced into England during or just after the Norman Conquest, this name was a complimentary nickname for someone who was especially courteous or courtly. Shakespeare used the name for one of the characters in *Taming of the Shrew*.

Famous names: Curtis LeMay (World War II general)
Curtis Strange (golfer)

Nicknames: **Curt, Kurt**

Other spelling: **Curtiss**

Curtiss (see **Curtis**)

Cy Nickname for **Cyril** or **Cyrus**. This nickname has become a name in its own right, possibly because of its association with Cy Young, an outstanding baseball pitcher whose name was given to an annual award for the best pitcher in the major leagues.

Cyrek (see **Cyril**)

Cyril Greek *kyrios*, "lord, master." Because of its association with the name Christ, Cyril has had religious connotations since the time of Jesus. There have been several saints of this name, including Cyril of Alexander, who was instrumental in clarifying what is now Roman Catholic dogma regarding the

Trinity. Another St. Cyril is known as the Apostle to the Slavs and for his translations of liturgical books. He is credited with inventing the Cyrillic alphabet, which is still used in Russia and some Slavic countries. He was also noted for his insistence on using Slavonic in the mass, a departure from Orthodox practice that caused him and his brother St. Methodius to break with Pope Nicholas I and led to the establishment of the Greek Orthodox Church.

Famous name: Cyril Ritchard (actor)

Nicknames: **Cy, Cyrek** (Czech), **Lilo**

Variations: **Cirilio** (Portuguese), **Cirill** (Hungarian), **Cirillo** (Italian), **Cirilo** (Spanish), **Cyrill** (German), **Cyrille** (French), **Kiril** (Bulgarian), **Kirill** (Russian), **Kurillos** (Greek), **Kyrylo** (Ukrainian)

Cyrill, Cyrille (see Cyril)

Cyrus Persian *Kurush,* perhaps from *kuru,* "throne," through Greek *Kyros,* referring to the great Persian king mentioned in the Old Testament. Cyrus is a biblical name that is seldom used in the United States today. Cyrus foretold great victories and befriended the Israelites; he issued a proclamation allowing them to return to the Holy Land.

Famous names: Cyrus McCormick (inventor)
                Cyrus Roberts Vance (diplomat)

Nickname: **Cy**

Variations: **Ciro** (Portuguese, Italian, and Spanish), **Kyros** (Greek)

Dain (see **Dana**)

Dakota Name of an American Indian nation, later the name of two states in the northern Great Plains. The names of almost all the American states have been used as given names from time to time, but Dakota is the first one to become generally popular. Although its "-a" ending would normally make it thought of as a name for girls by most English speakers, the masculine image of the West overcomes this; the name sounds as if it were originally a nickname for a cowboy from the Dakotas. The name is flourishing all over the United States; between 1989 and 1991, Dakota rose from 231st on the list of American names for boys to 100th. It is now also being regularly given to girls.

Dale Old English *dael,* "valley, hollow." This name started out as a place name. Like "hill," "crag," "ford," and "moor," it became a surname and then a given name. In the United States, both boys and girls are named Dale, but it is still primarily a male name.
Famous names: Dale Berra (baseball player)
Dale Carnegie (author)
Other spelling: **Dayle**

Dallas Old English *dalhous,* "house in the valley"; also, Scottish place name, "meadow house." This name is currently being used as a first name for both boys and girls, although historically it has been a surname. Because of Dallas, Texas, which was named for George Mifflin Dallas, vice-president of the United States under James K. Polk, the name evokes the Old West.
Famous name: George Dallas Green (baseball manager)

Dalton Old English *daeltun,* "valley farm." This place name developed first into a surname and later into a first name. Dalton is quickly increasing in popularity, jumping from 361st to 108th place among American names for boys between 1989 and 1991.

    Famous names: Dalton Jones (baseball player)
                       Dalton Trumbo (novelist)

Dame (see **Damian, Damon**)

Damek (see **Damian**)

Damian, Damien Greek *damazein,* "to tame." This name got its start early in the Christian Era. It shows how much the early Christians esteemed placidity and contemplation. Several saints were named Damian, including St. Damian, who became widely known for his healing powers and medical skills. Along with his brother, St. Cosmas, he is the patron saint of doctors. His day is September 26. Geoffrey Chaucer used the name in "The Merchant's Tale." The name also appears in Sir Walter Scott's *Ivanhoe.* Scott appropriately gave the name to a young man studying for Holy Orders. The given name became popular in the United States around 1975 and has remained so, despite its use as the name of the Antichrist in the *Omen* film series.

    Nickname: **Dame, Damek** (Polish)

    Variations: **Damiano** (Italian), **Damon, Demyan** (Russian and Ukrainian)

Damiano (see **Damian**)

Damon Classical Greek form of **Damian.** This name was very popular among Elizabethan and Jacobean writers, probably because of Damon, a young herder of goats in Virgil's *Eclogues.* It became a stock name in pastoral poems and plays. The play *Damon and Pithias* by Richard Edwards was produced in 1571. Fifty years later, John Banim and Richard Lalor Shell published a tragedy with the same name. Colly Cibber produced the pastoral farce *Damon and Phillida* in 1729. The name became popular in the late 1960s, especially with African-American parents.

    Famous names: Damon Runyon (writer)
                       Damon Evans (actor)

    Variations: **Dame, Damian, Damien** (English)

Dan Hebrew "judge"; also, a form of **Daniel.** Dan is sometimes used as a separate name and not always thought of as a nickname for Daniel. In the Old Testament, Dan is the son of Jacob; his mother was Bilhah, Rachel's maid. The biblical city Dan, the northernmost point of Palestine, was the inspiration for the naming of the Dan River by William Byrd; Danville, Virginia, takes its name from the river.

Famous names: Dan Quayle (U.S. vice-president)
Dan Rather (TV newscaster)

Nicknames: **Dannie, Danny**

Dana Perhaps Old English "a Dane." Surnames sometimes signify nationalities, such as Walsh for a person from Wales and Dana for a Dane. This name has survived since the Danes invaded and settled parts of the British Isles.

Famous names: Dana Andrews (actor)
Dana Carvey (comedian)

Variations: **Dain, Dane**

Dandie, Dandy (see **Andrew**)

Dane Middle English, "a Dane," or Old English, "a valley."

Famous name: Dane Clark (actor)

Variation: **Dana**

Daniel Hebrew "God is my judge." In the Old Testament, Daniel is the author of the Book of Daniel. Because he refused to obey an order of Darius of Persia, Daniel was thrown into a den of lions, but he was saved through the intercession of God. This well-known biblical story has assured the popularity of the name, especially in Protestant countries. Another biblical Daniel is the son of David and Abigail. In the United States, Daniel ranks among the top 20 names given to boys.

Famous names: Daniel Boone (pioneer)
Daniel Defoe (novelist)
Daniel K. Inouye (U.S. senator)
Daniel Webster (statesman)

Nicknames: **Dan, Dannie, Danny**

Variations: **Danielek** (Polish), **Danielus** (Lithuanian), **Daniil** (Greek and Rumanian), **Danilo** (Serbian), **Danko** (Czech), **Danylo** (Ukrainian)

Danielek (see **Daniel**)

Danielus (see **Daniel**)

Daniil (see **Daniel**)

Danilo (see **Daniel**)

Danko (see **Daniel**)

Dannie, Danny Forms of **Dan** or **Daniel**. Danny is frequently given as an official name in its own right, especially in the American South.

Famous names: Danny DeVito (actor)
Danny Glover (actor)
Danny Kaye (comedian)

Dante Italian *durante,* "lasting." This Italian name is closely associated with Dante Alighieri, the author of the *Divina Commedia.* Today it is a popular name with African-Americans, who usually spell it **Donte** or **Dontay.**

Famous name: Dante Gabriel Rossetti (artist)

Variations: **Dontay, Donte, Durand, Durante**

Danylo (see **Daniel**)

D'Arcy, D'arcy (see **Darcy**)

Darcy French *d'Arcy,* "from Arcy"; a French place name perhaps meaning "bear den." Norman d'Arcei, a friend of William the Conqueror, brought this name to England. Darcy is also claimed by Ireland, where the name is an Anglicized form of the Gaelic *O Dorchaidhe,* "dark one's descendant." Jane Austen gave the name to Elizabeth Bennet's aristocratic suitor in *Pride and Prejudice.* In the United States, Darcy is now primarily used for girls, so it may not continue to be thought of as a name for boys.

Famous name: D'arcy Raymond Flowers (baseball player)

Variations: **Arcy, D'Arcy, D'arcy**

Daren, Darin (see **Darren**)

Darius Latin form of Persian *Darayavahush,* "he who upholds the good." Darius the Great, ruler of the Persian empire (522–486 B.C.), allowed the Jews to rebuild the temple in Jerusalem. His prominence in the Old Testament led some of the early Puritans to give this name to their sons. In the 20th century,

Darius has been most popular in the African-American community, and that popularity is still increasing; in 1991, Darius was the 25th most common name given to nonwhite boys born in the United States.

Famous names: Darius James (novelist)
Darius Kasparaitis (hockey player)

Darl (see **Darryl**)

Darrel, Darrell (see **Darryl**)

Darren Probably from Irish Gaelic *Dubhdara,* perhaps meaning "black oak"; this would have originally been a nickname for a strong or stout-hearted person. This name was unheard of until actor Darren McGavin began appearing in movies and on television during the 1950s; he now occasionally shows up on *Murphy Brown* as the title character's father. Between 1964 and 1972, the name was also featured as that of Darrin Stephens, the mortal husband on the television series *Bewitched.* The program and the name were soon exported to England, where Darren became much more popular than it had ever been in the United States; it was a top ten name in England and Wales throughout the 1970s. Darren was never as popular in the United States; although it has been well used since the 1960s, it's gradually declining.

Other spellings: **Daren, Darin, Darrin, Darron**

Darrin, Darron (see **Darren**)

Darryl, Daryl Middle English *deAyrel,* "from Airelle," a town in northern France. Like **Darcy,** Darrel was originally a Norman French surname that was often used by English and American novelists around 1900 because of its aristocratic air. When Darryl F. Zanuck later helped found 20th Century Fox and became Hollywood's most famous movie producer, he inspired thousands of other parents to give the name to their sons. Darryl became especially popular with African-American parents, and it was second only to Michael as a black male name in the 1960s. More recently, the mute brothers Darryl and Darryl got lots of laughs on *Newhart.*

Famous names: Derrel McKinley "Bud" Harrelson (baseball player)
Darryl Strawberry (baseball player)

Other spellings: **Darrel, Darrell, Daryle**
Variations: **Darl, Dorrell**

Daryle (see **Darryl**)

Dave (see **David**)

Davey (see **David**)

David Hebrew *Dodavehu,* "darling or beloved of God"; originally a
   lullaby word. This name has just fallen below the American top
   ten list for boys after being there for more than 50 years. In the
   Bible, David was the second king of Israel and the author of
   many of the Psalms. While he was still a boy, he killed the giant
   Goliath. Charles Dickens used the name for the title character
   of *David Copperfield.*
   Famous names: David Ben-Gurion (statesman)
              David Livingstone (explorer)
              David Souter (U.S. Supreme Court justice)
              David Mark Winfield (baseball player)
   Nicknames: **Dave, Davey**
   Variations: **Davide** (Italian), **Davyd** (Russian and Ukranian),
       Dawid (Polish and Yiddish), **Dewey, Dovydas**
       (Lithuanian), **Taavetti** (Finnish)

Davide (see **David**)

Davyd (see **David**)

Davon (see **Devin**)

Dawid (see **David**)

Dayle (see **Dale**)

Dean Greek *deka,* "ten," through Middle English *deen,* "leader of
   ten," from which dean of a college derives; also, Old English
   dene, "valley."
   Famous names: Dean Acheson (U.S. secretary of state)
              Dean Rusk (U.S. secretary of state)
   Nickname: **Dino**
   Other spelling: **Deane**

DeAndre This is the most common of the many African-American
   names for boys formed by putting the prefix "De-" in front of
   another name. Such forms began to occur regularly in the

1970s and were at their height of popularity in the 1980s. They are just beginning to recede today, but **DeAndre** was still the 57th most common name for African-American boys in 1991. Other popular "De-" forms include **DeAngelo, DeJuan, DeMario, DeMarco, DeMarcus,** and **DeShawn.**

Other spellings: **Deondray, Deondre**

Deane (see **Dean**)

DeAngelo (see **DeAndre**)

Dederick (see **Derek**)

Dee Welsh "holy one." Dee is also often a nickname for names that begin with the letter "D." Dee Brown is the author of the classic work on American Indian history *Bury My Heart at Wounded Knee.*

DeJuan (see **DeAndre**)

Del (see **Delbert, Delmore**)

Delbert Variation of *Adelbert,* the Dutch form of **Albert.** This American name first developed in upstate New York among descendants of the original Dutch settlers of New Netherland. Today, it's not popular.

Famous names: Delbert Bernard Unser (baseball player)
Delbert Quentin "Babe" Wilber (baseball player and manager)

Nicknames: **Bert, Del**

Delisle (see **Lyle**)

Delmar Perhaps Latin "from the sea."

Delmore Perhaps a variation of **Delmar.**

Famous name: Delmore Schwartz (writer)
Nickname: **Del**

DeMarco, DeMarcus, DeMario (see **DeAndre**)

Demetrius Greek "belonging to Demeter, the Earth Mother, goddess of fertility." This name has been extremely popular with African-Americans in the 1980s and early 1990s.

Demyan (see **Damian**)

Den (see **Dennis**)

Denes, Denis (see **Dennis**)

Dennis French *Denys* from Latin *Dionysius* and Greek *Dionusios,* the god of Nysa, a Greek mountain, and the god of wine. St, Dennis is first mentioned in Acts as Dionysius the Areopagite. According to tradition, he was the first bishop of Athens and was martyred during the persecution of Christians in A.D. 95. His day is October 9. The name also belonged to several other saints and a pope. As a first name, Dennis was extremely popular in the United States during the 1940s and 1950s, but its use has since faded, perhaps because of its identification with the mischievous comic strip character Dennis the Menace.

    Famous names: Saint Denys (patron saint of France)
                    Denis Diderot (encyclopedist)
                    Dennis Dale McLain (baseball pitcher)
                    Dennis Quaid (actor)
                    Dennis Weaver (actor)

    Nicknames: **Den, Denny**

    Other spelling: **Denys**

    Variations: **Denes** (Hungarian), **Denis** (French), **Dionigi** (Italian), **Dion, Dionisio** (Spanish and Portuguese), **Dionisiy** (Russian), **Dionizy** (Polish), **Dionys** (German), **Dionysios** (Greek), **Dwight**

Denny (see **Dennis**)

Denys (see **Dennis**)

Deodoro (see **Theodore**)

Deon (see **Dion**)

Deondray, Deondre (see **DeAndre**)

Derek Dutch *Diederick* or *Direk* from Old German *Theodoric, theuda* [people] + *ricja* [rule]. This name came to England during the 15th century when there was an increased flow of trade with the Dutch. It was used only sporadically until the late 20th century when it suddenly became very popular.

    Famous names: Derek Brewer (actor)
                    Derek Nimmo (actor)
                    Derek Walcott (winner of the 1992 Nobel Prize in literature)

Variations: **Dederick, Derrick, Dieter** (German), **Dietrich** (German), **Dirk** (Dutch), **Theodorick**

Dermot (see **Derry**)

Derrick Form of **Derek.** This spelling is particularly popular with African-Americans.
Famous name: Derrick Coleman (basketball player)

Derry Short form of Irish **Dermot,** Gaelic *Diarmit,* name of an ancient hero considered the "greatest lover in Irish literature"; also, an Irish place name, perhaps meaning "oaks."

DeShawn (see **DeAndre**)

Devin, Devon Irish Gaelic *daimine,* "fawn"; Old French *devin,* "excellent"; or an English county name, "land of the Dumnonii tribe." These two spellings are pronounced the same by white Americans, as they are in Britain, but African-Americans often accent Devon on the second syllable. Both spellings are now used for boys and girls in the United States.
Famous name: Devon White (baseball player)
Variation: **Davon**

Dew (see **Dewey**)

DeWayne (see **Duane**)

Dewey Perhaps a form of *Dewi,* Welsh variation of **David.** This name was often used in the 19th century, but is now known mostly as the name of one of Donald Duck's nephews.
Nickname: **Dew**

Dex (see **Dexter**)

Dexter Old English *deghstre,* "dyer." By pure coincidence, this English surname has the same form as Latin *dexter,* meaning "right-handed" or "skillful," and very occasionally parents who know Latin may choose it for that reason.
Famous name: Dexter Ford (insurance executive)
Nicknames: **Dex**

Dick Form of **Benedict or Richard.** Dick Whittington is the orphan boy who became the mayor of London.

Famous names: Dick Butkus (football player)
                    Dick Clarence Clark (U.S. senator)

Dickie, Dicky (see **Richard**)

Diego (see **James**)

Dieter (see **Derek**)

Dietrich (see **Derek**)

Dillon (see **Dylan**)

Dino Form of **Bernard** or **Dean** or of names ending in "-dino." Most
people still consider Dino a nickname.

Dion Form of **Dennis.** This is now a fairly popular name with
African-Americans, although the spelling **Deon** is more
common. Dion was one of Plato's students who became the
ruler of Syracuse in 356 B.C.
Famous names: Dion (musician)
                    Dion Boucicault (playwright)

Dionigi (see **Dennis**)

Dionisio (see **Dennis**)

Dionisiy (see **Dennis**)

Dionizy (see **Dennis**)

Dionys (see **Dennis**)

Dionysios (see **Dennis**)

Dirk (see **Derek**)

Doane (see **Duane**)

Doby Form of **Robert.**
Famous name: Larry Doby Johnson (baseball player)

Dodge (see **Roger**)

Dolf (see **Adolph**)

Dolfie (see **Adolph**)

Dolph (see **Adolph**)

Dom (see **Dominic**)

Domas (see **Thomas**)

Domenico (see **Dominic**)

Domingo (see **Dominic**)

Domingos (see **Dominic**)

Dominic Latin *dominicus,* "of the Lord"; usually refers to the
Lord's day, Sunday, and was given to children born on that
day. This name began to be used in England in the 13th
century, influenced directly by the fame of St. Dominic,
founder of the Order of Preachers, known now as the
Dominican Order. His day is November 17. It ranks 105th
among the names most often given to boys in the United States
and is popular with Italian-Americans.

Nicknames: **Dom, Mingo, Nick, Nicki, Nickie, Nicky, Nik**

Variations: **Domenico** (Italian), **Domingo** (Spanish), **Domingos**
(Portuguese), **Dominick** (English), **Dominik** (Polish and
Russian), **Dominiks** (Latvian), **Dominique** (French),
Domonkos (Hungarian)

Dominick, Dominik (see **Dominic**)

Dominiks (see **Dominic**)

Dominique French form of **Dominic.** This is now a popular name
with African-Americans because of the fame of basketball
player Dominique Wilkins, who was born in France while his
father was stationed there with the U.S. Army and was named
by his French nanny. Dominique was the 41st most popular
name given to African-American boys in 1991.

Domonkos (see **Dominic**)

Don Form of **Donald.** This name is primarily a nickname, but
occasionally it may refer to the Spanish title, which is the
equivalent of "mister" in English, or to the Italian title, which
is the equivalent of "lord."

Famous name: Don Raphael Flinn (baseball player)

Donald Scots Gaelic *Domhnall* and Old Irish *Domnall,* "world mighty." This name was very popular in both England and the United States between 1915 and 1965. King Donald was the first Christian king of Scotland. The nickname **Don,** used as a separate name, fits the current trend toward short names.
Famous name: Donald Sutherland (actor)
Nicknames: **Don, Donnie**
Variations: **Donaldas** (Lithuanian), **Donaldo** (Italian), **Donnell** (Irish)

Donaldas (see **Donald**)

Donaldo (see **Donald**)

Donnell (see **Donald**)

Donnie (see **Donald**),

Dontay, Donte (see **Dante**)

Doro (see **Theodore**)

Dorrell Variation of **Darryl.**
Famous name: Dorrell Norman Elvert Herzog (baseball manager)

Doug Form of **Douglas.**
Famous name: Doug Flutie (football player)

Dougie (see **Douglas**)

Douglas Gaelic *Dubhglas,* "dark blue stream." Douglas was originally the name of a river and later of a Scottish clan. The Douglas clan in Scotland dates back to at least the eighth century. Shakespeare depicts Archibald, the earl of Douglas, as one of the Scottish conspirators against Henry IV in *Henry the Fourth, Part One.* The name was used for both boys and girls in England during the 17th century, but only became widely popular for boys after 1920.
Famous names: Douglas Fairbanks, Jr. (actor)
Douglas MacArthur (general)
Nicknames: **Doug, Dougie**
Other spelling: **Douglass**

Douglass (see **Douglas**)

Dovydas (see **David**)

Drew Old German *Drogo,* "carry" or "ghost"; also, French *Dru,* "favorite"; also, a form of **Andrew.** This name was first introduced in England at the time of the Norman Conquest by Dru, a companion of William the Conqueror, and it has been moderately popular ever since. With the present great popularity of **Andrew,** Drew may well become more common in the near future.

Famous name: Drew Pearson (columnist)

Other spelling: **Dru**

Dru (see **Drew**)

Drystan (see **Tristram**)

Duane Irish Gaelic *Dubhain,* form of *dubh,* "black." This name was moderately popular in the United States from 1945 through 1965, but it has since developed a working-class image and has fallen out of fashion.

Famous names: Duane Eddy (musician)

Duane Lewis Wilson (baseball player)

Dwayne Hickman (actor)

Other spellings: **Dwain, Dwayne**

Variations: **DeWayne, Doane**

Duardo (see **Edward**)

Dudley Old English *Dudda's leah,* "Dudda's meadow or clearing." This name is primarily a surname. When used as a first name, it is usually a family name, such as the mother's maiden name that parents wish to pass on to their child.

Famous name: Dudley Moore (actor)

Dukarai Shona (Zimbabwe) "happiness." This African name parallels English names such as **Joy** or Tate (happy).

Duke Latin *dux,* "leader." This English title of high rank has become a surname, a nickname, and rarely, a given name.

Famous names: Edwin Donald "Duke" Snider (baseball player)

Edward Kennedy "Duke" Ellington (musician)

Nicknames: **Dukie, Duky**

Dukie, Duky (see **Duke**)

Dun (see **Duncan**)

Dunc (see **Duncan**)

Duncan Scottish form of Old Irish *Dunecan,* "brown warrior." This
name has always been associated with the Scots, although it
figured prominently in Icelandic sagas. King Duncan I of
Scotland is best known outside Scotland as the king who is
assassinated by the power-hungry Macbeth in Shakespeare's
tragedy. As a given name, it is still uncommon in the United
States.
Famous names: Duncan Hines (gourmet)
Duncan Phyfe (cabinetmaker)
Nicknames: **Dun, Dunc**
Variation: **Dunkanas** (Lithuanian)

Dunkanas (see **Duncan**)

Durand (see **Dante**)

Durante (see **Dante**)

Dustin Perhaps a Norman French form of Old Norse *Thorsteinn,*
"Thor's stone." Dustin has been a popular name in the United
States since the late 1970s, undoubtedly because of the fame of
actor Dustin Hoffman, who was himself named after Dustin
Farnum, a silent-movie star who acted mostly in Westerns. Its
popularity has passed its peak, but Dustin was still the 53rd
most common name given to American boys in 1991.

Dwain, Dwayne (see **Duane**)

Dwight Probably Middle English *Diot,* a form of *Dionysus* (see
Dennis). This name has never been popular in England. As a
surname, it emigrated to the United States from England in the
17th century and became an American first name in honor of
Timothy Dwight, an early president of Yale University. It
received its greatest use in the 1950s because of the popularity
of Dwight D. Eisenhower (34th U.S. president), but the use of
this name has fallen in recent years.
Famous name: Dwight Gooden (baseball pitcher)

Dyl (see **Dylan**)

Dylan Welsh "of the sea." Dylan was the Welsh god of the ocean waves. A popular name in Wales, it only began to be used in the United States in the 1950s, mostly through the influence of the singer Bob Dylan, who took his name from the Welsh poet Dylan Thomas. Its popularity had been slowly increasing until 1990, when the number of Dylans born in the United States suddenly tripled. This was undoubtedly because of the character Dylan McKay on the popular television series *Beverly Hills, 90210.* However, it should be noted that about 20 percent of parents are using the spelling Dillon, which may mean that baby boomers are also remembering the character of Marshal Matt Dillon from *Gunsmoke.* (Dillon is an English and Irish surname with at least five different origins.) In any event, Dylan in all its spellings was the 32nd most common name for American boys born in 1991 and may well be on its way to top ten status.

Nickname: **Dyl**

Variations: **Dillon, Dylon**

Dylon (see **Dylan**)

Eamon (see **Edmond, Emmons**)

Eanraig (see **Henry**)

Earl Old English *Eorl,* "noble man or warrior." This royal title was often used as a given name in the United States between 1870 and 1940, but it is now going out of fashion. Among English nobility, the title indicates a rank between marquis and viscount and corresponds to the title of count in other countries. Earl is one of the oldest titles, and it is mentioned in *Beowulf* where it has the meaning of minor king. The place name Arlington means "the town of the people of the earl."

Famous names: Earl Douglas Averill (baseball player)
Erle Stanley Gardner (mystery writer)
Earl "The Pearl" Monroe (basketball player)
Earl Warren (U.S. Supreme Court chief justice)
Early "Gus" Wynn (baseball pitcher)

Variations: **Earle, Erl, Erle**

Earle (see **Earl**)

Easton English place name and surname, "eastern farmstead or village." As **Weston** has become a popular name, a few American parents are starting to use Easton as a name for their sons.

Ebert (see **Everett**)

Eckbert (see **Egbert**)

Ector (see **Hector**)

Ed Nickname of **Edgar, Edmond, Edward,** or **Edwin.** Ed is very rarely used as a separate name.

    Famous names: Ed McMahon (TV personality)
                  Ed Sullivan (TV personality)
                  Ed Wynn (actor)

Eddie Form of names beginning with "Ed-," including **Edgar, Edmond, Edward,** and **Edwin.** Eddie is fairly often given as an official first name, especially in the American South. It was originally a nickname and became a favorite with entertainers.

    Famous names: Eddie Albert (actor)
                  Eddie Murphy (comedian)

Eddy (see **Edward, Edwin**)

Edelmar (see **Elmer**)

Edgar Old English *Eadgar,* "prosperous spearman," from *ead* [wealth] + *gar* [spear]. This name has been popular since the tenth-century reign of Edgar of England, a widely respected and extremely successful and influential ruler. Shakespeare used the name for the loyal son of the duke of Gloucester in *King Lear.* Edgar is a popular name with Hispanic-American parents today.

    Famous names: Edgar Cayce (psychic)
                  J. Edgar Hoover (FBI director)
                  Edgar Lee Masters (poet)
                  Edgar Allan Poe (writer)

    Nicknames: **Ed, Eddie**

    Variations: **Edgard** (French and Portuguese), **Edgardo** (Italian and Spanish), **Edgars** (Latvian), **Garek** (Czech)

Edgard (see **Edgar**)

Edgardo (see **Edgar**)

Edgars (see **Edgar**)

Edmond, Edmund Old English *Eadmund,* "prosperous protector," from *ead* [wealth] + *mund* [protection]. Before the Norman Conquest, several English kings and two saints, St. Edmund of Abingdon and St. Edmund the Martyr, were named Edmund. The name has been used continuously by royalty in England, despite changes in the ruling household. Edmund was the bastard and disloyal son of the duke of Gloucester in Shakespeare's *King Lear*.

Famous names: Edmund Burke (statesman)
Sir Edmund Hillary (mountaineer)
Edmund Muskie (politician)
Edmond Rostand (playwright)
Edmund Spenser (poet)
Edmund Wilson (literary critic)

Nicknames: **Ed, Eddie, Mundy**

Variations: **Eamon** (Irish), **Edmondo** (Italian), **Edmundo** (Spanish and Portuguese), **Edmunds** (Latvian), **Mundek** (Polish), **Odon** (Hungarian)

Edmondo (see **Edmond**)

Edmundo (see **Edmond**)

Edmunds (see **Edmond**)

Edo (see **Edward**)

Edouard (see **Edward**)

Eduard (see **Edward**)

Eduardo Spanish form of **Edward,** frequently used by Hispanic-American parents.

Famous name: Eduardo Matos Moctezuma (archaeologist)

Eduardos (see **Edward**)

Eduino (see **Edwin**)

Edvard, Edvardas (see **Edward**)

Edvino (see **Edwin**)

Edvins (see **Edwin**)

Edward Old English *Eadweard,* "wealthy guardian," from *ead* [wealth] + *weard* [guardian]. This very old name has often been the name of the king of England. Several King Edwards ruled West Saxony and England before the Norman Conquest, and eight have sat on the throne since. The latest was Edward VIII, who abdicated after less than a year on the throne to marry

Wallis Simpson. Edward VII, who succeeded his mother, Queen Victoria, gave his name to the Edwardian era, which corresponds to his reign from 1901 to 1910.

Famous names: Edward Fitzgerald (translator)
Edward Gibbon (author)
Edward Lear (painter and poet)
Edward R. Murrow (TV reporter)
Edward G. Robinson (actor)
Edward Steichen (photographer)

Nicknames: **Duardo, Ed, Eddie, Eddy, Edo, Ned, Ted**

Variations: **Edouard** (French), **Eduard** (German, Estonian, Rumanian, Russian, Ukrainian, and Yiddish), **Eduardo** (Spanish), **Eduardos** (Greek), **Edvard** (Danish, Norwegian, and Slovenian), **Edvardas** (Lithuanian), **Ewart, Odoardo** (Italian)

Edwin Old English *Eadwine,* "rich friend," from *ead* [wealth] + *wine* [friend]. The first Edwin of historical record was the king of Northumbria, who converted to Christianity in 627. After he was killed at the battle of Heathfield, he was canonized St. Edwin. His day is October 12. This name fell into almost total disuse until it was revived in the late 19th century, influenced by *The Mystery Edwin Drood,* an unfinished novel by Charles Dickens. Like **Edgar,** Edwin is popular with Hispanic-American parents today but is out of fashion with other ethnic groups.

Famous names: Edwin Booth (actor)
Edwin Lee Mathews (baseball player)
Edwin Arlington Robinson (poet)

Nicknames: **Ed, Eddie, Eddy, Ned, Ted**

Variations: **Eduino** (Spanish), **Edvino** (Italian), **Edvins** (Latvian)

Eemeli (see **Emil**)

Egbert Old English "bright as a sword" from *ecg* [sword] + *beorht* [bright]. In the ninth century, Egbert became the first king of all England. There is only one St. Egbert, and he was honored by the Church for persuading the Celts to adopt Roman liturgical practices. His day is April 24, the day of his death.

Nicknames: **Bert, Bertie, Egg**

Variations: **Eckbert** (German), **Egberto** (Italian)

Egberto (see **Egbert**)

Egg (see **Egbert**)

Egidio (see **Giles**)

Egidius (see **Giles**)

Ekoka Bakwerri (Cameroon) "great chief."

Eldin (see **Eldon**)

Eldon Old English "Ella's hill." This rare name has become well known to fans of the television comedy *Murphy Brown,* where Robert Pastorelli plays Eldin Bernecky, a house painter turned nanny.
Variation: **Eldin**

Elfred (see **Alfred**)

Eli Hebrew "height"; also, a short form of **Elijah** or **Elisha.** Eli was the high priest who advised Hannah, the barren wife of Elkanah, to go in peace and God would grant her petition to have a child, which God did. The child was Samuel, who Eli trained in the ways of the Lord. The name Eli did not come into general use until the 17th century when the Puritans turned to the Old Testament for names. Old Eli is no longer a popular nickname for Yale University; the name of the institution's first benefactor was Elihu Yale.
Famous names: Eli Wallach (actor)
     Eli Whitney (inventor)
Other spelling: **Ely**

Elia (see **Elijah**)

Elias (see **Elijah**)

Eliasz (see **Elijah**)

Elie (see **Elijah**)

Elijah Hebrew "Yahweh is my God." Elijah was the Hebrew prophet who appeared before Ahab, the king of Israel, and predicted that God would punish his people with a great drought because the king practiced idolatry. Later, Elijah ended the famine by praying to God and denouncing Ahab for having murdered Naboth. At the end of his life, Elijah was carried to heaven in a chariot of fire. The name was popular during the

Middle Ages and then dropped from use. It was revived in the 17th century by the Puritans, and it's still used today.

Famous name: Elie Wiesel (novelist)

Variations: **Eli, Elia** (Italian), **Elias** (Czech, English, German, Greek, Hungarian, Portuguese, Spanish, and Yiddish), **Eliasz** (Polish), **Elie** (French), **Elliot, Elliott, Ellis, Illes** (Hungarian)

Eliot, Eliott (see **Elliot**)

Elisee (see **Elisha**)

Eliseo (see **Elisha**)

Elisha Hebrew "God is salvation." Elisha was the Hebrew prophet who succeeded Elijah. He performed many miracles, including raising a person from the dead, causing an axe to float in water, curing leprosy, and predicting the conclusions of sieges.

Famous names: Elisha Cook, Jr. (actor)
  Elisha Harrison "Camp" Skinner (baseball player)

Variations: **Eli, Elisee** (French), **Eliseo** (Spanish and Italian)

Elliot, Elliott Middle English form of **Elijah;** or Old English *Athelgeat,* "noble Geat (a Germanic tribe)," or *Aelfweald,* "elf rule"; or Scots Gaelic *eileach,* "mound." This British surname of many origins has long been used as a first name in the United States. Eliot Ness, real-life leader of a squad of Treasury agents in the 1930s, had his struggle with gangster Al Capone dramatized in several films, in the controversial late 1950s to early 1960s television series *The Untouchables,* and in the contemporary version of that series. Elliott was also the name of the young hero of Steven Spielberg's 1982 movie *E.T.—The Extra-Terrestrial.* However, this did not prevent Elliott from falling from 158th to 204th place on the list of American names given to boys born between the years 1989 and 1991.

Famous names: Elliott Gould (actor)
  Elliot Richardson (statesman)

Other spellings: **Eliot, Eliott**

Ellis Medieval English form of **Elijah.**

Famous name: Ellis Fergason "Cot" Deal (baseball pitcher)

Nickname: **Elly**

Ellwood (see Elwood)

Elly (see Ellis, Elmer, Elroy, Elwood)

Elmar (see Elmer)

Elmer Old English *Aethelmaer* from *aethel* [noble] + *maer* [famous].
This name almost never occurs in England; it is strictly
American. The name has become unpopular in recent years
because it reminds most people of a comic country hick. The
cartoon character Elmer Fudd does not improve the name's
image; neither does the preacher Elmer Gantry in Sinclair
Lewis's novel of that same name.
   Famous names: Elmer Ellsworth "Hickory" Johnson (baseball
                        player)
                    Elmer Rice (playwright)
   Nickname: **Elly**
   Variations: **Edelmar** (German), **Elmar** (Hungarian), **Elmers**
        (Latvian)

Elmers (see Elmer)

Elroy Old French "the king." This name is very rare in the United
States, but it's familiar to fans of the television cartoon series
The Jetsons as the name of the young son of the family who,
like most children on television, is much smarter than any of
the adults in the vicinity.
   Famous name: Elroy Leon Face (baseball pitcher)
   Nickname: **Elly**
   Variation: **Leroy**

Elsdon Old English *Ellis's dene,* "Ellis's valley." This name is very
rare, perhaps because it is so difficult to pronounce.
   Famous name: Elsdon C. Smith (lawyer and expert on
                        surnames)

Elton English place name *Aeltun,* "eel town" or "Ella's village or
farm." Elton has been a surname since the Middle Ages, when
it was common for a person to be named after the place where
he lived or, more commonly, where his family lived.
   Famous names: Elton John (entertainer)
                    Elton Langford (baseball player)

Elvin (see Alvin)

Elvis Perhaps a Welsh version of *Ailbhe,* an Irish name from Celtic *albho,* "white," although as likely to be a Southern invention blending the names of **Alvin** and **Ellis.** It's surprising that Elvis is still such a rare name despite the great hero worship of Elvis Presley. However, Irish singer Declan Patrick McManus did rename himself Elvis Costello in honor of "The King," and a few American parents choose this name every year.

Elwin (see **Alvin**)

Elwood Form of **Ellwood,** English place name meaning either "elder tree wood" or "elves' forest."
Famous name: Elwood George English (baseball player)
Nicknames: **Elly, Wood, Woody**
Variation: **Ellwood**

Ely (see **Eli**)

Em (see **Emil, Emmett, Emmons**)

Emanoil, Emanuel (see **Emmanuel**)

Emanuele, Emanuelis (see **Emmanuel**)

Emens (see **Emmons**)

Emerson Middle English "son of *Amery,*" a Norman French form of Germanic *Amalrich* from *amal* [bravery] + *ric* [power]. This surname undoubtedly became a first name in the United States during the 19th century in honor of Ralph Waldo Emerson, the famous poet and essayist. Although it is not very popular today, a few parents are still naming their sons Emerson, perhaps after beloved uncles or grandfathers.
Famous name: Emerson Fittipaldi (race car driver)

Emil, Emile German and French forms of Latin *Aemilius,* a Roman family name, possibly connoting "rival." This name has a Christian background. As a feminine name, it occurs in the works of Boccaccio, Chaucer, and Jane Austen. Aemilius is a noble Roman in Shakespeare's *Titus Andronicus.* Jean-Jacques Rousseau presented his treatise on education in *Emile,* in which he advised parents to bring up their children according to the laws of nature.
Famous names: Emil Jannings (actor)
              Emile Zola (novelist)

Nicknames: **Em, Emilek** (Czech and Polish), **Emmy**

Variations: **Eemeli** (Finnish), **Emilio** (Spanish and Italian)

Emilek (see **Emil**)

Emilio Spanish and Italian form of **Emil.** This name is regularly
used by Hispanic-Americans and has recently become well
known through the fame of actor Emilio Estevez. He is the son
of actor Martin Sheen, whose original name was Ramon
Estevez.

Emmanuel Hebrew "God is with us." This is the name of the future
Messiah prophesied in the Old Testament Book of Isaiah and
identified with Jesus in the Gospel of Matthew in the New
Testament. Emanuel Leutze was the artist who created the
famous painting "Washington Crossing the Delaware." This
name has long been more common in continental Europe than
in any English-speaking country, but in the United States
today, it is popular with Hispanic-Americans and African-
Americans.

Famous name: Emmanuel Lewis (actor)

Variations: **Emanoil** (Rumanian), **Emanuel** (Czech, Polish, and
Scandinavian), **Emanuele** (Italian), **Emanuelis**
(Lithuanian), **Emmanuil** (Russian), **Immanuel** (Dutch),
Manu (Finnish), **Manuel** (Spanish)

Emmanuil (see **Emmanuel**)

Emmet (see **Emmett**)

Emmett Middle English "son of **Emma.**" This is one of the few
British surnames based on a woman's, rather than a man's, first
name. Irish-Americans began to use Emmett as a name for
boys in the 19th century in honor of Robert Emmet, a hero in
the Irish struggle for independence who was executed by the
British in 1803. The first name then spread to other ethnic
groups, but the name is not popular in the United States today.

Famous names: Emmett Kelly (clown)
Emmett R. "Snags" Heidrick (baseball player)

Nicknames: **Em, Emmy**

Other spelling: **Emmet**

Emmon (see **Emmons**)

Emmons Origin and meaning uncertain. After the Norman Conquest, this name began to appear in England as Emagyne, Imayn, Emens, Emmines, and Emonie. It could have evolved from an Old German name meaning "strength" or "iron," but it might be derived from **Edmund** through **Eamon,** a contracted form. The suffix "-s" means "son of," so Emmons means "son of Emmon."

Famous names: Walter Emmons Alston (baseball manager)
Emmons Joseph "Chick" Bowen (baseball player)

Nicknames: **Em, Emmy**

Variations: **Eamon, Emens, Emmon**

Emmy (see **Emil, Emmett, Emmons**)

Enoch Hebrew "experienced, educated." Enoch was the eldest son of Cain, although some biblical scholars suggest that he may have been Abel's son, because Enoch is listed in the Book of Genesis only as a grandson of Adam. The name was popular with the Puritans. "Enoch Arden," a poem by Alfred, Lord Tennyson, recounts the story of the sailor who returns home and finds his wife married to his friend. He does not reveal himself and dies of a broken heart.

Variation: **Hanoch** (Hebrew)

Enos Hebrew "man." Enos was the son of Seth and a grandson of Adam. Although nothing more is written about Enos in the Bible, the name has been used in England, Ireland, and the United States since Puritan times. However, Enos is a very uncommon name today.

Famous name: Enos Bradsheer "Country" Slaughter (baseball player)

Enrico (see **Henry**)

Enrique Spanish form of **Henry.**

Famous name: Enrique Batiz (conductor)

Eoin (see **John**)

Erberto (see **Herbert**)

Eric Old Norse, possibly from *ei* [always] + *rikr* [ruler]. In England, this name is a result of Danish colonization, but Eric is popular in the United States because it is a common name in all Scandinavian countries. The name has been quite fashionable since the 1960s and was still the 25th most common name for American boys born in 1991.

Famous names: Eric Clapton (singer)
　　　　　　　　Eric Fingerhut (member of Congress)
　　　　　　　　Erich Maria Remarque (author)
　　　　　　　　Eric the Red (Norwegian navigator who explored Greenland)
　　　　　　　　Erich von Stroheim (movie director)

Nicknames: **Ric, Rick, Rickie, Ricky**

Variations: **Erich** (German and Slovakian), **Erico** (Portuguese and Italian), **Erik** (Danish and Swedish), **Eriks** (Latvian), **Erkki** (Finnish)

Erich (see Eric)

Erico (see Eric)

Erik (see Eric)

Eriks (see Eric)

Erkki (see Eric)

Erl, Erle (see Earl)

Erman (see Herman)

Ermanno (see Herman)

Ern (see Ernest, Erwin)

Ernek (see Ernest)

Ernest German *Ernst,* "serious, earnest." This name is a relative latecomer to England; it was introduced in the 18th century by the royal family of Hanover. Edward Bulwer Lytton published his novel *Ernest Maltravers* in 1827. Oscar Wilde used the name to launch one pun after another in his play *The Importance of Being Earnest.* This name was very popular in the United States during the Victorian era, but it has fallen out of fashion since 1930.

Famous names: Ernest Hemingway (novelist)
　　　　　　　　Ernest F. Hollings (U.S. senator)

Ernest Jones (biographer)
Ernie Kovacs (comedian)
Ernst Lubitsch (movie director)

Nicknames: **Ern, Ernie**

Variations: **Ernek** (Czech), **Ernestas** (Lithuanian), **Ernesto** (Portuguese, Italian, and Spanish), **Erno** (Hungarian), **Ernst** (German, Russian, Slovakian, Swedish, and Ukrainian)

Ernestas (see **Ernest**)

Ernesto (see **Ernest**)

Ernie (see **Ernest**)

Erno (see **Ernest**)

Ernst (see **Ernest**)

Ervin (see **Erwin**)

Ervins (see **Erwin**)

Erwin Old English *Eoforwine* from *eofor* [boar] + *wine* [friend]. This name is sometimes mistaken as a variation of Irvin or Irving, but Erwin is an entirely different name.

Nicknames: **Ern, Erwinek** (Polish)

Variations: **Ervin** (Czech and Slovakian), **Ervins** (Latvian), **Irwin, Irwyn**

Erwinek (see **Erwin**)

Esaias (see **Isaiah**)

Esdras (see **Ezra**)

Esra (see **Ezra**)

Esteban Spanish form of **Stephen**.

Famous names: Esteban Krotz (anthropologist)
Esteban Torres (member of Congress)

Estefon (see **Stephen**)

Estephano (see **Stephen**)

Estevan (see Stephen)

Ethan Hebrew "strength, permanence, and firmness." In the Old Testament, one Ethan was the son of Zerah, and another Ethan was the son of Kushaiah. The name was not used until the 18th century when it was taken up by the Puritans, mostly in the United States. They generally took names for their children from the Bible, sometimes by opening the book at random and placing a finger upon the page; the child was named whatever name the finger touched. Edith Wharton used this name for the hero of her tragic novella *Ethan Frome*. Ethan increased rapidly in popularity at the end of the 1980s and is now well into the top 100 names chosen for boys in the United States. Some of this increase was probably because Ethan was the name of Elliot and Nancy's son on the late 1980s television series *thirtysomething*. During the same period, Ethan Allen Cord (played by actor Lee Horsley) was also the chief character on the television Western *Paradise*.

Famous names: Ethan Allen (American Revolution hero)
Ethan Coen (film director)

Etienne (see Stephen)

Ettore (see Hector)

Eugen (see Eugene)

Eugene Greek *Eugenios*, "well born"; Latin *Eugenius*. Popes and princes have chosen this name because of its connotation of nobility, and their choice has increased its popularity with common people. St. Eugenius of Carthage was noted for his piety and goodness. Pope Eugene III helped unite the Eastern Church with the Church of Rome. Prince Eugene de Savoie Carignan was a great Austrian general; he led the Second Crusade and helped the duke of Marlborough to victory over Louis XIV and contributed more to the popularity of this name than anyone else.

Famous names: Eugene V. Debs (political activist)
Eugene Ionesco (playwright)
Eugene Joseph McCarthy (U.S. senator)
Eugene O'Neill (playwright)
Eugene Ormandy (conductor)

Nicknames: **Gene, Geno**
Variations: **Eugen** (German and Rumanian), **Eugenio**

(Portuguese, Italian, and Spanish), **Eugeniusz** (Polish), **Evgen** (Slovenian), **Evgenije** (Serbian), **Yevgeni** (Russian)

Eugenio (see **Eugene**)

Eugeniusz (see **Eugene**)

Ev (see **Evan, Everett**)

Evan Welsh form of **John.** Before Christian times, a Welsh king named Evan made a law that gave him the right to all the women in his kingdom. After more than 1000 years, the oppressive law was repealed at the request of King Malcolm's queen, and the subjects were allowed to give the king a money payment instead of their wives. The name Evan is becoming steadily more popular, especially in the eastern United States, and ranked 69th nationwide for American boys born in 1991.

Famous name: Evan Hunter (novelist)

Nicknames: **Ev, Van**

Variation: **Yvaine** (English)

Evarardo (see **Everett**)

Everett Old German *Eburhart,* "brave as a boar," from *ebur* [wild boar] + *hartu* [strong]. This name entered England at the time of the Norman Conquest. Then, as now, it only occasionally appeared as a first name.

Famous names: Everett Dirksen (U.S. senator)
C. Everett Koop (U.S. Surgeon General)

Nickname: **Ev**

Variations: **Ebert** (German), **Evarardo** (Italian and Spanish), **Everhard** (German), **Evert** (Swedish), **Evrard** (French)

Everhard (see **Everett**)

Evert (see **Everett**)

Evgen (see **Eugene**)

Evgenije (see **Eugene**)

Evrard (see **Everett**)

Ewan (see **Owen**)

Ewart Norman French form of **Edward** or Middle English *ewehirde,* "shepherd of ewes."

Ewen (see **Owen**)

Ez (see **Ezra**)

Ezekiel Hebrew "the strength of God." The biblical prophet Ezekiel wrote during the Babylonian exile around 580 B.C. He is famous for his vision of God riding in a chariot carried by four fantastic creatures, and his book contains many other vivid visual images. Ezekiel was often found as a first name in colonial New England, but today it is most popular with Hispanic-Americans.
Famous name: Zeke Mowatt (football player)
Nickname: **Zeke**
Variation: **Ezequiel** (Spanish and Portuguese)

Ezequiel (see **Ezekiel**)

Ezra Hebrew "help." With permission from King Artaxerxes, Ezra, a Hebrew scribe and priest, led the Israelites out of exile to rebuild the temple in Jerusalem. Ezra is the author of the Book of Ezra and is believed to have written other books in the Bible as well. The name is still used occasionally today in all parts of the United States.
Famous name: Ezra Pound (poet)
Nicknames: **Ez, Ezzie**
Variations: **Esdras** (Spanish), **Esra** (Finnish)

Ezzie (see **Ezra**)

Fabian Late Latin *Fabianus,* derived from Latin *faba,* "bean." This Roman family name may have originally designated a farmer's favorite crop. St. Fabian was a pope who was martyred in A.D. 250 during a persecution of the Christians by the emperor Decius. This name has never been very popular in English-speaking countries but does receive regular use in the Hispanic-American community. Many Americans will remember Fabian, the Philadelphia teenager who was an overnight singing sensation in the late 1950s. His full name is Fabian Forte.

Fariji Swahili "consolation." This African abstract name has been chosen recently by a few African-American families.

Farrell Irish Gaelic *fearghal,* "brave." This name was common in medieval Ireland and was brought to the United States by Irish immigrants in the 19th century.

Farris (see Ferris)

Fay (see Lafayette)

Fayette (see Lafayette)

Fede (see Frederick)

Federico (see Frederick)

Fedor (see Theodore)

Fee (see Felix)

Fele (see Felix)

Feles (see Felix)

Felice (see Felix)

Feliks (see Felix)

Feliksas (see Felix)

Felipe (see Philip)

Felippe (see Philip)

Felix Latin *felix*, "happy." Felix was once an extremely popular name and was the name of four popes and many saints. In the Bible, Felix was a procurator of Judea who was influenced by St. Paul's preaching, but when Felix was removed from his post, he left Paul in prison. It follows that popes chose the name for its Latin meaning, not to honor the actions of the historic Felix. On the long-running television comedy *The Odd Couple,* based on a play by Neil Simon, Tony Randall played the fastidious Felix Unger. Felix the Cat lives up to his name with his jovial attitude toward life. This name is not generally popular in the United States.

    Famous names: Felix Frankfurter (U.S. Supreme Court justice)
                    Felix Jose (baseball player)
                    Felix Mendelssohn (composer)

    Nicknames: **Fee, Fele, Feles, Pito**

    Variations: **Bodog** (Hungarian), **Felice** (Italian), **Feliks** (Polish, Russian), **Feliksas** (Lithuanian)

Feodor (see Theodore)

Ferd (see Ferdinand)

Ferdek (see Ferdinand)

Ferdie (see Ferdinand)

Ferdinand Gothic "daring adventurer" from *fard* [journey] + *nand* [ready]. This royal name moved south from Germany. It belonged to kings of Aragon, Austria, Leon, Castile, Spain, the Holy Roman Empire, Naples, Portugal, and the two Sicilies, some 23 in all, making Ferdinand the all-time most popular name for kings. Ferdinand II of Spain helped launch Christopher Columbus on his voyage to the Americas. Cortez, whose first name, Hernando, is a variation of Ferdinand, later exploited the riches of the New World for Spain. Shakespeare used the name Ferdinand for Miranda's suitor in *The Tempest* and for the king of Navarre in *Love's Labour's Lost.* John Webster made Ferdinand the brother and murderer of the duchess in *The Duchess of Malfi,* and in *The Duenna* by Richard Sheridan, Ferdinand is the lover of Clara.

Famous name: Fernando Magellan (navigator)

Nicknames: **Ferd, Ferdie**

Variations: **Ferdek** (Polish), **Ferdinandas** (Lithuanian), **Ferdinando** (Italian), **Ferdinandos** (Greek), **Ferdys** (Czech), **Fernand** (French), **Fernando** (Spanish), **Nandor** (Hungarian)

Ferdinandas (see **Ferdinand**)

Ferdinando (see **Ferdinand**)

Ferdinandos (see **Ferdinand**)

Ferdys (see **Ferdinand**)

Ferenc (see **Francis**)

Ferg (see **Fergus**)

Ferghus (see **Fergus**)

Fergus Old Irish "manly vigor" from *fer* [man] + *gus* [vigor]. Although this name is strongly associated with Ireland, Ferguss was the king of Scotland who repelled invasions of the Picts and Britons in 330 B.C. He was later drowned, and Carrickfergus was named to commemorate him. Several saints were named Fergus.

Famous name: Ferguson G. "Fergy" Malone (baseball player)

Nicknames: **Ferg, Fergy, Gus**

Variations: **Ferghus, Ferguson, Ferris**

Ferguson (see **Fergus**)

Fergy (see **Fergus**)

Fernand French form of **Ferdinand.** This shortened form of Ferdinand is occasionally used in the United States, especially by descendants of French-Canadians in New England.

Fernandino (see **Fernando**)

Fernando Spanish form of **Ferdinand**. Although **Ferdinand** is almost never found in the modern United States, Fernando is still quite popular within the Hispanic-American community.
Famous name: Fernando Valenzuela (baseball player)
Nicknames: **Ferni, Nando, Nano**
Variations: **Fernandino, Hernando**

Ferni (see **Fernando**)

Ferris Irish surname based on **Fergus**. In Scotland, this name is associated with the Ferguson clan, formerly MacFergus. In the United States, it is a rare but occasionally used name among Irish-Americans. The 1986 movie *Ferris Bueller's Day Off* may inspire some of its fans to use the name.
Famous name: Ferris "Burrhead" Fain (baseball player)
Variation: **Farris**

Fess Short form of **Festus**.
Famous name: Fess Parker (actor)

Festus Latin "firm, steadfast." Festus is a Roman family name. Sextus Pompeius Festus was a second-century lexicographer; Porcius Festus was a Roman procurator in Palestine who refused to turn St. Paul over to the Jews. After giving St. Paul a hearing, Festus sent him to Rome to appeal to the Caesar. In the television series *Gunsmoke,* Ken Curtis played Festus Haggen.
Famous name: Festus Edward Higgins (baseball pitcher)
Nickname: **Fess**

Feyo (see **Alfredo**)

Fico (see **Frederick**)

Filib (see **Philip**)

Filip (see **Philip**)

Filippino (see **Philip**)

Filippo (see **Philip**)

Filippos (see **Philip**)

Fin (see **Finlay**)

Finlay Gaelic "fair-haired warrior." This Scottish surname is used
occasionally as a given name.
Nicknames: **Fin, Lee**

Fito (see **Alfred, Alfredo**)

Fletch (see **Fletcher**)

Fletcher Old French "a maker of arrows." This occupational name
is an uncommon given name.
Famous name: Fletcher Knebel (novelist)
Nickname: **Fletch**

Flint Old English "rock." This name probably began as a nickname,
meaning "hard as a rock." It is both a surname and a given
name, and even though it is very rare at the present time, the
popularity of similar-sounding male names such as **Clint** and
Trent may bring it more use. Older baby boomers may recall
this as the name of Flint McCullough, the scout on the
television Western *Wagon Train,* played by actor Robert
Horton. Flint Castle in Wales is the scene of the meeting
between Henry Bolingbrook and Richard II in Shakespeare's
Richard II.
Famous name: Charles Flint "Shad" Rhem (baseball pitcher)

Flip (see **Philip**)

Floren (see **Florian**)

Florian Latin "blooming." This name has a similar derivation to
the girl's name **Florence**. Although it was introduced into
England just after the Norman Conquest, it's been much more
popular in Germany and Poland than it has ever been in any
English-speaking country.
Famous name: Peter Florian Dembowski (educator)
Variations: **Floren, Flory**

Flory (see **Florian**)

Floyd English variation of Welsh **Lloyd**, "gray." The change in
spelling resulted when native English speakers tried to
pronounce the Welsh "Ll-," a sound that exists in few other
languages besides Welsh. This name was extremely popular in

the United States during the late 19th century, but most parents today seem to find it too old-fashioned. Many Americans will immediately identify this name with the character of Floyd Lawson, the Mayberry barber on *The Andy Griffith Show,* played by actor Howard McNear.

Famous name: Floyd Patterson (boxer)

Other spelling: **Floyde**

Floyde (see **Floyd**)

Foma (see **Thomas**)

Foncho (see **Alfonso**)

Fonz (see **Alfonso**)

Fonzie (see **Alfonso**)

Fonzo (see **Alfonso**)

Forester (see **Forrest, Foster**)

Forrest Old English "forest" or "forester." Forrest started out as a place name or an occupational name. As a given name, it became popular in the late 19th century in the American South, where it was chosen to commemorate the exploits of Confederate general Nathan Bedford Forrest during and after the Civil War.

Famous names: Forrest Sawyer (newscaster)

Forrest Tucker (actor)

Nickname: **Foss**

Variations: **Forester, Foster**

Forrester (see **Foster**)

Forster (see **Foster**)

Foss (see **Forrest, Foster**)

Foster This English surname has four possible derivations from Middle English words for "foster-parent," "keeper of the woods," "sheep-shearer," or "saddle-tree maker."

Famous name: Foster Brooks (entertainer)

Nickname: **Foss**

Variations: **Forester, Forrest, Forrester, Forster**

Fount (see **Fountain**)

Fountain Old French *fontane* from Latin *fontanus,* "of a spring." This name may be associated with the Fountain of Youth, a legendary spring for which Ponce de Leon and other explorers searched in vain.

Variation: **Fount**

Foy Old French *foi,* "faith." Foy was used until the 17th century when Faith took over as the preferred form of this religious name. In *The Faerie Queene* by Edmund Spenser, the allegorical character Sansfoy represents people without faith. Foy has always been an extremely rare name in the United States.

Fran (see **Francis, Frank**)

Franc (see **Frank**)

Francesco (see **Francis**)

Francis Latin *Franciscus,* "Frenchman," from Old German *franc,* "free." Francis has been the name of several kings and many saints. St. Francis of Assisi is the most famous saint with this name. Born Giovanni, he is said to have been given the name Francesco because of his fluency in French. His father called him a madman and brutally disinherited the future saint. Francis's life of poverty and devotion caused many disciples to follow him. His day is October 4. St. Francis Xavier is credited with carrying the teachings of the Church to countries in the Far East. The name became popular in England beginning with the 16th century and has been used consistently since that time.

Famous names: Francis Bacon (essayist)
Francis Beaumont (playwright)
Sir Francis Drake (admiral)
Francis Scott Key Fitzgerald (novelist)
Franz Josef Haydn (composer)
Francis Scott Key (author of "The Star-Spangled Banner")

Nicknames: **Fran, Franek, Frank, Frannie, Franny**

Variations: **Ferenc** (Hungarian), **Francesco** (Italian), **Francisco** (Portuguese and Spanish), **Franciszek** (Polish), **Francois** (French), **Franjo** (Serbian), **Frans** (Swedish), **Frantisek** (Czech), **Frantiskos** (Greek), **Franz** (German)

Francisco Spanish and Portuguese form of **Francis.** This name has retained its popularity with Hispanic-Americans.
Famous name: Francisco Toledo (painter)
Nicknames: **Chico, Cisco, Paco, Pancho**

Franciszek (see **Francis**)

Franco (see **Frank**)

Francois (see **Francis**)

Franek (see **Francis**)

Franjo (see **Francis, Frank**)

Frank Old French *franc,* "free man"; also, a form of **Francis** or **Franklin.** Although this name is sometimes used as a nickname, it's also a separate name.
Famous names: Frank Capra (movie director)
　　　　　　　Frank Sinatra (singer)
　　　　　　　Frank Lloyd Wright (architect)
　　　　　　　Frank Zappa (musician)
Nicknames: **Fran, Frankie, Franky**
Variations: **Franc** (Bulgarian), **Franco** (Italian), **Franjo** (Serbian), **Franz** (German), **Pranas** (Lithuanian)

Frankie, Franky (see **Frank, Franklin**)

Franklin Middle English *frankeleyn,* "a free landowner." In England in the 14th and 15th centuries, Franklin was a title that designated a landlord who was of free but not noble birth. Geoffrey Chaucer gave one of the stories in *The Canterbury Tales* to the Franklin, a successful landowner. Two presidents have had this name, and it is always associated with Benjamin Franklin, statesman and inventor.
Famous names: Franklin Pierce (14th U.S. president)
　　　　　　　Franklin Delano Roosevelt (32nd U.S. president)
Nicknames: **Frank, Frankie, Franky, Linn**

Frannie, Franny (see **Francis**)

Frans (see **Francis**)

Frantisek (see **Francis**)

Frantiskos (see **Francis**)

Franz (see **Francis, Frank**)

Fred Form of **Alfred** or **Frederick**. This name has been used in its own right in both England and the United States since the middle of the 19th century and was among the top 20 names for American boys born from 1875 through 1900. By 1991, however, it had fallen to 462nd on the list and showed little sign of revival. Fred is the name of Ebenezer Scrooge's nephew in Charles Dickens's novel *A Christmas Carol.*
Famous names: Fred Astaire (dancer and actor)
Fred Dryer (football player and actor)
Fred MacMurray (actor)
Fred Savage (actor)

Freddie, Freddy Forms of **Alfred** or **Frederick.** On official birth certificates in the United States, this name is now somewhat more common than **Fred,** especially in the South.
Famous names: Freddy Fender (country singer)
Freddie Mercury (rock musician)

Fredek (see **Frederick**)

Frederic (see **Frederick**)

Frederick Old German *Frithuric* from *frithu* [peace] + *ricja* [rule]. Frederick has long been a royal name in Germany. When Hanover became the royal house of England, the name came along with it. Frederick, the prince of Wales, was the son of George II of England. Gilbert and Sullivan used the name for the boy who is apprenticed by his nurse to pirates instead of pilots in *The Pirates of Penzance.* This name has been declining in use in both England and the United States since the 1930s.
Famous names: Frederic Chopin (composer and pianist)
Frederick Landis "Fat Freddie" Fitzsimmons (baseball pitcher)
Fredric March (actor)
Frederic Remington (painter)
Nicknames: **Fede, Fico, Fred, Freddie, Freddy, Fredek** (Polish), **Fredi, Frico, Fritz, Fritzchen, Ikoy, Ric, Rick, Rickie, Ricky, Riki**
Variations: **Federico** (Portuguese, Spanish, and Italian), **Frederic** (French), **Friderik** (Serbian), **Friedrich** (German), **Frigyes** (Hungarian)

Fredi (see **Frederick**)

Fredo (see **Alfred, Alfredo**)

Frico (see **Frederick**)

Friderik (see **Frederick**)

Friedrich (see **Frederick**)

Frigyes (see **Frederick**)

Fritz (see **Frederick**)

Fritzchen (see **Frederick**)

Fulop (see **Philip**)

Fulton Old English "place with birds" from *fugol* [bird, fowl] + *tun* [enclosure]. The modern use of this name honors Robert Fulton, a 19th-century American inventor and civil engineer. His many patents include a steamboat that could navigate the Hudson River from New York City to Albany. Many counties and towns along that river and other rivers in the United States were named for him.
Famous name: Fulton J. Sheen (TV preacher)

Fyodor (see **Theodore**)

Gabe (see **Gabriel**)

Gabor (see **Gabriel**)

Gabriel Hebrew "man of God," the name of an archangel. This angel first appeared to Daniel in the Old Testament and then to Mary in the New Testament announcing the impending birth of Jesus. Because of Gabriel's association with messages from God, in 1921 Pope Benedict XV declared him the patron saint of letter carriers and telephone operators. The name Gabriel was rare in the United States before the 20th century because many Anglo-Saxon Protestants thought it was sacrilegious to name children after angels. But the present huge popularity of **Michael** has encouraged American parents to reconsider the names of other angels, and Gabriel reached 92nd on the list of names given to newborn sons in 1991.

Famous names: Gabriel Byrne (actor)
Gabriel Faure (composer)
Gabriel Garcia Marquez (1982 Nobel prize winner for literature)
Gabriel Spera (poet)

Nickname: **Gabe**

Variations: **Gabor** (Hungarian), **Gabriele** (Italian), **Gavrylo** (Ukrainian), **Kaapo** (Finnish)

Gabriele (see **Gabriel**)

Gage Old Norman French *gauge,* used as a name for an official who checked legal weights and measures in medieval times. Gage is quickly becoming more common as a name for American boys.

Gahiji Rwandan "the hunter." This African warrior's name is sometimes chosen by African-American parents.

Gale British surname of several different derivations, including Middle English *gaile,* "jovial"; Norman French *Galon* from Old Germanic *walh,* "foreigner"; and Old Norman French *gaiole,* "jailer." This last name became a first name in America in the late 19th century, when many short British surnames were taken up generally as names for boys. It was never especially popular and now has almost died out because it is pronounced the same as the girl's name **Gail,** with which it has no etymological connection.
Famous names: Gale Gordon (actor)
Gale Sayers (football player)

Galen Probably a Latin form of Greek *galene,* "calm." Galen was a highly respected second-century Greek physician.
Variation: **Gaylon**

Gallard (see **Gaylord**)

Galway Irish Gaelic *galimh,* "stony." Galway Bay, along with the county and city of Galway, is a place that many Irish-Americans remember with nostalgia. In the 17th century, before England conquered Ireland, this port had an extensive trade with Spain. As a first name, Galway is extremely rare.
Famous name: Galway Kinnell (poet)

Gamaliel Hebrew "God is my reward." In the Old Testament, Gamaliel was the son of Pedahzur and prince of Manasseh. In the New Testament, he was the rabbi who taught Saul of Tarsus (St. Paul). The name was popular with the Puritans, beginning in the 17th century.

Famous name: Warren Gamaliel Harding (29th U.S. president)

Gar (see **Garret, Garth**)

Garald (see **Harold**)

Garek (see **Edgar**)

Garner (see **Warner**)

Garrelt (see **Gerald**)

Garret (see **Garrett**)

Garrett Middle English form of both **Gerald** and **Gerard.** This name seems to be the 1990s replacement for **Gary.** In 1991, it was the 76th most often used name for boys in the United States, and it is quickly becoming more popular.

Famous name: Garrett A. Hobart (U.S. vice-president)

Nicknames: **Gar, Gary**

Other spelling: **Garret**

Variation: **Jarrett**

Garry (see **Gary**)

Garth Old Norse *garthr,* "enclosure," through Middle English *garth,* "garden, yard." This surname has been used as a first name since the early 19th century, but it has never been especially popular, even though Garth has been a well-used name for fictional characters. There is a Garth in Maxwell Anderson's play *Winterset.* Garth was the name of the character played by actor Martin Mull in the television series *Mary Hartman, Mary Hartman* as well as the name of the popular character played by Dana Carvey in the movie *Wayne's World,* based on sketches from *Saturday Night Live.* With the huge popularity of country singer Garth Brooks the name has been inching upward in use, but it was still only 560th on the list of American names for boys in 1991.

Famous names: Garth Ellis Griffith (railroad executive)
Garth Hudson (musician)

Nickname: **Gar**

Gary Old English *gari,* "spear," or a short form of **Garrett.** This name was one of the top ten names for boys during the 1940s and 1950s in the United States. It owed its popularity to Gary Cooper, two-time Oscar winner for *Sergeant York* and *High Noon.* His original name was Frank Cooper; the name Gary was suggested to him by his agent, Nan Collins, who had been born in Gary, Indiana. Gary was also formerly often used to Americanize such European names as Garibaldi. As an official name, Gary has receded in popularity, but it will often be heard as a nickname for **Garrett** among boys born in the 1990s.

Famous names: Gary Edmund "The Kid" Carter (baseball
catcher)
Gary Hart (U.S. senator)
Garry Moore (comedian)

Other spelling: **Garry**

Gaspar (see **Casper**)

Gaspare (see **Casper**)

Gauthier (see **Walter**)

Gautier (see **Walter**)

Gav (see **Gavin**)

Gaven (see **Gavin**)

Gavin Scottish form of Welsh *Gwalchgwyn,* "white hawk." Gavin, or Gawain, was the first knight of King Arthur's Round Table. He is considered to be the most courteous of the knights. Gawain is also the hero of "Sir Gawayne and the Grene Knight," the finest of the Arthurian romances. William Faulkner's character Gavin Stevens plays an integral but ironic part in several of his novels. Gavin's nephew, Gowann Stevens, is a young man who becomes drunk and is unable to shield Temple Drake from Popeye. Both names allude to the knight's exemplary morals.
Famous name: Gavin McLeod (actor)
Nickname: **Gav**
Variations: **Gaven, Gawain, Gawayne**

Gavrylo (see **Gabriel**)

Gawain (see **Gavin**)

Gawayne (see **Gavin**)

Gay (see **Gaylord**)

Gayelord (see **Gaylord**)

Gaylon (see **Galen**)

Gaylord Norman French *Gailhard* from Germanic *gail* [gay, joyous] + *hard* [hardy, strong]. This unusual name is usually chosen by families in which it is traditional.
Famous name: Gaylord Jackson Perry (baseball pitcher)
Nicknames: **Gay, Lord**
Variations: **Gallard, Gayelord**

Gellert (see **Gerard**)

Gelo (see **Angelo**)

Gene Form of **Eugene.** Gene began to be thought of as a separate name at the beginning of the 20th century. It was fairly popular during the 1940s and 1950s but is now out of fashion.

Famous names: Orvon Gene Autry (singer and actor)
Gene Kelly (dancer)
Gene Tunney (boxer)

Geno (see **Eugene**)

Geoff (see **Geoffrey**)

Geoffrey Old German *Guafrid,* "peaceful land"; or *Walahfrid,* "peaceful traveler"; or *Gisfrid,* "pledge of peace"; in Norman French, all three of these names became *Jeufroi,* which was taken into Middle English as *Geffrey.* Geoffrey Chaucer, author of *The Canterbury Tales,* is the best-known literary Geoffrey. Geoffrey is the traditional British spelling of this name, but in the United States **Jeffrey** is the more popular form; less than ten percent of American parents use the British spelling.

Famous names: Geoffrey Holder (dancer and choreographer)
Geoffrey Horne (actor)

Nicknames: **Geoff, Jeff**

Variations: **Geoffroi** (French), **Geoffroy** (French), **Goffredo** (Italian), **Jeffrey**

Geoffroi (see **Geoffrey**)

Geoffroy (see **Geoffrey**)

Geordie (see **George**)

George Greek *georgos,* "farmer." This name dates back to ancient Greece. Virgil celebrated the pleasures of farming in the Georgics, a poetic treatise on agriculture. St. George, a Roman military tribune who was martyred at Lydda, Palestine, was the favorite saint of Edward III of England. In 1349, the king dedicated the Order of the Garter to St. George, thereby making him the patron saint of England. George, the duke of Clarence, was the brother of Edward IV and brother to

Richard III, who had him murdered. The name, however, did not move into common use in England until the royal house of Hanover ascended the throne of Great Britain; there have been four kings named George since then. In the United States, George remained a very popular name after the Revolution because of the first president, George Washington. It was one of the top five names for American boys until about 1930. It has steadily lost ground since and was 90th on the popularity list in 1991. Hispanic-Americans and Greek-Americans are the groups most fond of the name today.

Famous names: George Balanchine (choreographer)
George Gordon, Lord Byron (poet)
George Bush (41st U.S. president)
George Cohan (lyricist)
George Washington Carver (educator)
George Gershwin (composer)
Jerzy N. Kosinski (novelist)
George Orwell (author)
George Herman "Babe" Ruth (baseball great)
George Bernard Shaw (playwright)

Nicknames: **Geordie** (Scottish)**, Georgie, Orito, Yoyi, Yoyo**

Variations: **Georges** (French), **Georgios** (Greek), **Goran** (Swedish), **Gyorgy** (Hungarian), **Jerzy** (Polish), **Jorge** (Portuguese and Spanish), **Jurgen** (German), **Yrjo** (Finnish), **Yuri** (Russian and Ukrainian)

Georges (see **George**)

Georgie (see **George**)

Georgios (see **George**)

Gerald Old German *Gairovald,* "spear ruler," from *ger* [spear] + *vald* [rule]. This name existed in England before the Norman Conquest. In the eighth century, St. Gerald founded monasteries and a convent. His day is March 13. This was a popular American name during the first half of the 20th century, but the use Gerald is declining. Its nickname Jerry is now given more often as a first name than is Gerald itself.

Famous name: Gerald Rudolph Ford, Jr. (38th U.S. president)

Nicknames: **Gerry, Jerry**

Variations: **Garrelt** (Dutch), **Garrett** (English), **Geralde** (French), **Geraldo** (Portuguese, Italian, and Spanish),

Geraldos (Greek), Geralds (Latvian), Geraud (French), Gerhold (Dutch and German), Gerold (German), Giraldo (Italian), Giraud (French), Jerrold

Geralde (see **Gerald**)

Geraldo (see **Gerald**)

Geraldos (see **Gerald**)

Geralds (see **Gerald**)

Gerard Old German *Gairhard,* "spear-brave," from *ger* [spear] + *hardu* [hard]. This name arrived in England with the Norman Conquest. Seven saints have been named Gerard, and three other Gerards have been blessed but not canonized. In the historical novel *The Cloister and the Hearth* by Charles Reade, the love story of Gerard, Erasmus's father, plays an important part in the plot.

Famous names: Gerard Depardieu (actor)
　　　　　　　　Gerard Manley Hopkins (poet)

Nicknames: **Jerry, Gerry**

Variations: **Garrett, Gellert** (Hungarian), **Gerardo** (Portuguese, Italian, and Spanish), **Gerhard** (German and Swedish)

Gerardo Spanish, Italian, and Portuguese form of **Gerard.** The recent success of the Ecuadorian-born rap musician Gerardo has inspired many Hispanic-American parents to choose this name for their sons.

Geraud (see **Gerald**)

Geremia (see **Jeremiah**)

Gerhard (see **Gerard**)

Gerhold (see **Gerald**)

Gerold (see **Gerald**)

Gerome (see **Jerome**)

Geronimo (see **Jerome**)

Gerrie (see **Gerry, Jerry**)

Gerry Form of **Gerald, Gerard,** or **Jeremiah;** variation of **Jerry.** This spelling is much less common than **Jerry.**

Famous name: Gerry E. Studds (member of Congress)

Other spelling: **Gerrie**

Geyo (see **Roger**)

Giacobbe (see **Jacob**)

Giacomo (see **James**)

Gian (see **John**)

Gianni (see **John**)

Gide (see **Giles**)

Giermo (see **William**)

Gigo (see **Roderick, Rodrigo**)

Gil (see **Giles**)

Giles Greek *aigidion,* "kid (young goat)," through Latin *Aegidius* and French *Gide, Gilles;* associated with soldiers because shields were made of goatskin. St. Giles, a seventh-century Greek monk, left his homeland to avoid the publicity that his miracles had caused and went to France where he became a hermit. His asceticism won him renown there as well, and he performed a miracle for Charlemagne. He is the patron saint of cripples and beggars (having been both) and also of Edinburgh, Scotland. In England, more than 100 churches were named for him. His day is February 16. John Barth used the name in his novel *Giles Goat-Boy;* the title is a pun on the meaning of the name. Paul Guillaume, a French 20th-century novelist, is better known as Andre Gide.

Famous name: Giles Fletcher (writer)

Variations: **Egidio** (Italian), **Egidius** (German), **Gide** (Provencal), **Gil** (Portuguese and Spanish), **Gill** (Norwegian), **Gilles** (French), **Gillis** (Danish), **Gyles** (English)

Gill (see **Giles**)

Gilles (see **Giles**)

Gillis (see **Giles**)

Giordano (see **Jordan**)

Giosia (see **Josiah**)

Giosue (see **Joshua**)

Giovanni Italian form of **John.** This Italian name is now extremely
   popular in the United States with parents of Hispanic ancestry;
   it reached 224th place on the list of names given to American
   boys born in 1991.

Giraldo (see **Gerald**)

Giraud (see **Gerald**)

Girolamo (see **Jerome**)

Giuda (see **Judah**)

Giuliano (see **Julian, Julius**)

Giulio (see **Julian**)

Giuseppe (see **Joseph**)

Giustino (see **Justin**)

Glen (see **Glenn**)

Glenn Celtic *gleann,* "wooded valley, dale, glen." This place name
   and surname became a popular given name in the 19th century,
   perhaps because Sir Walter Scott used it often in his novels,
   especially in *The Monastery,* which chronicles the Glendenning
   family. Glenn was particularly well used in the 1950s and
   1960s, but its popularity has now receded. In 1991, it was the
   196th most popular name for American boys.
   Famous names: Glenn Ford (actor)
                 Glenn Gould (pianist)
   Nickname: **Glenny**
   Other spelling: **Glen**
   Variations: **Glyn** (Welsh), **Glynn** (Scottish)

Glenny (see **Glenn**)

Glyn, Glynn (see **Glen**)

Godofredo (see **Godfrey**)

Godefroy (see **Godfrey**)

Godfrey Norman French from Germanic *god* [God] + *fred* [peace].
Since the Middle Ages, Godfrey and **Geoffrey** have sometimes
been confused, but they probably were originally separate
names. Both Godfrey and Geoffrey were brought to England
during the Norman Conquest. Godfrey is only very rarely
chosen by parents in the United States. Godfrey Cass is the
wealthy dissolute young man who is Eppie's biological father in
British novelist George Eliot's *Silas Marner,* one of the most
commonly read books in American high-school literature
classes.

Famous name: Godfrey Cambridge (comedian)

Variations: **Godofredo** (Portuguese), **Godefroy** (French),
Goffredo (Italian), **Gotfrid** (Russian and Serbian),
Gotfrids (Latvian), **Gotfryd** (Polish), **Gottfrid** (Swedish),
Gottfried (German)

Goffredo (see **Geoffrey, Godfrey**)

Gome (see **Gomer**)

Gomer Hebrew "to complete, accomplish." In the Bible, Gomer
was the son of Japheth. The use of this name has always been
extremely rare, even in colonial New England when the
Puritans used many obscure biblical names. It is remembered
today because of the 1960s television series *Gomer Pyle,
U.S.M.C.,* which starred Jim Nabors in the title role.

Nickname: **Gome**

Goncalvo (see **Gonzalo**)

Gontier (see **Gunnar**)

Gonzaleo (see **Gonzalo**)

Gonzalez (see **Gonzalo**)

Gonzalo Spanish, a Visigothic name with a first syllable from
Germanic *gund* [strife]. The meaning of the second part of the
name is disputed; "disposed to," "elf," and "safe" have been

suggested as possibilities. Gonzalo was an extremely common name in medieval Spain, and **Gonzalez** ("son of Gonzalo") is one of the top ten Hispanic surnames in the United States today. Gonzalo is no longer one of the top Spanish first names, but it is still being regularly used in the Hispanic-American community.

Nickname: **Gonzi**

Variations: **Goncalvo** (Portuguese), **Gonzaleo, Gonzoyo**

Gonzi (see **Gonzalo**)

Gonzoyo (see **Gonzalo**)

Goran (see **George**)

Gordie, Gordy (see **Gordon**)

Gordon Uncertain origin, but may come from a French place name *Gourdon* or from Celtic *gor* [spacious] + *din* [fort]. Gordon became a popular given name in England in the 19th century because of the exploits of Charles George Gordon, a general and adventurer known as "Chinese Gordon" and "Gordon Pasha." He was killed at Khartoum on January 26, 1885, by the Mahdi fighters who stormed the city. Gordon's Gin is named after him. Gordon is a Scottish clan name; its members are renowned for their military abilities, which are usually proved by their leading English soldiers into battle. During the 1950s, Gordon was an especially popular name in Canada, undoubtedly due to Canadian admiration for hockey star Gordie Howe, who was the National Hockey League's most valuable player six times between 1952 and 1963.

Famous names: Gordon Lightfoot (musician)
                        Gordon MacRae (actor)

Nicknames: **Gordie, Gordy**

Gotfrid, Gotfryd (see **Godfrey**)

Gotfrids (see **Godfrey**)

Gottfrid (see **Godfrey**)

Gottfried (see **Godfrey**)

Goyo (see **Gregory**)

Grade (see **Grady**)

Grady Irish *Grada,* "noble" or "illustrious." This name is used in the southern part of the United States, especially with people with Scottish or Irish ancestors.

Famous name: Grady Nutt (comedian)

Nickname: **Grade**

Graeme (see **Graham**)

Graham Old English *Grantham* from *grand* [gravel] + *ham* [home or village]. This name was taken from England to Scotland in the 12th century by William de Graham, a Norman baron, and became the name of a major Scottish clan. Graham was extremely popular as a first name all over Great Britain and in Australia during the 1950s and 1960s. Although not popular with American parents, it still is in regular use in the United States, being the 340th most common name given to American boys born in 1991. Graham crackers were named after Sylvester Graham, an American physician.

Famous names: Graham Greene (novelist)
Graham Kerr (chef)
Graham Nash (musician)

Variations: **Graeme, Gram**

Gram (see **Graham**)

Grant Norman French *graunt,* "tall, large." Like **Graham,** Grant is a surname that migrated from England to Scotland in medieval times, becoming much more common in Scotland than it had been in England. The name came to England with the Norman Conquest. In the 19th century, Grant became a first name in the United States when parents began to name their sons in honor of Ulysses S. Grant, commander of the Union Army during the Civil War and 18th president of the United States. The name still gets steady use, being 154th on the popularity list in both 1990 and 1991.

Famous names: Grant Tinker (television producer)
Grant Wood (painter)

Variation: **LeGrand**

Greg, Gregg Forms of **Gregory.** These short forms are occasionally given as names in their own right.

Famous names: Greg LeMond (bicyclist)
Greg Louganis (Olympic diver)
Greg Morris (actor)

Gregoire (see **Gregory**)

Gregor (see **Gregory**)

Gregory Greek *Gregorios,* "watchful." Sixteen popes and many saints have been named Gregory. Gregory I was pope for 14 years in the sixth century; he was instrumental in converting many Europeans to the Christian faith. Before he became pope, he had planned to go to the British Isles, but he was kept in Rome by Pope Pelagius II who needed Gregory as an administrator. When Gregory became pope, he sent Augustine and 40 monks to England, and in 597, Athelbert and 10,000 of his subjects were baptized. In 1582, Pope Gregory VIII established the Gregorian calendar, which we now use.
Famous names: Gregory Hines (dancer and actor)
Gregory Peck (actor)
Nicknames: **Greg, Gregg**
Variations: **Goyo** (Spanish), **Gregoire** (French), **Gregor** (Czech, German, and Norwegian), **Grigor** (Bulgarian)

Griff (see **Griffin**)

Griffin Form of Welsh *Gruffudd,* perhaps "strong prince"; or Middle English *griffin,* "gryphon." A gryphon is a mythical animal with the head and wings of an eagle and the body of a lion; many medieval coats of arms included gryphons. Although still fairly uncommon as a first name, Griffin seems to be slowly increasing in use in the United States. Griffin Mill is the name of the antihero in Robert Altman's 1992 film *The Player,* which satirized the Hollywood entertainment industry.
Nickname: **Griff**

Grigor (see **Gregory**)

Grove (see **Grover**)

Grover Old English "one who lives by a grove." The fame of President Grover Cleveland made this one of the top 50 names for American boys for a few years around 1890, but now it is a rare name mostly given to boys being called after a father or grandfather. A blue muppet named Grover, a member of the cast of *Sesame Street,* has made parents fondly aware of the name even if they don't choose to use it.

Famous names: Stephen Grover Cleveland (22nd and 24th
           U.S. president)
           Grover Cleveland "Pete" Alexander (baseball
           pitcher)

Nickname: **Grove**

Gualterio (see **Walter**)

Gualtiero (see **Walter**)

Guglielmo (see **William**)

Guido (see **Guy**)

Guillaume (see **William**)

Guillermo (see **William**)

Guillo (see **William**)

Guirmo (see **William**)

Gulielm (see **William**)

Gun (see **Gunnar**)

Gunder (see **Gunnar**)

Gunn (see **Gunnar**)

Gunnar Old Norse *Gunnarr,* "battle warrior"; or Old German *Gundher,* "battle army." In the Germanic saga *The Nibelungenlied,* Gunnar is Brunhild's husband and Kriemhild's brother. The name was primarily used in the United States by Scandinavian-Americans until recently, but now seems to be catching on with other parents, perhaps because of the fame of rock singer Gunnar Nelson.

Famous name: Gunnar Hansen (actor)

Nicknames: **Gun, Gunn, Gunny**

Variations: **Gontier** (French), **Gunder** (Danish), **Gunner, Gunter**
    (Dutch and Hungarian), **Gunther** (German)

Gunner (see **Gunnar**)

Gunny (see **Gunnar**)

Gunter (see **Gunnar**)

Gunther (see **Gunnar**)

Gus Form of **Augustus, Fergus,** or **Gustav.** Some parents choose this name without reference to the longer names, but it is fairly unusual.
    Famous name: August Rodney "Gus" "Blackie" Mancuso
                           (baseball catcher)
    Nickname: **Gussy**

Gussy (see **Augustus, Gus, Gustav**)

Gust (see **Gustav**)

Gustaf (see **Gustav**)

Gustav Old Norse from *Gautr* [a tribal name] + *stafr* [staff]. This Scandinavian name spread to other countries during the reign of Gustavus Adolphus (Gustaf II) of Sweden. He inherited wars with Poland, Germany, and Denmark when he ascended the throne in 1611.
    Famous names: Gustave Flaubert (novelist)
                          Gustav Mahler (composer)
    Nicknames: **Gus, Gussy, Gust, Gusti, Tabo, Tavito, Tavo**
    Variations: **Gustaf** (Swedish), **Gustave** (French), **Gustavo** (Italian, Portuguese, and Spanish), **Gustavus** (Latin), **Gusts** (Latvian), **Kustaa** (Finnish)

Gustave (see **Gustav**)

Gustavo (see **Gustav**)

Gustavus (see **Gustav**)

Gusti (see **Gustav**)

Gustino (see **Justin**)

Gusts (see **Gustav**)

Gutierre (see **Walter**)

Guy Old German *Wido,* either "wood" or "wide," through French

Guy. The name Guy came to England during the time of the Norman Conquest and was in common use until 1605 when Guy Fawkes decided to kill King James I and members of Parliament by blowing up the Parliament building. He and his fellow conspirators managed to fill a cellar with gunpowder, but before anything blew up, they were caught and executed. The event is known as the Gunpowder Plot, and Guy Fawkes Day is still celebrated in England. The name Guy then went out of fashion until 1815 when Sir Walter Scott revived it for his novel *Guy Mannering.* Guy was among the top 50 names for American boys in the 1880s, but it went out of fashion again when "guy" became a slang term for "man."

Famous name: Guy de Maupassant (writer of short stories)

Variations: **Guido** (Italian, Spanish, and Portuguese), **Gvidas** (Lithuanian), **Gvidon** (Bulgarian, Croatian, and Russian)

Gvidas, Gvidon (see **Guy**)

Gyles (see **Giles**)

Gyorgy (see **George**)

Hadrian (see **Adrian**)

Hakeem (see **Akeem**)

Hal Originally a medieval form of **Harry** or **Henry;** later also a form of **Harold**. Prince Hal, the rakish son of Henry IV of England and the boon companion of Falstaff, is depicted in Shakespeare's *Henry IV, Part I* and *Henry IV, Part II*. But in *Henry V,* he has grown up to become a courageous and responsible king.

    Famous names: Hal Lanier (baseball player)
                     Hal Linden (actor)
                     Hal Williams (actor)

Ham (see **Hamilton, Hamlin**)

Hamilton Old English "bare or cleared hill" from *hamel* [scarred] + *dun* [hill]. This place name and surname became a first name in the United States in honor of Alexander Hamilton, the first secretary of the Treasury of the United States and one of the most popular political figures during George Washington's presidency. He was killed in a duel with Aaron Burr in 1804.

    Famous names: Hamilton Fish Kean (U.S. senator)
                     Hamilton Jordan (adviser to President Carter)

    Nicknames: **Ham, Tony**

Hamish (see **James**)

Hamisi Swahili "born on Thursday." Day names are common in many cultures. In Daniel Defoe's novel *Robinson Crusoe*, Friday is the native man who assists Crusoe. In Spanish-speaking countries, Dominic and its many variations mean "born on Sunday."

Hamlin Norman French *Hamblin,* a diminutive form of Germanic *Haimo,* "home." The name arrived in England after the Norman Conquest and soon became popular as Hamlen, Hamlyn, Hamblen, Hamblin, and Hambling. All these forms died out as first names around 1500 but survive as surnames today. The American writer Hamlin Garland, whose stories about life in the Dakotas are now considered classics, was born in 1860 and named after Hannibal Hamlin, who was vice-president of the United States at the time.
Nickname: **Ham**

Hamp (see **Hampton**)

Hampton Old English *Hamtun,* "homestead"; *Hammtun,* "farm at the river bend"; or *Heantun,* "high-town." This name is connected with royalty in England. Hampton Court is a royal palace that was built on the Thames River by Cardinal Woolsey, archbishop of York and primate of England. When he fell into disfavor, Henry VIII took over Woolsey's palace for himself.
Famous name: Clarence Hampton Etchison (baseball player)
Nickname: **Hamp**

Handy (see **Hannibal**)

Hanibal (see **Hannibal**)

Hank This name existed in medieval England as a short form of *Jehankin,* itself from *Jehan,* a Middle English form of **John.** The name died out in England, but in America it is now used as a nickname for **Henry.** This probably came about when English speakers had contact with the early Dutch settlers in New Netherland (New York), because *Hannek* and *Henk* are common pet forms of **Hendrik,** the Dutch version of **Henry.**
Famous names: Henry Louis "Hank" Aaron (baseball player)
Hank Williams (country musician)

Hannes (see **John**)

Hannibal Phoenician "one favored by the god Baal." Hannibal, a Carthaginian general, crossed the Alps in 218 B.C. and defeated the Romans. He did not follow up his victory by sacking Rome, but returned to Carthage.
Famous name: Hannibal Hamlin (U.S. vice-president)

Nickname: **Handy**

Variations: **Anibal, Hanibal**

Hanoch (see **Enoch**)

Hans Danish, Dutch, and German form of **John.** Many Americans will remember reading the story of the Dutch boy Hans Brinker and his silver skates.

Famous names: Hans Christian Andersen (writer)
Hans Conried (actor)

Hansel (see **John**)

Harald (see **Harold**)

Haraldo (see **Harold**)

Haralds (see **Harold**)

Harbert (see **Herbert**)

Harding Old English *Hearding,* "son or follower of *Heard.*" Heard was an Old English name meaning "hardy, strong, brave." This surname was first used as a given name to honor President Warren Harding.

Harley Old English "hares' glade."

Famous name: Harley Martin Kilgore (U.S. senator)
Variation: **Arley**

Harlow Old English "army hill."

Famous name: Harlow Shapeley (astronomer)
Variations: **Arlow, Harlowe**

Harlowe (see **Harlow**)

Harman (see **Herman**)

Harmon (see **Herman**)

Harold Old English *Hereweald* from *here* [army] + *weald* [power]; also, Old Norse *Harivald.* Harold II was the last Saxon king of England. He reigned for only a few months because he broke the oath he had made to William the Conqueror, duke of Normandy. Harold's army met William's at the battle of Hastings on October 14, 1066, where the Saxons were defeated and Harold was killed. The story is retold by Tennyson in his poem *Harold.* Lord Byron used the name in his long poem *Childe Harold,* on which Berlioz based his opera *Harold in Italy.*

Famous names: Harold Christian Hagen (member of Congress)
　　　　　　　Harold Lloyd (comedian)
　　　　　　　Harold Macmillan (prime minister of Great Britain)

Nicknames: **Hal, Harry**

Variations: **Garald** (Russian), **Harald** (German and Scandinavian), **Haraldo** (Portuguese and Spanish), **Haralds** (Latvian)

Haroun (see **Aaron**)

Harrison Middle English *Herryson,* "son of Henry." This name has recently increased in use due to the great popularity of film actor Harrison Ford.

Harry Originally a form of **Henry**; in modern times, also a form of **Harold**. In Elizabethan England, the name Henry was pronounced Harry, but when spelling became more uniform, Harry became a separate name. Although singer Harry Belafonte has done very well, another singer named Harry changed his name to Bing Crosby.

Famous names: Harry Golden (journalist)
　　　　　　　Harry Houdini (magician)
　　　　　　　Harry S Truman (33rd U.S. president)

Variations: **Arrigo** (Italian), **Hal**

Harvey Breton *Haerveu,* "battle-worthy." This warrior's name came to England during the Norman Invasion. Today, however, Harvey is not associated with fierceness but with the gentle, imaginary rabbit in Mary Chase's play *Harvey,* which was made into a movie starring James Stewart. St. Harvey lived during the sixth century and was known for his piety. Because he was blind, he is invoked for eye trouble. His day is June 17.

Famous names: Harvey Firestone (industrialist)
　　　　　　　Harve Presnell (actor)

Variations: **Herve** (French), **Hervey**

Haskel (see **Haskell**)

Haskell Old Norse *Asketill* from *oss* [god] + *ketill,* "sacrificial cauldron." Many Celtic and Germanic myths mention a divine cauldron where warriors who have been slain in battle can be brought back to life by the gods. Haskell is practically nonexistent as a first name today. Baby boomers are likely to associate it with Eddie Haskell, a teenage character in the 1950s television series *Leave It to Beaver.*

Nickname: **Hasky**

Variation: **Haskel**

Hasky (see **Haskell**)

Hayden Old English *heg denu,* "hay valley," English place name; or Irish Gaelic *Eideain,* "armor." This name suddenly came out of nowhere in 1990, reaching 221st place on the popularity chart in 1991. That may not sound like very much, but it means that in the first three years of the 1990s alone at least four thousand American boys were named Hayden, probably many more than had been so named in the previous three decades. This explosion of Haydens must have been inspired by Hayden Fox, the title character of the television series *Coach,* which debuted in February 1989.

Haywood Old English "enclosed wood" or "high wood." When this name is used as a first name, it is usually a family name.

Famous names: Haywood Cooper Sullivan (baseball player)
Heywood Brown (literary critic)

Nicknames: **Wood, Woodie, Woody**

Variation: **Heywood**

Hebert (see **Herbert**)

Heck (see **Hector**)

Hector Greek *Hektor,* "one who holds fast" or "restrainer." In Homer's *Iliad,* Hector, the brave son of Priam, was killed by Achilles, and his body was dragged three times around the wall of Troy. In England, the name is part of the legend of King Arthur. Sir Hector was the foster father of the king, and Sir Hector de Mares was a knight of the Round Table. Shakespeare depicted Hector as the sensible older brother of Paris and Troilus in his play *Troilus and Cressida.* In the United States today, Hector is a very popular name with Hispanic-Americans, but is only very rarely found in other ethnic groups.

Famous names: Hector Berlioz (composer)

Hector Dilan Cruz (baseball player)
Hector Hugh Munro (humorist)

Nickname: **Heck**

Variations: **Ector** (Greek), **Ettore** (Italian), **Heitor** (Portuguese), **Hektor** (Polish, Czech, and Scandinavian), **Hektoras** (Lithuanian)

Heinrich (see **Henry**)

Heinz (see **Henry**)

Heitor (see **Hector**)

Hektor (see **Hector**)

Hektoras (see **Hector**)

Hendrik, Hank (see **Henry**)

Henrey (see **Henry**)

Henri (see **Henry**)

Henrico (see **Henry**)

Henrik (see **Henry**)

Henry Old German *Haimirich* from *haimi* [home] + *ric* [ruler, protector]. Henry is a royal name in England, France, and Germany. Henry I of England, the fourth son of William the Conqueror, ruled for more than 30 years. His grandson Henry II established English common law. Henry VIII is said to be the founder of the modern English state. Several German emperors were also named Henry, and four French kings named Henri died violently.

Famous names: Henry Albert Bauer (baseball player)
Henry Fonda (actor)
Henry Ford (industrialist)
Henry Hudson (explorer)
Henry James (novelist)
Henry Wadsworth Longfellow (poet)
Henry L. Mencken (editor)
Henry David Thoreau (author)

Nicknames: **Hal, Hank, Harry**

Other spelling: **Henrey**

Variations: **Andrique, Eanraig** (Scottish), **Enrico** (Italian),
   Enrique (Spanish), **Heinrich** (German), **Heinz** (German),
   Hendrik (Danish and Dutch), **Henri** (French), **Henrico,
   Henrik** (Swedish), **Henryk** (Polish), **Jindrich** (Czech),
   Kiki, Kiko, Quico, Quiqui

Henryk (see **Henry**)

Herb (see **Herbert**)

Herbert Old German *Hariberct* from *harja* [army] + *berhta* [bright].
   Famous names: Herbert Hoover (31st U.S. president)
                 Herbert Spenser (philosopher)
   Nicknames: **Bert, Bertie, Herb, Herbie**
   Variations: **Erberto** (Italian), **Harbert** (Dutch), **Hebert**
      (French), **Herberto** (Spanish), **Heribert** (German and
      Slovakian), **Heriberto** (Spanish), **Hoireabard** (Irish)

Herberto (see **Herbert**)

Herbie (see **Herbert**)

Heribert (see **Herbert**)

Heriberto (see **Herbert**)

Herm (see **Herman**)

Herman Old German *Harimann* from *harja* [army] + *mann* [man].
   This name was popular in the 19th century.
   Famous names: Herman Hesse (novelist)
                 Herman Melville (novelist)
   Nicknames: **Herm, Hermie, Hermy**
   Variations: **Armand** (French), **Armando** (Spanish), **Armant,
      Armin, Arminio** (Italian), **Armond, Erman** (Rumanian),
      Ermanno (Italian), **Harman, Harmon, Hermann** (Danish
      and German), **Hermino** (Spanish and Portuguese**)**

Hermann (see **Herman**)

Hermie, Hermy (see **Herman**)

Hermino (see **Herman**)

Hernando (see **Fernando**)

Hersch (see **Herschel**)

Herschel German and Yiddish "deer."
Famous name: Hershel Walker (football player)
Nicknames: **Hersch, Hersh, Hirsch, Hirsh**
Other spelling: **Hershel**

Hersh (see **Herschel**)

Hershel (see **Herschel**)

Herve (see **Harvey**)

Hervey (see **Harvey**)

Hesus (see **Jesus**)

Hewart (see **Howard**)

Hewie (see **Hugh**)

Heywood (see **Haywood**)

Hi (see **Hiram**)

Hieronym (see **Jerome**)

Hieronymus (see **Jerome**)

Hiram Perhaps a form of Hebrew *Ahiram,* "brother of the exalted."
In the Bible, Hiram is the king of Tyre. He sent cedar trees, as
well as carpenters and masons, to King David to build him a
house. Later, Hiram cut down the cedars of Lebanon to build
David's son, Solomon, a palace. The name was in regular use
in the northern United States from the 17th century to the late
19th century. The form **Hyrum** is still regularly given to boys in
Utah in honor of Hyrum Smith, brother of the Mormon
prophet Joseph Smith, who was martyred in Illinois in 1844.
Famous name: Hiram Johnson (U.S. senator)
Nickname: **Hi**
Variation: **Hyrum**

Hirsch, Hirsh (see **Herschel**)

Hobart (see **Hubert**)

Hoibeard (see **Hubert**)

Hoireabard (see **Herbert**)

Holden Old English *Holedene,* "deep valley," from *hol* [hollow] + *denu* [valley]. This unusual name was chosen by J. D. Salinger for the teenage antihero of *The Catcher in the Rye.*

Holles (see **Hollis**)

Hollings (see **Hollis**)

Hollins (see **Hollis**)

Hollis Old English *holegn,* "holly." This name could be thought of as a masculine form of **Holly** and given to boys born around Christmas.
Variations: **Holles, Hollings, Hollins**

Homer Greek *Homeros,* meaning uncertain, perhaps "hostage" or "blind." Homer became a fairly popular American name in the early 19th century when names from classical Greek and Roman literature were in vogue. At the same time, many American towns and cities received classical names such as Rome, Athens, Ithaca, Troy, and Utica. The name is almost never found in England and has once more become rare in the United States as well. Homer is best known as the name of the father of the television cartoon family *The Simpsons.* This will probably ensure that American boys named Homer will remain very scarce for at least another generation.
Famous name: Homer (Greek poet)
Variations: **Homere** (French), **Homero** (Spanish), **Homeros** (Greek), **Omero** (Italian)

Homere (see **Homer**)

Homero (see **Homer**)

Homeros (see **Homer**)

Hood Old English *hod,* "hood," originally a nickname for someone who made hoods or who wore a distinctive hood. This name goes at least as far back as Robin Hood, the legendary English outlaw. Hood is extremely rare as a first name and when found is usually when a mother's maiden name is given to her son.
Famous name: Hood Roberts (linguist)

Hoop (see **Hooper**)

Hooper Old English "one who fits hoops on barrels."
Nickname: **Hoop**

Horace Latin *Horatius,* a Roman family name, which may be related to *hora,* "time." The Roman poet Horatius Flaccus is known as Horace.
Famous names: Horace Greeley (journalist)
Horace Gregory (poet)
Horace Mann (educator)
Horace Walpole (writer)
Variations: **Horacio** (Spanish), **Horatio, Horatius** (Estonian and German), **Oracio, Orasio, Orazio** (Italian), **Racho**

Horacio (see **Horace**)

Horatio Variation of **Horace.** Captain Horatio Hornblower is the hero of the well-known stories by C. S. Forester.
Famous names: Horatio Alger (author)
Horatio Nelson (British admiral)

Horatius (see **Horace**)

Houston Old English and Scottish "Hugh's town." Samuel Houston was president of the Republic of Texas. This name honors him.

Howard Old German *Huguard* from *hug* [heart, mind] + *hard* [hardy, brave]; or Old Norse *Haward* from *ha* [high] + *vard* [guardian]. This aristocratic English surname became a popular first name in wealthy American families during the 1870s and by 1900 had spread to all social classes. Howard has been going out of fashion since 1950, but some parents are still choosing it for their sons; it was the 364th most common name for boys born in 1991. Howard Hughes, the wealthy industrialist, was in the public eye throughout his life. As a young man, he was a dashing playboy; as an old man, a bizarre recluse.
Famous names: Howard Fast (novelist)
Howard Keel (singer)
Nicknames: **Howie, Ward**
Variations: **Hewart**

Howie (see **Howard**)

Hoyt Possibly Irish "spirit, mind."

    Famous names: Hoyt Axton (country singer)
                      Hoyt Wilhelm (baseball player)

    Other spelling: **Hoyte**

Hoyte (see **Hoyt**)

Hristo (see **Christian**)

Hristofor (see **Christopher**)

Hub (see **Hubert**)

Hubbard (see **Hubert**)

Hube (see **Hubert**)

Hubert Old German *Hugubert* from *hug* [heart, mind] + *berht* [bright, famous]. The eighth-century St. Hubert is the patron saint of hunters.

    Famous names: Hubert Alfred Evans (baseball player)
                      Hubert Humphrey (U.S. vice-president)
                      Hubert Wilkins (polar explorer)

    Nicknames: **Bert, Hub, Hube, Hubi, Hubie**

    Variations: **Hobart, Hoibeard** (Irish), **Hubbard, Huberto** (Spanish), **Hugbert** (German), **Uberto** (Italian)

Huberto (see **Hubert**)

Hubi, Hubie (see **Hubert**)

Hud (see **Hugh**)

Huet (see **Hugh**)

Huey (see **Hugh**)

Hugbert (see **Hubert**)

Hugh Probably Old German *huga,* "heart, mind, spirit." This name was popular in England and France during the Middle Ages because of St. Hugh of Lincoln, England, a medieval bishop noted for his charity and his defense of the Church against the crown, and because of Hugh Capet, founder of the Capetian dynasty in France.

    Nicknames: **Hewie, Huey, Hughie, Hughy**

Variations: **Aodh** (Irish), **Aoidh** (Scottish), **Hud, Huet, Hugo** (Danish, Dutch, German, Spanish, and Swedish), **Hugon** (Polish and Spanish), **Hugonas** (Lithuanian), **Hugues** (French), **Hutch, Huugo** (Finnish), **Ugo** (Italian), **Ugon** (Greek)

Hughie, Hughy (see **Hugh**)

Hugo Latin form of **Hugh**. Residents of the Caribbean and South Atlantic states will long associate this name with Hurricane Hugo, the September 1989 storm that took 504 lives.

Famous name: Hugo Frank Bezdek (baseball manager)

Hugon (see **Hugh**)

Hugonas (see **Hugh**)

Hugues (see **Hugh**)

Humfredo (see **Humphrey**)

Humfrey (see **Humphrey**)

Humfrid (see **Humphrey**)

Humfried (see **Humphrey**)

Humfry (see **Humphrey**)

Humph (see **Humphrey**)

Humphrey Norman French *Humfrey;* form of Old German *Hunfrid* from *hun* [bear cub, young warrior] + *frid* [peace]. Even the well-loved actor Humphrey Bogart wasn't able to attract many parents to this little-used name. It dates at least to the 12th century in England and was the name of the unfortunate duke of Gloucester, the son of Henry IV, who founded one of the first libraries at Oxford University and later was starved to death in the Tower of London.

Nicknames: **Humph, Numps**

Other spellings: **Humfrey, Humfry**

Variations: **Humfredo** (Spanish), **Humfrid** (Swedish), **Humfried** (German), **Hunfredo** (Spanish), **Hunfried** (German), **Onfredo** (Italian), **Onfroy** (French)

Hunfredo (see **Humphrey**)

Hunfried (see **Humphrey**)

Hunter Middle English *huntere,* "huntsman." This name is now increasing in popularity rather rapidly, in just the two years prior to 1991 rising from 255th to 155th place on the list of names for newborn boys in the United States. Perhaps some of its success can be traced to the 1980s television series *Hunter,* which starred former professional football player Fred Dryer as Rick Hunter, a sergeant in the Los Angeles Police Department. Like most of television's tough cop characters, he was normally addressed as "Hunter," not "Rick," and so parents looking for new names with decidedly masculine images may have been encouraged to choose Hunter for their sons. The rugged outdoor associations of the word *hunter* also contribute to the name's image.

Famous name: Hunter S. Thompson (journalist)

Husto (see **Justin**)

Hutch (see **Hugh**)

Huugo (see **Hugh**)

Hyrum (see **Hiram**)

Iago Italian and Welsh forms of **James.** In Shakespeare's *Othello*, Iago is the evil servant who convinces the Moor that his wife has been unfaithful.

Iain (see **Ian, John**)

Ian Scottish form of **John.**
>   Famous name: Ian Fleming (writer)
>   Other spelling: **Iain**

Ibrahim (see **Abraham**)

Ichabod Hebrew *Ikabhoth,* "where is the glory?" In the Old Testament, the pregnant wife of Phinehas goes into labor when she learns that her husband has been killed in battle; she herself then dies in childbirth after naming her son Ichabod. Because of this story, it became the custom among the Puritans in colonial New England to name boys whose mothers died in childbirth Ichabod. The name itself had almost died out by the 19th century when Washington Irving wrote *The Legend of Sleepy Hollow* and named its comic schoolmaster hero Ichabod Crane. Ichabod is therefore a name most Americans have heard of but that none would consider actually conferring upon a newborn son.

Iggy (see **Ignatius**)

Ignac (see **Ignatius**)

Ignace (see **Ignatius**)

Ignacy (see **Ignatius**)

Ignat (see **Ignatius**)

Ignatius Form of *Egnatius,* Roman family name of Etruscan origin and unknown meaning, but altered to resemble Latin *ignis,* "fire." Several saints were named Ignatius, including St. Ignatius of Antioch, who was killed by lions in the Roman arena, and St. Ignatius Loyola, who founded the Society of Jesus, the Jesuits. The name is fairly popular with Greek-Americans.
    Famous names: Inigo Jones (architect)
                  Ignace Jan Paderewski (statesman and musician)
                  Ignazio Silone (novelist)
    Nickname: **Iggy**
    Variations: **Ignac** (Czech), **Ignace** (French), **Ignacy** (Polish), **Ignat** (Bulgarian), **Ignaz** (German), **Ignazio** (Italian), **Inigo**

Ignaz (see **Ignatius**)

Ignazio (see **Ignatius**)

Igor Russian form of Scandinavian *Ivar* from Old Norse *yr* [yew] + *herr* [army].
    Famous names: Igor Sikorsky (aviation pioneer)
                  Igor Stravinsky (composer)

Ike (see **Isaac**)

Ikey, Ikie (see **Isaac**)

Ikoy (see **Frederick**)

Illes (see **Elijah**)

Immanuel (see **Emmanuel**)

Inigo (see (**Ignatius**)

Ingemar (see **Ingmar**)

Ingmar Scandinavian from *Ing* [a Norse fertility god] + *maerr* [famous]. This name has become known in the United States through movie director Ingmar Bergman.
    Famous name: Ingemar Johansson (boxer)
    Variation: **Ingemar**

Ioan (see **John**)

Ioannes (see **John**)

Ioel (see **Joel**)

Iordache (see **Jordan**)

Iordanos (see **Jordan**)

Iosef (see **Joseph**)

Ioseph (see **Joseph**)

Ira Hebrew "watchful" or "young ass."
Famous name: Ira Gershwin (lyricist)

Irv (see **Irving**)

Irvin (see **Irving**)

Irvine (see **Irving**)

Irving Scottish place name and surname, probably meaning "green
river." Like **Byron, Emerson,** and **Milton,** Irving is a surname
that became a first name out of admiration for a famous
author: Washington Irving, the early 19th-century American
writer most remembered for *The Legend of Sleepy Hollow,*
which was made into a popular Disney animated film. In 20th-
century America, Irving is stereotyped as a Jewish name. In the
19th century, Jewish immigrant parents gave their son or
daughter a Hebrew name, usually in honor of a deceased
relative, to be used in the synagogue. The parents also gave the
child an "American" name on the birth certificate to help him
or her assimilate into the larger society. It was the custom,
however, to pick an "American" name that started with the
same letter as the Hebrew name. There are many biblical
Hebrew names starting with "I," such as **Isaiah, Israel,** and
Isaac, but when most Jews first came to the United States, the
only obviously "American" name starting with "I" was Irving.
Thus, Irving quickly became a predominantly Jewish name in
the United States, which, ironically, defeated the purpose of
parents who wanted to give their son an American name that
wouldn't immediately type him as Jewish.
Famous names: Irving Berlin (composer)
                    Irving Stone (writer)

Nickname: **Irv**

Variations: **Irvin, Irvine, Irwin**

Irwin Variation of **Irving** or **Erwin**.

Famous names: Irwin Edman (philosopher)
Irwin Shaw (playwright)

Other spelling: **Irwyn**

Irwyn (see **Erwin, Irwin**)

Isaac Hebrew "laughter." In the Old Testament, Isaac was cherished by his mother, Sarah, because the Lord granted her wish to have a child when she feared she was too old to bear children. But after giving Sarah and her husband, Abraham, this child, the Lord demanded that Abraham sacrifice his son to show his faith. Just before he was about to slay Isaac, the Lord appeared and spared the boy, explaining that Abraham's willingness to obey was testimony enough. Isaac is gradually becoming more popular and was 118th on the list of names given American boys in 1991.

Famous names: Isaac Asimov (author)
Isaac Newton (mathematician and physicist)
Isaac Singer (novelist)
Isaac Stern (violinist)
Izaak Walton (writer)

Nicknames: **Ike, Ikey, Ikie, Zak**

Other spellings: **Isac, Isacc, Ysaac, Ysac**

Variations: **Isaak** (German, Greek, and Russian), **Isacco** (Italian), **Itzhak, Izaak** (Dutch and Polish), **Yitzchak** (modern Hebrew), **Yitzhak**

Isaak (see **Isaac**)

Isac, Isacc (see **Isaac**)

Isacco (see **Isaac**)

Isaia (see **Isaiah**)

Isaiah Hebrew "Yahweh is salvation." The Book of Isaiah was written by a prophet who lived seven centuries before Jesus. Isaiah is now popular with African-American parents.

Famous name: Isiah Thomas (basketball player)

Other spelling: **Isiah**

Variations: **Esaias** (Danish and Swedish), **Isaia** (Italian and Rumanian), **Isais** (Spanish and Portuguese)

Isais (see **Isaiah**)

Isiah (see **Isaiah**)

Israel Hebrew *Yisrael,* "God perseveres" or "wrestling with God." This name was given to Jacob after he successfully wrestled with an angel, and his descendants were called the people of Israel. The land of Israel was the biblical kingdom of God's chosen people, the Israelites.
Famous names: Israel Goldiamond (psychologist)
Israel Kaplan (educator)
Variations: **Israele** (Italian), **Izrael** (Polish and Hungarian), **Izraelis** (Lithuanian), **Srul** (Yiddish)

Israele (see **Israel**)

Issa Arabic and Swahili form of **Jesus.**

Itzhak Variation of **Isaac.**
Famous name: Itzhak Perlman (violinist)

Iuda (see **Judah**)

Ivan Russian variation of **John.** Ivan was the name of six Russian tsars. The 14th-century Ivan I was the grand prince of Moscow. The 15th-century Ivan III, called Ivan the Great, helped to unify Russia by preventing the Tartars from overrunning the country. The 16th-century Ivan IV, known as Ivan the Terrible, was actually the first tsar of unified Russia. Although he took control of Siberia and brought order to the central government, he was known for his personal cruelty.
Famous names: Ivan Lendl (tennis player)
Ivan Reitman (film director)

Ives (see **Yves**)

Izaak (see **Isaac**)

Izrael (see **Israel**)

Izraelis (see **Israel**)

Jaan (see **John**)

Jace (see **Jason**)

Jack Form of **John,** from Middle English *Jankin, Jackin.* Jack was considered an independent name in England as early as the 14th century. This name abounds in children's nursery rhymes, including "Jack and the Beanstalk," "Jack Sprat," "Jack and Jill," and "Little Jack Horner."

Famous names: Jack Benny (comedian)
Jack Dempsey (boxer)
Jack Kerouac (writer)
Jack Lemmon (actor)
Jack London (novelist)
Jack Nicholson (actor)
Jack Nicklaus (golfer)

Nickname: **Jackie**

Variation: **Jock** (Scottish)

Jackie Form of **Jack.**

Famous names: Jackie Gleason (comedian)
Jackie Mason (comedian)
Jackie Roosevelt Robinson (baseball player)
Jackie Wilson (singer)

Other spelling: **Jacky**

Jackson Middle English *Jakson,* "son of **Jack.**"

Famous names: Jackson Browne (singer)
Jackson Pollock (painter)

Jacky (see **Jackie, John**)

Jacob Hebrew *Ya'aqob,* "may God protect," later interpreted as "supplanter." In the Book of Genesis, Jacob was the son of Isaac and Rebecca. He was a devious man who tricked his father into giving him the inheritance that rightfully belonged to his brother, Esau. With the power he had acquired, Jacob formed the tribe of Israel. He is also remembered for his vision of a stairway to heaven, called Jacob's ladder. In English history, the Jacobites rallied to the cause of James Stuart of Scotland, who became king after the death of Elizabeth I. Three centuries later, the extremists in the French revolution were called the Jacobins. Jacob is the fashionable "J" name today; it was 20th on the national list of names given American boys in 1991 and is already in the top ten in several Western states.
Famous name: Jacob Javits (U.S. senator)
Nicknames: **Jake, Jakie**
Variations: **Giacobbe** (Italian), **Jacobo** (Spanish), **Jacques** (French), **Jakob** (German), **James**

Jacobo Spanish form of **Jacob.**
Famous name: Jacobo Timerman (author)

Jacques French form of **Jacob** or **James.**
Famous names: Jacques Cousteau (explorer)
Jacques David (painter)

Jago (see **James**)

Jaime (see **James**)

Jake (see **Jacob, James**)

Jakie (see **Jacob**)

Jakob (see **Jacob**)

Jamaal, Jamahl (see **Jamal**)

Jamal Arabic "beauty, handsomeness." This name, popular in most of the Arab world, has also become the most popular Muslim name in the African-American community. Jamal was the 44th most common name given African-American boys in 1991. The similar Arabic names **Jamel** and **Jamil** (meaning "handsome") are also popular. The resemblance of these names to **James,** which has long been especially well used, has undoubtedly contributed to their quick acceptance.

Famous name: Jamaal Wilkes (basketball player)

Other spellings: **Jamaal, Jamahl**

Jamel (see **Jamal**)

James English form of **Jacob.** This name developed from Late Latin *Iacomus,* a form of the original Latin *Iacobus.* In the New Testament, two of Jesus' apostles were named James. Legend says that one of them was a brother of Jesus and the first bishop of Jerusalem; he is thought to be the author of the Epistle of St. James. The other James was John's brother and a witness to Jesus' betrayal; like John the Baptist, he was beheaded by King Herod. James I of England was a fairly unpleasant man. Because he wanted to become heir to the English throne, he didn't object to the execution of his mother, Mary Stuart, the queen of Scotland, whose supporters attempted to make her queen of England. When James finally succeeded to the throne, he alienated the court by trying to acquire power for the throne at a time when Parliament was taking control of the government. James II of England reigned for only three years. When he was suspected of trying to return the country to Roman Catholicism, his daughter Mary and her husband, William of Orange, were encouraged to take over the English throne, which they did in the Glorious Revolution. Two literary giants also share this name: James Joyce of Ireland, author of *A Portrait of the Artist as a Young Man* and *Ulysses,* and American James Baldwin, author of *Go Tell It on the Mountain, Another Country,* and *The Fire Next Time.* In American history, the name is presidential. James Madison, the father of the Constitution and one of the authors of the Federalist papers, was the fourth president. James Monroe was the fifth president and the author of the Monroe Doctrine. James Polk was the 11th president and the designer of the doctrine of manifest destiny. James Buchanan was the 15th president, and James Garfield was the 29th president. The fictional spy James Bond and actor James Dean, who gained fame with the movie *Rebel Without a Cause,* provide dashing images for this traditional name.

Famous names: James Fenimore Cooper (novelist)
James Garner (actor)

James Hargreaves (inventor)
James Earl Jones (actor)
James Oglethorpe (founder of Georgia)
James Stewart (actor)
James Taylor (singer)
James Thurber (cartoonist)

Nicknames: **Jake, Jamey, Jamie, Jamy, Jay, Jem, Jemmy, Jim, Jimmy**

Variations: **Diego** (Spanish), **Giacomo** (Italian), **Hamish** (Scottish), **Iago** (Italian and Welsh), **Jacques** (French), **Jago** (Cornish), **Jaime** (Spanish), **Jayme** (Portuguese), **Santiago** (Spanish), **Seamas** (Irish), **Shamus** (Irish)

Jameson Middle English *Jamesson,* "son of **James.**" American parents who like James but want to name their sons something slightly unusual have begun to choose this name; actor Jameson Parker of the television series *Simon & Simon* has popularized this name.

Other spelling: **Jamison**

Jamey, Jamie, Jamy (see **James**)

Jamil (see **Jamal**)

Jamison (see **Jameson**)

Jan Dutch, Scandinavian, Polish, and Czech form of **John.**

Famous name: Jan Vermeer (painter)

Janek (see **John**)

Janis (see **John**)

Janne (see **John**)

Janos (see **John**)

Jared Perhaps Hebrew "descent" or Akkadian "servant." In the Book of Genesis, Jared is the father of Enoch and grandfather of Methuselah. The only other information given about him is that he lived to age 962, making him second only to his own grandson in longevity. Perhaps because the name sounds more attractive in English than the name Methuselah, 17th-century Puritan parents in both England and New England began to call their sons Jared to express their hope that their children have long and healthy lives. There is also a Jared in the Book of Mormon who has a nameless brother—always referred to as "the Brother of Jared"—who is an even more important person; he receives a vision of Christ and is told about Jesus' future coming in the flesh. This kept the name well used in Utah for years after it almost disappeared from use in the rest of the United States. Jared revived strongly all over the United States in the late 1960s when Jarrod Barkley (played by actor Richard Long) appeared as Barbara Stanwyck's self-controlled lawyer son on the television Western *The Big Valley*. Many parents probably saw Jared as an updated version of **Gerald;** ironically, **Jarrod** is a rare English surname based on Gerald. Jared, and not Jarrod, became the more common spelling because parents were familiar with that version. American parents have felt free to respell this name, and forms such as **Jarod, Jarred, Jerad, Jerod, Jerrid, Jerrod,** and the like have always been well used alongside the two main spellings. Jared's peak period of popularity has now passed, but in 1991 it was still 49th on the list of names given newborn American boys.

Famous names: Jared Diamond (ornithologist and linguist)
Jared Sparks (historian)

Jarod, Jarred (see **Jared**)

Jarrett (see **Garret**)

Jarrod (see **Jared**)

Jas (see **Casper**)

Jasius (see **John**)

Jason Greek "the healer"; used in New Testament times as a Greek form of **Joshua.** In Greek mythology, Jason led the Argonauts on their quest for the Golden Fleece. He later married the sorceress Medea, who helped him fulfill his quest. His life turned to tragedy when Medea, suspecting Jason of infidelity, killed their children. Although the name used to be unusual, it came back into use in the late 1960s. It then rapidly became one of the most popular names for boys in the United States, being the second most popular name in the late 1970s. But Jason's popularity began to recede quickly around 1980, and it was only 51st on the list for newborn boys in 1991. The murdering monster character called Jason in the *Friday the 13th* series of "slasher" films may have contributed to this quick fall.

Famous names: Jason Bateman (actor)
Jason Robards (actor)

Nicknames: **Jace, Jay**

Jasper (see **Casper**)

Javiel (see **Xavier**)

Javier (see **Xavier**)

Jay Old French *jai,* "blue jay," from Latin *gaius,* "rejoiced in"; also, a form of **James, Jason,** or other names beginning with "J."

Famous names: Jay Leno (comedian)
Jay McInerney (novelist)
Jay Ward (movie producer)

Jayme (see **James**)

Jean French variation of **John.** Although this is primarily a feminine name in the United States, parents interested in art should remember that five prominent French painters were named Jean: Chardin, Corot, Fragonard, Ingres, and Millet.

Famous names: Jean Anouilh (playwright)
Jean Arthur Dubuc (baseball player)
Jean Luc Godard (movie director)
Jean Baptiste Racine (dramatist)

Jeff Form of **Jeffrey, Geoffrey.**

Famous names: Jeff MacNelly (cartoonist)
Jeff Smith (cooking expert)

Jeffery (see **Jeffrey**)

Jeffrey Variation of **Geoffrey.** This spelling is much more popular in the United States than the original English form, Geoffrey.

Famous names: Jeffrey Hunter (actor)
Jeffrey Leonard (baseball player)

Nickname: **Jeff**
Other spellings: **Jeffery, Jeffry**
Variations: **Joffre, Joffrey** (French)

Jeffry (see **Jeffrey**)

Jehan (see **John**)

Jem (see **James**)

Jemmy (see **James**)

Jen (see **John**)

Jens (see **John**)

Jerad (see **Jared**)

Jeremiah Hebrew "may God raise up, exalt." Jeremiah was a biblical prophet who wrote the Book of Lamentations as well as the Old Testament book named after him.
   Nicknames: **Gerry, Jerrie, Jerry**
   Variations: **Geremia** (Italian), **Jeremias** (German and Spanish), **Jeremie** (French), **Jeremio, Jeremy** (English), **Yirmeya** (modern Hebrew)

Jeremias (see **Jeremiah**)

Jeremie (see **Jeremiah, Jeremy**)

Jeremio (see **Jeremiah**)

Jeremy English form of **Jeremiah.** This version of the name dates to at least the 13th century in England. Jeremy became a fashionable American name in the 1970s, and although its popularity is now slowly fading, it was still among the top 50 names for boys in 1991.
   Famous names: Jeremy Bentham (philosopher)
   Jeremy Irons (actor)
   Other spelling: **Jeremie**

Jerod (see **Jared**)

Jeroen (see **Jerome**)

Jerome Greek *Hieronymos,* "holy name." The fourth-century St. Jerome translated the Old Testament from Hebrew into Latin. The Germans retained the Greek form of this name, Hieronymos, so perhaps the German painter Hieronymus Bosch is the best-known Jerome in the art world. Composer Jerome Kern is remembered for his musical *Showboat.*
   Famous name: Jerome Robbins (choreographer)
   Nicknames: **Jerrie, Jerry**
   Other spelling: **Gerome**

Variations: **Chombo, Chomo, Geronimo** (Italian), **Girolamo** (Italian), **Hieronym** (Slovakian), **Hieronymus** (German, Dutch, and Scandinavian), **Jeroen** (Dutch), **Jeromo, Jeronim** (Slovenian and Croatian), **Jeronimo** (Spanish)

Jeromo (see **Jerome**)

Jeronim (see **Jerome**)

Jeronimo (see **Jerome**)

Jerrid (see **Jared**)

Jerrie (see **Jeremiah, Jerome, Jerry**)

Jerrod (see **Jared**)

Jerrold (see **Gerald**)

Jerry Form of **Gerald, Gerard, Jeremiah,** or **Jerome.**
Famous names: Jerry Lewis (comedian)
Jerry West (basketball player)
Other spellings: **Gerrie, Gerry, Jerrie**

Jerzy (see **George**)

Jesito (see **Jesus**)

Jess (see **Jesse**)

Jesse Hebrew "God exists." In the Bible, Jesse was the father of David, who became king of Israel. In the 19th century, the famous outlaw Jesse James plundered the West. In the 1936 Olympics in Berlin, African-American athlete Jesse Owens won four gold medals for the United States, disputing Adolf Hitler's theory of Aryan superiority. In the 1980s, civil rights leader Jesse Jackson became the first African-American to run for president.
Famous names: Jesse Colin Young (singer)
Jesse Kornbluth (writer)
Jesse Orosco (baseball player)
Other spellings: **Jessie, Jessy**
Variations: **Jess, Yishai** (modern Hebrew)

Jessie, Jessy (see **Jesse**)

Jesus Aramaic and Greek form of **Joshua,** Hebrew "God saves." People in many cultures have considered this name to be too sacred for general use, but it has always been popular in Spanish-speaking countries and with Hispanic-Americans.

Famous name: Jesus Alou (baseball player)

Variations: **Hesus, Issa, Jesito**

Jewel Old French *juel,* "gem stone." The names of precious stones often become given names to symbolize the preciousness of human life. Such names are usually feminine, but Jewel has been used for both boys and girls. William Faulkner used the name for one of the male characters in *As I Lay Dying.*

Famous name: Jewel Willoughby Ens (baseball player)

Jim (see **James**)

Jimeno (see **Simon**)

Jimi Form of **Jimmy.**

Famous name: Jimi Hendrix (musician)

Jimmie (see **Jimmy**)

Jimmy Form of **James.** Although his legal name is James Earl Carter, the 39th president of the United States is more comfortable with his nickname, Jimmy.

Famous names: Jimmy Breslin (columnist)

Jimmy Connors (tennis player)

Other spellings: **Jimi, Jimmie**

Jindrich (see **Henry**)

Joao (see **John**)

Jock Scottish form of **Jack** or **John,**

Jody Form of **Joseph.** This name owes its use as an official form to Marjorie Kinnan Rawlings's 1938 novel *The Yearling,* where Jody is a boy who raises a pet fawn and then is told to shoot the deer once it becomes a buck. The book is frequently taught in American public schools. Although still occasionally given to boys, Jody has been primarily used for girls in the United States since the 1970s.

Famous name: Jody Powell (assistant to President Carter)

Joe Form of **Joseph.** This name has often been associated with athletes, but award-winning actor Joe Mantegna appears to be expanding that image.

Famous names: Joe DiMaggio (baseball player)
Joe Frazier (boxer)
Joe Louis (boxer)
Joe Namath (football player)

Joel Hebrew "the Lord is God." In the Bible, Joel was a Hebrew
prophet. The name is steadily used without being overly
popular.
Famous names: Joel Grey (actor)
Joel Chandler Harris (writer)
Variations: **Ioel, Yoel** (Hebrew)

Joey (see **Joseph**)

Joffre, Joffrey (see **Jeffrey**)

Johan (see **John**)

Johann, Johannes German forms of **John.** Two of the world's
great composers share this name: Johann Sebastian Bach and
Johannes Brahms.

John Hebrew *Johanan,* "God has favored" or "God is gracious."
For the last six centuries, this has been one of the most popular
names for boys in most European countries. In the Bible, John
the Baptist was a cousin of Jesus. He was imprisoned for
denouncing King Herod, and he was beheaded at the request of
the king's niece, Salome. St. John the Evangelist was a brother
of James and one of the apostles. He is probably the author of
the Gospel of John and three of the Epistles. Among
Christians, the name has always been revered. It is the name of
more than 20 popes and more than 80 saints. John XXIII, who
was elected pope in 1958, called the Second Vatican Council,
which radically changed the Roman Catholic church. Pope
John Paul II, formerly Karol Jozef Wojtyla, was the first non-
Italian pontiff to be chosen pope in more than 450 years. The
name John has not been especially popular among royalty, and
only one John has sat on the English throne. In 1199, John I, a
son of Henry II and Eleanor of Aquitaine, was crowned
following the death of his brother Richard. John I's many
frustrated attempts to regain a hold on British territory led to a
revolt among the rebel lords who forced John to sign the
Magna Charta, which paved the way for a representational
government in Great Britain. Parents who love poetry have

good reason to consider this name. Four of England's greatest poets are John Milton, John Donne, John Keats, and John Dryden. It also has great presidential connections through John Adams, John Quincy Adams, John Tyler, and John F. Kennedy. Astronaut John Glenn was the first American to orbit the earth, and musician John Lennon is considered to be one of the finest composers of rock music.

Famous names: John Alden (Mayflower pilgrim)
John Barrymore (actor)
John Brown (abolitionist)
John Galbraith (economist)
Sir John Gielgud (actor)
John Irving (writer)
John Le Carre (writer)
John McEnroe (tennis player)
John Singleton Mosby (Confederate cavalry officer)
John Updike (writer)
John Wayne (actor)

Nicknames: **Jack, Jackie, Jacky, Johnnie, Johnny**

Other spelling: **Jon**

Variations: **Eoin** (Irish), **Evan** (Welsh), **Gian** (Italian), **Gianni** (Italian), **Giovanni** (Italian), **Hannes** (Afrikaans), **Hans** (Danish, Dutch, and German), **Hansel** (Bavarian), **Iain** (Scottish), **Ian** (Scottish), **Ioan** (Rumanian), **Ioannes** (Greek), **Ivan** (Slavic), **Jaan** (Estonian), **Jan** (Czech, Danish, and Dutch), **Janek** (Czech), **Janis** (Latvian), **Janne** (Finnish), **Janos** (Hungarian), **Jasius** (Lithuanian) **Jean** (French), **Jehan** (Belgian), **Jen, Jens** (Danish, Norwegian, and Swedish), **Joao** (Portuguese), **Jock** (Scottish), **Johan** (Danish), **Johann** (German), **Johannes** (German), **Jovan** (Serbian), **Juan** (Spanish), **Juha** (Finnish), **Seainin** (Irish), **Sean** (Irish), **Shane** (Irish), **Vanni** (Italian), **Vanya** (Russian), **Yahya** (Arabic), **Yehochanan** (modern Hebrew), **Yochanan** (Yiddish)

Johnathan, Johnathon (see **Jonathan**)

Johnnie (see **John, Johnny**)

Johnny Form of **John.**

Famous names: Johnny Bench (baseball player)
Johnny Carson (TV personality)

Johnny Mathis (singer)
Johnny Weissmuller (swimmer)
Other spelling: **Johnnie**

Jojo Fante (Ghana) "born on Monday."

Jon (see **John, Jonathan**)

Jona (see **Jonah**)

Jonah Hebrew "dove." Most people remember the prophet Jonah because he was swallowed by a big fish and regurgitated still alive three days later. He also preached against excessive and intolerant religious views and taught that Yahweh was the God of the Gentiles as well as of the Israelites. Jonas Salk, a 20th-century medical researcher, discovered the polio vaccine.
Variations: **Jona, Jonas**

Jonas (see **Jonah**)

Jonatan (see **Jonathan**)

Jonathan Hebrew "God has given" or "God's gift." In the Old Testament, Jonathan is the son of King Saul who swears to remain David's closest friend, even though Saul hates David and wants to kill him. When Jonathan falls in battle, a grieving David utters the famous lament, "your love to me was wonderful, passing the love of women." David and Jonathan therefore became the biblical symbol of true friendship. Nevertheless, Jonathan was a rare name until the Puritans in colonial New England began to use it. Indeed, it was such a common name around Boston in 1776 that the British referred to all American Revolutionary soldiers as "Brother Jonathan." The name then went out of fashion until the 1950s, when parents looking for alternatives to **John** began to make it popular again. Jonathan peaked in use around 1985 but still was 18th on the list for American boys born in 1991. Surprisingly, Jonathan has recently been especially popular with Hispanic-Americans, in spite of its having almost no tradition of use in Spanish-speaking countries.
Famous names: Jonathan Swift (political satirist)
Jonathan Winters (comedian)
Nickname: **Jon**
Other spellings: **Johnathan, Johnathon, Jonathon**
Variation: **Jonatan** (Spanish, Slavic, and Hungarian)

Jonathon (see **Jonathan**)

Jordan Hebrew *Yarden*, from *yarad*, "to descend," the name of the river that flows from the Sea of Galilee to the Dead Sea. This became a first name in the 12th century when soldiers returning from the Crusades brought home vials of water from the Jordan that were later used in the baptism of their children. As a result, Jordan became a popular name for children of both sexes in several western European countries. In England, the name disappeared for girls and became rare for boys by 1600. In the United States, the name began to revive around 1970 and, remarkably, has once again become popular for both sexes. However, more than twice as many boys as girls were receiving the name in the early 1990s. Jordan was the 32nd most common name for white American boys and 20th for African-American boys by 1991. The slightly greater popularity with African-Americans may mean that some parents are responding to basketball star Michael Jordan's incredible popularity by giving his last name, rather than his first name, to their sons. Jordan seems destined to become one of the most fashionable American names.

   Famous names: Jordan Knight (singer)
                  Jordan A. Schwarz (historian)
                  Jordan H. Sobel (philosopher)

   Other spellings: **Jorden, Jordon**

   Variations: **Giordano** (Italian), **Iordache** (Rumanian), **Iordanos** (Greek), **Jourdain** (French)

Jorden, Jordon (see **Jordan**)

Jorge Spanish form of **George**.

   Famous name: Jorge Luis Borges (writer)

Jose (see **Joseph, Josiah**)

Joseba (see **Joseph**)

Josef (see **Joseph**)

Joseph Hebrew "the Lord shall add (children)." In the Old Testament, Joseph was the favorite son of Jacob. He was sold into slavery in Egypt by his brothers, but because he interpreted the dreams of the pharaoh, he became powerful in the court and urged a relaxation of the repression of his people. In the New Testament, Joseph was the husband of Mary and the mother of Jesus. Two Holy Roman emperors, Joseph I and Joseph II, reigned in the 18th century. Inspired by the ideas of the Enlightenment, Joseph II freed the serfs. In North America, Chief Joseph of the Nez Pierce tribe rebelled against a treaty that would have forced his people to be resettled. In 1877, Chief Joseph led his tribe on a long, harrowing march from Oregon to Canada, but they were stopped within miles of the border. In the Soviet Union, Joseph Stalin, a disciple of Lenin, wrested control away from the Politburo in 1929 and established a virtual dictatorship that lasted until his death in 1953. Through the use of powerful secret police, exile, and executions, he eliminated people he considered to be the enemies of the state. After Stalin's death, his policies were denounced. The term *yellow journalism* reflects the aggressive newspaper style of publisher Joseph Pulitzer, who introduced tabloids to the United States. Pulitzer is perhaps better remembered for his endowment of the Pulitzer Prizes.

Famous names: Joseph Conrad (author)
Joseph Kennedy (industrialist and statesman)
Joseph Losey (film director)
Joseph Mankiewicz (movie producer and director)
Joseph Smith (founder of the Mormons)
Joseph Turner (painter)

Nicknames: **Jody, Joe, Joey**

Variations: **Giuseppe** (Italian), **Iosef** (Greek), **Ioseph** (Gaelic), **Jose** (Spanish), **Joseba** (Basque), **Josef** (Czech, Dutch, German, and Scandinavian), **Jozef** (Polish), **Jozsef** (Hungarian), **Juozas** (Lithuanian), **Juuso** (Finnish), **Osip** (Russian), **Pepe, Pepito, Seosamh** (Irish), **Yosef** (Hebrew), **Yusef** (Arabic), **Yusuf** (Arabic)

Josh (see **Joshua, Josiah**)

Joshua Hebrew "God saves." Joshua was Moses' successor as the leader of the Israelites and led the nation into the Land of Promise. The Book of Joshua recounts the settling of Canaan. This name was regularly used among the Puritans in colonial New England. Joshua was revived in the 1970s and is now one of the most popular American names; in 1991, it reached third place on the list of names given newborn boys in the United States.

Famous name: Sir Joshua Reynolds (painter)

Nickname: **Josh**

Variations: **Giosue** (Italian), **Jason, Jesus, Josua** (German), **Josue** (French and Spanish), **Yehoshua** (modern Hebrew)

Josia (see **Josiah**)

Josiah Hebrew "God heals." Josiah, the king of Judah, destroyed idols and other evidence of the worship of false gods. He was slain by the pharaoh Necho at the battle of Megiddo. The name was popular among the Puritans from the 17th century until the latter part of the 19th century. Josiah seems to be undergoing a slow revival now that such similar names as **Joshua** are fashionable again. A historical example of the name is Josiah Wedgewood, founder of the famous pottery.

Nicknames: **Jose, Josh**

Variations: **Josia** (Swedish), **Josias** (French, German, and Spanish), **Jozsias** (Hungarian), **Giosia** (Italian)

Josias (see **Josiah**)

Josua (see **Joshua**)

Josue (see **Joshua**)

Jourdain (see **Jordan**)

Jovan (see **John**)

Jozef (see **Joseph**)

Jozsef (see **Joseph**)

Jozsias (see **Josiah**)

Juan (see **John**)

Juda (see **Judah**)

Judah Hebrew "praise." Judah was one of the great Hebrew prophets. He was the fourth son of Jacob and Leah and was the founder of the tribe of Judah, the most powerful of the 12 tribes of Israel. This name was used somewhat by the Puritans in the 17th century, but it has never really been popular, probably because it is too similar to **Judas** (which is, in fact, simply the New Testament form of Judah).

Variations: **Giuda** (Italian), **Iuda** (Bulgarian), **Juda, Jude** (English)

Judas (see **Judah**)

Jude (see **Judah**)

Juha (see **John**)

Jule (see **Julius**)

Jules French form of **Julius.** French author Jules Verne is
    considered the father of science fiction.
    Famous name: Jules Feiffer (cartoonist)

Julian Latin *Julianus,* "belonging to Julius." Julian was a common
    name among early Christians. Several saints are named Julian,
    including Julian the Hospitaller, medieval patron of both
    innkeepers and travelers. Julian seems to be slowly increasing
    in popularity.
    Famous names: Julian Bond (legislator)
                Julian Lennon (singer)
    Variations: **Giulio, Giuliano** (Italian), **Julianus** (Finnish and
        German), **Juliao** (Portuguese), **Julien** (French), **Julion**

Julianus (see **Julian**)

Juliao (see **Julian**)

Julien (see **Julian**)

Julio (see **Julius**)

Julion (see **Julian**)

Julius Roman clan name, perhaps from *Jovilios,* "descended from
    Jove (Jupiter)." Of all the ancient Romans, Julius Caesar is the
    best known. Pope Julius II was the patron of the artists
    Michelangelo and Raphael. Julius Marx found success as
    comedian Groucho Marx.
    Famous name: Julius Erving (basketball player)
    Variations: **Giulio** (Italian), **Jule, Jules** (French), **Julio**
        (Spanish), **Yul**

Juma Swahili "born on Friday."

Juozas (see **Joseph**)

Jurgen (see **George**)

Jus (see **Justin**)

Just (see **Justin**)

Justin Latin *Justinus,* derivative of *Justus,* "the just." St. Justin
Martyr, who was executed at Rome in A.D. 165, is generally
credited with being the first Christian philosopher. He was
known for holding public debates with non-Christians where
he defended his faith from charges of immorality and atheism
because Christians refused to sacrifice to the emperor. Before
1970, Ireland was the only country where the name Justin was
frequently found, but it then exploded in use all over the
English-speaking world. Justin has been among the top 15
names given to American boys since 1982.

Nicknames: **Jus, Just**

Variations: **Giustino** (Italian), **Gustino, Husto, Justinas**
(Lithuanian), **Justino** (Spanish and Portuguese), **Justinus**
(Dutch and Scandinavian), **Justyn** (Czech and
Ukrainian), **Jusztin** (Hungarian)

Justinas (see **Justin**)

Justino (see **Justin**)

Justinus (see **Justin**)

Justyn (see **Justin**)

Jusztin (see **Justin**)

Juuso (see **Joseph**)

Kaapo (see **Gabriel**)

Kain, Kaine (see **Kane**)

Kane Irish Gaelic *Cathain,* "battle"; also, Old French *cane,* "reed," or *Caen,* "battle plain." This surname has recently become quite popular as a first name in Australia, but it is still uncommon in the United States, perhaps because it sounds like **Cain,** the name of the first murderer in the Bible.
Other spellings: **Cain, Kain, Kaine, Kayne**

Kareem Arabic "noble." The royal connotations of this name certainly suit Kareem Abdul-Jabbar, the long-reigning king of the basketball courts.
Other spellings: **Karim, Karime**

Karel (see **Charles**)

Karim, Karime (see **Kareem**)

Karl German variation of **Charles.** German-born political scientist Karl Marx and his colleague Friedrich Engels published *The Communist Manifesto* in 1848. They promoted the theory of dialectical materialism that predicted conflict between the capitalist class and the working class. Marx saw an advanced stage of socialism, or communism, replacing capitalism.
Famous names: Karl August Drews (baseball pitcher)
              Karl Lagerfeld (fashion designer)
              Karl Malden (actor)
              Karl Menninger (psychiatrist)
              Karl Shapiro (poet)
Variation: **Carl**

Karlis (see **Charles**)

Karol (see **Charles**)

Karolek (see **Charles**)

Karolis (see **Charles**)

Karoly (see **Charles**)

Kaspar (see **Casper**)

Kayne (see **Kane**)

Keefe Irish *Caomh,* "kind, gentle." Driven from their homeland by the Normans, the Keefes migrated to what is now County Cork, Ireland, and are known as Pobal O'Keeffe. This surname is very common in County Cork and is fairly common among people of Irish descent in the United States. Keefe is still quite rare as a first name, but the popularity of similar names such as **Keenan** and **Kiefer** may lead to its discovery by American parents looking for the proverbial "different but not *too* different" name for a son.
> Famous name: Keefe Brasselle (actor)

Keefer (see **Kiefer**)

Keenan, Keenen Irish Gaelic *Cianain,* a form of *Cian,* "enduring." This name is quickly becoming more popular, rising from 356th to 244th place on the list of names given American boys in the two years prior to 1991.
> Famous names: Keenen Ivory Wayans (comedian and
> producer)
> Keenan Wynn (actor)

Keifer (see **Kiefer**)

Keith Scottish place name; origin and meaning unknown but may come from Gaelic "the wind" or "the forest." Keith was a very popular name in the 1960s and, although its peak has now passed, it is still well used.
> Famous names: Keith Hernandez (baseball player)
> Keith Richards (musician)

Kelcey (see **Kelsey**)

Kelemen (see **Clement**)

Kelly Irish Gaelic *Ceallagh,* uncertain meaning, perhaps "church-goer," "bright-headed," or "strife." Although Kelly has been hugely popular as a female name in the United States since the 1960s, it has remarkably never gone out of style for boys. Kelly is holding steady at around 300th place on the list of names given American boys.

    Famous names: Kelly Gruber (baseball player)
                     Kelly Slater (surfing champion)

Kelsay (see **Kelsey**)

Kelsey Probably Old English *Ceolsige* from *ceol* [ship] + *sige* [victory]. This was primarily a name for boys since about 1980. It has also become very popular for girls and is rapidly dying out as a masculine form.

    Famous names: Kelsey Grammer (actor)
                     Kelsie B. Harder (expert on American place names)

    Other spellings: **Kelcey, Kelsay, Kelsie**

Kelsie (see **Kelsey**)

Ken Form of **Kenneth.**

    Famous names: Ken Kesey (writer)
                     Ken Rosewall (tennis player)
                     Ken Russell (film director)

Kenneth Scots Gaelic *Coinneach,* "handsome," or *Cinaed,* "fire-born." In the ninth century, Kenneth McAlpine was the first king to rule both the Picts and the Scots in the area now known as Scotland.

    Famous names: Sir Kenneth Clark (art critic)
                     Kenneth Clark (psychologist)
                     Kenneth Grahame (author)

    Nicknames: **Ken, Kenney, Kennie, Kenny**

Kenney, Kennie (see **Kenneth**)

Kenny Form of **Kenneth** or **Kent.**

    Famous names: Kenny Loggins (musician)
                     Kenny Rogers (singer)

Kent Name of a county in southeastern England, probably from
Celtic "coast" or "border." This English place name and
surname has been much more popular as a first name in the
United States and Canada than it has been in England itself.
Famous names: Kent McCord (actor)
Kent Taylor (actor)
Nickname: Kenny

Kerby (see **Kirby**)

Keresztely (see **Christian**)

Kester (see **Christopher**)

Keven (see **Kevin**)

Kevin Irish *Caemgen,* "comely birth, beloved child." The sixth-
century St. Kevin was known as a hermit and is one of the
patron saints of Dublin. This common Irish name has been
popular in the United States since the 1960s. It received
favorable exposure through Kevin Arnold, the chief character
on *The Wonder Years,* the nostalgic television series that helped
many baby boomers relive their childhood.
Famous names: Kevin Dobson (actor)
Kevin Kline (actor)
Kevin Ramsey (dancer)
Other spelling: **Keven**

Khristian (see **Christian**)

Kiefer German "barrel-maker" or "pine tree." When Canadian
actors Donald Sutherland and Shirley Douglas had a son in
1966, they decided that the last name of their friend—novelist,
screenwriter, and film producer Warren Kiefer—would be
perfect as a first name for their little boy. Now Kiefer
Sutherland has grown up and started making a name for
himself in the movies, and many other parents are deciding to
give the name to their sons.
Other spellings: **Keefer, Keifer**

Kiki (see **Henry**)

Kiko (see **Henry**)

Kile (see **Kyle**)

Kim Form of **Kimball,** Old English *Cynebeal* from *cyne* [royal] + *beald* [bold], or Welsh *Cynbel* from *cyn* [chief] + *bel* [war]. The best-known Kim is the title character of Rudyard Kipling's novel about an Irish boy growing up in India, whose full name is Kimball O'Hara.

   Famous name: Kim Warwick (tennis player)

Kimball (see **Kim**)

King Old English *cyning,* "king, tribal leader."

   Famous names: King Camp Gillette (inventor and
                       manufacturer)
                   King Vidor (film director)

Kingsley Old English "king's meadow." This name is too overtly "royal" to have wide appeal to Americans, who prefer less obviously royal names, such as **Sarah, Diana,** and **Andrew.**

   Famous name: Kingsley Amis (author)

Kirby Old English "church village" from *ciric* [church] + *by* [village].

   Famous name: Kirby Puckett (baseball player)
   Other spelling: **Kerby**

Kiril (see **Cyril**)

Kirill (see **Cyril**)

Kirk Scottish form of Old English *ciric,* "church."

   Famous name: Kirk Douglas (actor)

Kit Form of **Christian** or **Christopher.**

   Famous name: Kit Carson (scout)

Klaudiusz (see **Claud**)

Klaus (see **Nicholas**)

Klavdii (see **Claud**)

Klemens (see **Clement**)

Klemensas (see **Clement**)

Klement (see **Clement**)

Klementos (see **Clement**)

Kliment (see **Clement**)

Klymentiy (see **Clement**)

Knut Danish, from Old Norse *Knutr,* "knot," originally a nickname for a short but tough Viking. A Danish invader named Cnut, or Canute, ruled England in the 11th century. He is the king who tested his power by commanding the waves to be still. Knute Rockne, the famous University of Notre Dame football coach, was the first to modernize the game by stressing the forward pass.

   Famous name: Knut Hamsun (novelist)

   Variations: **Canute, Cnut**

Kodie, Kody (see **Cody**)

Kolos (see **Claud**)

Kolya (see **Nicholas**)

Konrad Old German *Conrad,* "bold counsel."

   Famous names: Konrad Adenauer (chancellor of former
                              West Germany)
                              Konrad Lorenz (ethologist)

   Nicknames: **Con, Conny, Kurt**

   Other spelling: **Conrad**

Korey, Kory (see **Corey**)

Kris Form of **Christian** or **Christopher**. Kris Kringle is the Bavarian equivalent of Santa Claus, or St. Nicholas.

   Famous name: Kris Kristofferson (singer)

Krishna Hindi from Sanskrit "dark, black." In Hindu teachings, Krishna is an incarnation of Vishnu and a proponent of selfless actions. He is usually pictured playing a flute.

   Famous name: Krishna Mennon (statesman)

Kriss (see **Christopher**)

Kristaps (see **Christopher**)

Kristian (see **Christian**)

Kristjanis (see **Christian**)

Kristof (see **Christopher**)

Kristoffer (see **Christopher**)

Krizas (see **Christian**)

Krys (see **Christian**)

Krystian (see **Christian**)

Kumar Hindi "youth" from Sanskrit *kumara,* "boy, son." This name is popular in India, where it serves as both a last name and a given name. The central character in Frank Scott's *The Jewel and the Crown* is named Kumar.

Famous name: Anil Kumar Chopra (educator)

Kurillos (see **Cyril**)

Kurt Form of **Curtis** or **Konrad.**

Famous names: Kurt Russell (actor)
Kurt Vonnegut (writer)
Kurt Weill (composer)

Other spelling: **Curt**

Kustaa (see **Gustav**)

Kwame Akan (Ghana) "born on Saturday." Kwame Nkrumah led the West African nation of Ghana to independence in 1957; it was the first African colony to receive its freedom from a European power. Kwame is one of the first genuinely African names to be regularly used by African-American parents.

Famous name: Kwame Holman (television journalist)

Kyle Scots Gaelic *caol,* "narrows, strait." This Scottish surname was only occasionally given as a first name before the 1950s, but it was among the top 25 names for boys in the United States in 1991.

Famous names: Kyle MacLachlan (actor)
Kyle Rote (football player)

Other spelling: **Kile**

Kyros (see **Cyrus**)

Kyrylo (see **Cyril**)

Labhrainn (see **Lawrence**)

Labhras (see **Lawrence**)

Lad Middle English *ladde,* "servant, young man, boy." This is practically nonexistent as a first name anywhere in the English-speaking world.

Variations: **Ladd, Ladde** (Scottish), **Laddie**

Ladd (see **Lad**)

Ladde, Laddie (see **Lad**)

Lafayette French place name and surname, "beech tree grove." This name honors the memory of Marie Jean Paul Roch Yves Gilbert Motrier, the marquis de Lafayette. At the age of 20, Lafayette was granted the rank of major general in the American Revolutionary Forces. He served throughout the war as a leader of troops and as an aide to General George Washington. For his services, he was honored as an American hero. During his tour of the country in 1825, he was met by demonstrations of frenzied enthusiasm without parallel in U.S. history. Many counties and towns were named for him.

Famous name: Lafayette Fresco "Tommy" Thompson (baseball player)

Nicknames: **Fay, Lafe**

Variation: **Fayette**

Lafe (see **Lafayette**)

Lafredo (see **Alfred, Alfredo**)

Laine (see **Lane**)

Lal Hindi "beloved boy" from Sanskrit "to play, caress." Lal
Bahadur Shastri was prime minister of India during the 1960s.

Lamar French *la mare,* "the pool or pond."
Famous name: LaMarr Hoyt (baseball player)
Variation: **LaMarr**

LaMarr (see **Lamar**)

Lammond, Lamond (see **Lamont**)

Lamont Medieval Scottish *Lagman* from Old Norse *Logmadr,* "law
man." The resemblance of this name to French *le mont,* "the
mountain," is accidental. Many Americans will remember this
name from Lamont Sanford, the son on the 1970s television
series *Sanford and Son,* played by Demond Wilson.
Nicknames: **Monte, Monty**
Variations: **Lammond, Lamond**

Lance Old German *Lanzo,* "land," later associated with French
lance, "light spear"; also, a short form of **Lancelot.**
Famous names: Lance Alworth (football player)
Lance Armstrong (bicyclist)
Lance Loud (gossip columnist and actor)

Lancelot Origin uncertain, but perhaps from Old Norman French
Ancelot, "young servant." In the Arthurian romances, Sir
Lancelot was a French knight who came to King Arthur's
court. Although he fell in love with the king's wife, Guinevere,
he rallied to Arthur's side to battle Mordred.
Famous name: Lancelot Hogben (mathematician)
Nickname: **Lance**

Landon Probably a form of *Langdon,* Old English "long hill." The
use of Landon as a first name in the United States is steadily
increasing, perhaps in honor of Michael Landon, the actor and
producer of family-oriented television programs who died in
1991.
Famous name: Landon Turner (basketball player)

Lane English "path" or "roadway."
Famous name: Lane Bradford (actor)

Other spelling: **Laine**
Variation: **Laney**

Laney (see **Lane**)

Langston Old English "long or tall stone," originally a place name indicating the presence of an ancient stone monument.
Famous name: Langston Hughes (poet)

Lanny (see **Lawrence**)

Larkin (see **Lawrence**)

Larrance (see **Lawrence**)

Larrie (see **Lawrence**)

Larry Form of **Lawrence**. This name started out as a nickname for Lawrence, but it became a popular independent name in the 1940s. Although it is now becoming less fashionable, Larry was still given by American parents considerably more often than Lawrence on birth certificates in 1991.
Famous names: Larry Bird (basketball player)
Larry Hagman (actor)
Larry Holmes (boxer)
Larry King (commentator)
Larry McMurtry (novelist)
Larry Rivers (painter)

Lars (see **Lawrence**)

Launo (see **Nicholas**)

Laurance (see **Lawrence**)

Lauren (see **Lawrence**)

Laurence (see **Lawrence**)

Laurenco (see **Lawrence**)

Laurens, Laurenz (see **Lawrence**)

Laurent (see **Lawrence**)

Laurentius (see **Lawrence**)

Lauri (see **Lawrence**)

Laurie (see **Lawrence**)

Laurits (see **Lawrence**)

Lavrentij (see **Lawrence**)

Law (see **Lawrence**)

Lawrance (see **Lawrence**)

Lawrence Latin *Laurentius* from *Laurentum,* an ancient Roman town that may have derived its name from *laurus,* "laurel or bay tree." The ancient Greeks revered the laurel tree and used its leaves for wreaths to celebrate victory. There were three St. Lawrences. The first lived during the third century and suffered a terrible martyrdom by being roasted to death. Friar Laurence is the friendly priest who marries Romeo and Juliet. Laurence Sterne is the author of the 18th-century novel *Tristram Shandy.*
  Famous names: Lawrence Durrell (novelist)
            Lawrence Ferlinghetti (poet)
            Laurence Harvey (actor)
            Sir Laurence Olivier (actor)
  Nicknames: **Lanny, Larrie, Larry, Lauren, Laurie, Law, Lawry, Lon, Lonnie, Lonny, Loren, Lorin, Lorry**
  Other spellings: **Larrance, Laurance, Laurence, Lawrance**
  Variations: **Labhrainn** (Scottish), **Labhras** (Irish), **Larkin, Lars** (Scandinavian), **Laurenco** (Portuguese), **Laurens** (Dutch), **Laurent** (French), **Laurentius** (Latin), **Laurenz** (German), **Lauri** (Finnish), **Laurits** (Danish), **Lavrentij** (Russian), **Lenz** (Swiss), **Lorens** (Scandinavian), **Lorenz** (German), **Lorenzo** (Italian and Spanish), **Lorinc** (Hungarian), **Lovre** (Croatian), **Wawrzyniec** (Polish)

Lawry (see **Lawrence**)

Lea (see **Lee**)

Leao (see **Leo**)

Lee Old English *leah,* "meadow"; also, nickname for **Ashley, Bentley, Bradley, Finlay, LeGrand, Leland, Leo, Leroy, Morley,** or **Wesley.** This is one of the few names that Americans still commonly give to both boys and girls. The name was formerly more popular in the southern part of the United States, where it honors both General Robert E. Lee and his father Henry "Light Horse Harry" Lee. Surprisingly, this very American name was one of the top ten names for boys born in England during the early 1980s.

Famous names: Lee J. Cobb (actor)
Lee Iacocca (industrialist)
Lee Marvin (actor)
Lee Strasberg (acting teacher)
Lee Trevino (golfer)

Other spellings: **Lea, Leigh**

Leeland (see **Leland**)

Leeroy (see **Leroy**)

LeGrand Old French *le grand,* "great, tall, large." This name started out as a nickname for a remarkably big man and later became a French and English surname. It is only rarely used as a first name today, although **Grant,** which is derived from the same French word, is fairly popular in that role.

Nickname: **Lee**

Variation: **LeGrant**

LeGrant (see **LeGrand**)

Leigh Spelling variation of **Lee.** Although this spelling is now usually reserved for girls in the United States, it still is occasionally given to boys.

Famous name: Leigh Hunt (essayist)

Leith Scots Gaelic *lite,* "wet," originally the name of a river near Edinburgh, Scotland. This Scottish surname occurs very occasionally as a first name in the southern part of the United States, where many people from Scotland settled.

Leland Old English "fallow land." This British place name and surname became a given name that symbolizes professionalism, good taste, and wealth in the 19th century because of the fame of A. Leland Stanford, the railroad magnate and philanthropist who founded Stanford University in California. The name's upper-crust image is now being reinforced by the character Leland McKenzie, senior partner of the legal firm featured on the television program *L.A. Law,* played by Richard Dysart.

Famous name: Leland Hayward (movie producer)
Nickname: **Lee**
Other spelling: **Leeland**

Lem (see **Lemuel**)

Lemmie, Lemmy (see **Lemuel**)

Lemuel Hebrew, probably meaning "belonging to the Lord."
Although parts of the Book of Proverbs are credited to
Lemuel, nothing else is known about him. The name became
popular in England in the 17th century under the influence of
the Puritans who sometimes named children by opening the
Bible and placing a finger on a name. Jonathan Swift used this
name for the central character of *Gulliver's Travels*.
Nicknames: **Lem, Lemmie, Lemmy**

Len Form of **Leonard**.
Famous name: Len Deighton (novelist)

Lenard (see **Leonard**)

Lencho (see **Lorenzo**)

Lennard (see **Leonard**)

Lennart (see **Leonard**)

Lennie, Lenny (see **Leonard**)

Lennox Scottish *Leunaichs*, "place of elms," from Gaelic
leamhanach.
Other spelling: **Lenox**

Lenox (see **Lennox**)

Lenz (see **Lawrence**)

Leo Latin "lion." Thirteen popes were named Leo, including Leo
the Great who prevented the Huns from sacking Rome. Six
emperors of Constantinople were also called Leo. The
continuing popularity of the name probably stems from its
association with the lion, long considered the king of beasts.
Russian author Count Leo Tolstoy is certainly considered a
lion of the literary world. His novels include *War and Peace*
and *Anna Karenina*.

Famous names: Leo Buscaglia (author)
Leo Szilard (nuclear physicist)

Nickname: **Lee**

Variations: **Leao** (Portuguese), **Leon** (French, Slavic, Spanish, and Irish), **Leonas** (Lithuanian), **Leone** (Italian), **Leonon, Leos** (Czech and Slovakian), **Lionel**

Leon Form of **Leo**. Leon Blum founded the modern French Socialist Party. Parents with an ear for unusual music might like this name, which is shared by musicians Leon Redbone and Leon Russell.

Leonard Old German "lion hard." In the sixth century, St. Leonard converted his master, Clovis, a powerful Frank king. This may explain why the name was formerly common in parts of France. Leonard was a popular name in both Britain and America during the first half of the 20th century, but its really fashionable period was over by 1950.

Famous names: Leonard Bernstein (composer and conductor)
Leonard Lyons (columnist)
Leonard Nimoy (actor and director)

Nicknames: **Len, Lennie, Lenny**

Other spellings: **Lennard, Leonerd**

Variations: **Lenard** (Hungarian), **Lennart** (Scandinavian), **Leonardo** (Italian, Portuguese, and Spanish), **Leonardus** (Dutch), **Leonhard** (German), **Lienhard** (Swiss)

Leonardo Italian, Spanish, and Portuguese form of **Leonard**. Most adults will recognize this name as that of one of the greatest artists of all time. Italian-born Leonardo da Vinci is remembered for his majestic paintings, including the "Mona Lisa" and "The Last Supper," but he is also the epitome of the Renaissance man. He was not only a painter but a sculptor, an architect, and an engineer. His sketches and engineering plans brought him renown in his own time, and 500 years after his death, his models for airplanes and designs for engines are still being studied. Most children of the 1990s, however, will probably first think of one of the Teenage Mutant Ninja Turtles when they hear this name. The creators of those idolized cartoon heros named the turtle after the great da Vinci.

Variation: **Lionardo**

Leonardus (see **Leonard**)

Leonas (see **Leo**)

Leone (see **Leo**)

Leonel (see **Lionel**)

Leonerd (see **Leonard**)

Leonhard (see **Leonard**)

Leonid Russian form of *Leonidas,* an ancient Greek name meaning "son of the lion."
   Famous name: Leonid Brezhnev (statesman)

Leonon (see **Leo**)

Leos (see **Leo**)

LeRoi (see **Leroy**)

Leroy, LeRoy Old French *le roi,* "the king." This name was generally popular in the United States during the late 19th century, but since 1920 it has been primarily used in the African-American community.
   Famous name: LeRoy Burrell (Olympic sprinter)
            Leroy Kelly (football player)
   Nicknames: **Lee, Roy**
   Variations: **Elroy, Leeroy, LeRoi**

Les (see **Leslie, Lester**)

Lesley, Lesly (see **Leslie**)

Leslie Scottish clan name of uncertain origin; possible meanings include "garden by the pool" and "court of hollies." This once-popular name for boys is now used primarily for girls.
   Famous names: Leslie Dunkling (onomatologist)
            Leslie Fiedler (literary critic)
            Leslie Howard (actor)
            Leslie Nielsen (actor)
            Sir Leslie Stephen (author)
   Nickname: **Les**
   Other spellings: **Lesley, Lesly**

Lester Old English form of *Leicester* from *Ligore* [a tribal name of uncertain meaning] + *cester* [from Latin *castra,* "city"]. This aristocratic British surname has been used as a first name in England since about 1840. In the United States, it was popular in the late 19th century, but its use has since faded. In the 20th century, it seems to have appealed more to parents in the South than the North. William Faulkner used the name for a farm boy in *The Sound and the Fury.*

Famous names: Lester B. Pearson (prime minister of Canada)
Lester Thurow (economist)

Nickname: **Les**

Levi Hebrew "joined in harmony." In the Old Testament, Levi was a son of Jacob and Leah. Levi Eshkol was the prime minister of Israel from 1963 to 1969 and led the Six-Day War. Levi is becoming more fashionable and is especially popular with parents in the western United States.

Other spelling: **Levy**

Levy (see **Levi**)

Lew (see **Llewellyn, Louis**)

Lewelyn (see **Llewellyn**)

Lewie (see **Louis**)

Lewis Variation of **Louis.** Lewis Carroll is remembered for his books *Alice in Wonderland* and *Through the Looking-glass.* General Lew Wallace wrote *Ben Hur* in 1880.

Famous name: Lewis Powell (U.S. Supreme Court justice)

Licho (see **Luis**)

Lienhard (see **Leonard**)

Lile (see **Lyle**)

Lilo (see **Cyril**)

Lin (see **Lincoln, Lynn**)

Linc (see **Lincoln**)

Lincoln English place name *Lindocolonia* from Celtic "lake" and Latin "colony." This surname became an American first name during the Civil War in honor of Abraham Lincoln, 16th president of the United States.

Famous names: Lincoln Ellsworth (polar explorer)
Lincoln Steffens (journalist)

Nicknames: **Lin, Linc**

Linden (see **Lyndon**)

Lindon (see **Lyndon**)

Linn (see **Franklin, Lynn**)

Linus Latin form of Greek *Linos,* in mythology a musician who was one of the tutors of Hercules. St. Linus, the second pope, was martyred in A.D. 76. Given the enduring popularity of cartoonist Charles Schultz, it's surprising that more parents don't name their sons after Linus, the brother of Lucy in the popular comic strip "Peanuts."

Famous name: Linus Pauling (chemist)

Lionardo (see **Leonardo**)

Lionel Medieval French and English form of **Leo.**

Famous names: Lionel Barrymore (actor)
Lionel Richie (musician)
Lionel Trilling (literary critic)

Variations: **Leonel** (Spanish), **Lionello** (Italian)

Lionello (see **Lionel**)

Lisle (see **Lyle**)

Lito (see **Angelo, Charles**)

Ljudvig (see **Louis**)

Llewellyn Form of Welsh *Llywelyn,* an ancient name of uncertain origin, possibly meaning "resembling the god of light." The modern Welsh spelling has been altered to include the word *llew,* "lion." Llewellyn I and Llewellyn II ruled Wales in the 13th century. The English royal title Prince of Wales originated with them. Llywelyn ab Gruffydd supported Simon de Monfort against Henry III of England and was defeated in 1265. When he refused to pay homage to Edward I, the English captured Wales and killed Llywelyn. The Welsh have kept the name alive as a statement of their independent spirit.

Famous name: Llewellyn Lloyd (author)
Nickname: **Lew**
Variations: **Lewelyn, Llewelyn**

Llewelyn (see **Llewellyn**)

Lloyd Welsh *Llwyd,* "gray" or "holy." This name was popular between 1900 and 1940 in the United States, but is now out of fashion. David Lloyd George, who is usually referred to as Lloyd George, was prime minister of Great Britain during World War I.
Famous names: Lloyd Bentsen (politician)
Lloyd Bridges (actor)
Variations: **Floyd, Loyd**

Lodewijk (see **Louis**)

Lodovico (see **Louis**)

Logan Scots Gaelic "little hollow." This Scottish place name and surname is now quickly rising in popularity as a first name, especially in the western United States. In 1991, Logan was the 78th most common name given to all American boys and was well into the top 50 names in states such as Utah and Nebraska. Perhaps the most famous bearer of this Scottish name in American history was an American Indian. The Cayuga chief Tahgahjute (perhaps meaning "long eyelashes") adopted the name Logan around 1750 in honor of James Logan, a Pennsylvania Quaker known as a friend of American Indians. Chief Logan later moved to Ohio, where his family was massacred by settlers in 1774. This caused him to go to war against the British. He refused to attend the signing of the peace treaty ending this minor war in 1775, but sent a letter so eloquent in its description of the injustices done Native Americans that he became a heroic figure to many of the same settlers he had been fighting. The towns of Logansport, Indiana, and Logan, West Virginia, were named for Chief Logan.
Famous name: Logan Jackson (activist for the homeless)

Lon Form of **Alonso, Lawrence,** or **Mahlon.**
Famous name: Lon Chaney (actor)

Lonnie, Lonny (see **Alonso, Lawrence, Mahlon**)

Loral Origin unknown; perhaps a masculine form of **Laurel** or **Lorelei.**
Famous name: Loral Wyatt (football player)

Lord (see **Gaylord**)

Loren (see **Lawrence, Lorin**)

Lorencho (see **Lorenzo**)

Lorenjo (see **Lorenzo**)

Lorens, Lorenz (see **Lawrence**)

Lorenzino (see **Lorenzo**)

Lorenzo Spanish and Italian form of **Lawrence.** In the 15th century, Lorenzo de' Medici was the ruler of Florence and a patron of the arts.
Famous name: Lorenzo Lamas (actor)
Variations: **Lencho** (Mexican), **Lorencho, Lorenjo, Lorenzino, Renzo**

Lorin Form of **Lawrence.**
Famous names: Lorin Hollander (pianist)
Lorin Maazel (conductor)
Variation: **Loren**

Lorinc (see **Lawrence**)

Lorn, Lorne From *Lorn,* a Scottish place name of unknown meaning. Lorne Michaels was the original producer of television's *Saturday Night Live* between 1975 and 1980 and has been again since 1985.
Famous name: Lorne Greene (actor)

Lorry (see **Lawrence**)

Lotario (see **Lothair**)

Lothaire (see **Lothair**)

Lothair Old German from *hlud* [fame] + *heri* [army]. This was the name of two Holy Roman Emperors; the French province of Lorraine was named after Lothair I in the early Middle Ages. This name has always been quite rare in English-speaking countries, although **Lothar** has been common in Germany.

Variations: **Lotario** (Spanish and Italian), **Lothaire** (French), **Lothar** (German), **Lothario**

Lothar (see **Lothair**)

Lothario (see **Lothair**)

Lou Form of **Louis.**

Famous names: Lou Brock (baseball player)
Lou Costello (comedian)
Lou Gehrig (baseball player)
Lou Rawls (singer)

Louie (see **Louis**)

Louis French form of Old German *Hludwig,* "famous warrior," through Latin *Ludovicus.* Many prominent Frenchmen, including 18 kings, share this name. Louis I was a ninth-century Holy Roman Emperor who divided his kingdom and paved the way for the nation of France. Louis IX was canonized as a saint for his efforts on behalf of the Crusades. Louis XV, the Sun King, who reigned from 1643 to 1715, built the palace of Versailles. Louis XVI, who inherited the financial problems caused by the wars his father had fought, died on the guillotine during the French Revolution. The 17th-century explorer Louis Joliet explored the Mississippi River with Father Marquette. French chemist Louis Pasteur is noted for his many contributions to science and medicine, including the life-saving theory that diseases are spread by bacteria. Louis Braille invented an alphabet for blind readers like himself. Louis (and **Lewis**) became very popular in the United States during the last half of the 19th century and was still the 138th most common name given to American boys in 1991.

Famous names: Louis Armstrong (musician)
Louis Brandeis (U.S. Supreme Court justice)
Louis Leakey (paleontologist)
Louis Skidmore (architect)
Louis Sullivan (architect)
Louis Comfort Tiffany (glass manufacturer)

Nicknames: **Lew, Lewie, Lou, Louie**

Other spelling: **Lewis**

Variations: **Alois, Aloisius** (Latin), **Aloys** (French), **Aloysius,**

Clodoveo (Spanish), Clovis (Latin), Ljudvig (Russian and Ukrainian), Lodewijk (Dutch), Lodovico (Italian), Ludis (Latvian), Ludovic (Scottish), Ludvig (Scandinavian), Ludvik (Czech), Ludwig (German), Ludwik (Polish), Luigi (Italian), Luis (Spanish), Luiz (Portuguese), Luthais (Scots Gaelic)

Lovell (see **Lowell**)

Lovre (see **Lawrence**)

Lowe (see **Lowell**)

Lowell Norman French *lovel,* "wolf cub." The use of this surname as a first name probably originally honored the 19th-century American poet and essayist James Russell Lowell. At that time, it was common for parents to name sons after their favorite authors; see **Byron, Homer, Irving,** and **Milton** for other examples.
Famous name: Lowell Thomas (commentator)
Variations: **Lovell, Lowe**

Loyd (see **Lloyd**)

Luc (see **Luke**)

Lucas Latin form of **Luke.** Lucas is now slightly more common than Luke on birth certificates in the United States, reaching 98th on the list of names given American boys in 1991. Most American boys by this name are undoubtedly called Luke in everyday life, however.
Famous name: Lucas Samaras (artist)

Lucho (see **Luis**)

Lucian Form of Latin *Lucianus,* "bringing light." Lucian was a second-century satirist, and St. Lucian was a third-century martyr. Lucian Freud, a grandson of Sigmund Freud, the founder of psychoanalysis, is considered one of the greatest modern artists in Great Britain.
Variations: **Luciano** (Italian), **Lucien** (French)

Luciano Italian and Spanish form of **Lucian.** Opera fans might want to choose this name to honor tenor Luciano Pavarotti.

Lucien (see **Lucian**)

Lucio (see **Lucius**)

Lucius Latin *lux,* "light." **Lucy** and **Lucia,** the feminine forms of
this name, are more common than this name for boys.
Famous names: Lucius Benjamin Appling (baseball player)
Lucius Seneca (Roman philosopher)
Nickname: **Luke**
Variation: **Lucio** (Italian, Spanish, and Portuguese)

Ludi (see **Ludwig**)

Ludis (see **Louis**)

Ludovic (see **Louis**)

Ludvig (see **Louis**)

Ludvik (see **Louis**)

Ludwig German form of **Louis.** This name has never been popular
outside of Austria, Switzerland, and Germany, despite the
admiration for one of the world's greatest composers, Ludwig
van Beethoven.
Famous names: Ludwig Erhard (chancellor of former West
Germany)
Ludwig Wittgenstein (philosopher)
Nicknames: **Ludi, Lutz**

Ludwik (see **Louis**)

Luigi Italian form of **Louis.**
Famous name: Luigi Pirandello (playwright)

Luis Spanish form of **Louis.** Luis is one of the most popular
traditional Spanish names with Hispanic parents in the United
States. The American physicist Luis W. Alvarez won the
Nobel Prize in physics in 1968. He later developed the now
widely accepted theory that a meteor impact caused the
extinction of the dinosaurs.
Famous names: Luis Aparicio (baseball player)
Luis Bunuel (movie director)
Nicknames: **Licho, Lucho**

Luither (see **Luther**)

Luiz (see Louis)

Lukas (see Luke)

Luke Greek *Loukas,* "a person from Lucania"; in the United States, also used as a nickname for **Lucius** or **Luther.** The original popularity of Luke was based almost entirely on St. Luke, who wrote the third Gospel. He is the patron saint of physicians and painters. The most famous modern Luke is undoubtedly Luke Skywalker, hero of the fabulously successful *Star Wars* movie trilogy. Luke has been an extremely popular name in both Australia and England since about 1975. Although it hasn't been as successful in the United States, the name is being used more frequently than in the past and was 107th on the list of names given American boys born in 1991. And if Luke and **Lucas** were counted together, they would have been 66th that year.

Famous names: Luscious Luke Easter (baseball player)
Luke Perry (actor)

Variations: **Luc** (French), **Lucas** (Latin and Dutch), **Lukas** (German, Scandinavian, and Czech)

Lutalo Luganda (Uganda) "warrior."

Lute (see Luther)

Lutero (see Luther)

Luthais (see Louis)

Luther Old German from *liut* [people] + *heri* [army]. Parents who choose this name usually wish to honor Martin Luther, the originator of Protestantism.

Famous names: Luther Burbank (horticulturist)
Luther Vandross (singer)

Nicknames: **Luke, Lute**

Variations: **Luither** (German), **Lutero** (Spanish), **Lutherio, Luto**

Lutherio (see Luther)

Luto (see Luther)

Lutz (see Ludwig)

Lyel, Lyell (see Lyle)

Lyle French *l'isle,* "the island."
  Famous names: Lyle Alzado (football player)
  Lyle Lovett (musician)
  Other spellings: **Lile, Lyel, Lyell**
  Variations: **Delisle, Lisle**

Lyman Old English "man living at the pasture." Lyman Beecher was one of the leading proponents of the abolition of slavery and presumably a strong influence on his daughter, Harriet Beecher Stowe, who wrote *Uncle Tom's Cabin.* Lyman Frank Baum created Dorothy, her mismatched crew, and the Yellow Brick Road in his book *The Wonderful Wizard of Oz.*
  Famous name: Lyman Hall (signer of the Declaration of Independence)

Lyn (see **Lyndon, Lynn**)

Lyndon Old English "hill of linden trees." Lyndon Baines Johnson was the 36th U.S. president.
  Nickname: **Lyn**
  Other spellings: **Linden, Lindon**

Lynn Celtic "stream, pool." This English place name and surname began to be used as a first name for boys around 1880. In the 20th century, it was also used for girls and is now only very rarely given to boys.
  Famous name: Lynn Swann (football player)
  Other spellings: **Lin, Linn, Lyn, Lynne**

Lynne (see **Lynn**)

Mac Scottish "son of." Mac is a prefix that corresponds to the suffixes "-son" and "-sen"; all mean "son of." Mac is a nickname for names that begin with Mac or Mc, a nickname for **Macaulay** and **Maximilian,** and a name on its own.
Other spelling: **Mack**

Macaulay Irish and Scottish "son of *Amalgaid* or **Olaf.**" The latter derivation gives evidence that many of the Vikings who raided Scotland and Ireland during the Middle Ages ended up settling there. Macaulay is still very rare as a first name, but if the child actor Macaulay Culkin retains his popularity, it may very well be used more often in the upcoming years.
Nicknames: **Mac, Mack**
Variations: **McAulay, McAuley, McCaulay, McCauley**

Mace (see **Mason**)

Mack (see **Mac, Macaulay, Maximilian**)

Maddy (see **Madison**)

Madison Middle English "son of **Maud**" or "son of **Matthew.**" James Madison, the fourth president of the United States, is the source of this name. He was president during the War of 1812, and along with John Hay and Alexander Hamilton, Madison was the author of the Federalist papers.
Famous name: Madison Jones (novelist)
Nickname: **Maddy**

Mahlon Hebrew "illness." In the Bible, Mahlon was the eldest son of Elimelech and Naomi and was the husband of Ruth. The name began to appear in the 17th century under the influence of the Puritans and still is used occasionally.

Famous name: Mahlon Pitney (U.S. Supreme Court justice)

Nicknames: **Lon, Lonnie, Lonny**

Variation: **Malon**

Maksymilian (see **Maximilian**)

Mal (see **Malcolm**)

Malcolm Gaelic *maol-Columb,* "servant of Columb," from Latin *columbia,* "dove." This was the name of four Scottish kings. In Shakespeare's play *Macbeth,* Malcolm III joined with Macduff to defeat Macbeth. Malcolm has never been a very popular name in the United States, but recently many African-American parents have chosen it to honor slain civil rights leader Malcolm X.

Famous names: Malcolm Cowley (editor)
Malcolm Forbes (publisher)
Malcolm Jamal Warner (actor)

Nickname: **Mal**

Malon (see **Mahlon**)

Manny (see **Manuel**)

Manu (see **Emmanuel**)

Manuel Spanish form of **Emmanuel.**

Famous name: Manuel da Falla (composer)

Nickname: **Manny**

Marc French form of **Mark.**

Famous names: Marc Blitzstein (composer)
Marc Chagall (painter)

Marco Italian form of **Mark.** Venetian Marco Polo explored the Far East in the 13th century and introduced spaghetti and gunpowder to European culture.

Marcos (see **Mark**)

Marcus This original Latin form of **Mark** has long been especially common in the African-American community. This is undoubtedly because of admiration for Marcus Garvey, the

Jamaican-born civil rights leader who founded a back-to-Africa movement in the early 20th century. He was one of the first to promote the idea of black pride. Americans from other ethnic backgrounds may more readily associate this name with *Marcus Welby, M.D.,* television's favorite family doctor in the 1970s.

Marek (see **Mark**)

Marin Latin *marinus,* "sailor." Parents who have sailing for a pastime might consider giving this name to their son.
Variation: **Maryn** (Polish)

Mario Italian and Spanish form of *Marius,* a Roman clan name probably related to Mars, the god of war, but in modern times often used as a masculine form of **Maria.**
Famous name: Mario Cuomo (politician)

Mark Latin *Marcus,* a Roman forename probably derived from Mars, god of war. Marcus Antonius and Marcus Brutus had opposite opinions about Julius Caesar. Marcus Aurelius, the Roman emperor, was a Stoic philosopher as well as a savage persecutor of Christians. St. Mark is the author of the second Gospel. In Venice, home of St. Mark's Cathedral, the name has enduring popularity. When writer Samuel Clemens was looking for a pen name, he found inspiration not in these historical Marks but in an expression of Mississippi boatmen. "Mark Twain" is the minimum safe depth of two fathoms.
Famous names: Mark Rothko (painter)
Mark Spitz (swimmer)
Mark Van Doren (editor and poet)
Variations: **Marc** (French), **Marco** (Italian), **Marcos** (Spanish), **Marcus, Marek** (Czech and Polish), **Markku** (Finnish), **Marko** (Serbo-Croatian and Ukrainian), **Markos** (Greek), **Markus** (Danish, Dutch, German, and Swedish), **Marques** (Portuguese), **Morkus** (Lithuanian)

Markku (see **Mark**)

Marko (see **Mark**)

Markos (see **Mark**)

Markus (see **Mark**)

Marques (see Mark)

Marquis Medieval Latin *marchensis,* "count of a borderland," an English and French title of nobility. Marquis was used occasionally as a first name by white Americans in the early 20th century, but now it is almost exclusively an African-American name. In 1991, this was the 61st most common name given to nonwhite boys in the United States. African-Americans also give the name **Marquise** to their sons, although technically that is the title for a woman who holds the rank of a marquis.

Marquise (see Marquis)

Marsh (see Marshall)

Marshal (see Marshall)

Marshall Old French *marshal,* "horse groom" and later "a leader of men." The military sound of this name has made it unpopular today, but it was more common before the 1950s.
Famous names: Marshall Field (merchant)
Marshall McLuhan (writer)
Nickname: **Marsh**
Other spelling: **Marshal**

Mart (see Martin)

Martainn (see Martin)

Marten (see Martin)

Martie (see Martin)

Martijn (see Martin)

Martin Latin *Martinus,* form of *Martius,* "of Mars." Among Roman Catholics, Martin was a popular name in the Middle Ages. Four popes took this name, perhaps in honor of the fourth-century St. Martin, the bishop of Tours and the patron saint of France. The name is revered by Protestants because of Martin Luther, who inspired the Reformation. Charles Dickens used the name for the title character of *Martin Chuzzlewit.*
Famous names: Martin Buber (philosopher)
Martin Luther King, Jr. (civil rights activist)

Martin Short (comedian)
Martin Van Buren (8th U.S. president)
Nicknames: **Mart, Martie, Marty**
Other spellings: **Marten, Marton**
Variations: **Martainn** (Scots Gaelic), **Martijn** (Dutch), **Martino** (Italian), **Morten** (Danish and Norwegian)

Martino (see **Martin**)

Marton (see **Martin**)

Marty Form of **Martin.** Parents who grew up watching the *Mickey Mouse Club* may remember the boy adventurers Spin and Marty.
Famous name: Marty Robbins (singer)

Marv, Marve (see **Marvin**)

Marven (see **Marvin**)

Marvin Old English *Maerwine* from *maer* [famous] + *wine* [friend].
Famous names: Marvin Gaye (musician)
Marvin Hagler (boxer)
Marvin Kaplan (actor)
Nickname: **Marv**
Other spelling: **Marven**
Variations: **Marve, Mervyn, Merwyn**

Maryn (see **Marin**)

Mason Old French *masson,* "a stonecutter."
Famous name: Mason Adams (actor)
Nickname: **Mace**

Massimiliano (see **Maximilian**)

Mat (see **Matthew**)

Mata (see **Matthew**)

Matej (see **Matthew**)

Mateo (see **Matthew**)

Mateusz (see **Matthew**)

Mathias (see **Matthew**)

Mathieu (see **Matthew**)

Mats Swedish form of **Matthew**.
> Famous name: Mats Wilander (tennis player)

Matt Form of **Matthew**. Actor James Arness played the Western marshal Matt Dillon on the television series *Gunsmoke*.
> Famous name: Matt Dillon (actor)

Mattaus (see **Matthew**)

Matteo (see **Matthew**)

Matthaeus (see **Matthew**)

Mattheus (see **Matthew**)

Matthew Hebrew *Matisyahu*, "gift of the Lord." St. Matthew, a former tax collector and one of the 12 apostles, was the author of the first Gospel. The name has enduring popularity in England and the United States. In the 19th century, Admiral Matthew Perry opened Japan to trade to the West. Matthew has been among the top five names given to American boys since 1980.
> Famous names: Matthew Arnold (poet)
> Mathew Brady (photographer)
> Matthew Broderick (actor)

> Nicknames: **Mat, Matt, Mattie, Matty**

> Variations: **Mata** (Scottish), **Matej** (Bulgarian and Slovenian), **Mateo** (Spanish), **Mateusz** (Polish), **Mathias, Mathieu** (French), **Mats** (Swedish), **Mattaus** (German), **Matteo** (Italian), **Matthaeus** (Danish), **Mattheus** (Dutch), **Matthias, Matti** (Finnish), **Mattias** (Swedish), **Matvei** (Russian), **Matyas** (Czech and Hungarian)

Matthias (see **Matthew**)

Matti (see **Matthew**)

Mattias (see **Matthew**)

Mattie, Matty (see **Matthew**)

Matvei (see **Matthew**)

Matyas (see **Matthew**)

Mauri (see **Maurice**)

Maurice Latin *Mauricius,* form of *Maurus,* "a Moor." St. Moritz, the fashionable Swiss ski resort, is named for St. Maurice, a third-century martyr. Although this name hasn't been popular for some time, it became common in the African-American community during the 1960s and was still 67th on the list of names given nonwhite boys in the United States in 1991.

Famous names: Maurice Chevalier (entertainer)
Maurice Ravel (composer)
Maurice Sendak (illustrator)

Nicknames: **Maurie, Maury**

Variations: **Mauri** (Finnish), **Mauricio** (Spanish), **Maurits** (Danish and Dutch), **Maurizio** (Italian), **Maurycy** (Polish), **Mavriki** (Russian), **Meurig** (Welsh), **Moric** (Hungarian), **Moritz** (German), **Morris, Morse**

Mauricio (see **Maurice**)

Maurie (see **Maurice**)

Maurits (see **Maurice**)

Maurizio (see **Maurice**)

Maury (see **Maurice**)

Maurycy (see **Maurice**)

Mavriki (see **Maurice**)

Max Form of **Maximilian** or **Maxwell.** Celebrities often set trends, and since movie producer and director Steven Spielberg and actress Amy Irving named their son Max, this name has become somewhat more popular.

Famous names: Max Beckmann (painter)
Sir Max Beerbohm (writer)
Max Ernst (painter)
Max John Flack (baseball player)

Max Lerner (columnist)
Max von Sydow (actor)
Max Weber (sociologist)

Maxie (see **Maximilian**)

Maximilian Latin *Maximilianus,* a diminutive of *Maximus,* "the greatest." The Romans bestowed the title Maximus on their great warriors. Ironically, St. Maximilian was martyred in the third century because he refused to be drafted into the Roman army. In France, Maximilien Robespierre was one of the leaders of the French Revolution. A few decades later, Austrian Archduke Maximilian was quite popular at home, but the Mexicans did not appreciate his being given the title of Emperor of Mexico by Napoleon, and they executed him.

Famous name: Maximilian Schell (actor)

Nicknames: **Mac, Mack, Max, Maxie, Maxy**

Variations: **Maksymilian** (Polish and Ukrainian), **Massimiliano** (Italian), **Maximilien** (French), **Maximiliano** (Spanish), **Maximilianus** (Dutch), **Miksa** (Hungarian)

Maximiliano (see **Maximilian**)

Maximilianus (see **Maximilian**)

Maximilien (see **Maximilian**)

Maxwell Scottish place name, "Magnus's well." This surname became a first name in Scotland in the 19th century.

Famous name: Maxwell Anderson (playwright)

Nickname: **Max**

Maxy (see **Maximilian**)

McAulay, McAuley (see **Macaulay**)

McCaulay, McCauley (see **Macaulay**)

Meical (see **Michael**)

Mel Usually a form of **Melvin** or **Samuel,** but this is not the case for the Australian actor Mel Gibson. He was named after St. Mel, a nephew of St. Patrick who first wrote down the story of his uncle's evangelization of Ireland. The original meaning of St.

Mel's name is unknown, but if Mel Gibson retains his reputation, there's a chance that this name may become popular.

Famous names: Mel Allen (sportscaster)
Mel Brooks (producer)

Melvin Perhaps a masculine form of **Malvina,** a name invented by Scottish poet James Macpherson in the 1700s; or, less likely, from Irish Gaelic *maoillmhin,* "gentle chief."

Famous names: Melvin Belli (lawyer)
Melvyn Douglas (actor)

Nicknames: **Mel, Vinnie, Vinny**

Other spelling: **Melvyn**

Melvyn (see **Melvin**)

Mensah Ewe (Ghana) "third son."

Menz (see **Clement**)

Merrill Gaelic "sea-bright," related to the girl's name **Muriel;** or from Old English *myrige* [merry] + *hyll* [hill], British place name.

Famous names: Merrill Moore (psychiatrist and poet)
Merrill Proudfoot (civil rights activist)

Variation: **Meryl**

Mervyn (see **Marvin**)

Merwyn (see **Marvin**)

Meryl (see **Merrill**)

Meurig (see **Maurice**)

Micah Hebrew "who is like Yahweh?" Micah is considered one of the minor prophets in the Old Testament. The famous vision of a peaceful world, "They shall beat their swords into plowshares, and their spears into pruning hooks; nation shall not lift up sword against nation, neither shall they learn war any more," is from the Book of Micah. This name has hardly been used in English-speaking countries until recently, but some American parents are now beginning to discover Micah as an alternative to the popular **Michael.**

Famous name: Micah L. Sifry (journalist)

Michael Hebrew "who is like the Lord?" The Archangel Michael leads the great battle described in the Revelation of St. John the Divine. The name of the Italian painter Michelangelo refers to the archangel. Emperors of Constantinople, Rumanian kings, and the first Romanov tsar of Russia shared this name. Since 1960, Michael has been the most popular name for boys in the United States, and it is extending its lead over other names even today. Michael is popular with Americans from all ethnic, racial, and religious backgrounds. Probably the two most celebrated Michaels in the world today are both African-Americans: basketball star Michael Jordan and singer Michael Jackson. French experts on names credit Jackson's popularity for making **Mickael** recently replace **Michel** as the common form of this name in France. Michael is also tending to replace **Miguel** in Brazil.

Famous names: Michael Bennett (choreographer)
Michael Bolton (singer)
Michael Caine (actor)
Michael Douglas (actor)
Michael Dukakis (politician)
Michael J. Fox (actor)
Michael Redgrave (actor)

Nicknames: **Mick, Mickey, Mickie, Micky, Mike**

Variations: **Meical** (Welsh), **Micah, Michail** (Russian), **Michal** (Polish), **Micheal** (Irish and Scottish), **Michel** (French), **Michele** (Italian), **Mickael** (modern French), **Miguel** (Spanish and Portuguese), **Mihael** (Greek), **Mihai** (Rumanian), **Mihaly** (Hungarian), **Mihhail** (Estonian), **Mikael** (Swedish), **Mikel** (Basque), **Mikelis** (Latvian), **Mikhail** (Russian), **Mikko** (Finnish), **Mitchell, Mykolas** (Lithuanian)

Michail (see **Michael**)

Michal (see **Michael**)

Micheal (see **Michael**)

Michel, Michele (see **Michael**)

Mick (see **Michael**)

Mickael (see **Michael**)

Mickey, Mickie, Micky Form of **Michael.** This nickname for Michael may be best known through Walt Disney's cartoon creation Mickey Mouse, but this association isn't exclusive, thanks to baseball player Mickey Mantle, writer Mickey Spillane, and actors Mickey Rooney and Mickey Rourke.

Migel (see **Miguel**)

Miguel Spanish and Portuguese form of **Michael.** The Spanish writer Miguel de Cervantes Saavedra, author of *Don Quixote,* is probably the most famous Miguel. This is still a very popular name with Hispanic parents and was 157th on the list of names given to all boys born in the United States in 1991.
Variation: **Migel**

Mihael (see **Michael**)

Mihai (see **Michael**)

Mihaly (see **Michael**)

Mihhail (see **Michael**)

Mikael (see **Michael**)

Mike Form of **Michael.**
Famous names: Mike Marshall (baseball player)
Mike Todd (film producer)

Mikel (see **Michael**)

Mikelis (see **Michael**)

Mikhail Russian form of **Michael.** This name has long been extremely popular in Russia. Americans are now familiar with it because of two famous Mikhails: Baryshnikov, the ballet dancer and choreographer, and Gorbachev, leader of the Soviet Union before its collapse. As a result, a few American boys are now being named Mikhail each year.
Nicknames: **Mischa, Misha, Mishenka**

Mikko (see **Michael**)

Miklos (see **Nicholas**)

Mikolaj (see **Nicholas**)

Mikolas (see **Nicholas**)

Miksa (see **Maximilian**)

Mil (see **Milton**)

Milan (see **Miles**)

Miles Norman French *Milo* possibly from Slavic *mil,* "mercy," or
Latin *miles,* "soldier." Miles Standish was a leader in the
founding of New England, but he is better known through
Henry Wadsworth Longfellow's poem "The Courtship of Miles
Standish."
Famous name: Miles Davis (jazz musician)
Other spelling: **Myles**
Variations: **Milan** (Czech and Hungarian), **Mille** (French),
Milo, Milos (Slovenian and Rumanian)

Mille (see **Miles**)

Milo (see **Miles**)

Milos (see **Miles**)

Milt (see **Milton**)

Milton Old English "mill town" or "middle town." This surname
became a first name in honor of John Milton, the 17th-century
English poet who wrote *Paradise Lost.* In the first decade of
television, comedian Milton Berle made this name familiar but
did nothing to increase the popularity of the name.
Famous names: Milton Avery (artist)
Milton Friedman (economist)
Nicknames: **Mil, Milt, Milty**

Milty (see **Milton**)

Mincho (see **Benjamin**)

Mingo (see **Dominic**)

Miron (see **Myron**)

Mischa (see **Mikhail**)

Misha (see **Mikhail**)

Mishenka (see **Mikhail**)

Mitch (see **Mitchell**)

Mitchell Middle English form of **Michael.**
Famous name: Mitch Miller (band leader)
Nickname: **Mitch**

Moe (see **Moses**)

Moise (see **Moses**)

Moisei (see **Moses**)

Moises, Moisis (see **Moses**)

Mojzesz (see **Moses**)

Mojzis (see **Moses**)

Moke (see **Moses**)

Monchi (see **Moses**)

Moncho (see **Simon**)

Monro (see **Monroe**)

Monroe Gaelic *mun-Rotha,* "mouth of the Roe" (a river in Ireland).
Surnames of presidents have often been used for first names.
James Monroe was the fifth president of the United States.
Other spellings: **Monro, Munroe, Munrow**

Montague A place name from Mont Aigu, France, which means
"pointed hill." Drogo de Montacute brought the name to
England in 1066.

Monte, Monty Form of **Lamont** or **Montgomery.**
Famous names: Monty Hall (television game show host)
Monte Markham (actor)

Montgomery French place name, "Gumric's hill." Gumric itself is
an Old Germanic name from *gum* [man] + *ric* [powerful].
Famous names: Montgomery Clift (actor)
Montgomery Ward (merchant)
Nicknames: **Monte, Monty**

Mooses (see **Moses**)

Morgan Welsh, either *mor* [sea] or *mawr* [great] + *can* [bright]. This is one of the few names now being commonly given to both boys and girls in the United States.
Famous name: Morgan Freeman (actor)

Moric (see **Maurice**)

Moritz (see **Maurice**)

Morkus (see **Mark**)

Morley Old English "marsh meadow." Morley has a long tradition as a place name and surname in England. It was in use there before the Norman Invasion. It became somewhat popular as a first name during the 18th and 19th centuries, when many authors, statesmen, and artists were named Morley. Queen Anne of England used the pseudonym Mrs. Morley.
Famous name: Morley Safer (journalist)
Nickname: **Lee**

Morrie (see **Morris, Seymour**)

Morris Form of **Maurice.** This name has never been popular in the United States, and now that a cat-food company has made it famous as the name of a cat, it seems unlikely that many parents, with the possible exception of feline fanatics, will choose this name for their sons.
Famous name: Morris Fishbein (physician and editor)
Nickname: **Morrie**

Morrison Middle English *Morisson,* "son of **Maurice.**"
Famous name: Morrison Remick Waite (U.S. Supreme Court chief justice)

Morse (see **Maurice**)

Mort Form of **Mortimer** or **Morton.**
Famous name: Mort Sahl (comedian)

Morten (see **Martin**)

Mortie (see **Mortimer**)

Mortimer French place name *Mortemer* in Normandy, "dead sea."

Famous name: Mortimer Adler (philosopher and educator)
Nicknames: **Mort, Mortie**

Morton Old English "marshy farmstead."
Famous name: Morton Downey, Jr. (television talk show host)
Nickname: **Mort**

Mose (see **Moses**)

Moses Probably Egyptian "child." As an infant, Moses was taken from the Nile River by the daughter of Pharoah. Because the ancient Hebrews didn't understand the meaning of the Egyptian name he was given, they interpreted it as meaning "saved, drawn out of the water." In the Old Testament, Moses was the law giver of the Israelites and led them to the promised land, which he could not enter. He died after having viewed it. This name was used by Jews throughout the Middle Ages. In the 17th century, the Puritans made it popular. But in the late 19th century, it, along with other Puritan names, fell into disuse. It is still rare today despite the revival of many other biblical names.

Famous names: Moses Austin (Texas pioneer)
Moses Cleaveland (founder of Cleveland)
Moshe Dayan (defense minister of Israel)
Moses Malone (basketball player)

Nicknames: **Moe, Moke, Monchi** (Spanish), **Mose, Mosie, Moss**
Variations: **Moise** (French and Rumanian), **Moisei** (Bulgarian), **Moises** (Spanish), **Moisis** (Greek), **Mojzesz** (Polish), **Mojzis** (Slovakian), **Mooses** (Estonian and Finnish), **Moshe** (Hebrew), **Moyses** (Portuguese), **Moze** (Lithuanian), **Mozes** (Dutch and Hungarian)

Moshe (see **Moses**)

Mosie (see **Moses**)

Moss Form of **Moses.**
Famous name: Moss Hart (playwright)

Moyses (see **Moses**)

Moze (see **Moses**)

Mozes (see **Moses**)

Mundek (see **Edmond**)

Mundy (see **Edmond**)

Munroe, Munrow (see **Monroe**)

Murray Celtic "sea settlement" or from Irish Gaelic *Giolla Mhuire,* "servant of the Virgin Mary."
Famous name: F. Murray Abraham (actor)
Other spelling: **Murry**

Murry (see **Murray**)

Mykola (see **Nicholas**)

Mykolas (see **Michael**)

Myles (see **Miles**)

Myron Greek "myrrh, perfume."
Variation: **Miron** (Slavic and Spanish)

Nado (see **Bernard**)

Naldo (see **Reinaldo**)

Nando (see **Fernando**)

Nandor (see **Ferdinand**)

Nano (see **Fernando**)

Nat (see **Nathan**)

Natal (see **Noel**)

Natale (see **Noel**)

Natan (see **Nathan**)

Nataneal, Nataniel (see **Nathaniel**)

Nate (see **Nathan**)

Nathan Hebrew "the given." In the Old Testament, the prophet Nathan was the one man who could stand up to King David. He chastised him for sending Bathsheba's husband into battle. Nathan has been a popular Jewish name for centuries. Nathan Hale was the often-quoted American Revolutionary hero who said on the gallows, "I regret I have but one life to give for my country." Like other biblical names, Nathan became extremely popular in the 1980s.

Nicknames: **Nat, Nate, Natty**

Variation: **Natan** (Polish, Spanish, and Italian)

Nathanael (see **Nathaniel**)

Nathaniel Hebrew "the Lord has given." Nathaniel was a popular
name in New England during the 18th and 19th centuries.
Along with **Nathan,** it has recently been revived. The present
trend is for **Nathan** to be more popular with white parents
while **Nathaniel** is used more by Hispanic-Americans and
African-Americans.
Famous names: Nathanael Greene (American Revolutionary
general)
Nathaniel Hawthorne (novelist)
Nathanael West (novelist)
Variations: **Nataneal** (Spanish), **Nataniel** (Polish), **Nathanael**

Natty (see **Nathan**)

Nayo (see **Bernard**)

Neacail (see **Nicholas**)

Neal (see **Neil**)

Neale (see **Neil**)

Neall (see **Neil**)

Nealson (see **Nelson**)

Necho (see **Andrew**)

Necolas (see **Nicholas**)

Ned Form of **Edward** or **Edwin.**
Famous name: Ned Beatty (actor)

Neel (see **Neil**)

Neil Irish Gaelic *Niall,* uncertain meaning, perhaps "cloud,"
"passionate," or "chief." Neil is a name that has never been
hugely popular in the United States, but it also never seems to
go completely out of style. Neil is therefore a good choice for
parents searching for a solid but unfaddish name.
Famous names: Neil Armstrong (astronaut)
Neil Diamond (singer)
Neil Sedaka (singer)
Neil Simon (playwright)

Other spellings: **Neal, Neale, Neall, Neel, Neill, Niel**

Variations: **Nial, Niall** (Irish and Scottish), **Nigel, Njal**
(Scandinavian)

Neill (see **Neil**)

Nels (see **Niels**)

Nelson English "son of **Neil**." South African civil rights activist
Nelson Mandela, jailed for more than 25 years, has given this
first name worldwide recognition.

Famous names: Nelson Algren (novelist)
Nelson Eddy (singer)

Variations: **Nealson, Niles**

Nevil, Nevile (see **Neville**)

Neville French *Neuville,* "the new town."

Famous names: Neville Chamberlain (statesman)
Neville Marriner (conductor)
Nevil Shute (novelist)

Other spellings: **Nevil, Nevile**

Nial, Niall (see **Neil**)

Niccolo (see **Nicholas**)

Nicholas Greek *Nikolaos* from *nike* [victory] + *laos* [people]
through Latin *Nicolaus.* So many miracles are credited to the
fourth-century St. Nicholas that he has become the patron of
Russian schoolchildren, sailors, and pawnbrokers. In a
convoluted way, St. Nicholas is connected to the mythical
character Santa Klaus. Klaus is the German shortened form of
Nikolaus, and German and Dutch immigrants brought Sinter
Klaus and the tradition of giving gifts on St. Nicholas's feast
day, December 6, to the United States. Eventually, Santa Claus
came to deliver gifts on Christmas Eve. Nicholas has long been
a popular name in Europe. It was the name of five popes and
two Russian emperors. In England, the name goes back to
before the Norman Invasion. Its long-established roots have
given rise to many variations, including **Cole** and **Colin,** which
are now popular independent names. Famous Italians of this
name include Niccolo Machiavelli, author of *The Prince,* a
philosophy of politics, and violinist Niccolo Paganini. The

Polish thinker Nicolaus Copernicus revolutionized astronomy with his then-heretical theory that the earth revolved around the sun. Charles Dickens used the name for the title character of *Nicholas Nickleby*. Although Nicholas has enjoyed only moderate popularity in the past, it became very fashionable in the 1980s and was among the top ten names given to American boys by 1991. Nicholas Bradford, a character on the family-oriented television series *Eight Is Enough* played by Adam Rich, may have had something to do with the name's increased use.

Famous name: Nicholas Poussin (painter)

Nicknames: **Nick, Nicki, Nickie, Nicky, Nicol, Nik, Nikky**

Variations: **Claus, Colacho, Cole, Colin** (Celtic), **Klaus** (Danish and German), **Kolya** (Russian), **Launo** (Finnish), **Miklos** (Hungarian), **Mikolaj** (Polish), **Mikolas** (Czech), **Mykola** (Ukrainian), **Neacail** (Scots Gaelic), **Necolas, Niccolo** (Italian), **Nico** (Greek and Italian), **Nicola** (Italian), **Nicolaas** (Dutch), **Nicolao** (Portuguese), **Nicolas** (French and Spanish), **Nicolo** (Italian), **Nidzo** (Serbian), **Niels** (Danish), **Niilo** (Finnish), **Niklas** (Scandinavian), **Niko** (Dutch and Slovenian), **Nikolai** (Russian), **Nikolaos** (Greek), **Nikolaus** (German), **Nils** (Swedish and Norwegian)

Nick Form of **Dominic** or **Nicholas**.

Famous name: Nick Nolte (actor)

Nicki, Nickie, Nicky (see **Dominic, Nicholas**)

Nico (see **Anthony, Nicholas**)

Nicol (see **Nicholas**)

Nicola (see **Nicholas**)

Nicolaas, Nicolas (see **Nicholas**)

Nicolao (see **Nicholas**)

Nicolo (see **Nicholas**)

Nidzo (see **Nicholas**)

Niel (see **Neil**)

Niels Danish form of **Nicholas.** There is a natural tendency for Americans to confuse this name with **Neil,** but the true Scandinavian form of Neil is **Njal.** Niels Bohr, the Danish physicist who won the Nobel Prize in 1922, was a leading figure in the development of quantum theory that led to the atomic age.

Variations: **Nels** (Swedish), **Nils** (Norwegian and Swedish)

Nigel (see **Neil**)

Niilo (see **Nicholas**)

Nik (see **Dominic, Nicholas**)

Nikita Russian form of Greek *Aniketos,* "unconquerable."

Famous name: Nikita Khrushchev (statesman)

Nikky (see **Nicholas**)

Niklas (see **Nicholas**)

Niko (see **Nicholas**)

Nikolai (see **Nicholas**)

Nikolaos (see **Nicholas**)

Nikolaus (see **Nicholas**)

Niles (see **Nelson**)

Nils (see **Nicholas, Niels**)

Njal (see **Neil**)

Noah Hebrew, perhaps "rest." The story of Noah and his ark is probably the best-known tale in Western civilization, although essentially the same story occurs in most other cultures. Because of Noah's goodness and righteousness, God favored him and let him in on the secret that the world was going to be destroyed by a flood. Noah was given directions on building a boat and told how to select those who were to be saved from the flood. After the flood, the descendants of Noah repeopled the world. The name came into vogue in the 17th century when it was used by the Puritans. It went out of fashion in the 19th century, but is very slowly reviving in the United States today.

Noah was the 205th most common name given to American boys born in 1991.

Famous names: Noah Beery (actor)
Noah Webster (lexicographer)

Variation: **Noe** (French and Spanish)

Noam Hebrew "pleasantness." This name is a masculine variation of **Naomi.** Because it has no biblical reference, it was not used by the Puritans, and consequently, the name continues to be used primarily by European Jews.

Famous name: Avram Noam Chomsky (linguist)

Nobby (see **Norbert**)

Noe (see **Noah**)

Noel Latin *natalis,* "birth," through Old French *noel* or *nowel;* traditionally used as a name for children born on Christmas Day. For a boy born on Christmas Day, Noel is an apt name, even though it is less popular than Christopher.

Famous name: Sir Noel Coward (playwright)

Other spellings: **Nowel, Nowell**

Variations: **Natal** (Spanish), **Natale** (Italian)

Nolan Irish Gaelic *Nuallain* from *nuall,* "shouter, chariot-fighter, champion."

Famous name: Nolan Ryan (baseball pitcher)

Variation: **Noland**

Noland (see **Nolan**)

Noldy (see **Arnold**)

Noll (see **Oliver**)

Nolly (see **Oliver**)

Norbert Old German, perhaps "aurora borealis" from *nord* [north] + *berht* [bright]. St. Norbert was struck by lightning and began to hear the words of God. He reformed his life, became a monk, and established the Order of Premonstrants. Norbert is a very unusual name in the modern United States.

Famous name: Norbert Beverly Enzer (child psychologist)

Nicknames: **Bert, Bertie, Nobby**

Norm Form of **Norman.**
  Famous name: Norm Cash (baseball player)

Norman Old English "north man." This name has roots in England, but not until the 19th century did it attained a slight degree of popularity in the United States.
  Famous names: Norman Jewison (movie director)
  Norman Lear (movie producer)
  Norman Mailer (writer)
  Norman Rockwell (painter)
  Nicknames: **Norm, Normie, Normy**
  Variation: **Normand**

Normand (see **Norman**)

Normie, Normy (see **Norman**)

Norris Old Norman French *norreis,* "person from the north."
  Famous names: Norris Cotton (U.S. senator)
  Norris McWhirter (editor, *Guinness Book of World Records*)

Nort (see **Norton**)

Norton Old English "north town." Norton is fairly common as a surname. Several Nortons have served in Congress; others have contributed to the arts and to education.
  Nickname: **Nort**

Nowel, Nowell (see **Noel**)

Numps (see **Humphrey**)

Oba Yoruba (Nigeria) "king."

Odoardo (see **Edward**)

Odo (see **Otto**)

Odon (see **Edmond, Otto**)

Ogden Old English "from the oak valley" from *ac* [oak] + *denu* [dale or valley]. Perhaps the harsh sound of this name or simply that it is a name beginning with "O" is responsible for the current lack of enthusiasm for this name.
Famous name: Ogden Nash (poet)
Variation: **Ogdon**

Ogdon (see **Ogden**)

Olaf Old Norse *Anleifr* from *anu* [ancestor] + *leifr* [heir, descendant]. St. Olaf was the first Christian king of Norway and the first of many royal Olafs, which probably accounts for the name's enduring popularity throughout Scandinavia. Most American Olafs have Scandinavian ancestors.
Variations: **Amblaoibh** (Irish), **Olav** (Norse), **Oliver**

Olav (see **Olaf**)

Oliva (see **Oliver**)

Oliver Uncertain meaning; perhaps Old German *Alfihar*, "elf-host"; a French form of **Olaf**; or Old French "olive tree." The olive tree was essential to Greek and Roman cultures, and with the advance of the Roman Empire, the name spread quickly to northern Europe and England, where it was listed in the

Domesday Book. Shakespeare used the name for the brother of Orlando in his play *As You Like It,* but in the 17th century, Oliver Cromwell's ruthless reign tainted the name. In the 18th century, one of the few instances of the name is that of novelist Oliver Goldsmith. In the 19th century, Charles Dickens brought a new image to the name with his novel *Oliver Twist,* which is about an orphan boy who finds happiness.

Famous names: Oliver Wendell Holmes (U.S. Supreme Court justice)
Oliver Stone (movie director)

Nicknames: **Noll, Nolly, Olley, Ollie, Olly**

Variations: **Oliva** (French Canadian), **Oliverio** (Italian and Spanish), **Olivier** (French), **Olivo**

Oliverio (see **Oliver**)

Olivier (see **Oliver**)

Olivo (see **Oliver**)

Olley, Ollie, Olly (see **Oliver**)

Omar Arabic "thriving, prospering, long-lived" or Hebrew "speaker." This name had a literal application for at least two men who prospered in their chosen professions and whose reputations have been long-lived: 12th-century Persian poet Omar Khayyam and U.S. Army General Omar Bradley, commander of the Normandy Invasion.

Famous name: Omar Sharif (actor)

Variation: **Amar**

Omero (see **Homer**)

Ondrej (see **Andrew**)

Onfredo (see **Humphrey**)

Onfroy (see **Humphrey**)

Oracio (see **Horace**)

Oral Latin *oral,* "spoken," from *os,* "mouth." This seems to be an appropriate name for a preacher and television evangelist such as Oral Roberts, who was named by an aunt who simply liked the sound of the word.

Famous name: Oral Clyde Hildebrand (baseball pitcher)

Orasio (see **Horace**)

Orazio (see **Horace**)

Orban (see **Urban**)

Orel From a Czech surname meaning "eagle." This name has never been popular. In 1988, Orel Hershisher, a baseball pitcher, won the Most Valuable Player Award in the World Series, the Cy Young Award, and many other top honors, including the record for pitching the most scoreless innings in a row. Sports fans may want to name a son for this baseball player.

Orien (see **Orion**)

Orion Greek "son of light." In Greek mythology, Orion was a mighty hunter. Poseidon, his father, gave him the power to walk on water. Instead of wooing the daughter of the king of Chios, he seduced her. The king was furious, so he got Orion drunk and had him blinded. He wandered the earth until the sun restored his eyesight, then Orion challenged Artemis to a hunt, and the goddess immediately killed him. The constellation Orion is easily recognized by the row of stars that make up Orion's belt.
Variation: **Orien**

Orito (see **George**)

Orland (see **Roland**)

Orlando Italian form of **Roland.** Orlando is the hero of Shakespeare's play *As You Like It* and the name Virginia Woolf chose for the title character of her fictional biography of her friend Vita Sackville-West. Although originally an Italian name, this name is now popular with Hispanic-Americans.
Famous name: Orlando Cepeda (baseball player)

Orsino (see **Orson**)

Orson Old Norman French "bear cub" from Latin *ursus,* "bear." The prominence of movie director and actor Orson Welles, whose movie credits include *Citizen Kane* and *The Magnificent Ambersons* as well as his famous "War of the Worlds" radio broadcast, did nothing to increase the popularity of this unusual name.

Famous name: Orson Bean (actor)

Variations: **Orsino, Ursin** (Danish, French, Russian, and Rumanian), **Ursino** (Italian and Spanish), **Urson, Ursyn** (Ukrainian)

Orv (see **Orville**)

Orvie (see **Orville**)

Orville French "gold town." This name was invented by Fanny Burney for the hero of her novel *Evelina*. The name was made popular in the United States by Orville Wright, who with his brother, Wilbur, flew the first motor-driven airplane.

Famous name: Orville Redenbacher (entrepreneur)

Nicknames: **Orv, Orvie**

Osborn Old English *Osbeorn* from *os* [god] + *beorn* [bear, warrior]. This is an old name in England that is found mostly in Northumberland. It has been in general use since long before the Norman Conquest.

Nicknames: **Oz, Ozzie**

Variation: **Osborne, Ozburn**

Osborne (see **Osborn**)

Oscar Irish Gaelic from *os* [deer] + *cara* [friend]. Scottish researcher James Macpherson revived this name in the 18th century through his supposed translations of the third-century poems by Ossian. (Most modern scholars believe that Macpherson wrote the poems himself and merely claimed that they were translations of ancient writings.) These works were popular throughout western Europe, and Napoleon Bonaparte insisted that his godson, Oscar Bernadotte, be given this name. He later became king of Sweden. Oscar is the pet name for the awards given by the Academy of Motion Picture Arts and Sciences. The gold-covered statuettes supposedly got this name in 1931 when the librarian of the Academy, Margaret Herrick, said that she thought the trophies looked like her uncle Oscar.

Famous names: Oscar Hammerstein (librettist)
Oscar Robertson (basketball player)
Oscar Wilde (playwright)

Nicknames: **Ossie, Ozzie**

Other spelling: **Oskar**

Osip (see **Joseph**)

Oskar (see **Oscar**)

Osman Turkish form of Arabic *Uthman*, "young bustard." A bustard is a Middle Eastern bird similar to a crane. The Turkish sultan Osman founded the Ottoman Empire in 1517.

Ossie (see **Oscar, Oswald**)

Osvaldo (see **Oswald**)

Oswald Old English *Osweald*, "divinely powerful," from *os* [god] + *weald* [power]. This very old name dates to at least the seventh century through the king of Northumbria, who was killed in a battle with the Welsh army. The name is unusual in the United States, although the nickname Ozzie became a household name through Ozzie Nelson in the 1950s television comedy *The Adventures of Ozzie and Harriet*, while rock singer Ozzy Osborne made it a name for the 1980s.
Famous names: Ossie Davis (actor)
　　　　　　　 Oswald Spengler (philosopher)
Nicknames: **Ossie, Oz, Ozzie, Wallie, Wally**
Variation: **Osvaldo** (Spanish)

Otao (see **Otto**)

Otho (see **Otto**)

Otis Middle English *Otes, Odes*, "son of **Otto** or *Odo*," the latter from Old Norse *odd*, "point of a weapon." This surname became a first name in the United States in honor of James Otis, an 18th-century Massachusetts patriot thought to have been the first to use the phrase "taxation without representation."
Famous names: Otis Redding (singer)
　　　　　　　 Otis Skinner (actor)

Oto (see **Otto**)

Otone (see **Otto**)

Otti (see **Otto**)

Otto Old German *asdo*, "rich." Otto von Bismarck, chancellor of the German empire, is known for engineering the unification of Germany in the 19th century.

Famous name: Otto Klemperer (conductor)

Variations: **Odo** (Latin and Polish), **Odon, Otao** (Portuguese), **Otho, Oto** (Bulgarian and Croatian), **Otone** (Italian), **Otti** (Estonian), **Otton** (French, Greek, and Russian)

Otton (see **Otto**)

Owain (see **Owen**)

Owen Probably a Welsh form of **Eugene.** This name has Welsh roots and is known to history through the 12th-century general Owen of Gwynedd and the 15th-century rebel Owen Glendower, who failed to achieve his bid for Welsh independence. Today, the name is not very popular, although it is among the top 500 names given American boys.

Famous names: Owen Feltham (poet)
                    Owen J. Roberts (U.S. Supreme Court justice)
                    Owen Wister (novelist)

Variations: **Ewan, Ewen, Owain**

Owodunni Yoruban (Nigeria) "it's nice to have money."

Oz (see **Osborn, Oswald**)

Ozburn (see **Osborn**)

Ozzie (see **Osborn, Oscar, Oswald**)

Paal (see **Paul**)

Paavo (see **Paul**)

Pablo Spanish form of **Paul.**
Famous names: Pablo Casals (conductor)
Pablo Picasso (painter)

Paco (see **Francisco**)

Paddy (see **Patrick**)

Padraig (see **Patrick**)

Padrig (see **Patrick**)

Pal (see **Paul**)

Panchito (see **Pancho**)

Pancho Spanish form of **Francisco.**
Famous names: Pancho Gonzalez (tennis player)
Pancho Villa (bandit)
Variations: **Panchito, Pancholo, Panzo**

Pancholo (see **Pancho**)

Panzo (see **Pancho**)

Paolo (see **Paul**)

Par (see **Peter**)

Parcifal (see **Percival**)

Park (see **Parker**)

Parker Old English "a gamekeeper." This is an occupational name, like Baker. Parker has received more attention since the high-school sitcom *Parker Lewis Can't Lose* appeared on the Fox network in the fall of 1990.
Famous name: Parker Stevenson (actor)
Nickname: **Park**

Parnel (see **Parnell**)

Parnell A Norman French contraction of Latin *Petronilla,* perhaps "little rock," the name of an early Christian martyr who was legendarily the daughter of St. Peter. Parnell is one of the few European surnames from medieval times to be based on a woman's rather than a man's first name. The name is associated with Irish politics and literature. Charles Stewart Parnell was an Irish nationalist leader, and some Irish-Americans choose to name their sons after him.
Famous name: Pernell Roberts (actor)
Variations: **Parnel, Pernell**

Parsifal (see **Percival**)

Parzival (see **Percival**)

Pascal French form of Latin *Paschalis,* "relating to Easter or the Hebrew Passover." This name honors Good Friday, and boys born on that day traditionally were named Pascal. The Sunday following Good Friday is Easter, the day for hunting eggs, which used to be called Pascal eggs. Pascal is hardly used in English-speaking countries, but it was very popular in France during the 1960s. It's the name of the little boy in the French children's book *The Red Balloon.*
Variations: **Paschal, Pascoe** (Cornish), **Pascual** (Spanish), **Pasquale** (Italian)

Paschal (see **Pascal**)

Pascoe (see **Pascal**)

Pascual (see **Pascal**)

Pasquale (see **Pascal**)

Passi (see **Sebastian**)

Pat Form of **Patrick**.
> Famous name: Pat Metheny (musician)

Patrice (see **Patrick**)

Patricio (see **Patrick**)

Patricius (see **Patrick**)

Patrick Latin *patricius,* "member of the nobility." St. Patrick, the patron saint of Ireland, was born in England and educated in France. In A.D. 432, he came to Ireland to preach the Gospel. Until the 17th century, most people in Ireland held St. Patrick in such high esteem that his name wasn't used. Although this name is often thought to be exclusively Irish, Scots claim it as well. In the United States, the statesman and orator Patrick Henry urged the declaration of war against the English crown with his famous speech, "Give me liberty or give me death." The name has been popular in both England and the United States during the 20th century and was the 42nd most common name given to American boys born in 1991. Since 1975, Patrick has also become a popular name in Germany.
> Famous names: Patrick Duffy (actor)
>> Patrick Ewing (basketball player)
>> Patrick J. Leahy (U.S. senator)
>> Patrick Stewart (actor)
>
> Nicknames: **Paddy, Pat, Patsy, Patty, Ticho** (Spanish)
> Variations: **Padraig** (Irish Gaelic), **Padrig** (Welsh), **Patrice** (French), **Patricio** (Spanish and Portuguese), **Patricius** (Dutch), **Patrik** (Czech, Finnish, Swedish, and Hungarian), **Patriss** (Latvian), **Patrizio** (Italian), **Patryk** (Polish)

Patrik (see **Patrick**)

Patriss (see **Patrick**)

Patrizio (see **Patrick**)

Patryk (see **Patrick**)

Patsy (see **Patrick**)

Patty (see **Patrick**)

Paul Greek *paulos,* "small." St. Paul, a Jew who had persecuted Christians, became one of Christianity's most ardent advocates after his conversion. Through his epistles, Paul's beliefs and his interpretations of Christianity became the foundation of much of the religion. Paul is also the name of six popes. Paul was not a common name in England before the 20th century, but was very popular in Russia, Italy, Spain, and France. Painters Paul Cezanne, Paul Gauguin, and Paul Klee lent the name artistic roots, while the American Revolutionary hero Paul Revere gave the name stature in the United States. The name has been particularly popular among actors, including Paul Muni, Paul Newman, Paul Robeson, Paul Scofield, and Paul Winfield.

Famous names: Paul Harvey (commentator)
Paul Hindemith (composer)
Paul McCartney (musician)
Paul Verlaine (poet)
Paul Volcker (economist)
Paul Wylie (figure skater)

Nickname: **Paulie, Pava** (Russian)

Variations: **Paal** (Estonian), **Paavo** (Finnish), **Pablo** (Spanish), **Pal** (Hungarian, Scots Gaelic, and Swedish), **Paolo** (Italian), **Paulo** (Portuguese), **Paulos** (Greek), **Paulus** (Latin and Dutch), **Paval** (Bulgarian and Slovenian), **Pavao** (Serbo-Croatian), **Pavel** (Czech and Russian), **Pavlo** (Ukrainian), **Pawel** (Polish), **Pol** (Irish Gaelic), **Polo** (Italian), **Poul** (Danish), **Povilas** (Lithuanian)

Paulie (see **Paul**)

Paulo (see **Paul**)

Paulos (see **Paul**)

Paulus (see **Paul**)

Pava (see **Paul**)

Paval (see **Paul**)

Pavao (see **Paul**)

Pavel (see **Paul**)

Pavlo (see **Paul**)

Pawel (see **Paul**)

Peadar (see **Peter**)

Peder (see **Peter**)

Pedro Spanish and Portuguese form of **Peter.** This name is still used
fairly often by Hispanic-Americans.
Famous names: Pedro Almodovar (film director)
Pedro Guerrero (baseball player)
Variations: **Perico, Pero, Peyo, Pico**

Pekka (see **Peter**)

Pello (see **Peter**)

Pentti (see **Benedict**)

Pepe (see **Joseph**)

Pepito (see **Joseph**)

Per (see **Peter**)

Perce (see **Percival**)

Perceval (see **Percival**)

Percival Origin uncertain, but may come from French *perce-val,*
"valley piercer." This name was invented by Chretien de Troyes
in the 12th century. He used it for a knight who was on a quest
for the Holy Grail. The story is retold in Malory's *Morte
d'Arthur* and also in Tennyson's *Idylls of the King.*
Famous name: Percival Lowell (astronomer)
Nicknames: **Perce, Percy**
Other spelling: **Perceval**
Variations: **Parcifal** (Dutch), **Parsifal** (Italian, Polish, and
Czech), **Parzival** (German and Hungarian)

Percy French place name "Persius's estate" or a form of **Percival.** In
medieval England, this was considered a good name for a
rugged masculine knight, but in modern times Percy has lost its
macho image.
Famous name: Percy Bysshe Shelley (poet)

Perico (see **Pedro**)

Perkin (see **Peter**)

Pernell (see **Parnell**)

Pero (see **Pedro**)

Perry Old English *pyrige,* "pear tree." The many books, television shows, and movies about the exploits of defense attorney Perry Mason overshadow any other connotations of this name.

Famous names: Perry Como (singer)
Perry Ellis (fashion designer)
Perry King (actor)
Perry Miller (historian)

Pershing American form of German *Pfoersching,* "a person who grows or sells peaches." This name is very unusual today. It honors General John Joseph "Blackjack" Pershing, commander of the U.S. Expeditionary Forces in World War I. The name was given to sons of soldiers who fought under his command.

Famous name: Robert Pershing "Bobby" Doerr (baseball player)

Pervis (see **Purvis**)

Petar (see **Peter**)

Pete Form of **Peter.**

Famous names: Pete Rose (baseball player)
Pete Seeger (musician)

Peter Greek *petros,* "rock." St. Peter, once a fisherman, was one of the 12 apostles and is regarded as the first pope, which is why so many churches were named after him. In Russia, three tsars were named Peter. Peter I, called Peter the Great, attempted to westernize his country in the 18th century. Peter II and Peter III each ruled for only a few years. Four famous Peters reigned in the art world: Pieter Bruegel, Piet Mondrian, Pierre Auguste Renoir, and Peter Paul Rubens. Pyotr Ilyich Tchaikovsky is known as one of the world's great composers. In the 20th century, the name became very popular in England and Australia, perhaps because of James Barrie's *Peter Pan.* Peter was also popular in the United States between 1940 and 1975. Although now going out of fashion, it was still 86th on the list of names given American boys born in 1991.

Famous names: Peter Jennings (broadcast journalist)
　　　　　　　 Peter O'Toole (actor)
　　　　　　　 Peter Sellers (actor)
　　　　　　　 Peter Ustinov (actor)

Nicknames: **Pete, Petey, Petie**

Variations: **Par** (Swedish), **Peadar** (Gaelic), **Peder** (Danish), **Pedro** (Spanish), **Pekka** (Finnish), **Pello** (Basque), **Per** (Scandinavian), **Perkin, Petar** (Bulgarian), **Peto** (Hungarian), **Petr** (Czech), **Petras** (Lithuanian), **Petro** (Ukrainian), **Petros** (Greek), **Petru** (Rumanian), **Petrus** (Dutch and German), **Petter** (Norwegian), **Pierce, Piero** (Italian), **Pierre** (French), **Piers, Piet** (Dutch), **Pieter** (Dutch), **Pietro** (Italian), **Piotr** (Polish), **Pyotr** (Russian)

Petey, Petie (see **Peter**)

Peto (see **Peter**)

Petr (see **Peter**)

Petras (see **Peter**)

Petro (see **Peter**)

Petros (see **Peter**)

Petru (see **Peter**)

Petrus (see **Peter**)

Petter (see **Peter**)

Peyo (see **Pedro**)

Peyton Old English "Paega's farm." Peyton Randolph of Virginia was the first president of the Continental Congress in 1774, and the name Peyton has been in steady use ever since, especially in the southern United States, but it has never been overly popular.

Phil Form of **Philip.**
　　Famous names: Phil Collins (singer)
　　　　　　　　　 Phil Donahue (talk show host)
　　　　　　　　　 Phil Mahre (skier)
　　　　　　　　　 Phil Silvers (actor)

Philip, Phillip Greek *Philippos,* "horse lover." In the New

Testament, Philip was one of the apostles. Philip of Macedon was the father of Alexander the Great. In both France and Spain, the name has a long association with royalty, including six French and five Spanish kings. The most famous was Philip II, who united the Iberian peninsula and ruled over an empire that also included Milan, Naples, Sicily, the Netherlands, and much of the New World. In England today, Philip Mountbatten is the consort of Queen Elizabeth II and the duke of Edinburgh. Phillip Sharp of MIT was cowinner of the Nobel Prize in medicine in 1993.

Famous names: Philip Johnson (architect)
Philip Roth (writer)
Philip Sheridan (Civil War general)
Sir Philip Sidney (poet)

Nicknames: **Flip, Phil, Pip**

Variations: **Felipe** (Spanish), **Felippe** (Portuguese), **Filib** (Scots Gaelic), **Filip** (Scandinavian, Polish, and Czech), **Filippino** (Italian), **Filippo** (Italian), **Filippos** (modern Greek), **Fulop** (Hungarian), **Philipp** (German), **Philippe** (French), **Philippus** (Dutch), **Pilib** (Irish), **Pilypas** (Lithuanian), **Pylyp** (Ukrainian)

Philipp (see **Philip**)

Philippe (see **Philip**)

Philippus (see **Philip**)

Pico (see **Pedro**)

Pierce Middle English variation of **Peter**.
Famous names: Pierce Brosnan (actor)
Pierce Butler (U.S. Supreme Court justice)

Piero (see **Peter**)

Pierre French form of **Peter**.
Famous names: Pierre Corneille (author)
Pierre Curie (scientist)
Pierre Renoir (painter)

Piers Middle English form of **Peter**. The long poem *Piers Plowman* by William Langland is one of the few pieces of medieval English literature that has survived to be widely read today. Its title character exhibits a work ethic and sense of fair play that is still admired in the modern world.

Famous name: Piers Anthony (science fiction and fantasy author)

Piet (see **Peter**)

Pieter (see **Peter**)

Pietro (see **Peter**)

Pilib (see **Philip**)

Pilypas (see **Philip**)

Piotr (see **Peter**)

Pip (see **Philip**)

Pito (see **Felix**)

Placi (see **Placido**)

Placid, Placide (see **Placido**)

Placido Italian, Spanish, and Portuguese form of Latin *Placidus,* "untroubled, unworried, faithful."

Famous name: Placido Domingo (singer)

Nicknames: **Placi, Plasio**

Variations: **Placid** (English and Russian), **Placide** (French), **Placyd** (Polish and Ukrainian), **Plakidos** (Greek)

Placyd (see **Placido**)

Plakidos (see **Placido**)

Plasio (see **Placido**)

Plato English form of Greek *Platon,* "broad shouldered." The famous Greek philosopher Plato was a student of Socrates and the teacher of Aristotle. This name is popular with Greek-Americans.

Variation: **Platon**

Platon (see **Plato**)

Pol (see **Paul**)

Polo (see **Paul**)

Poncho (see **Alfonso**)

Ponso (see **Alfonso**)

Porter Middle English *porter* from Old French *portier,* "gate-keeper, door-keeper." This occupational surname has been sporadically used as a given name on both sides of the Atlantic since the 19th century.
Famous name: Porter Wagoner (country singer)

Poul Danish form of **Paul.**
Famous name: Poul Anderson (science fiction and fantasy
author)

Povilas (see **Paul**)

Pranas (see **Frank**)

Prescott English place name from Old English *preost* [priest] + *cot,* "cottage, dwelling." This surname became a first name in New England in honor of William Prescott, a Connecticut leader in the Revolutionary War. It is still occasionally found today. Prescott Bush, a U.S. senator from Connecticut in the early 20th century, was the father of George Bush, the 41st president of the United States.

Preston Old English "priest's town." Preston is in steady, regular use as an American first name and was the 170th most common name given to boys born in the United States in 1991.
Famous names: Preston Foster (actor)
Preston Sturges (director and screenwriter)

Prince Latin *princeps,* "the first." Prince was a fairly common name among slaves before the Civil War and has been traditionally passed down in a few African-American families, including that of singer Prince. His original full name was Prince Roger Nelson.

Purvis Latin *providere,* "provider," through Anglo-French *purveier.* This was originally a name for the official in charge of gathering supplies for a medieval monastery.
Famous name: Pervis Ellison (basketball player)
Other spelling: **Pervis**

Pylyp (see **Philip**)

Pyotr (see **Peter**)

Quaashie Ewe (Ghana) "born on Sunday,"

Quantavious, Quantavius This African-American creation, which seems to blend the sounds of African names such as **Quaashie** with an ending from the Latin name *Octavius,* "eighth son," is becoming more popular in the African-American community in the southeastern United States.
Variation: **Quintavious**

Quentin Latin "the fifth." This was a popular name with the Romans, who traditionally used it for a fifth son. St. Quentin was martyred in the fifth century. The movies have made most Americans familiar with San Quentin, the maximum security prison in California. Quentin is having a minor revival in the United States today, but **Quinton** is even more popular.
Famous names: Quentin Bell (writer)
                Quentin Burdick (U.S. senator)
                Maurice Quentin De La Tour (painter)
Variations: **Quintin, Quinton**

Quico (see **Henry**)

Quina (see **Achilles**)

Quincy French "fifth son's place." This surname became a first name in honor of John Quincy Adams, the sixth U.S. president.
Famous names: Quincy Howe (journalist)
                Quincy Jones (musician)
Nickname: **Quinn**

Quinn Irish Gaelic *O Cuinn,* "descendant of *Conn*"; Conn may have meant "wise"; also, a form of **Quinton** or **Quincy.** Quinn enjoys steady but not spectacular use as a first name in the United States.

Famous names: Quinn Martin (television producer)
Quinn Redeker (actor)

Quint Short form of **Quinton.** Fans of television Westerns may remember that Burt Reynolds played Quint Asper, the blacksmith, on *Gunsmoke* between 1962 and 1965.

Quintavious (see **Quantavius**)

Quintin (see **Quentin, Quinton**)

Quinton Form of **Quentin** or English place name, "queen's manor." Quinton has more popularity as a first name now than ever before in history; it was 198th on the list of names given American boys born in 1991.

Famous names: Quintin Dailey (basketball player)
Quintin Smith (football player)

Variations: **Quinn, Quint, Quintin**

Quiqui (see **Henry**)

Quito (see **Achilles**)

Rab (see **Robert**)

Rabbie (see **Robert**)

Racho (see **Horace**)

Radolf (see **Ralph**)

Rafael Spanish and Portuguese form of **Raphael.** This name is quite common among Hispanic-Americans and reached 211th on the list of names given boys in the United States in 1991.
Famous name: Rafael Palmeiro (baseball player)

Rafail (see **Raphael**)

Rafal (see **Raphael**)

Rafe (see **Ralph, Raphael**)

Raffaello (see **Raphael**)

Raghnall (see **Reginald, Ronald**)

Ragnvald (see **Reginald**)

Raimo (see **Raymond**)

Raimondo (see **Raymond**)

Raimund (see **Raymond**)

Raimundo (see **Raymond**)

Ralf, Ralfs (see **Ralph**)

Ralph Norman French *Raulf*, form of Old German *Radulf* from *rat* [counsel] + *wulf* [wolf]. This name was extremely common in the United States between 1870 and 1920 and remained popular until 1950. Ralph has now lost much of its popularity and was only 347th on the list of names given American boys in 1991. Television didn't help the name: Ralph Kramden of *The Honeymooners* and Ralph Malph of *Happy Days* may have been lovable in their own way, but few parents want to name their sons after these characters.

Famous names: Ralph Waldo Emerson (essayist)
                 Ralph Lauren (fashion designer)
                 Ralph Nader (consumer advocate)
                 Sir Ralph Richardson (actor)

Nicknames: **Rafe, Ralphie**

Other spelling: **Ralf**

Variations: **Radolf** (German), **Ralfs** (Latvian), **Raoul** (French), **Raul** (Italian and Spanish), **Rauli** (Finnish)

Ralphie (see **Ralph**)

Ramon (see **Raymond**)

Ramsay (see **Ramsey**)

Ramsey Old English *Hramesege*, "wild-garlic island." This very old place name connotes solidity and strength.

Famous names: Ramsey Clark (U.S. attorney general)
                 James Ramsay MacDonald (prime minister of Great Britain)

Variation: **Ramsay**

Rand (see **Randall**)

Randall Middle English form of Old English *Randwulf* from *rand* [shield-rim] + *wulf* [wolf]. This name was only rarely used before the 20th century, but it became very popular in the United States during the 1940s. Randall's popularity has been fading since 1965, but it was still 141st on the list of names given American boys in 1991. The short form **Randy** is now almost as common as Randall itself.

Famous names: Randall Cunningham (football player)
                 Randall Jarrell (poet)

Nicknames: **Rand, Randey, Randi, Randie, Randy**

Variations: **Randell, Randle, Randolf, Randolfo** (Spanish), **Randolph, Ranolfo** (Italian)

Randell (see **Randall**)

Randey, Randi, Randie (see **Randall, Randy**)

Randle (see **Randall**)

Randolf, Randolfo (see **Randall**)

Randolph This form of **Randall** died out as a first name after the Middle Ages but survived as a surname. It was revived again as an American first name in the late 18th century, probably in honor of the aristocratic Randolph family of Virginia. The Randolphs spawned many prominent politicians, including Edmund Randolph, the first attorney general of the United States. As a first name, Randolph has been much rarer than Randall during the 20th century, however.

Famous names: Randolph Caldecott (illustrator)
Randolph Scott (actor)

Randy Form of **Randall.** Randy is now independently as popular as Randall, being the 145th most common name given American boys in 1991. Randy is almost never used as a first name in England because the British commonly use the word *randy* to mean "oversexed" or "lecherous" and are therefore amazed that Americans consider it an appropriate name for a baby.

Famous names: Randy Newman (musician)
Randy Quaid (actor)
Randy Travis (singer)

Other spellings: **Randey, Randi, Randie**

Ranolfo (see **Randall**)

Raoul (see **Ralph**)

Raphael Hebrew "God cures" or "God has healed." In Jewish literature, Raphael is an archangel and the teacher of Tobias. In his narrative poem *Paradise Lost,* John Milton made Raphael the representative God sent to instruct Adam and to warn him not to eat fruit from the Tree of Knowledge.

Famous name: Raphael Sanzio (painter)

Variations: **Rafael** (Spanish), **Rafail** (Russian), **Rafal** (Polish), **Rafe, Raffaello** (Italian)

Rashad Arabic "good spiritual guidance." Rashad is now the second most commonly given Islamic name in the African-American community (after **Jamal**) and was 76th on the list of names given nonwhite American boys in 1991.

Rasheed Arabic "rightly guided, mature." Although not as popular as **Rashad,** this name is also now frequently found among African-Americans.

Raul (see **Ralph**)

Rauli (see **Ralph**)

Raven Old English *hraefn,* "raven." This is now primarily a feminine name in the United States, but it is still used rarely for boys. The late Raven McDavid was one of the foremost authorities on the dialects or accents of American English.

Ray Form of **Raymond;** also, French *rei,* "king." This name was more popular earlier in the 20th century than it is today. Parents might want to name a baby after Ray Kroc, the man who built McDonald's fast-food chain into a fabulously successful enterprise.

Famous names: Ray Bolger (dancer and actor)
                   Ray Bradbury (writer)
                   Ray Charles (musician)
                   Ray Milland (actor)

Raymond Old German *Raginmund* from *ragan* [advice] + *mund* [guardian or protector]. This name dates to the Crusades. Raymond was a very common name in England and the United States through the 1950s. Although its use is now fading, it was still the 94th most common name given American boys in 1991.

Famous names: Raymond Burr (actor)
                   Raymond Chandler (novelist)
                   Raymond Massey (actor)

Nickname: **Ray**

Variations: **Raimo** (Finnish), **Raimondo** (Italian), **Raimund** (German), **Raimundo** (Spanish and Portuguese), **Ramon** (Spanish), **Reamonn** (Irish)

Read, Reade (see **Reid**)

Reamonn (see **Raymond**)

Red Nickname for a person with red hair or a red complexion.
> Famous names: Red Buttons (comedian)
> Redd Foxx (comedian)
> Red Grange (football player)
> Red Skelton (comedian)

> Other spelling: **Redd**

Redd (see **Red, Reid**)

Rede (see **Reid**)

Reed (see **Reid**)

Reg (see **Reginald**)

Reggie Form of **Reginald.**
> Famous names: Reggie Jackson (baseball player)
> Reggie Lewis (basketball player)

Reggy (see **Reginald**)

Reginald Old English *Regenweald* from *ragan* [advice] + *weald* [power]. Reginald has never been a popular name with white Americans, who much prefer its Scottish variation, **Ronald.** It was, however, extremely popular between 1940 and 1980 in the African-American community. The traditional song "O Promise Me" was composed by Reginald de Koven.

> Famous name: Reginald F. Lewis (first African-American to head a Fortune 500 corporation)

> Nicknames: **Reg, Reggie, Reggy**

> Variations: **Raghnall** (Irish), **Ragnvald** (Scandinavian), **Reinald** (Dutch and German), **Reinaldo** (Spanish), **Reinhold** (Danish and Swedish), **Reino** (Finnish), **Reinold** (Dutch and German), **Reinwald** (German), **Renald, Renaldo** (Spanish), **Renaud** (French), **Renault** (French), **Reynold, Rinaldo** (Italian), **Ronald** (Scottish)

Regis Old Provencal "ruler." Regis originally became a first name in France in honor of St. Jean-Francois Regis, a 17th-century French Jesuit known for his work with prostitutes and the poor. This is a very rare name in America, but it is nevertheless well known because of television talk show host Regis Philbin.

Reid Old English *hreod,* "reeds"; also, Old English *read,* "red."
Famous names: Reid R. Keays (geologist)
Reid Nagle (financial analyst)
Other spellings: **Read, Reade, Redd, Rede, Reed**

Reilly (see **Riley**)

Reinald (see **Reginald**)

Reinaldo Spanish form of **Reginald.**
Famous name: Reinaldo Arenas (novelist)
Variations: **Naldo, Reynaldo**

Reinhold (see **Reginald**)

Reino (see **Reginald**)

Reinold (see **Reginald**)

Reinwald (see **Reginald**)

Remington Old English *Rimingtun,* "town on the boundary
stream." This very old English place name was used for the
central character of the television series *Remington Steele.* The
show's writers were probably thinking about Remington
firearms rather than the English heritage of this name.

Renald (see **Reginald**)

Renaldo (see **Reginald**)

Renaud (see **Reginald, Ronald**)

Renault (see **Reginald**)

Rene French form of Latin *Renatus,* "reborn." In the United States,
this name is primarily used by Hispanic parents.
Famous names: Rene Clair (movie director)
Rene Descartes (philosopher)

Renzo (see **Lorenzo**)

Reuben Hebrew "behold a son." In the Old Testament, Reuben is
Jacob's oldest son. This name was popular with the Puritans,
but today it is used most often by Americans of Hispanic
ancestry.

Famous name: Ruben Dario (poet)
Nickname: **Rube**
Variations: **Reuven, Ruben** (Spanish), **Ruvim** (Russian and Rumanian)

Reuven (see **Reuben**)

Rex Latin "king." This was not used as a name in English-speaking countries before the 19th century.
Famous names: Rex Harrison (actor)
Rex Reed (drama critic)
Variations: **Rexford, Rey** (Spanish), **Roi, Roy**

Rexford Origin unknown, perhaps a variation of **Rex.**
Famous name: Rexford Tugwell (political scientist)

Rey (see **Rex, Roy**)

Reynaldo (see **Reinaldo**)

Reynold (see **Reginald**)

Rezso (see **Rudolf**)

Rhisiart (see **Richard**)

Ric (see **Eric, Frederick**)

Ricardo Spanish form of **Richard.**
Famous name: Ricardo Montalban (actor)

Riccardo (see **Richard**)

Ricciardo (see **Richard**)

Rich (see **Richard**)

Richard Old English "strong ruler." *Ricard* is the Old English version of this name, but the French spelling Richard became popular in England after Eleanor of Aquitaine named her second son Richard. Despite his fame as the crusader Richard I, Coeur de Lion (Richard the Lionhearted), another Richard did not ascend the English throne for more than one hundred years. Richard II began his reign when he was ten years old, but it didn't take him long to attempt to assert his power by ordering his enemies slain. His insistence on the divine right of

kings, and his seizure of enemies' land, led to his murder at age
33. For a king who reigned only slightly more than two years,
Richard III, the last of the Plantagenets, is quite well known.
Shakespeare's play by the same name depicts him as a monster
who is directly responsible for the murder of his two young
nephews, who were heirs to the throne. Richard III was slain at
the Battle of Bosworth, and Henry VII became king,
establishing the Tudor dynasty. It is likely that the Tudors
encouraged the evil portrayal of Richard III to strengthen their
position on the throne. For whatever reason, Richard III
caused this name to be unpopular in England for several
centuries. By the 18th century, the name was back in fashion,
as evidenced by English playwright Richard Sheridan,
American admiral Richard Byrd, and many other historically
well-known Richards. In the 20th century, Richard Nixon, the
37th president of the United States, blighted the name when he
resigned in dishonor over the Watergate scandal. Richard's
popularity is now falling away gradually, but it was still the
39th most common name given American boys born in 1991.

Famous names: Richard Burton (actor)
               Richard Rogers (composer)
               Richard Wagner (composer)
               Richard Widmark (actor)

Nicknames: **Dick, Dickie, Dicky, Rich, Richie, Rick, Rickie,
Ricky, Ritchie**

Variations: **Rhisiart** (Welsh), **Ricardo** (Spanish), **Riccardo**
(Italian), **Ricciardo** (Italian), **Rickert** (German), **Rico,
Rikard** (Scandinavian), **Riku** (Finnish), **Risteard** (Irish
Gaelic), **Ryszard** (Polish)

Richie (see **Richard**)

Rick Form of **Cedric, Eric, Frederick, Richard,** or **Roderick.**
Famous names: Rick Mahler (baseball player)
               Rick Moranis (actor)
               Rick Nelson (singer)

Rickert (see **Richard**)

Rickie, Ricky Usually a short form of **Richard,** but can also be
from **Cedric, Eric, Frederick, Roderick,** or any other name
containing the syllable "-ric." Ricky became common as a
separate name in the 1950s, probably because television
featured two cute kids named Ricky: the character Ricky

Ricardo, Jr., of *I Love Lucy* and Ricky Nelson of *The Adventures of Ozzie and Harriet.* Attractive child characters are often especially effective at creating name fashions. Ricky has remained a popular official name, especially in the South, and was 139th on the list of names given American boys born in 1991.

Famous names: Ricky Graham (motorcycle racer)
Ricky Van Shelton (country singer)
Ricky Watters (football player)

Rico (see **Richard**)

Rikard (see **Richard**)

Riki (see **Frederick**)

Riku (see **Richard**)

Riley Irish Gaelic *Raghailligh,* perhaps "valiant"; or Middle English *Ryeley,* "rye field," a place name. This surname has recently begun to increase in popularity as an American first name, perhaps as parents begin to search for alternatives to the extremely popular name **Ryan.** Riley was the 223rd most common name given to American boys in 1991, and some girls are also being given the name now.

Famous name: Riley E. Dunlap (environmental sociologist)
Other spellings: **Reilly, Rylee, Ryley**

Rinaldo (see **Reginald**)

Ringo Perhaps a nickname for one who wears a distinctive ring.

Famous name: Ringo Starr (musician and actor)

Risteard (see **Richard**)

Ritchie (see **Richard**)

Roald Norwegian from Old Norse *hrothr,* "fame," + *valdr,* "ruler." This name has never been common in England or the United States.

Famous name: Roald Dahl (writer)

Rob Form of **Robert.** The famous Scottish pirate Rob Roy was also known as Robert the Red.

Famous name: Rob Lowe (actor)

Robart (see **Robert**)

Robat (see **Robert**)

Robb (see **Robert**)

Robbie, Robby (see **Robert**)

Robert Old English *Hreodbeorht,* "shining in fame," from *hrothi* [fame] + *berhta* [bright]. After the Norman Conquest, the Old English name, which appears in the Domesday Book, was replaced by the Norman-French version, Robert. It's been an extremely popular name ever since, particularly in Scotland, where the national hero Robert Bruce and the poet Robert Burns are honored. English poet Robert Herrick, writer Robert Louis Stevenson, American general Robert E. Lee, American poets Robert Frost and Robert Lowell, and politician Robert Kennedy all add distinction to the name. Many famous actors have also been named Robert, including Robert De Niro, Robert Duvall, Robert Redford, Robert Taylor, and Robert Wagner.

> Nicknames: **Bert, Bob, Bobbie, Bobby, Doby, Rabbie, Rob, Robb, Robbie, Robby, Robin**

> Variations: **Beto, Rab** (Scottish), **Robart** (Bulgarian), **Robat** (Welsh), **Robertas** (Lithuanian), **Roberto** (Italian, Portuguese, and Spanish), **Robrecht** (Dutch), **Roibeard** (Irish Gaelic), **Roope** (Finnish), **Rovertos** (Greek), **Rupert, Rupprecht** (German)

Robertas (see **Robert**)

Roberto Spanish and Italian form of **Robert.** This name is very popular with Hispanic-American parents.

> Famous name: Roberto Clemente (baseball player)

Robin Form of **Robert.** Although this name began as a diminutive of Robert, Robin has been an independent name for many centuries, as evidenced by the legendary Robin Hood. It continued to be used as a pet form of Robert in the 16th century when Elizabeth I wrote letters to her Robin, Lord Robert Dudley, earl of Leicester.

> Famous names: Robin Cousins (figure skater)
> Robin Williams (actor)

Robrecht (see **Robert**)

Rocco Italian from Old German *hrok,* "rest." This name became popular in Italy because of St. Rocco, a 14th-century Frenchman who abandoned a pilgrimage to Rome to care for plague victims in Lombardy. Naturally, most Italian-Americans named Rocco are called **Rocky** by their friends and neighbors.
Famous name: Rocco "Rocky" Domenico Colavito (baseball player)
Variations: **Roch** (French), **Roque** (Spanish and Portuguese)

Roch (see **Rocco**)

Rock When actor Roy Fitzgerald began his Hollywood career, his agent renamed him Rock Hudson after the Rock of Gibraltar. Even at the height of Hudson's fame, however, Rock was always an extremely rare name, with American parents preferring to put **Rocky** on birth certificates.

Rocky This name is usually a form of **Rocco** (or, rarely, **Rockwell**) in the modern United States, but it may also have been independently invented as a nickname for a tough customer. Rocky is still given often enough to be among the top 500 names for white American boys.
Famous name: Rocky Marciano (boxer)
Nickname: **Rock**

Rockwell Old English *Hrocwella,* "rocky spring," a place name.
Famous name: Rockwell Kent (artist)
Nickname: **Rocky**

Rod Form of **Roderick** or **Rodney**.
Famous names: Rod Laver (tennis player)
Rod Serling (writer)
Rod Steiger (actor)
Rod Taylor (actor)

Roddie (see **Roddy, Roderick**)

Roddy Form of **Roderick** or **Rodney**.
Famous name: Roddy McDowell (actor)
Other spelling: **Roddie**

Roderic, Roderich (see **Roderick**)

Roderick Old German *Hrodric,* "famous ruler," from *hrod* [fame] + *ric* [power]. This name was brought to England in medieval times by Scandinavian settlers and was revived there in the 19th century. In the United States today, Roderick is fairly common in the African-American community, reaching 115th on the list of names given nonwhite boys in 1991. *Roderick Hudson* is a novel by Henry James.

Nicknames: **Rick, Rickie, Ricky, Rod, Roddie, Roddy**

Other spellings: **Roderic, Rodrick**

Variations: **Gigo, Roderich** (German), **Roderyk** (Polish and Ukrainian), **Rodrigo** (Spanish, Italian, and Portuguese), **Rodrigue** (French), **Rurik** (Russian)

Roderyk (see **Roderick**)

Rodge (see **Roger**)

Rodger (see **Roger**)

Rodney Old English "Hroda's island," a place name.

Famous names: Rodney Dangerfield (comedian)
Rodney Scott Hudson (actor)

Nicknames: **Rod, Roddy**

Rodolfo (see **Rudolf**)

Rodolphe (see **Rudolf**)

Rodrick (see **Roderick**)

Rodrigo Spanish, Italian, and Portuguese form of **Roderick**. Rodrigo was hugely popular in medieval Spain, which is why *Rodriguez,* "son of Rodrigo," is the most common Spanish surname in the United States. Although its period of top status is long past, Rodrigo is still found regularly in the Hispanic-American community. Pierre Corneille's well-known drama *Le Cid* is about Rodrigo de Bivar.

Nicknames: **Gigo, Ruy**

Rodrigue (see **Roderick**)

Rodzers (see **Roger**)

Roeland (see **Roland**)

Roelof (see **Rudolf**)

Rog (see **Roger**)

Rogelio (see **Roger**)

Roger Old English *Hrothgar* from *hrothi* [fame] + *gar* [spear]. This name dates to the Domesday Book and has always been a favorite with British royalty, although never the name of a king. The name almost disappeared for a few centuries, but it was revived in the 18th century. Roger has been fairly popular during the 20th century and was still 173rd on the list of names given American boys in 1991. Roger Williams was the founder of Rhode Island and an advocate of religious freedom and universal democracy.

    Famous names: Roger Ebert (film critic)
               Roger Maris (baseball player)
               Roger Moore (actor)
               Roger Staubach (football player)

    Nicknames: **Rog, Rodge**

    Other spelling: **Rodger**

    Variations: **Dodge, Geyo, Rodzers** (Latvian), **Rogelio** (Spanish), **Rogerio** (Spanish), **Rogero** (Portuguese), **Rojelio, Rudiger** (German), **Ruggiero** (Italian), **Rutger** (Dutch)

Rogerio (see **Roger**)

Rogero (see **Roger**)

Rogers Middle English *Rogeres,* "son of **Roger.**" There are many common English surnames formed by adding "-s" to a first name, such as Williams, Roberts, and Daniels, but Rogers is almost the only one of these that is regularly turned back into a first name in the United States. This may be because of admiration for Will Rogers (1879–1935), the famous American humorist.

    Famous name: Rogers Hornsby (baseball player)

Roi (see **Rex, Roy**)

Roibeard (see **Robert**)

Rojelio (see **Roger**)

Roland Old German *Hrodland,* "famous throughout the country," from *hrodi* [fame] + *landa* [land]. The story of Roland, the most famous knight of Charlemagne, is retold in the French classic *Chanson de Roland.* The name is quite unusual in North America today.

Famous names: Roland Barthes (philosopher)
Roland Young (actor)

Nicknames: **Rollie, Rolly, Rowe**

Variations: **Orland, Orlando** (Italian), **Roeland** (Dutch), **Rolando** (Italian), **Rolann** (Irish Gaelic), **Rolant** (Welsh), **Roldan** (Spanish), **Roldao** (Portuguese), **Rowland**

Rolando (see **Roland**)

Rolann (see **Roland**)

Rolant (see **Roland**)

Roldan (see **Roland**)

Roldao (see **Roland**)

Rolf Old German *Hrodulf,* "famous wolf," from *hrod* [fame] + *wulf* [wolf]. This name, which is often confused with **Ralph,** is actually a medieval Norman French version of **Rudolf.**

Variations: **Rolfe, Rollo, Rolph**

Rolfe (see **Rolf**)

Rollie (see **Roland**)

Rollo Latin form of **Rolf.** Viking Rollo, a Norman duke, brought this name to England.

Famous name: Rollo May (psychologist)

Rolly (see **Roland**)

Rolph (see **Rolf**)

Romain (see **Roman**)

Roman Latin *Romanus,* "a Roman." This name, which has long been common in Latin and Slavic countries, is coming into general use in the United States. This may be partly due to Roman Brady, a popular character on the daytime soap opera *Days of Our Lives.*

Variations: **Romain** (French), **Romano** (Italian), **Romanos** (Greek), **Romanus** (Dutch), **Romo** (Finnish)

Romano (see **Roman**)

Romanos (see **Roman**)

Romanus (see **Roman**)

Romeo Italian form of Latin *Romaeus,* "pilgrim to Rome." Shakespeare immortalized this name in *Romeo and Juliet,* but Romeo's name has never been popular.

Romo (see **Roman**)

Ron Form of **Ronald.**
Famous names: Ron Howard (actor and movie director)
Ron Reagan, Jr. (actor)

Ronald Scottish form of **Reginald.** This form of Reginald has long been the most popular variation of that name in English-speaking countries. In the United States, it was especially well used from 1940 to 1960. In 1980, Ronald Reagan was elected 40th president of the United States. He was the first Ronald to hold the office, but this didn't stop the name from falling in popularity throughout the 1980s. In fact, Reagan probably had more boys named after him while he was an actor than after he went into politics. The clown Ronald McDonald, spokesperson for the fast-food chain, is the second most recognized fictional character by American children, surpassed only by Santa Claus.
Famous name: Ronald Colman (actor)
Nicknames: **Ron, Ronnie, Ronny**
Variations: **Raghnall** (Irish), **Renaud** (French), **Ronaldo** (Italian)

Ronaldo (see **Ronald**)

Ronnie, Ronny (see **Aaron, Ronald**)

Roope (see **Robert**)

Roosevelt Dutch "field of roses." In the 18th and 19th centuries, surnames of presidents, such as Washington, Jefferson, and Madison, were commonly used as first names. In the 20th century, only Theodore Roosevelt and Franklin Delano

Roosevelt achieved the kind of stature that inspired many parents to use their surname to name their children.

Famous name: Roosevelt Grier (football player)

Nickname: **Rosie**

Roque (see **Rocco**)

Rory Irish Gaelic *Ruaidri*, "red king." Rory O'More was a famous Irish chieftain.

Famous names: Rory Calhoun (actor)
Rory Sparrow (basketball player)

Rosie (see **Roosevelt**)

Ross From of Old German *Rozzo*, "fame," or *hros*, "horse"; also, Celtic *rhos*, "moorland." Because of billionaire entrepreneur and presidential candidate Ross Perot, it will be difficult for a while for many Americans to hear this name and not think of pie charts and the federal budget. Ross was the 199th most common name given to boys in the United States in 1991.

Famous names: Ross Hunter (film producer)
Ross Martin (actor)

Rovertos (see **Robert**)

Rowe (see **Roland**)

Rowland (see **Roland**)

Roy Gaelic *ruadh*, "red," later also interpreted as Old French *roy*, "king." For parents who like a name that offers little chance for a nickname, this is a good choice. Roy is also used as a nickname for **Leroy** and **LeRoy.**

Famous names: Roy Blount, Jr. (writer)
Roy Campenella (baseball player)
Roy Lichtenstein (painter)
Roy Marston (actor)
Roy Rogers (actor)
Roy Scheider (actor)

Variations: **Rex, Rey** (Spanish), **Roi** (French)

Royce Middle English *Royse*, form of Germanic *Rothais* from *hrod* [fame] + *haidis* [type, sort].

Rube (see **Reuben**)

Ruben (see **Reuben**)

Ruddy (see **Rudyard**)

Rudgerd Old German "red spear" or "fame spear." This compound
name came to England at the time of the Norman Invasion,
but it has never been popular.
Nickname: **Rudy**

Rudiger (see **Roger**)

Rudolf, Rudolph German "famous wolf." This name was a
favorite of Austrian nobility. Rodolfo is the hero of Puccini's
opera *La Boheme,* and Rudolf Rassendyll is the hero of *The
Prisoner of Zenda* by Anthony Hope. Modern Americans will
immediately associate this name with the Christmas song
"Rudolf the Red-Nosed Reindeer," which may be why it's not
often given to boys today.
Famous names: Rudolph Bing (conductor)
       Rudolf Friml (composer)
       Rudolph Nureyev (dancer)
       Rudolph Valentino (film star)
Nickname: **Rudy**
Variations: **Rezso** (Hungarian), **Rodolfo** (Italian and Spanish),
Rodolphe (French), **Roelof** (Dutch), **Rolf** (English and
Scandinavian)

Rudy Form of **Rudgerd** or **Rudolf.**
Famous name: Rudy Vallee (entertainer)

Rudyard Old English "pond with red carp."
Famous name: Rudyard Kipling (poet)
Nickname: **Ruddy**

Ruf (see **Rufus**)

Rufe (see **Rufus**)

Ruffo (see **Rufus**)

Rufo (see **Rufus**)

Rufus Latin *Rufus,* "man with red hair." At the end of his Letter to
the Romans in the New Testament, St. Paul wrote, "Greet
Rufus, chosen in the Lord." This positive biblical reference led

to Rufus being used as a name by the Puritans in colonial New England. William II of England was known as Rufus because of his red hair.

Variations: **Ruf** (French and Bulgarian), **Rufe, Ruffo** (Italian), **Rufo** (Spanish, Portuguese, and Croatian), **Rufusz** (Hungarian), **Ryffe** (Finnish)

Rufusz (see **Rufus**)

Ruggiero (see **Roger**)

Runako Shona (Zimbabwe) "handsome."

Rupert Low German and Dutch variation of **Robert,** brought to England by Prince Rupert of the Rhine, who was a general for his uncle Charles I during the English civil war in the 1600s.

Famous names: Rupert Brooke (poet)
                Rupert Murdoch (publisher)

Variation: **Ruperto** (Italian)

Ruperto (see **Rupert**)

Rupprecht (see **Robert**)

Rurik (see **Roderick**)

Russ Form of **Russell.**

Famous name: Russ Tamblyn (dancer)

Russel (see **Russell**)

Russell Norman French *Rousel,* "one with red hair." This aristocratic English surname began to be used as a first name in the United States before 1800. Russell was among the top 50 names for American boys born between 1900 and 1950, but it had fallen to 152nd place on the popularity charts by 1991.

Famous names: Russell Baker (columnist)
                Russell Crouse (screenwriter)

Nicknames: **Russ, Rusty**

Other spelling: **Russel**

Rusty (see **Russell**)

Rutger (see **Roger**)

Rutherford Old English "cattle ford." Rutherford B. Hayes was elected 19th president of the United States by a margin of only one vote in the electoral college.

Ruvim (see **Reuben**)

Ruy (see **Rodrigo**)

Ryan Probably Irish Gaelic *Rigan,* "little king." This name jumped into prominence in the 1980s, perhaps due to the overall popularity of Irish names as well as the appeal of actor **Ryan** O'Neal. In 1991, Ryan had fallen below the top ten list of names given American boys for the first time in a decade.

Ryffe (see **Rufus**)

Rylee, Ryley (see **Riley**)

Ryszard (see **Richard**)

Sahar (see **Zachariah**)

Sailbheastar (see **Sylvester**)

Sakarias (see **Zachariah**)

Sal Form of **Salvador.**
    Famous name: Sal Mineo (actor)

Sallie (see **Salvador**)

Salomo (see **Solomon**)

Salomon (see **Solomon**)

Salomone (see **Solomon**)

Salvador Spanish form of Latin *salvator,* "savior." Like the name
    Jesus, this name is popular in Spanish-speaking countries, but
    it's unusual elsewhere.
    Famous name: Salvador Dali (artist)
    Nicknames: **Chavo, Sal, Sallie**
    Variations: **Chabalito, Salvadore, Salvatore** (Italian), **Salwator**
        (Polish), **Spas** (Russian, Bulgarian, and Ukrainian),
        Spejus (Lithuanian), **Szalvator** (Hungarian)

Salvadore (see **Salvador**)

Salvatore Italian form of **Salvador.** This name was formerly very
    popular in Sicily and Calabria, parts of Italy that were once
    ruled by Spain. In the United States, Salvatore is now being
    used by Hispanic-Americans as well as Italian-Americans.

Salwator (see **Salvador**)

Sam Form of **Samuel.** Uncle Sam, the symbol for the United States that became popular during World War II, is the best-known Sam in history. This name is enjoying some renewed popularity, perhaps because of the character Sam Malone on the television show *Cheers* played by Ted Danson.

Famous names: Sam Elliott (actor)
               Sam Levene (actor)
               Sam Rayburn (politician)
               Sam Shepard (playwright)

Sami Arabic "elevated, sublime"; or a form of **Samuel.**

Famous name: Sami Frey (actor)

Sammie (see **Samuel**)

Sammy Form of **Samuel.**

Famous name: Sammy Davis, Jr. (actor and singer)

Samu (see **Samuel**)

Samuel Hebrew "name of the Lord." The prophet Samuel wrote two books of the Old Testament that cover an important era in the early history of Israel. Like other biblical names, Samuel came into frequent use after the Protestant Reformation. Men of letters named Samuel include Samuel Butler, author of *The Way of All Flesh;* lexicographer and essayist Samuel Johnson; diarist Samuel Pepys; and Samuel Clemens, who wrote under the pen name Mark Twain. Samuel Adams was a leader of the American Revolution, and Samuel Houston was president of the Republic of Texas. Samuel is slowly but steadily returning to popularity in the United States; it reached 46th on the list of names given American boys born in 1991.

Famous names: Samuel Barber (composer)
               Samuel Beckett (author)
               Samuel Taylor Coleridge (poet)
               Samuel Goldwyn (movie producer)
               Samuel Gompers (labor leader)
               Samuel Morse (inventor)

Nicknames: **Mel, Sam, Sammie, Sammy**

Variations: **Sami** (Arabic), **Samu** (Hungarian), **Samuele** (Italian), **Samuelo, Samuil** (Russian, Greek, and Bulgarian), **Sawel** (Welsh), **Shmuel** (modern Hebrew)

Samuele (see **Samuel**)

Samuelo (see **Samuel**)

Samuil (see **Samuel**)

Sandor (see **Alexander**)

Sandy Form of **Alexander** and names beginning with "San-."
   Famous name: Sandy Koufax (baseball player)

Santiago (see **James**)

Sarge (see **Sargent**)

Sargent Latin *servient,* "server" or "attendant," through Old
   French *serjant.* The same word later became English *sergeant,*
   an enlisted person's rank in the army. This unusual name
   became better known during the Kennedy presidency; the
   president's brother-in-law, Sargent Shriver, was the first
   director of the Peace Corps and later unsuccessfully ran for the
   vice-presidency on the McGovern ticket.
   Nickname: **Sarge**
   Other spelling: **Sergeant**

Sawel (see **Samuel**)

Schuyler Dutch "teacher." Along the Hudson River, Dutch names
   still occur for both places and people. This name has become
   fairly well known as a given name because of Philip John
   Schuyler, a soldier and statesman who served in the French and
   Indian Wars and the American Revolution, participated in the
   Continental Congress, and became a U.S. senator. Three
   counties in New York are named for him.
   Famous name: Schuyler Colfax (U.S. vice-president)
   Nickname: **Sky**
   Variations: **Skylar, Skyler**

Scot (see **Scott**)

Scottie, Scotty (see **Scott**)

Scott Old English "a Scotsman," possibly from Old Welsh *ysgthru,*
   "carved, tatooed." This was the middle name of two famous
   Americans, Francis Scott Key, author of the national anthem,

and writer F. Scott Fitzgerald, Key's second cousin three times removed. The name was very popular in the 1960s and 1970s. African-Americans, however, avoid naming their sons Scott, in spite of the fame of African-American composer Scott Joplin. The name's popularity is now fading; it was 59th on the list for American boys born in 1991.

Famous names: Scott Carpenter (astronaut)
Scott Fletcher (baseball player)
Scott Glenn (actor)
Scott Turow (author)

Nicknames: **Scottie, Scotty**

Other spelling: **Scot**

Seainin (see **John**)

Seamus (see **James**)

Sean Irish form of **John**. Sean became extremely popular with Americans from all ethnic and racial backgrounds in the 1970s. Sean's popularity is now falling, but very slowly, and it was still the 26th most common name given to American boys in 1991.

Famous names: Shaun Cassidy (actor)
Sean Connery (actor)
Sean O'Casey (playwright)
Sean Penn (actor)

Other spellings: **Shaun, Shawn**

Variation: **Shane**

Seb (see **Sebastian**)

Sebastian Greek *sebastos,* "old, venerable," through Latin *Sebastianus,* "man from Sebastia." St. Sebastian was a Roman martyred in the third century by being shot with arrows; this became a favorite subject for religious art. In Shakespeare's *Twelfth Night,* Sebastian is Viola's twin. This name was very rare in English-speaking countries until recently, but it may be about to become popular; in the United States, Sebastian rose from 335rd to 213th on the list of names for boys between 1989 and 1991.

Famous names: Sebastian Cabot (actor)
Sebastian Coe (track athlete)

Variations: **Baste** (Scandinavian), **Bastien** (French), **Basto** (Italian), **Passi** (Estonian), **Seb, Sebastiano** (Italian),

Sebastien (French), **Sevastian** (Rumanian and Russian), **Sevastianos** (Greek)

Sebastiano (see **Sebastian**)

Sebastien (see **Sebastian**)

Segismundo (see **Sigmund**)

Seosamh (see **Joseph**)

Serge (see **Sergio**)

Sergeant (see **Sargent**)

Sergei (see **Sergio**)

Sergio Spanish, Italian, and Portuguese form of *Sergius,* a Roman clan name perhaps from an Etruscan word for "servant." This name seems to be becoming more popular in the Hispanic-American community.
Famous names: Sergio Leone (film director)
                    Sergio Mendes (musician)
Variations: **Serge** (French and Finnish), **Sergei** (Russian)

Sessylt (see **Cecil**)

Seth Hebrew "appointed." Seth was the third son of Adam and Eve. This name is gradually becoming more common and reached 79th place among American boys born in 1991. It's certainly used much more often than **Cain** or **Abel,** the names of Seth's older brothers.
Famous name: Seth Thomas (clockmaker)

Sevastian (see **Sebastian**)

Sevastianos (see **Sebastian**)

Seymore (see **Seymour**)

Seymour Old English place name from *sae* [sea] + *mere* [pond]; or a form of Norman French *St. Maur.*
Famous name: Seymour Harris (economist)
Nickname: **Morrie**
Other spelling: **Seymore**

Shamus (see **James**)

Shane Variation of **Sean**. This name was practically nonexistent until the classic Western film *Shane* was released in 1953. Parents in both Great Britain and the United States then began giving the name to their sons. Although Shane's popularity is slowly falling off, it was still the 65th most common name given to American boys in 1991.

    Famous names: Shane Black (screenwriter)
                      Shane White (historian)

Shaun, Shawn (see **Sean**)

Sheldon Old English *scylf-dun,* "flat or slightly sloping hill." This name was more popular in the 19th and early 20th centuries than it is today.

    Famous names: Sheldon Cheney (writer)
                      Sheldon Glashow (physicist)

    Nicknames: **Shelley, Shelly**

Shelley, Shelly Old English *scelf-leah,* "woodland clearing on a ledge"; also, a form of **Sheldon.**

    Famous name: Shelley Berman (comedian)

Sherm (see **Sherman**)

Sherman Old English *scearramann,* "man who shears cloth or sheep." This first name derived from a surname often honors Civil War General William Tecumseh Sherman. During the Eisenhower administration, Sherman Adams, an aide to the president, was considered to be the most powerful man in Washington, until he was forced to resign for accepting gifts.

    Nicknames: **Sherm, Shermie**

Shermie (see **Sherman**)

Shimon (see **Simon**)

Shlomo (see **Solomon**)

Shmuel (see **Samuel**)

Shomari Swahili "forceful."

Sid Form of **Sidney.**

    Famous name: Sid Caesar (comedian)

Sidney Old English *sidenieg*, "wide, well-watered land," English place name. Algernon Sidney was an English aristocrat who opposed King Charles II. He was executed in 1683 after being convicted of treason in a rigged trial. In 1776, American orators used Sidney's fate as an example of the tyranny of British royalty, and so Sidney became a fairly popular given name in the United States in the early 19th century. This popularity was later reinforced by Sydney Carton, the hero of Charles Dickens's *A Tale of Two Cities.* Today, Sidney is fast disappearing as a name for American boys, but is becoming quite fashionable for girls.

Famous names: Sidney Lanier (poet)
Sidney Perelman (humorist)
Sidney Poitier (actor)
Sidney Sheldon (novelist)

Nicknames: **Sid, Syd**

Other spelling: **Sydney**

Siegmund (see **Sigmund**)

Siemen (see **Simon**)

Sig (see **Sigmund**)

Sigismond (see **Sigmund**)

Sigismondo (see **Sigmund**)

Sigismund (see **Sigmund**)

Sigmond (see **Sigmund**)

Sigmund Old German *Sigumund*, "victorious protector." This name has become synonymous with Sigmund Freud, the founder of psychoanalysis.

Nicknames: **Sig, Zig, Ziggy**

Other spellings: **Siegmund, Sigmond**

Variations: **Segismundo** (Spanish), **Sigismond** (French), **Sigismondo** (Italian), **Sigismund** (German), **Zygmunt** (Polish)

Silvester, Silvestre (see **Sylvester**)

Silvestro (see Sylvester)

Silvestru (see Sylvester)

Silvo (see Sylvester)

Sim (see Simon)

Simao (see Simon)

Simeon (see Simon)

Simon Hebrew *Shimeon,* "he listens"; also, Greek *Simon,* "snub nose (a nickname)." In honor of Simon Bolivar, who fought for the independence of South America from Spain and Portugal, this is an extremely popular name in many countries in Latin America.
Famous name: Simon Rattle (conductor)
Nickname: **Sy**
Variations: **Chimone, Jimeno, Moncho, Shimon** (modern Hebrew), **Siemen** (Dutch), **Sim** (Scots Gaelic), **Simao** (Portuguese), **Simeon, Simone** (Italian), **Siomon** (Irish Gaelic), **Szymon** (Polish), **Ximon**

Simone (see Simon)

Sinclair English form of *Saint Clair,* French place name.
Famous name: Sinclair Lewis (novelist)

Singh Hindi from Sanskrit "lion."

Siomon (see Simon)

Sky (see Schuyler)

Skylar, Skyler (see Schuyler)

Sly (see Sylvester)

Sol (see Solomon)

Solamh (see Solomon)

Sollie, Solly (see Solomon)

Solomon Hebrew *Shlomo* from *shalom,* "peace." King Solomon, the son of David and Bathsheba, was the ruler of Israel about three thousand years ago. During his reign, many palaces and temples were built, and Israel began trading with other countries. The Song of Solomon, considered to be one of the most beautiful Hebrew poems, is attributed to him. The revival of biblical names, however, has not affected this name, and it is no longer popular.

Famous name: Solomon Rapaport (playwright)

Nicknames: **Sol, Sollie, Solly**

Variations: **Salomo** (Dutch and German), **Salomon** (French, Polish, and Spanish), **Salomone** (Italian), **Shlomo** (Hebrew), **Solamh** (Gaelic), **Sulayman** (Arabic), **Zalman** (Yiddish)

Spas (see **Salvador**)

Spejus (see **Salvador**)

Spence (see **Spencer**)

Spencer Middle English "steward" or "storekeeper." This surname became a first name in the 19th century, perhaps in honor of Herbert Spencer, a celebrated philosopher who applied Darwin's theory of evolution to social problems and coined the phrase "survival of the fittest." Spencer is now one of the 100 most popular names for American boys.

Famous name: Spencer Tracy (actor)

Nickname: **Spence**

Other spelling: **Spenser**

Spenser (see **Spencer**)

Srul (see **Israel**)

Staffan (see **Stephen**)

Stan Form of **Stanley.**

Famous names: Stan Laurel (comedian)
Stan "The Man" Musial (baseball player)
Stan Smith (tennis player)

Stanleigh (see **Stanley**)

Stanley Old English "rocky meadow." This surname began to be used as a first name about two hundred years ago.

Famous names: Stanley Kramer (movie director)
Stanley Kubrick (movie director)
Nickname: **Stan**
Other spellings: **Stanleigh, Stanly**

Stanly (see Stanley)

Steaphan (see Stephen)

Steef (see Stephen)

Stefan Scandinavian and German form of **Stephen.**
Famous name: Stefan Edberg (tennis player)

Stefano (see Stephen)

Stefanos (see Stephen)

Steffan (see Stephen)

Stepan (see Stephen)

Stephan (see Stephen)

Stephen Greek *stephanos,* "crown." The Book of Acts in the Bible relates the stoning of St. Stephen, who is considered the first Christian martyr. A few popes took this name; in Hungary, there were five kings named Stephen; in England, one King Stephen. But there are probably more famous Stephens in the last one hundred years than during any time in history, including composer Stephen Collins Foster, who wrote "Oh! Susannah"; writer Stephen Crane, author of *The Red Badge of Courage;* Stephen Biko, the slain South African civil rights activist; American composer Stephen Sondheim, who is known for *Sweeney Todd, Sunday in the Park with George,* and *Into the Woods;* poet Stephen Spender; and English physicist Stephen Hawking. Either spelled Stephen or **Steven,** this was one of the top ten American names for boys between 1955 and 1980 and was still 16th on the list for boys born in 1991.
Famous names: Stephen Vincent Benet (poet)
Stephen Collins (actor)
Stephen Decatur (hero of the War of 1812)
Stephen King (author)
Nicknames: **Steve, Stevie**
Other spelling: **Steven**

Variations: **Esteban** (Spanish), **Estefon, Estephano** (Portuguese), **Estevan** (Spanish), **Etienne** (French), **Staffan** (Swedish), **Steaphan** (Scots Gaelic), **Steef** (Dutch), **Stefan** (Scandinavian, German, and Polish), **Stefano** (Italian), **Stefanos** (Greek), **Steffan** (Welsh), **Stephan** (French), **Stepan** (Russian), **Stiofan** (Irish Gaelic), **Szczepan** (Polish)

Sterling Old English *stearling,* "a starling"; Middle English *sterrling,* "little star, pure silver coin"; or from a Scottish place name.

Famous names: Sterling Hayden (actor)
Sterling Marlin (auto racer)
Sterling Seagrave (biographer)

Other spelling: **Stirling**

Steve Form of **Stephen.**

Famous names: Steve Allen (TV personality)
Steve Martin (comedian)
Steve McQueen (actor)
Steve Miller (musician)
Steve Sax (baseball player)

Nickname: **Stevie**

Steven Variation of **Stephen.** This has been the more common spelling of the name in the United States since the 1950s.

Famous name: Steven Spielberg (movie producer and director)

Stevie Form of **Stephen** or **Steve.**

Famous name: Stevie Wonder (musician)

Stew (see **Stuart**)

Stewart Variation of **Stuart.**

Famous name: Stewart Udall (politician)

Stiofan (see **Stephen**)

Stirling (see **Sterling**)

Stoffel (see **Christopher**)

Strom German "stream." Strom Thurmond, a well-known U.S. senator, received the maiden name of his mother, Gertrude Strom, as his given name.

Stu (see **Stuart**)

Stuart Old English *stigweard,* "steward of the manor," from *stig* [hall] + *ward* [guard]. This name is derived from a surname. Parents probably started to use it during the reign of the Scottish Stuarts on the English throne.
Famous name: Stuart Taylor, Jr. (journalist)
Nicknames: **Stew, Stu**
Other spelling: **Stewart**

Sulayman (see **Solomon**)

Sy Form of **Simon** or **Sylvester.**

Syd (see **Sidney**)

Sydney (see **Sidney**)

Sylvester Latin "of the woods." Although the feminine form **Sylvia** has been popular for centuries, this masculine form of a Roman surname is not chosen by many parents.
Famous name: Sylvester Stallone (actor)
Nicknames: **Sly, Sy**
Other spelling: **Silvester**
Variations: **Sailbheastar** (Irish Gaelic), **Silvestre** (French and Spanish), **Silvestro** (Italian), **Silvestru** (Rumanian), **Silvo** (Finnish), **Sylwester** (Polish)

Sylwester (see **Sylvester**)

Szalvator (see **Salvador**)

Szczepan (see **Stephen**)

Szymon (see **Simon**)

Taavetti (see David)

Tabo (see Gustav)

Tad (see Thaddeus)

Tadeo (see Thaddeus)

Tadeusz (see Thaddeus)

Tam (see Thomas)

Tamas (see Thomas)

Tandy (see Andrew)

Tanner Old English *tannere,* "tanner of hides." Tanner has risen
from nowhere to become fairly common, especially in the
western United States. The reasons for the sudden interest in
this name are unknown, but the simultaneous increase in
Tanner, **Tyler, Taylor, Trevor,** and **Tucker** shows that a certain
sound pattern in names has become popular with American
parents. Tanner had risen to 122nd place on the national list
for American boys by 1991 and was positioned to become a top
name in the near future. However, Tanner has appealed mostly
to white parents and is being practically ignored by the
African-American community.

Tau Tswana (Botswana) "lion,"

Tavito (see Gustav)

Tavo (see Gustav)

Taylor Old French *tailleur,* "tailor," a word brought to England by the Normans. As **Tyler** has become a hugely popular name for American boys, Taylor has been pulled up along with it. A rare name before 1980, Taylor was 70th on the list of names given American boys in 1989 and 52nd in 1991. But unlike Tyler, Taylor is also newly fashionable as a name for girls in the United States, making today unique in that two names (**Jordan** and **Taylor**) are surging in popularity for both sexes at the same time. In 1991, about 20 percent more American girls than boys were named Taylor. This would normally mean that in a very few years, when most parents realize that Taylor has become common for girls, it will quickly fall in popularity as a name for boys. Or, perhaps Jordan and Taylor are a sign that many Americans are choosing one name for their future child without regard to gender.

Famous name: Taylor Hackford (film director)

Te (see **Clement**)

Tecumseh Shawnee "one who springs," connoting a panther. The famous Shawnee chief Tecumseh was a brilliant leader and an eloquent orator. He was given the rank of colonel in the British army and constantly fought against the encroachment of American colonists upon tribal land. He was killed in Ontario at the Battle of the Thames between the British and the Americans, who were under the command of William H. Harrison, later ninth president of the United States.

Famous names: William Tecumseh Fisher (baseball player)
William Tecumseh Sherman (general)

Ted Form of **Edward, Edwin,** or **Theodore.**

Famous names: Ted Koppel (broadcast journalist)
Ted Turner (business executive)

Teddie, Teddy (see **Theodore**)

Tel (see **Terence**)

Tente (see **Clement**)

Teodor (see **Theodore**)

Teodoro (see **Theodore**)

Terance (see **Terence**)

Terenc (see **Terence**)

Terence Latin *Terentius,* a Roman family name, possibly related to *Terensis,* the goddess of milling grain. This very old name has never been very popular in the United States except in the African-American community, where it now ranks 26th among the names given black boys. **Terrance** is now the most common spelling.

    Famous names: Sir Terence Rattigan (playwright)
                     Terence White (novelist)
    Nicknames: **Tel** (British), **Terri, Terrie, Terry**
    Other spellings: **Terance, Terrance, Terrence**
    Variations: **Terenc** (Czech), **Terencio** (Spanish), **Terentiu** (Rumanian), **Terenzio** (Italian), **Teresk** (Estonian), **Tero** (Finnish)

Terencio (see **Terence**)

Terentiu (see **Terence**)

Terenzio (see **Terence**)

Teresk (see **Terence**)

Tero (see **Terence**)

Terrance (see **Terence**)

Terrell Origin uncertain, but may go back to the same Old French word as **Tyrell.** This rare British surname has become a popular name for African-American boys, probably because it blends the sounds of **Terry** and **Darryl.** However, Terrell's prominence may also honor Mary Church Terrell (1863–1964), a founder of the NAACP and advocate for women's suffrage who led a fight to desegregate the restaurants and theaters of Washington, D.C. If this is the case, Mrs. Terrell holds the unique distinction of being a woman whose fame turned her last name into a first name for boys instead of girls. Terrell was among the top 50 names for African-American boys throughout the 1980s and was 58th in that community in 1991.

    Famous name: Terrell Buckley (football player)

Terrence (see **Terence**)

Terri, Terrie (see **Terence**)

Terry Form of **Terence;** or Old French *Thierri,* a form of *Theodoric* (see **Derek**).

    Famous names: Terry Bradshaw (football player)
                    Terry Mulholland (baseball pitcher)
                    Terry Sanford (U.S. senator)

Teuvo (see **Theodore**)

Thad (see **Thaddeus**)

Thaddaus (see **Thaddeus**)

Thaddeus Aramaic name of unknown meaning, but possibly an Aramaic form of Greek *Theodotos,* "given by God." Thaddeus was one of the 12 apostles. The Puritans often named their sons Thaddeus, but today it just barely makes the top 500 list among names for American boys.

    Famous name: Thaddeus Stevens (statesman)

    Nicknames: **Tad, Thad**

    Variations: **Tadeo** (Spanish), **Tadeusz** (Polish), **Thaddaus** (German)

Thaine (see **Thane**)

Thane Old English *thegn,* "warrior," "soldier," or "free man."

    Other spellings: **Thaine, Thayne**

Thayne (see **Thane**)

Theo (see **Theodore**)

Theodor (see **Theodore**)

Theodore Greek *Theodoros,* "gift of God," from *theo* [god] + *doros* [gift]. Because there are almost 30 saints named Theodore, it's surprising that the name did not begin to be used in America until the 19th century. Victorian Americans, however, were fond of this name. Theodore has continued to be more common in the United States than in England, probably because of Theodore Roosevelt, the 26th president. Children's writer Theodor Geisel was better known by his pen name, Dr. Seuss.

    Famous names: Theodore Bikel (singer)
                    Theodore Dreiser (novelist)

Nicknames: **Doro, Ted, Teddie, Teddy, Theo**

Variations: **Deodoro** (Portuguese), **Fedor** (Russian), **Feodor** (Slavic), **Fyodor** (Russian), **Teodor** (Polish and Serbian), **Teodoro** (Italian and Spanish), **Teuvo** (Finnish), **Theodor** (Danish, German, and Swedish), **Theodoros** (Greek), **Theodorus** (Dutch), **Tivadar** (Hungarian), **Todor** (Bulgarian)

Theodorick (see **Derek**)

Theodoros (see **Theodore**)

Theodorus (see **Theodore**)

Theron Greek "a hunter."

Thom (see **Thomas**)

Thomas Aramaic "twin." St. Thomas came to be known as Doubting Thomas because he would not believe in the resurrection of Jesus until he had touched his wounds. Thomas was later martyred. The name is also associated with several other religious figures. To keep the church on his side, King Henry II of England appointed his friend, Thomas Becket, archbishop of Canterbury. When Becket would not go along with what the king wanted because he was more loyal to his church than to his friend, Henry had Becket murdered on the doorstep of the cathedral. The 13th-century St. Thomas Aquinas was one of the great philosophers of the Middle Ages. St. Thomas More was executed when he refused to allow Henry VIII to interfere with the rulings of the church. English novelist Thomas Hardy and American poet Thomas Stearns Eliot are two literary Thomases. Thomas Jefferson was the third president of the United States and one of the framers of the Constitution.

Famous names: Thomas Paine (American Revolutionary pamphleteer)
Thomas Edison (inventor)
Thomas Mann (novelist)

Nicknames: **Tam** (Scottish), **Thom, Tom, Tommie, Tommy**

Variations: **Domas** (Lusatian), **Foma** (Russian), **Tamas** (Hungarian), **Toma** (Rumanian), **Tomas** (Irish Gaelic, Lithuanian, and Spanish), **Tomasz** (Polish), **Tomaz** (Slovenian), **Tommaso** (Italian), **Tomos** (Welsh), **Toms** (Latvian and German), **Tuomo** (Finnish)

Ticho (see **Patrick**)

Tim Form of **Timothy**.
> Famous names: Tim Allen (comedian)
> Tim Curry (actor)
> Tim Reid (actor)

Timmie, Timmy (see **Timothy**)

Timofei (see **Timothy**)

Timot (see **Timothy**)

Timotej (see **Timothy**)

Timoteo (see **Timothy**)

Timothee (see **Timothy**)

Timotheos (see **Timothy**)

Timotheus (see **Timothy**)

Timothy Greek *Timotheos,* "honor God." St. Paul's conversion of his friend St. Timothy gave this name Christian roots, but the name was not widely used until the Reformation. Timothy has ranked among the leading names for boys in both England and the United States since the 1950s.
> Famous name: Timothy Hutton (actor)
> Nicknames: **Tim, Timmie, Timmy**
> Variations: **Timofei** (Russian), **Timot** (Hungarian), **Timotej** (Czech), **Timoteo** (Italian, Portuguese, and Spanish), **Timothee** (French), **Timotheos** (Greek), **Timotheus** (German), **Tymoteusz** (Polish)

Tito (see **Albert, Andrew**)

Tivadar (see **Theodore**)

Tobal (see **Christopher**)

Tobalito (see **Christopher**)

Tod (see **Todd**)

Todd Old English *tod,* "a fox." Robert Todd Lincoln was the only one of Abraham and Mary Todd Lincoln's four sons to live to manhood. He became a lawyer and served as secretary of war and minister to Great Britain.

Famous names: Todd Bell (football player)
                Tod Stratton Sloan (psychologist)

Other spelling: **Tod**

Todor (see **Theodore**)

Tola (see **Bartholomew**)

Toli (see **Bartholomew**)

Tom Form of **Thomas.** Originally a pet form of Thomas, this name dates back to early nursery rhymes and novels, such as Henry Fielding's *Tom Jones,* published in 1749. It is one of the most popular nicknames today, as evidenced by actors Tom Berenger, Tom Cruise, Tom Hanks, Tom Hulce, and Tom Selleck, writer Tom Wolfe, playwright Tom Stoppard, television anchorman Tom Brokaw, and dozens of professional athletes.

Toma (see **Thomas**)

Tomas (see **Thomas**)

Tomasz (see **Thomas**)

Tomaz (see **Thomas**)

Tommaso (see **Thomas**)

Tommie, Tommy Forms of **Thomas.** English soldiers are nicknamed Tommies because the name used in examples on the forms that soldiers are required to fill out is Thomas Atkins.

Famous names: Tommy Lee Jones (actor)
                Tommy Tune (dancer)

Tomos (see **Thomas**)

Toms (see **Thomas**)

Toncho (see **Anthony**)

Tonek (see **Anthony**)

Toni (see **Anthony**)

Tonico (see **Anthony**)

Tonio (see **Anthony**)

Tony Form of **Anthony** or **Hamilton.** Like Tom, this nickname has long been an independent name.

Famous names: Tony Bennett (singer)
Tony Bill (actor)
Tony Danza (actor)
Tony Perkins (actor)
Tony Roberts (actor)

Travis Middle English *travers,* "toll collector, crossing guard." This surname originally became a first name in Texas in honor of William Travis, the commander of the ill-fated American forces at the Battle of the Alamo in 1836. The majority of Travises born before 1950 probably had Texas connections, but the most famous modern Travis is a fictional Floridian, private detective Travis McGee. He first appeared in John D. MacDonald's *The Deep Blue Good-By* in 1964 and has since been featured in many other mysteries. By 1975, Travis was a fashionable name in both the United States and Australia. The name has steadily held a position between 40th and 50th on the list of names given newborn American boys.

Famous name: Travis Tritt (country singer)

Trefor (see **Trevor**)

Trent English river and village name, perhaps from a pre-Celtic word for "flooder." Trent has been used as a first name in the United States since the start of the 20th century. In the 1970s and 1980s, Trent became more popular, but now that its derivative **Trenton** has passed it, the name is beginning to recede again as an official name on birth certificates. American gymnast Trent Dimas's magnificent gold medal performance on the horizontal bar at the 1992 Barcelona Olympics will long be remembered by fans of that sport.

Famous name: Trent Lott (U.S. senator)

Trenton Eighteenth-century American "Trent's Town," the name of the city in New Jersey founded by William Trent. According to George Stewart, author of *American Place-Names,* this was "one of the first instances of a developer naming a place after himself." Trenton does not exist as an English place name or surname, but it has been used as a first name in the United States since the 1950s and is becoming more popular. This probably happened because Americans who heard the name **Trent** assumed that it must be short for Trenton in the same way that **Clint** was derived from **Clinton,** although in this case it was the other way around. Trenton was the 190th most common name given to boys born in the United States in 1991.

Trev (see **Trevor**)

Trevor Welsh *Trefor* from *tref* [home] + *mor* [great or sea]. This Welsh place name and surname became very popular as a first name throughout Britain during the 1950s. Trevor has also been widely used in the United States since 1975, although it has never reached the heights of fashion that it did in England. It has been holding steady at about 70th place on the list of names given American boys.

Famous names: Trevor Boys (football player)
Trevor Howard (actor)

Nickname: **Trev**

Variation: **Trefor** (Welsh)

Tris (see **Tristram**)

Tristan Since 1980, this form of **Tristram** has caught the attention of parents in Britain and Australia because of a character in *All Creatures Great and Small,* a television series based on the best-selling books by Yorkshire veterinarian James Herriot. Since 1988, when the same series began to be aired in the United States, American parents have also discovered the name, and it was 276th on the popularity chart for American boys in 1991. In the United States, however, some girls as well as boys are now being named Tristan, probably because it rhymes with the fashionable **Kristen.**

Famous names: Tristan Platt (anthropologist)
Tristan Rogers (actor)

Tristin (see **Tristram**)

Tristram Celtic *drystan,* "tumult" or "loud noise." This unusual name dates back to the Arthurian romances, but is perhaps best known through Laurence Sterne's 18th-century novel *Tristram Shandy*.

Famous name: Tristram Speaker (baseball player)

Nickname: **Tris**

Variations: **Drystan, Tristan, Tristin, Trystan**

Troy Middle English *Troie,* "from [French town of] Troyes"; or
Irish Gaelic *troightheach,* "foot soldier"; or from the ancient
city in Asia Minor made famous by the Trojan War. Whatever
this name's origin, there is little doubt that its success is due to
movie actor Troy Donohue (who changed his name from Merle
Johnson). Troy has been reasonably popular as a first name
ever since the 1950s. Today the name is beginning to decrease
in use, but Troy was still 121st on the list of names given
American boys in 1991.

Famous name: Troy Aikman (football player)

Trystan (see **Tristram**)

Tuck (see **Tucker**)

Tucker Old English *tucian,* "to torment," through Middle English
touken, "to stretch (cloth)." The work of the tucker, one who
sews folds in cloth, is now done by machines in most parts of
the world. But this very old occupational name is still around,
even though the craft itself is obsolete.

Nickname: **Tuck**

Tuomo (see **Thomas**)

Turi (see **Arthur**)

Tuto (see **Arthur**)

Ty (see **Tyler, Tyrone**)

Tyehimba Tiv (Nigeria) "we stand as a people." This name may be
too hefty for a baby, but the nickname Ty might work very well
until he grows up.

Tyler Old English *tygeler* or Old French *tieuleor,* both meaning "tile
maker." This common occupational surname was rare as a first
name until recently, although it has occasionally been given
since the 19th century, especially in the South, in honor of John
Tyler, the tenth president of the United States. In the late
1970s, Tyler began to become fashionable, and the name was in
or near the top ten for boys in most states west of the
Mississippi by 1985. Its popularity quickly spread eastward; in

1991, Tyler reached the national top ten. Tyler's sudden boom is all the more remarkable because there doesn't seem to be any well-known person, fictional or real, whose fame could have started the name on its upward swing. It does have a sound similar to other fashionable names such as **Ryan** and **Kyle,** along with the ending of the very popular **Christopher,** and this must have commended it to parents looking for the proverbial "different but not too different" alternative.

Famous name: Tyler Mathisen (financial reporter)

Nickname: **Ty**

Tymoteusz (see **Timothy**)

Tyrell Possibly from Old French *tirel,* "stubborn person." This Norman French surname (in the spelling **Tyrrell**) was the name of a prominent white family in the Carolinas, but in modern times it has become a popular name for African-American boys by blending the sounds of **Tyrone** and **Terrell.**

Famous name: Tyrell Biggs (boxer)

Tyrone Irish Gaelic "Eoghan's territory," the name of a county in Northern Ireland. American matinee idol Tyrone Power was descended from a great-grandfather named Tyrone Power (also an actor) who was born in Ireland. Although the name Tyrone never caught on with white Americans, it was very successful in the African-American community from 1950 through 1980. Tyrone is now slowly going out of style.

Famous name: Tyrone Corbin (basketball player)

Nickname: **Ty**

Tyrrell (see **Tyrell**)

Ualan (see **Valentine**)

Ualtar (see **Walter**)

Uberto (see **Hubert**)

Ugo (see **Hugh**)

Ugon (see **Hugh**)

Uilleam (see **William**)

Uilliam (see **William**)

Uinseann (see **Vincent**)

Ulises (see **Ulysses**)

Ulisse (see **Ulysses**)

Ulysses Latin form of *Odysseus,* meaning uncertain. In the *Iliad*
and the *Odyssey,* Homer tells the story of Odysseus. The Irish
writer James Joyce used the name *Ulysses* as the title of his
famous book. Ulysses S. Grant led the Northern forces in the
Civil War and was the 18th president of the United States. In
modern times, Ulysses is the most common name for American
boys beginning with the letter "U," but it is still an unusual
name.
Variations: **Ulises** (Spanish), **Ulisse** (Italian)

Urbain (see **Urban**)

Urban Latin "the town." Although eight popes assumed this name,
almost no baby boys have been named Urban recently.

Famous name: Urban Clarence Faber (baseball player)

Variations: **Orban** (Hungarian), **Urbain** (French), **Urbano** (Italian and Spanish), **Urbanus** (German and Dutch), **Urpo** (Finnish), **Urvan** (Russian)

Urbano (see **Urban**)

Urbanus (see **Urban**)

Uriah Hebrew "God is light." In the Old Testament, Uriah is the soldier who King David had deliberately placed in the front ranks of an army attack so that he would be killed; David then married Uriah's widow, Bathsheba. The prophet Nathan later made David remorseful for his evil deed by telling the famous story of the rich man who slaughters his poor neighbor's one pet lamb rather than kill one from his own vast flocks. Uriah is the only "U" name besides Ulysses that is being used to any extent in the United States today, but it is still quite rare. For unknown reasons it seems to be somewhat more common in Colorado and New Mexico than elsewhere.

Famous name: Uriah Phillips Levy (U.S. naval commander)

Urpo (see **Urban**)

Ursin (see **Orson**)

Ursino (see **Orson**)

Urson (see **Orson**)

Ursyn (see **Orson**)

Urvan (see **Urban**)

Val Short form of **Valentine.**
    Famous name: Val Kilmer (actor)

Valente (see **Valentine**)

Valentijn (see **Valentine**)

Valentin (see **Valentine**)

Valentine Latin *Valentinus,* from *valens,* "strong, healthy." The
    third-century Roman St. Valentinus was martyred on February
    14, which is his feast day. The ancient Roman fertility festival,
    Lupercalia, was celebrated on approximately the same day. By
    merging the two festival days, St. Valentine became associated
    with love and romance. The name is unusual in the United
    States, but it was formerly popular in continental Europe.
    Nickname: **Val**
    Variations: **Ualan** (Scots Gaelic), **Valente** (Italian), **Valentijn**
        (Dutch), **Valentin** (French, German, and Spanish),
        Valentino (Italian), **Velten** (German Swiss)

Valentino (see **Valentine**)

Valmy French place name, a village in the Department of Marne a
    few miles east of Rheims. On September 20, 1792, the French
    under F. C. Kellermann won a battle against the Prussians.
    Kellermann was awarded the title Duc of Valmy for his
    leadership.
    Famous name: Valmy Thomas (baseball player)

Van Dutch or German prefix "from," placed before a surname, which is usually derived from a place name. This name has never been very popular, and now that it is what most people call a small, enclosed truck, Van is unlikely to be chosen by many parents.

Famous names: Van Heflin (actor)
Van Johnson (actor)
Van Morrison (musician)

Nickname: **Vanny**

Other spelling: **Vann**

Vance Old English *fenns,* "marshes." The initial "V" of this name shows that it originated in southwestern England. Vance has never been a really popular name, but it has been regularly used in the 20th century, especially in the American South.

Famous names: Vance Packard (writer)
Vance Randolph (folklorist)

Vann (see **Van**)

Vanni (see **John, Van**)

Vanny (see **Van**)

Vanya (see **John**)

Vareck (see **Varrick**)

Varnava (see **Barnaby**)

Varrick Origin unknown, but possibly a form of *Warwick,* Old English *waering* [weir] + *wic* [settlement, harbor], an English place name.

Famous name: Varrick Chittenden (folklorist)

Other spelling: **Vareck**

Variation: **Warrick**

Vartolomej (see **Bartholomew**)

Vartolomeu (see **Bartholomew**)

Vas (see **Basil**)

Vasili (see **Basil**)

Vasilios (see **Basil**)

Vasska (see **Basil**)

Vaughan Welsh *Fychan*, "small"; originally a nickname that
became a surname. This name was most used from 1940
through 1960.
Famous names: Vaughn Monroe (band leader)
               Ralph Vaughan Williams (composer)
Other spelling: **Vaughn**
Variation: **Von**

Vaughn (see **Vaughan**)

Vazul (see **Basil**)

Veit (see **Vito**)

Velten (see **Valentine**)

Venediktos (see **Benedict**)

Veniamin (see **Benjamin**)

Venya (see **Benjamin**)

Venyamin (see **Benjamin**)

Vergil (see **Virgil**)

Vern Form of **Vernon**. This name now conjures up the image of
Ernest P. Worrell, the comic character created by actor Jim
Varney, and his conversations with his long-suffering but never
seen or heard friend Vern.

Vernaldo (see **Bernard**)

Vernardino (see **Bernard**)

Vernardinos (see **Bernard**)

Verne (see **Vernon**)

Verney (see **Vernon**)

Vernon French place name from a Gaulish (ancient Celtic) word for
"alder trees." This name is well known through George
Washington's home, Mount Vernon, which was named for the
original landowner, Vernon Washington.

Famous names: Vernon Castle (dancer)
Vernon Jordan (director, National Urban League)
Vernon Scannell (poet)

Nicknames: **Vern, Verne, Verney**

Vicente (see **Vincent**)

Vicho (see **Victor**)

Vic, Vick Form of **Victor**.
Famous name: Vic Damone (singer)

Vicko (see **Vincent**)

Vico (see **Victor**)

Victo (see **Victor**)

Victor Latin "conqueror." Although this name dates to at least the 13th century in England, it wasn't popular until the 19th century. Victor Emmanuel was the first king of unified Italy. Victor Sifuentes was a lawyer on the television series *L.A. Law,* played by actor Jimmy Smits. Victor was the 115th most common name given to American boys in 1991.
Famous names: Victor Borge (pianist and comedian)
Victor Herbert (composer)
Victor Hugo (novelist)
Victor Mature (actor)

Nicknames: **Vic, Vick, Vico** (Spanish)

Variations: **Bictar, Vicho** (Mexican), **Victo, Victorio** (Spanish), **Vihtori** (Finnish), **Viktor** (German, Scandinavian, Czech, and Russian), **Viktoras** (Lithuanian), **Vitorio** (Portuguese), **Vittore** (Italian), **Vittorio** (Italian), **Wiktor** (Polish)

Victorio (see **Victor**)

Vihtori (see **Victor**)

Vikent (see **Vincent**)

Vikentij (see **Vincent**)

Viktor (see **Victor**)

Viktoras (see Victor)

Vila (see Billy)

Vilem (see William)

Vilhelm (see William)

Vili (see Billy)

Vilmos (see William)

Vilppu (see William)

Vin (see Vincent)

Vincas (see Vincent)

Vince Form of **Vincent.** Singer Vince Gill won the Country Music
  Association's Entertainer of the Year Award in 1993.

Vincenc (see Vincent)

Vincent Latin *vincens,* "conquering." The 17th-century St. Vincent
  de Paul founded the Lazarists and the Sisters of Charity. The
  Dutch painter Vincent van Gogh lived for many years in
  Arles, France, and is considered to be one of the greatest
  Impressionists. This name acquired new connotations through
  the late 1980s television series *Beauty and the Beast,* in which
  the beast Vincent was both gentle and ferocious. Vincent is
  among the 100 most popular names for American boys.
  Famous names: Vincent Canby (film critic)
              Vincent Price (actor)
  Nicknames: **Vin, Vince, Vinn, Vinnie, Vinny**
  Variations: **Chento, Uinseann** (Irish Gaelic), **Vicente** (Spanish),
      Vicko (Croatian), **Vikent** (Ukrainian), **Vikentij** (Russian
      and Bulgarian), **Vincas** (Lithuanian), **Vincenc** (Czech),
      Vincente (Italian and Portuguese), **Vincentiu** (Rumanian),
      Vincentius (Dutch), **Vincenzo** (Italian), **Vinzenz** (German),
      Wincenty (Polish)

Vincente (see Vincent)

Vincentiu, Vincentius (see Vincent)

Vincenzo (see Vincent)

Vinn (see **Vincent**)

Vinnie, Vinny Forms of **Melvin** or **Vincent.**
    Famous name: Vinny Testaverde (football player)

Vinzenz (see **Vincent**)

Virge (see **Virgil**)

Virgil Latin *Vergilius,* meaning unknown, but spelling altered in
    ancient times to conform with *virgo,* "maiden." The great
    Roman poet Virgil was the author of the *Aeneid.* Virgil became
    an American first name during the early 19th century when
    other classical names such as **Homer** were also in fashion.
    Famous names: Virgil "Gus" Grissom (astronaut)
                    Virgil Thompson (composer)
    Nickname: **Virge**
    Variations: **Vergil, Virgilio** (Italian and Spanish)

Virgilio (see **Virgil**)

Vito Italian, Spanish, and Portuguese form of Latin *Vitus,* "alive"
    or "lively."
    Famous names: Vito Marcantonio (member of Congress)
                    Vito Russo (film critic and author)
    Variations: **Veit** (German), **Wit** (Polish)

Vitorio (see **Victor**)

Vittore (see **Victor**)

Vittorio Italian form of **Victor.**
    Famous name: Vittorio de Sica (movie director)

Von (see **Vaughan**)

Wade Old English *Wada,* "to go," name of a sea giant in ancient Germanic legends; or Middle English *wade,* "ford." Wade became a fairly common first name in the American South after the Civil War because of Wade Hampton, a Confederate general who later became both the governor of South Carolina and a U.S. senator from that state. Wade is now given to boys in all parts of the United States. It was the 280th most popular name for American males born in 1991.

Famous name: Wade Boggs (baseball player)

Waldo Old German *Wald,* "rule." The rare use of this name in the United States may have been inspired by admiration for the writer Ralph Waldo Emerson (1803–1882). Today, the name is best known from the children's picture books where one must find Waldo in a drawing containing hundreds of different people.

Walgierz (see **Walter**)

Walker Old English *wealcere,* "a fuller." A walker thickens cloth by gathering and pleating it. The profession is now obsolete, but the surname is still given as a first name occasionally.

Famous names: Walker Evans (photographer)
Walker Percy (writer)

Wallace Norman French *waleis,* "foreigner, Celt, Welshman." William Wallace was a 13th-century national hero of Scotland. Wallace was first used as a given name in Scotland in his honor. The name is only rarely found in America today.

Famous names: Wallace Beery (actor)
Wallace Stegner (author)
Wallace Stevens (poet)

Nicknames: **Wallie, Wally**

Other spelling: **Wallis**

Wallie, Wally Form of **Oswald, Wallace,** or **Walter.** In the
television series *Our Miss Brooks,* actor Wally Cox played Mr.
Peepers, the science teacher.
> Famous name: Wally Schirra (astronaut)

Wallis (see **Wallace**)

Walt Form of **Walter.**
> Famous names: Walt Disney (animator and film producer)
> Walt Whitman (poet)

Walter Old German *Waldhar* from *vald* [rule] + *harja* [people]. This
name dates back to the Domesday Book in England. By the
16th century, it had become well known through the exploits of
Sir Walter Raleigh, who established one of the first English
settlements in North America. From 1850 to 1950, Walter was
one of the top 50 names for boys in the United States, but it
disappeared suddenly from popular name lists, and now it
seems dated. *The Secret Life of Walter Mitty,* James Thurber's
short story, which was made into a movie, is about the
frustrations of day-to-day life. The close association of the name
Walter with the simple little man who is the hero of the story
may help to explain why Walter is no longer a popular name.
> Famous names: Walter Cronkite (TV newscaster)
> Walter Lippman (journalist)
> Walter Payton (football player)
> Walter Reed (pathologist)
> Walter Reuther (labor organizer)

Nicknames: **Wallie, Wally, Walt, Wat**

Variations: **Balto, Bhaltair** (Scottish), **Gauthier** (French),
Gautier (French), **Gualterio** (Spanish), **Gualtiero** (Italian),
Gutierre (Spanish), **Ualtar** (Irish), **Walgierz** (Polish),
Walther (German), **Watkin**

Walther (see **Walter**)

Ward Old English *weard,* "guard"; also, a form of **Howard.** Many
baby boomers will associate this name with Ward Cleaver, the
father in the 1950s television sitcom *Leave It to Beaver,* played
by Hugh Beaumont.
> Famous name: Ward Bond (actor)

Warner Old German *Warinhari* from *Warin* [a tribal name of
uncertain origin] + *hari* [army]. This name is more common as

a surname, but mystery fans remember actor Warner Oland and the movies in which he played the famed Chinese sleuth Charlie Chan.

Famous name: Warner Robins (World War I flier)

Variations: **Garner** (Old French), **Werner** (German and Scandinavian)

Warren Old German *Warin,* a tribal name; also, Norman French *La Varenne,* "the game park." This very old name dates to the Domesday Book in England. Warren was fairly common in the United States during the early 20th century, but had fallen to 324th on the list of names given American boys by 1991. In 1993, *Forbes* magazine declared that Omaha, Nebraska, financier Warren Buffet was the wealthiest person in the United States. This may encourage parents who envision a successful business career for their sons to revive the name.

Famous names: Warren Burger (U.S. Supreme Court chief justice)
Warren G. Harding (29th U.S. president)
Warren Moon (football player)

Warrick (see **Varrick**)

Wat (see **Walter**)

Watkin (see **Walter**)

Wawrzyniec (see **Lawrence**)

Wayland Germanic, perhaps from *wig* [war] + *land* [territory]. In ancient Germanic legend, Wayland the Smith was king of the elves.

Variations: **Waylon, Wieland** (German)

Waylon Modification of **Wayland.** Country singer Waylon Jennings has reported that his parents named him Wayland at birth, but while he was still an infant changed it to **Waylon** because, as Church of Christ members, they didn't want it assumed that he was named after Wayland Baptist University in Texas.

Wayne Old English *waegen,* "cart, wagon," a nickname for either a driver or maker of carts. This name was especially popular in the United States during the 1950s and 1960s. Wayne was later exported to England, where it was one of the top 50 names for boys born between 1970 and 1986.

Famous names: Wayne Gretzky (hockey player)
                      Wayne Rogers (actor)
                      Wayne Shorter (jazz musician)

Webb Old English *webbe,* "a weaver." This is an occupational name that is used occasionally as a first name.
Variations: **Webbe, Webster**

Webbe (see **Webb**)

Webster (see **Webb**)

Wendel (see **Wendell**)

Wendell Old German *Wend* [a Slavic tribe living in eastern Germany]. This name is infrequently but steadily used.
Famous names: Wendell Davis (football player)
                      Wendell Phillips (abolitionist)
Variation: **Wendel** (German)

Werner German and Scandinavian form of **Warner.**
Famous name: Wernher von Braun (scientist)

Wes (see **Wesley, Weston**)

Wesley Old English "west meadow." Parents honor John Wesley, the founder of Methodism, when they give their babies this surname as a first name.
Famous name: Wesley Mitchell (economist)
Nicknames: **Lee, Wes**
Variations: **Westleigh, Westley**

Westleigh, Westley (see **Wesley**)

Weston Old English "west farm." This very old surname is now being more frequently used as an American first name.
Famous name: Weston Dickson Fisler (baseball player)
Nickname: **Wes**

Wieland (see **Wayland**)

Wiktor (see **Victor**)

Wiley Old English *Wilig,* an ancient river name perhaps meaning "tricky stream" for a brook that often flooded.

Famous name: Wiley Post (aviator)
Other spelling: **Wylie**

Wilfred Old English from *wil* [will] + *frid* [peace]. This name has always been unusual in the United States, but it was very popular in England between 1900 and 1940. Wilfrid is the name of the hero of two of Sir Walter Scott's novels, *Ivanhoe* and *Rokeby*.

Famous names: Wilfrid Hyde-White (actor)
Wilfred Leach (stage and film director)
Variations: **Wilfrid, Wilfried** (German)

Wilfrid, Wilfried (see **Wilfred**)

Wilhelm (see **William**)

Will Form of **Willard** or **William**. Referring to himself, Shakespeare wrote: "Make but my name thy love, and love that still/And then thou lovest me, for my name is Will."

Famous name: Will Rogers (humorist)

Willard Old English *Wilheard* from *will* [desire] + *heard* [hardy, brave]. Willard has been used more in America than in Britain.

Famous name: Willard Scott (TV weatherman)
Nicknames: **Will, Willi, Willie, Willy**

Willem Dutch form of **William**.

Famous name: Willem Dafoe (actor)

Willet (see **William**)

Willi, Willie, Willy Form of **Willard** and **William**.

Famous names: Willi Smith (fashion designer)
Willie Mays (baseball player)
Willie Nelson (singer)
Willie Shoemaker (jockey)

William Old German *Wilahelm* from *wil* [will, desire] + *helm* [helmet]. For seven hundred years, between 1200 and 1900, William and John alternated between first and second place among names for boys in both Britain and the United States. The name came to England with William the Conqueror, who led the Norman Invasion of Great Britain. In the 11th century, William II, known as Rufus, came to the throne after his father. He was succeeded by his brother Henry I. For centuries, no other first-born royal Williams outlived their fathers, so despite a proliferation of Prince Williams, there was no other King William until William of Orange and his wife, Mary, were encouraged to depose James II. William IV briefly reigned after the death of his brother George IV, but was succeeded by his niece Queen Victoria. In the late 19th century during the reign of William I, king of Prussia, the German statesman Otto von Bismarck organized the unification of Germany. William II of Germany encouraged the fervent nationalism that led to World War I and his deposition in 1918. There are also many famous literary Williams, including the great dramatist William Shakespeare, poets William Wordsworth, William Blake, and William Butler Yeats, and American novelist William Faulkner. William Henry Harrison was the ninth president of the United States; William McKinley, the 20th; William Howard Taft, the 27th; and William Jefferson "Bill" Clinton, the 42nd.

Famous names: William Harvey (anatomist)
　　　　　　　William Holden (actor)
　　　　　　　William Hurt (actor)
　　　　　　　William Penn (founder of Pennsylvania)
　　　　　　　William Tell (Swiss hero)

Nicknames: **Bill, Billie, Billy, Guillo, Guirmo, Will, Willi, Willie, Willy, Wim** (Dutch)

Variations: **Giermo, Guglielmo** (Italian), **Guillaume** (French), **Guillermo** (Spanish), **Gulielm** (Rumanian), **Uilleam** (Scottish), **Uilliam** (Irish), **Vilem** (Czech), **Vilhelm** (Scandinavian), **Vilmos** (Hungarian), **Vilppu** (Finnish), **Wilhelm** (German), **Willem** (Dutch), **Willet, Wilmot**

Wilmot (see **William**)

Wim Dutch form of **William**.
　　Famous name: Wim Wenders (film director)

Win (see **Winn, Winston, Winthrop**)

Wincenty (see **Vincent**)

Winn Old English *Wine*, "friend"; also, a form of **Winston**.
　　Nicknames: **Winnie, Winny**
　　Other spelling: **Win**

Winnie, Winny (see **Winn, Winston**)

Winston Old English *Wynnstan* from *wynn* [joy] + *stan* [stone]; or Old English "Wine's village." The Churchill family made this name famous long before World War II brought the British prime minister to the attention of the world. In the 17th century, Sir Winston Churchill was the father of the first duke of Marlborough.

Nicknames: **Win, Winn, Winnie, Winny**

Winthrop Old English "Wynna's thorp," a place name, from *thorp,* "farm or village." This well-known New England surname conveys the idea of old wealth and colonial ancestors.

Famous name: Winthrop Ames (producer)

Nickname: **Win**

Winton (see **Wynton**)

Wit (see **Vito**)

Wood Form of **Elwood, Haywood,** or **Woodrow.** This rare name is now well known because of Wood Newton, the high-school football coach played by Burt Reynolds in the television series *Evening Shade.*

Woodie (see **Haywood, Woodrow, Woody**)

Woodrow Old English "a row of cottages along a wood" from *wudu* [wood] + *raw* [row]. Woodrow Wilson was the 28th president of the United States. He was born Thomas Woodrow Wilson; Woodrow was his mother's maiden name. The use of Woodrow as a first name is due solely to Wilson's fame.

Nicknames: **Wood, Woodie, Woody**

Woody Form of **Elwood, Haywood,** or **Woodrow.** This name has become well known through longtime Ohio State football coach Woody Hayes, musicians Woody Guthrie and Woody Herman, and movie director and actor Woody Allen.

Other spelling: **Woodie**

Wylie (see **Wiley**)

Wynton Alternate spelling of **Winton,** an English place name from Old English *wynn* [pasture] or *withigen* [willows] + *tun* [village]. Wynton is now occasionally given to boys in the United States, probably due to admiration for trumpeter Wynton Marsalis.

Xabiel (see **Xavier**)

Xabier (see **Xavier**)

Xaver (see **Xavier**)

Xavier Spanish form of Basque *Etcheberria,* "the new house."
Xavier became a first name in honor of St. Francis Xavier, who
helped establish the Society of Jesus (the Jesuits). This name
used to be confined to devout Roman Catholics, but it is now
becoming a common name with African-Americans because of
the fame of basketball player Xavier McDaniel. Xavier was the
62nd most common name given to nonwhite boys born in the
United States in 1991, and its popularity is still increasing.
Famous name: Xavier Cugat (bandleader)
Variations: **Javiel, Javier** (Spanish), **Xabiel, Xabier, Xaver**
(Czech, German, Swedish, and Hungarian), **Zavier**

Xeno (see **Xenos**)

Xenos Greek "stranger, foreigner."
Variation: **Xeno**

Ximon (see **Simon**)

Yahya (see **John**)

Yale Welsh *ial,* "fertile upland." In the early 18th century, Elihu Yale donated books and money to a new college that then took his name. When this surname is used as a first name, it often refers to Yale University.

Famous name: Yale Kamisar (lawyer)

Yasir Arabic "to be rich, to be easy."

Famous name: Yasir Arafat (Palestinian leader)

Yehochanan (see **John**)

Yehoshua (see **Joshua**)

Yevgeni (see **Eugene**)

Yirmeya (see **Jeremiah**)

Yishai (see **Jesse**)

Yitzchak, Yitzhak Modern Hebrew form of **Isaac.** Two prime ministers of Israel, Shamir and Rabin, have both had Yitzhak as a first name.

Yochanan (see **John**)

Yoel (see **Joel**)

Yosef (see **Joseph**)

Yoyi (see **George**)

Yoyo (see **George**)

Yrjo (see **George**)

Ysaac, Ysac (see **Isaac**)

Yul Form of **Julius.** Although the actor Yul Brynner, who was born in Vladivostok on the Pacific coast of Russia, liked to tell people that his first name came from a Mongolian word meaning "beyond the horizon," it was actually just a Russian version of **Jules,** the name of his Swiss-born grandfather.

Yuri Russian form of **George.** In 1961, Soviet cosmonaut Yuri A. Gagarin became the first person to orbit Earth.

Yusef (see **Joseph**)

Yusuf Arabic form of **Joseph.** This name is now regularly found in the African-American community.

Yvaine (see **Evan**)

Yves French form of Germanic *iv,* "yew tree." In ancient times, this name reminded people of hunting or warfare because bows were normally made out of yew wood. Yves was a popular name in France from the 1930s through the 1960s, but it is now out of fashion there. Although this name has never been common in English-speaking countries, it is well known as a place name because of the nursery rhyme that begins "As I was going to St. Ives, I met a man with seven wives."
Famous names: Yves Montand (actor)
　　　　　　　Yves Saint-Laurent (fashion designer)
Variations: **Ives, Yvon**

Yvon Old French *Ivon,* a form of **Yves.**

Zac (see **Zachariah, Zachary**)

Zacarias (see **Zachariah**)

Zacario (see **Zachariah**)

Zaccaria (see **Zachariah**)

Zach (see **Zachariah, Zachary**)

Zachar (see **Zachariah**)

Zachariah Form of **Zechariah.** In the King James version of the
Bible, this form is used in the Old Testament for one of the
kings of Israel, and the Greek form **Zacharias** is used in the
New Testament for the father of John the Baptist. Even though
more modern Bible translations call these two men Zechariah,
Zachariah is still the form more commonly given to American
boys. In fact, as **Zachary** has become fashionable, Zachariah is
also increasing in popularity and reached 217th on the list of
names given boys born in the United States in 1991.

Famous name: Zachariah Chandler (founder of the
Republican Party)

Nicknames: **Zac, Zach, Zack, Zak**

Variations: **Sahar** (Estonian), **Sakarias** (Finnish), **Zacarias**
(Spanish), **Zacario** (Mexican), **Zaccaria** (Italian), **Zachar**
(Bulgarian, Czech, Russian, and Ukrainian), **Zacharias**
(German), **Zachariasz** (Polish), **Zacharie** (French),
Zachary, Zaharius (modern Greek), **Zakarias** (Swedish
and Hungarian), **Zarko** (Serbo-Croatian)

Zacharias, Zachariasz (see Zachariah)

Zacharie (see Zachariah, Zachary)

Zachary Middle English form of **Zachariah.** Until recently, parents
almost never chose this name for their babies, despite the fame
of General Zachary Taylor, Old Rough and Ready, who was
the 12th president of the United States. But this name zoomed
from obscurity into prominence in the 1980s. It is now one of
the top 25 names for boys.
Nicknames: **Zac, Zach, Zack, Zak**
Other spellings: **Zacharie, Zackary, Zackery, Zackry**

Zack Form of **Zachariah** or **Zachary.** In the popular movie *An
Officer and a Gentleman,* actor Richard Gere played Zack.
Teenagers of the 1990s will connect this name with Zack
Morris, the girl-crazy student played by Mark-Paul Gosselaar
in the television series *Saved by the Bell.*

Zackary, Zackery, Zackry (see Zachary)

Zaharius (see Zachariah)

Zak (see Isaac, Zachariah, Zachary)

Zakarias (see Zachariah)

Zalman (see Solomon)

Zane English surname of unknown origin; possibly from a Danish
place name or a form of Old English *Saewine,* "sea friend."
Zane Grey was a New York dentist who wrote many best-
selling Western adventure novels, including *Riders of the Purple
Sage.* He was descended from the founders of Zanesville, Ohio,
and his first published novel, *Betty Zane,* was based on the lives
of his own ancestors. Grey's fame is solely responsible for the
present regular use of Zane as a first name for American boys.
Famous name: Zane Smith (baseball player)

Zarko (see Zachariah)

Zavier (see Xavier)

Zeb (see Zebadiah, Zebulon)

Zebadiah Hebrew "endowed by God." This is the name of nine different minor characters in the Old Testament.
>Nickname: **Zeb**
>Variation: **Zebedee**

Zebedee New Testament Greek form of **Zebadiah.** Zebedee was the father of the apostles James and John.

Zebulon Hebrew, perhaps "dwelling place." Zebulun was the sixth son of Jacob and Leah. The Puritans began to use the name in the 17th century.
>Famous name: Zebulon M. Pike (explorer)
>Nickname: **Zeb**
>Other spelling: **Zebulun**

Zebulun (see **Zebulon**)

Zechariah Hebrew "the Lord has remembered." In the Bible, the prophet Zechariah was the author of one of the books of the Old Testament.
>Variation: **Zachariah**

Zeke (see **Ezekiel**)

Zig (see **Sigmund**)

Ziggy Form of **Sigmund.**
>Famous name: Ziggy Marley (musician)

Zikomo Ngoni (Malawi) "thank you." This name is a lovely way to give thanks for the birth of a child.

Zubin Ancient Persian "the powerful sword." Although this name is still very rare, a few American parents who are fans of orchestra conductor Zubin Mehta have begun to give this name to their sons. Mehta was born in Bombay, India, into a Parsee family. The Parsees are descended from Zoroastrian Persians who fled from what is now Iran when it was conquered by Islamic forces in the seventh century.

Zygmunt (see **Sigmund**)

NAMES FOR GIRLS

Aakusta (see Augusta)

Abaigeal (see Abigail)

Abbey, Abbi, Abbie, Abby Short form of **Abigail.** Abby is now frequently given as an independent name in the United States.
Famous name: Abby Dalton (actress)

Abigail Hebrew *Avigayil,* "my father rejoices." In the Old Testament, Abigail was a wife of King David. This name was popular with the Puritans between 1550 and 1800, but then faded away when Abigail became associated with a lady's maid. The name is now becoming popular once again in the United States, especially along the East Coast.
Famous names: Abigail Adams (wife of John Adams, second president of the United States)
Abigail Thomas (author)
Abigail Van Buren (advice columnist)
Nicknames: **Abbey, Abbi, Abbie, Abby, Gail, Gale, Gayle**
Variation: **Abaigeal** (Irish Gaelic)

Abra Feminine form of **Abraham,** Hebrew "exalted father." Abra is a very unusual name for a girl.

Ada Form of **Adelaide;** or Old German *adal,* "noble"; or Hebrew *adah,* "ornament." In the Bible, Adah was one of the daughters of Adam and Eve, and the wife of Cain. George Gordon, Lord Byron, used the name in *Childe Harold's Pilgrimage.* Charles Dickens used the name in *Bleak House,* as did Vladimir Nabakov in *Ada.* This name was more popular in the 19th century than it is today, but its simple rhythm makes Ada an attractive alternative to **Anne** as a middle name.

Famous names: Ada Deer (Bureau of Indian Affairs director)
Ada Louise Huxtable (architecture critic)

Nicknames: **Adey, Adi, Adie**

Variation: **Adah** (Hebrew)

Adah Form of **Ada.**

Famous name: Adah Menken (actress)

Addie, Addy (see **Adela, Adelaide, Adeline, Adrienne**)

Adela Old German *athal,* "noble." William the Conqueror called one of his daughters Adela. The name has always been more popular in continental Europe than in England and the United States.

Famous name: Adela Rogers St. Johns (writer)

Nicknames: **Addie, Addy, Della**

Variations: **Adele** (French), **Adelia, Adelina** (Latin), **Adeline, Adelle**

Adelaida (see **Adelaide**)

Adelaide Old German *Adelhaid* from *adal* [noble] and *heid* [rank]. The names of British monarchs have always been popular with their subjects. Adelaide, wife of William IV, made this name popular in England and the Commonwealth in the 19th century. The capital of South Australia was named for her in 1836.

Famous name: Adelaide Ann Procter (poet)

Nicknames: **Ada, Addie, Addy, Heidi** (German)

Variations: **Adelaida** (Spanish and Portuguese), **Adelheid** (German)

Adele (see **Adela, Adeline**)

Adelheid (see **Adelaide**)

Adelia (see **Adela**)

Adelina (see **Adela, Adeline, Alina**)

Adelinda (see **Adeline**)

Adeline French diminutive of **Adela** or **Adele.** Adeline is a Norman name. Until the 15th century, it was more popular than

Adelaide in Great Britain. Although not often used in the United States, barbershop quartets have been singing about Adeline for many years, paving the way for the "Sweet Adelines," barbershop groups made up of women.

Famous name: Adeline Tintner (literary critic)

Nicknames: **Addie, Addy, Lena**

Variations: **Adelina** (Latin), **Adelinda, Alina, Aline**

Adelle (see Adela)

Adey, Adi, Adie (see Ada)

Adria, Adrian (see Adrienne)

Adriana, Adrianna Spanish and Italian form of **Adrienne.** Use of this name is growing quickly; by the late 1980s, Adriana was considerably more popular than **Adrienne** in the United States. Adriana Caselotti provided the title character's voice for *Snow White and the Seven Dwarfs* in 1937, the first full-length animated film; the film was re-released in 1993.

Adriane, Adrianne (see Adrienne)

Adrienne French feminine form of **Adrian,** Latin "from the Adriatic." Like other French names for girls, Adrienne became popular in the United States in the 1980s.

Famous name: Adrienne Rich (poet)

Nicknames: **Addie, Addy**

Variations: **Adria, Adrian, Adriana** (Italian and Spanish), **Adriane** (German), **Adrianna, Adrianne**

Ag (see Agatha, Agnes)

Agata (see Agatha)

Agate (see Agatha)

Agatha Greek *agathos,* "good." This name was very popular during the Middle Ages because of the third-century St. Agatha of Sicily. This Christian martyr suffered horrid tortures for rebuffing the advances of the consul Quintian and for refusing to repudiate her Christian faith. The veil of St. Agatha is believed to have saved the city of Catania, Sicily, from the nearby volcano, Mount Etna. This explains why St. Agatha is the patron saint of fire protection. The name is best known today because of Agatha Christie, creator of the famous fictional sleuths Jane Marple and Hercule Poirot.

Nicknames: **Ag, Aggi, Aggie, Aggy**

Variations: **Agata** (Irish, Italian, Polish, and Czech), **Agate** (Latvian and Norwegian), **Agathe** (French and German), **Agathi** (modern Greek), **Agda** (Swedish and Danish), **Agota** (Hungarian), **Agueda** (Spanish)

Agathe, Agathi (see **Agatha**)

Agda (see **Agatha**)

Aggi, Aggie, Aggy (see **Agatha, Agnes**)

Agna (see **Agnes**)

Agne (see **Agnes**)

Agnes Greek *hagnos,* "holy, pure." At the age of 13, St. Agnes was beheaded in Rome because she would not worship the goddess Minerva. She is the guardian of teenagers, and her symbol is the lamb. The saint's association with purity and innocence made Agnes a very popular name until the end of the 17th century. Poets John Keats and Alfred, Lord Tennyson, wrote poems celebrating St. Agnes's Eve (January 20). Agnes was one of the top 50 names for American girls born between 1880 and 1920, but it is very rarely used today.

Famous names: Agnes De Mille (choreographer)
      Agnes Moorehead (actress)

Nicknames: **Ag, Aggi, Aggie, Aggy, Nessa, Nessi, Nessie, Nesta, Nessy**

Variations: **Agna** (Norwegian), **Agne** (Lithuanian and Greek), **Agnesa** (Ukrainian and Bulgarian), **Agnese** (Italian), **Agnessa** (Russian), **Agneta** (Swedish), **Agnete** (German), **Agnieszka** (Polish), **Aigneis** (Irish Gaelic), **Anezka** (Czech), **Annice** (English), **Annis** (English), **Auno** (Finnish), **Ines** (Portuguese), **Inez** (Spanish), **Nancy** (medieval British), **Nezka** (Slovenian), **Ynes, Ynez** (Spanish)

Agnesa (see **Agnes**)

Agnese (see **Agnes**)

Agnessa (see **Agnes**)

Agneta (see **Agnes**)

Agnete (see **Agnes**)

Agnieszka (see **Agnes**)

Agota (see **Agatha**)

Agueda (see **Agatha**)

Aida Perhaps based on ancient Egyptian *'Iiti,* "she is arriving."
Verdi's opera *Aida* is about a slave girl in Egypt, who is really
the daughter of Amonasro, the king of Ethiopia. This name is
sometimes used in the Hispanic-American community.
Famous name: Aida Rios (oceanographer)

Aigneis (see **Agnes**)

Aileen Variation of **Eileen**.
Famous name: Aileen Quinn (actress)
Variations: **Aleen, Alene, Alyne**

Ailis (see **Alice**)

Aime, Aimee French "beloved" from Latin *amare,* "to love." This
name has never been very popular in France, but it is regularly
used in the United States as a spelling variation of **Amy,** which
has the same Latin derivation.
Famous names: Aimee Duvivier (artist)
                Aimee Semple MacPherson (evangelist)

Ain Arabic "eye." The metaphoric meaning of this name is
"precious."
Other spelling: **Ayn**

Aingeal (see **Angela**)

Aisha Arabic *A'isha,* "alive and well." Aisha was the third and
favorite wife of the prophet Mohammed. This name is now
popular with African-Americans. Although Aisha is technically
the "proper" Islamic spelling, **Iesha** was by far the more
common form among African-Americans by 1990.
Variations: **Asha** (Swahili), **Ashia, Asia, Ayesha, Iesha**

Alaina This modern blend of **Alana** and **Elaine** is steadily becoming popular and was among the top 300 names for American girls in 1991.

Famous name: Alaina Michaelson (social psychologist)

Variations: **Alaine, Alayna, Alayne**

Alaine (see **Alaina**)

Alamea Hawaiian "precious."

Alana, Alanna Usually a feminine form of **Alan,** perhaps Celtic "rock"; occasionally from Irish Gaelic *a leanbh,* "oh, child"; and in Hawaii, sometimes from Hawaiian *alana,* "awakening."

Variations: **Allene, Allyn, Lana, Lanna**

Alayna, Alayne (see **Alaina**)

Alba (see **Albina**)

Alberta Old German *athal* [noble] and *berhta* [bright]. This feminine form of Albert is not a favorite with American parents, although it was in regular use around 1900.

Nicknames: **Allie, Ally, Berta, Berti, Bertie, Berty, Birdie, Birdy**

Variations: **Albertina** (Portuguese, Spanish, and Swedish), **Albertine** (French), **Elberta** (English)

Albertina (see **Alberta**)

Albertine (see **Alberta**)

Albina Latin *albus,* "white." In 1992, French countess Albina de Boisrouvray gave $20 million to Harvard University to "promote the basic rights of the ill."

Variations: **Alba, Albinia, Aubine**

Albinia (see **Albina**)

Alda Perhaps a feminine form of **Aldous,** German "old" or "wise."

Aleen (see **Aileen**)

Alejandra (see **Alexandra**)

Aleka (see **Alexandra**)

Alena (see **Alina, Madeline**)

Alene (see **Aileen**)

Alessandra (see **Alexandra**)

Alethea Greek *aletheia,* "truth." This is not an ancient Greek name; it was coined in the 17th century in England by Puritan clergy who were reading the New Testament in its original Greek language.

Alex (see **Alexandra**)

Alexa This short form of the fashionable **Alexandra** is also becoming common as an independent name, reaching 120th place among American girls born in 1991.
Famous names: Alexa Grace (illustrator)
Alexa Riehle (experimental psychologist)

Alexandra Feminine form of Greek *Alexandros,* "protector of mankind." In Russia, many princesses were named Alexandra. The name's association with royalty goes back to Roman times with Queen Alexandra of Judaea, who died in 69 B.C. In England, Alexandra Rose Day (June 26) was designated in honor of Alexandra, the daughter of King Christian IV of Denmark who married Prince Albert (later King Edward VII). Since 1980, Alexandra and Alexandria have become fashionable names in the United States, and Alexandra was 45th on the list of names given to American girls in 1991. Romance novelist Alexandra Ripley made headlines when she was chosen to write *Scarlett,* the official sequel to *Gone with the Wind.*
Famous names: Alexandra Koltun (ballerina)
Alexandra Paul (actress)
Alexandra Stoddard (interior designer)
Nicknames: **Alex, Alix, Lexi, Lexie, Sandi, Sandie, Sandy, Sasha**
Variations: **Alejandra** (Spanish), **Aleka** (Greek), **Alessandra** (Spanish), **Alexa, Alexandria, Alexandrina, Alexandrine** (French), **Alexia, Lexine, Sandra, Sondra, Zandra**

Alexandria Form of **Alexandra.** Although both of these forms are popular with Americans from all ethnic backgrounds, the trend is for Alexandra to be more popular with whites while Alexandria is ahead among African-Americans, perhaps because of the well-known African city of Alexandria, Egypt.

Alexandria was the 74th most popular name for American girls born in 1991.

Alexandrina (see **Alexandra**)

Alexandrine (see **Alexandra**)

Alexia (see **Alexandra**)

Alexis Greek *Alexios,* "helper, defender." Although it was originally a male name and is still popular for Hispanic-American boys, Alexis is now almost exclusively a name for girls. The name is especially popular with African-Americans, for whom Alexis was the 12th most popular name for girls in 1991. On the television series *Dynasty,* Joan Collins played the character Alexis.
Famous name: Alexis Smith (actress)

Ali Form of **Alice, Alicia,** or **Alison.**
Famous name: Ali MacGraw (actress)

Alice Old French *Adalis, Alis,* from Old German *Adalhaidis,* "of noble rank." This name developed in the 12th century as an abbreviated form of **Adelaide.** The best-known fictional Alice is the central character of Lewis Carroll's *Alice's Adventures in Wonderland* and *Through the Looking Glass.* These books may have been responsible for the popularity of the name in the late 19th century. In keeping with Carroll's spunky Alice, the outspoken daughter of President Theodore Roosevelt also provoked imitation; even her preference for pastels was widely imitated and a new color, Alice-blue, was named in her honor. Alice is now fashionable again in Australia, but American parents prefer to use the forms **Alison, Alicia,** or **Alyssa.**
Famous names: Alice B. Toklas (writer)
Alice Walker (author)
Allyce Beasley (actress)
Nicknames: **Ali, Allie, Ally**
Other spellings: **Alis, Allyce, Alyce, Alys**
Variations: **Ailis** (Irish Gaelic), **Alicia** (Italian, Spanish, and Swedish), **Alisa** (Russian), **Alison, Alix** (French), **Alyssa**

Alicia Italian, Spanish, or Swedish variation of **Alice.** Alicia has been very fashionable as a name for American girls since the late 1970s and was still among the top 50 names in 1991.

Famous name: Alicia Markova (ballerina)
Nicknames: **Ali, Allie, Ally, Licia, Lisha**
Other spellings: **Alisha, Allycia, Alycia**

Alina Medieval short form of **Adeline** or **Adelina**. This name is fairly common in the Hispanic-American community.
Famous name: Alina Rodriguez (actress)
Other spelling: **Alena**

Aline (see **Adeline**)

Alis (see **Alice**)

Alisa Russian form of **Alice**, now regularly given in the United States as a blend of the sounds of **Alicia** and **Lisa**.

Alisha (see **Alicia**)

Alison Old French form of **Alice** brought to England by the Normans. Chaucer used the name Alison in "The Miller's Tale." Alison has been very fashionable in the United States since the 1970s.
Famous names: Alison Fraser (actress)
Alison Lurie (novelist)
Nicknames: **Ali, Allie, Ally**
Other spellings: **Allison, Allyson, Alyson**
Variation: **Allsun** (Irish Gaelic)

Alissa (see **Alyssa**)

Alix (see **Alexandra, Alice**)

Allegra Italian "lively, cheerful, gay, sprightly."
Famous name: Allegra Kent (ballerina)

Allene (see **Alana, Alanna**)

Allie, Ally Form of **Alberta, Alice, Alicia**, or **Alison**. This name showed a modest increase in popularity during the 1980s when the television series *Kate and Allie* was on the air.
Famous name: Ally Sheedy (actress)

Allison Form of **Alison**. This spelling is now more common in the United States than the traditional form.

Allsun (see **Alison**)

Allyce (see **Alice**)

Allycia (see **Alicia**)

Allyn (see **Alana, Alanna**)

Allyson (see **Alison**)

Alma Italian "soul"; Latin "nourishing, kind"; or Hebrew *almah,* "maiden." The Roman term *Alma Mater,* "bounteous mother," was used for several goddesses. In 1854, during the Crimean War, the British and French defeated the Russians in the Battle of Alma. The name was popular in England and the United States until the beginning of the 20th century.
Famous name: Alma Gluck (soprano)

Almira Spanish "the woman from the city of Almira."

Alva Irish Gaelic *Almha,* name of a legendary heroine of unknown meaning; or Hebrew *Alvah,* "foliage."

Alvina Feminine form of **Alvin,** Old English "elf friend."
Variation: **Elvina**

Alvira (see **Elvira**)

Alyce (see **Alice**)

Alycia (see **Alicia**)

Alyne (see **Aileen**)

Alys (see **Alice**)

Alyson (see **Alison**)

Alyssa Modern form of **Alice,** blending it with the sound of **Melissa.** Because the spelling Alyssa is ten times more common than **Alissa,** American parents may also see this name as a feminine form of the flower named alyssum, which comes from Greek *alyssos,* "curing madness"; in medieval Europe, it was believed that this plant could cure rabies in dogs. In any event, Alyssa became hugely popular in the United States during the 1980s, especially on the East Coast. In 1991, it was still 39th on the national list of names given to American girls.

Famous names: Alyssa Katz (film critic)
Alyssa Milano (actress)
Other spelling: **Alissa**

Ama Ewe (Ghana) "born on Saturday."

Amabel Latin *amabilis,* "lovable" or "loving." This name is much older than the more popular name **Annabel** or **Annabelle,** but few parents choose it today.
Variation: **Mabel**

Amada (see **Amy**)

Amalia (see **Amelia**)

Amalie (see **Amelia**)

Amalija (see **Amelia**)

Amanda Latin "worthy of love." In the 17th century, the writers of Restoration plays liked to invent pleasant names for their female characters, and Amanda is one of these names. The name first became popular in the United States during the 1840s, but then went out of fashion. During the early 20th century, Amanda had an elderly and unattractive image. However, it suddenly regained its popularity in England in the 1960s. This new fashion for Amanda was exported to the United States during the late 1970s, and Amanda has consistently held a place among the top five names given to American girls since 1983. Another factor in Amanda's revival may have been the fame of Amanda Blake, the actress who played Miss Kitty on the long-running television Western *Gunsmoke.* Indeed, the name has become a favorite among actresses, with Amanda Bearse, Amanda Donohoe, Amanda Pays, and Amanda Plummer all successfully making names for themselves.
Nicknames: **Manda, Mandi, Mandie, Mandy**
Variations: **Amandine** (French), **Amenda, Mandita** (Mexican)

Amandine (see **Amanda**)

Amaryllis Greek, perhaps from *amaryssein,* "to sparkle." In classical Greek and Roman poetry, this name was typically given to shepherdesses or other country maidens. In the 1780s, a newly discovered lilylike flower was named after one of these fictional maidens. The flower traditionally has the connotation of renewal. On the rare occasion Amaryllis is used as a name for girls today, it is probably thought of as a flower name, such as **Rose** or **Lily.** Most American girls now given this name have Hispanic parents.

Amata (see **Amy**)

Amatia (see **Amy**)

Amber Arabic *anbar,* "amber," a pale yellow or green fossil resin used to make jewelry. This relatively new name has recently become more popular than it has ever been. In the late 19th and early 20th centuries, jewel names were at the height of their popularity. But unlike **Pearl, Beryl,** and **Opal,** which are almost never used today, Amber has been one of the top 20 names for girls in the United States since 1984. In 1993, the film *Jurassic Park* made the gem amber suddenly fashionable because it featured the idea that dinosaur DNA from fossil mosquitos trapped in amber could be used to recreate the extinct creatures. This may help the name Amber extend its run of popularity for yet another decade.

Famous names: Amber Densmore (quilt artist)
　　　　　　　Amber Coverdale Sumrall (editor)

Amee (see **Amy**)

Amelia English form of German *Amalie,* probably from Old German *amal,* "work." This name was brought to England in the early 18th century when the German Hanoverian dynasty inherited the English throne. Since then, Amelia has been blended and confused with **Emily,** which has a different origin; the youngest daughter of King George III was called both Princess Amelia and Princess Emily, interchangeably. Amelia became popular outside the British royal family when Henry Fielding used it for the title character of his popular novel. Although Amelia went out of fashion in the United States by 1900, it now seems to be starting a minor revival, probably spurred by the success of **Emily, Amy,** and similar-sounding names.

Famous names: Amelia Curran (artist)
　　　　　　　Amelia Earhart (aviatrix)
Nicknames: **Mellie, Melly, Millie, Milly**
Variations: **Amalia** (Spanish, Italian, and Polish), **Amalie**

(German), **Amalija** (Serbian and Bulgarian), **Amelie** (French), **Amelija** (Russian), **Ameline, Emeline**

Amelie (see Amelia)

Amelija (see Amelia)

Ameline (see Amelia)

Amenda (see Amanda)

Ami (see Amy)

Amia (see Amy)

Amity Latin "friendship." This is a very rare name that is more often found in England than the United States.

Ammy (see Amy)

Amy English form of Old French *Amee,* "beloved." This name was popular in England during the 19th century. It became known in the United States because of the childhood classic *Little Women* by Louisa May Alcott and the 1933 movie based on the novel. The name didn't become really fashionable until the 1970s. At that point the name's popularity exploded, and it was second only to **Jennifer** as a name for American girls born in that decade. Amy's peak has now passed, and it was only 49th on the list for girls born in 1991.

Famous names: Amy Alcott (golfer)
　　　　　　　Amy Grant (singer)
　　　　　　　Amy Irving (actress)
　　　　　　　Amy Lowell (poet)
　　　　　　　Amy Madigan (actress)
　　　　　　　Amy Tan (novelist and screenwriter)

Other spellings: **Amee, Ami, Amye**

Variations: **Aime, Aimee** (French), **Amada** (Spanish), **Amata** (Italian, German, Swedish, Polish, and Hungarian), **Amatia** (Latin), **Amia, Ammy** (Norwegian)

Amye (see Amy)

Ana (see Anne)

Anabel (see Annabel, Annabelle)

Anais (see **Anne**)

Anastasia Feminine form of Greek *anastasis,* "resurrection."
Books and movies have been made about the legendary
Anastasia Romanov, daughter of Nicholas II. At least two
women have claimed to be Anastasia. Each says that she
escaped the massacre of the royal family by Bolsheviks during
the Russian Revolution, but neither woman's claim was ever
proved. The name has become associated with royalty and
romance.

Nicknames: **Anstey, Nastka** (Polish), **Nastya** (Russian), **Stacey,
Stacie, Stacy**

Variations: **Anstice, Nastasia, Nastassia, Nastassja**

Andela (see **Angela**)

Andi, Andie (see **Andrea**)

Andona (see **Antonia**)

Andrea Feminine form of **Andrew,** Greek "strong" or "manly."
Andrea is the male form of Andrew in Italian, but it became
popular in the United States and England as a name for girls in
the second half of the 20th century. Between 1960 and 1989, it
was one of the top 50 names for girls.

Famous names: Andrea Jaeger (tennis player)
Andrea Martin (comedienne)
Andrea McArdle (actress)

Nicknames: **Andi, Andie, Andy**

Variations: **Andree** (French), **Andreina** (Italian), **Andresa**
(Latvian), **Andria, Andrina**

Andree (see **Andrea**)

Andreina (see **Andrea**)

Andresa (see **Andrea**)

Andria, Andrina (see **Andrea**)

Andy (see **Andrea**)

Andzela (see **Angela**)

Ane (see **Anne**)

Anele (see **Angela**)

Anelja (see **Angela**)

Aneta (see **Anita**)

Anete (see **Antonia**)

Anezka (see **Agnes**)

Angel This was formerly a male name in English, as it still is in Spanish. For most Americans, however, Angel has now become a name for girls. Angel is now among the top 200 names given girls in the United States and is especially popular in the African-American community.
Famous name: Angel Martino (Olympic swimmer)

Angela Greek *angelos,* "angel" or "messenger." Although a favorite name in Italy and Spain from early Christian times, Angela did not come into regular use in England and America until the 18th century, partly because the Puritans rejected its use, regarding it as too sacred for use by mortals. Angela Merici founded the first order of women teachers, the Ursuline Order, but it wasn't until 1807, 300 years after her death, that she was canonized. Angela became a very popular name in both England and America during the 1960s and 1970s, but its popularity has now started to decrease.
Famous names: Angela Carter (author)
  Angela Lansbury (actress)
Nickname: **Angie**
Variations: **Aingeal** (Irish Gaelic), **Andela** (Czech and Croatian), **Andzela** (Latvian), **Anele** (Lithuanian), **Anelja** (Ukrainian), **Angele** (French), **Angelina** (Italian and Portuguese), **Angeline** (French), **Angelita** (Spanish), **Aniela** (Polish), **Anjela, Engel** (German)

Angele (see **Angela**)

Angelica Feminine form of Latin *angelicus,* "angelic." This name has a long literary history; it was used by Congreve in *Love for Love* and by Thackeray in *The Rose and the Ring.* Angelica is becoming more popular and was 150th on the list of names given girls born in the United States in 1991.
Famous name: Anjelica Huston (actress)
Variations: **Angelika** (German), **Angelique** (French), **Anjelica**

Angelika (see **Angelica**)

Angelina (see **Angela**)

Angeline (see **Angela**)

Angelique (see **Angelica**)

Angelita (see **Angela**)

Angie Pet form of **Angela** sometimes used independently.
Famous name: Angie Dickinson (actress)

Anni (see **Annie**)

Anica (see **Anne**)

Aniela (see **Angela**)

Aniko (see **Anne**)

Anilla (see **Anne**)

Anita Spanish form of **Anne.**
Famous name: Anita O'Day (singer)
Variations: **Aneta, Nita**

Anjelica (see **Angelica**)

Anjela (see **Angela**)

Anka (see **Anne**)

Anke (see **Anne**)

Ann English form of **Anne.** Ann was the original English spelling,
but it is now less common than Anne, probably because the
latter has been the form favored by the British royal family.
Famous names: Ann Beattie (author)
Ann Landers (advice columnist)
Ann Richards (governor of Texas)
Nicknames: **Annie, Anny, Nan, Nancy**

Anna Latin variation of **Anne** and **Hannah.** This is the normal form
of Anne in most Slavic and Germanic languages. Anna was
second only to Mary as a name for girls born in the United
States between 1875 and 1895. It has never been as common in

Britain. Anna went out of fashion in America for almost a century, but it became popular again around 1975. In the late 1980s, Hannah overtook Anna in popularity, but Anna was still 50th on the list of names given American girls in 1991. The tragic heroine of Count Leo Tolstoy's novel *Anna Karenina* may be the best-known Anna in literature.

Famous names: Anna Magnani (actress)
Anna Pavlova (ballerina)
Anna Quindlen (journalist)

Annabel, Annabelle A medieval Scottish form of **Amabel,** probably modified to resemble **Anna** and **Belle** (French "beautiful"). Annabel has recently been faddish with the British upper classes, but it is still rare in the United States. Due to Edgar Allan Poe's poem "Annabel Lee," this name will never be entirely unknown.

Famous name: Annabel Schofield (actress)

Other spellings: **Anabel, Annabella**

Annabella (see **Annabel, Annabelle**)

Annag (see **Anne**)

Annah (see **Anne**)

Anne French and English form of Hebrew **Hannah,** "God has favored me." Anne with an "e" developed in France and was adopted in England in the 12th or 13th century. The name was extremely popular from the 14th century on. Tradition has it that St. Anne was the mother of the Virgin Mary, although she is not mentioned in the Bible. The name has long been used by royalty, including Anne of Bohemia, the wife of Richard II; Anne Neville, the wife of Richard III; two wives of Henry VIII, Anne Boleyn and Anne of Cleves; Anne of Denmark, wife of James I of Scotland; and Queen Anne, the last reigning Stuart. Princess Anne is the daughter of Queen Elizabeth II of England. *Anne of Green Gables* by L. M. Montgomery was published in 1908. Today, many celebrated American women share the name, including three prominent authors who have garnered both critical acclaim and best-selling status: Anne Lindbergh, Anne Rice, and Anne Tyler. Although Anne's popularity as a first name has greatly diminished since 1960, it continues to be amazingly popular as a middle name. Probably one out of every ten American women alive today was given

Anne or **Ann** as a middle name at birth.

Famous names: Anne Archer (actress)
Anne Bancroft (actress)

Nicknames: **Anni, Annie, Anny, Nan, Nancy**

Other spelling: **Ann**

Variations: **Ana** (Spanish and Portuguese), **Anais** (Provencal), **Ane** (Danish), **Anica** (Rumanian), **Aniko** (Hungarian), **Anilla** (Hungarian), **Anita** (Spanish), **Anka** (Croatian and Slovenian), **Anke** (German), **Anna** (Latin, Germanic, and Slavic), **Annag** (Scots Gaelic), **Annah, Anneke** (Dutch), **Annette** (French), **Annick** (Breton), **Annika** (Danish and Swedish), **Annikki** (Finnish), **Annina, Anninka** (Russian and Czech), **Antje** (Frisian), **Anula** (Polish), **Anusia** (Polish), **Anuska** (Czech), **Hannah, Nana, Nanette, Nani, Nanni, Nannie, Nanny, Nina** (Italian), **Ninette** (French), **Ninon** (French), **Ona** (Lithuanian)

Anneke (see **Anne**)

Anne-Marie (see **Annemarie**)

Annemarie Combination of **Anne** and **Marie**. This name was popular with Roman Catholics during the 1950s and 1960s.

Variations: **Annmarie, Anne-Marie, Ann-Marie**

Annette French variation of **Anne**.

Famous names: Annette Bening (actress)
Annette Funicello (actress)
Annette O'Toole (actress)

Nickname: **Nettie**

Anni (see **Anne**)

Annice (see **Agnes**)

Annick (see **Anne**)

Annie Form of **Ann** or **Anne**. This name began as a nickname for Anne, but it became a name in its own right in the 19th century, long before the 1970 Broadway musical *Annie*. Diane Keaton played the title character in Woody Allen's movie *Annie Hall*. "Fair Annie" is an ancient ballad, and Sir Walter Scott used the name in *The Bride of Lammermoor*.

Famous names: Annie Dillard (writer)

Annie Leibovitz (photographer)
Annie Potts (actress)
Other spellings: **Anni, Anny**

Annika (see **Anne**)

Annikki (see **Anne**)

Annina (see **Anne**)

Anninka (see **Anne**)

Annis (see **Agnes**)

Ann-Marie (see **Annemarie**)

Annmarie (see **Annemarie**)

Anny (see **Ann, Anne, Annie**)

Anstey (see **Anastasia**)

Anstice (see **Anastasia**)

Antalka (see **Antonia**)

Antane (see **Antonia**)

Anthea Greek "flower." This name is the Greek equivalent of the Latin name **Flora** and the French name **Fleur.**
Other spelling: **Anthia**

Anthia (see **Anthea**)

Antje (see **Anne**)

Antoinette French form of **Antonia. Like** its male counterpart **Antoine,** Antoinette is especially popular among African-Americans, where it was among the top 100 names for girls throughout the 1980s. The Tony awards are named after Antoinette Perry, a Broadway actress, director, and producer.
Nicknames: **Nettie, Netty, Toni, Tonie, Tony**
Other spellings: **Antwanette, Antwonette**

Antonetta (see **Antonia**)

Antonia Feminine form of *Antonius,* Latin family name of unknown meaning. Although Antonia is regularly used in England, the name is unusual in the United States except in a shortened form, such as **Tonie** or **Tonia.**

Famous name: Antonia Fraser (historian and novelist)

Nicknames: **Nina, Toni, Tonia, Tonie, Tony, Tonya**

Variations: **Andona** (Mexican), **Anete** (Latvian), **Antalka** (Hungarian), **Antane** (Lithuanian), **Antoinette** (French), **Antonetta** (Scandinavian), **Antonie** (Czech and German), **Antonietta** (Italian), **Antonina** (Italian, Russian, Polish, and Czech)

Antonie (see **Antonia**)

Antonietta (see **Antonia**)

Antonina (see **Antonia**)

Antwanette, Antwonette (see **Antoinette**)

Anula (see **Anne**)

Anusia (see **Anne**)

Anuska (see **Anne**)

Aphra Hebrew *Aphrah,* a biblical place name meaning "dust." Aphra Behn was the first woman writer to make a living by her trade using her own name; she lived in the 17th century.

April Latin *aprilis,* the name of the month; perhaps from Latin *aperire,* "open to the sun," or from *Apru,* Etruscan name of the goddess Aphrodite. April is the most popular month name. American children today will probably immediately identify April as the name of the television reporter friend of the Teenage Mutant Ninja Turtles. In 1991, April Ulring Larson became the first woman Lutheran bishop in the United States.

Variations: **Apryl, Avril** (French)

Apryl (see **April**)

Arabella Possibly Latin *orabilis,* "able to be moved." Richard Strauss wrote the opera *Arabella.*

Aranka (see **Aurelia**)

Areta (see **Aretha**)

Aretha Possibly a form of Greek *arete,* "virtue." This name may stem from Arethusa, a nymph in Greek mythology who was transformed into a stream by the goddess Artemis.

Famous name: Aretha Franklin (singer)

Variations: **Areta, Aretta, Arette**

Aretta (see **Aretha**)

Arette (see **Aretha**)

Ariana, Arianna Latin form of Greek *Ariadne,* "very holy one"; in Greek mythology, the princess of Crete who helped Theseus escape from the Minotaur. This name is swiftly increasing in popularity, rising from 278th to 156th between 1989 and 1991 on the list of names for girls in America. Ariana's similarity in sound to **Ariel** is probably contributing to its sudden success.

Ariel Hebrew "lion of God." Shakespeare used this name for a magical spirit of the air in *The Tempest.* Although Ariel is a male name in both the Bible and Shakespeare's play, the creators of Disney's popular animated film *The Little Mermaid* called their heroine Ariel because the Shakespearean air sprite has a beautiful singing voice, just like the mermaid. The idea that Ariel was an appropriate female name probably came from Ariel Durant, the American historian who, with her husband, Will, wrote many best-selling books. In any event, the mermaid has inspired thousands of American parents to name their daughters Ariel; the name was the 67th most popular for girls born in the United States in 1991. Ariel may very well be on its way to the very top, for it has recently been reported that American elementary-school girls pick it as their favorite name for a future child of their own.

Variation: **Arielle**

Arielle This French feminine form of **Ariel** was actually regularly used as an American name for girls before Ariel itself began to be given to girls. However, Arielle became popular only after Ariel took off in the late 1980s. Arielle was the 179th most common name for girls in 1991.

Famous names: Arielle P. Kozloff (Egyptologist)
                       Arielle North Olson (children's book author)

Arleen (see **Arlene**)

Arlena (see **Arlene**)

Arlene Form of **Arline,** a name invented by composer M. W. Balfe
for the heroine of his opera *The Bohemian Girl.* Balfe may have
created the name as a partial anagram of Karolina, his wife's
name. Arlene was frequently given by American parents in the
middle decades of the 20th century, but the name isn't chosen
very often today.
Famous name: Arlene Blum (mountain climber)
Nicknames: **Arlie, Lena, Lina**
Variations: **Arleen, Arlena, Arleyne, Arlina, Arline**

Arleyne (see **Arlene**)

Arlie (see **Arlene**)

Arlina (see **Arlene**)

Arline (see **Arlene**)

Armida Italian feminine form of **Herman.**

Asha Swahili form of **Aisha;** also, a Hindu name from Sanskrit *asa,*
"wish, hope."

Ashia (see **Aisha**)

Ashlea, Ashlee, Ashleigh (see **Ashley**)

Ashley Old English "meadow with ash trees." This was a fairly
uncommon name for boys, but since 1984, Ashley has been one
of the top three names for girls born in the United States.
Ashley was an aristocratic English surname with connections
to the American South, which were reinforced by the best-
known fictional Ashley, the man who chose Melanie over
Scarlett in Margaret Mitchell's novel *Gone with the Wind.*
Upper-middle-class Southerners have long been accustomed to
giving family surnames (including such unlikely ones as
Winston and Langhorne) to daughters as well as to sons, and
so Ashley slowly became more popular as a name for girls in
the South, where it was fairly common by 1975. The name then
exploded in use all over the country, just as the similar
Southern surnames **Shirley** and **Beverly** had done in previous

decades. Remarkably, while Ashley was becoming successful for girls in the United States, it was becoming popular for boys in both Britain and Australia. In those countries, the spelling Ashley is considered masculine, but some girls are now being named **Ashleigh.**
Other spellings: **Ashlea, Ashlee, Ashleigh, Ashlie, Ashly**

Ashlie, Ashly (see Ashley)

Asia Name of the continent, from a Greek word meaning "east"; also, occasionally a form of **Aisha.**

Astra Greek "star."

Astrid Old Norse from *ass* [god] + *frithr* [beautiful]. This name was formerly very popular in Scandinavia.

Athena Greek "wise." In Greek mythology, Athena, the goddess of wisdom, was one of the most powerful deities. She was said to have sprung from the head of her father, Zeus. Many temples were founded in her honor, and Athens is named for her.
Famous names: Athina Onassis (heiress)
                Athene Seyler (actress)
Variations: **Athene, Athina, Thena**

Athene (see Athena)

Athina (see Athena)

Aubine (see Albina)

Aubrey French form of Old German *Albirich* from *alfi* [elf] + *ric* [ruler]. Aubrey was almost exclusively a male name and was especially popular in the American South, but since 1980, it has become a fashionable name for girls throughout the country.

Audie (see Audrey)

Audra Usually a form of **Audrey,** but also a popular Lithuanian name meaning "thunderstorm."

Audrey Old English *Aethelthryth,* "noble strength." St. Audrey (originally St. Ethelreda) was a seventh-century Anglo-Saxon saint who founded a monastery at Ely. Edda Hepburn van Heelmstra became the well-known actress Audrey Hepburn.
Other spellings: **Audrie, Audry, Audrye**

Variations: **Audie, Audra**

Audrie, Audry, Audrye (see **Audrey**)

Augusta Feminine form of Latin *August,* "venerable." Roman emperors took the title Augustus, and their female relatives were honored with the title Augusta. Both names were often used by royalty in Germany during the 16th and 17th centuries. In England, Augusta was popular during the 18th and 19th centuries because it was used by the reigning Hanover family. The wife of George IV was named Caroline Amelia Augusta, and their daughter was Charlotte Augusta.

Nicknames: **Gussie, Gusta**

Variations: **Aakusta** (Finnish), **Auguste** (German and Estonian), **Avgusta** (Russian)

Auguste (see **Augusta**)

Auli (see **Aurelia**)

Auno (see **Agnes**)

Aurelia Feminine form of Latin *Aurelius,* a Roman family name from *aureus,* "golden."

Variations: **Aranka** (Hungarian), **Auli** (Estonian), **Aurelie** (French), **Aurica** (Rumanian), **Aurilla, Oralie, Orelia**

Aurelie French form of **Aurelia.** This was the top name for girls born in France in the early 1980s.

Aurica (see **Aurelia**)

Aurilla (see **Aurelia**)

Aurora Latin "dawn."

Variations: **Aurore** (French), **Rora, Zora** (Slavic)

Aurore (see **Aurora**)

Autumn Latin *autumnus,* the season. This name seems to have been created in the early 20th century. Autumn is becoming more popular in the United States and was the 155th most common name given to American girls born in 1991.

Ava Possibly an Old German name of uncertain meaning, but more likely an American respelling of **Eva** to give the pronunciation

in English that the name has in other European languages.
Famous name: Ava Gardner (actress)

Aveline (see Evelyn)

Avgusta (see Augusta)

Avril (see April)

Ayesha (see Aisha)

Ayn (see Ain)

Aziza Swahili "precious."

Babbie (see **Barbara**)

Babette (see **Barbara, Elizabeth**)

Babs (see **Barbara**)

Bahati Swahili "luck."

Bailey For the original meanings of this name, see **Bailey** in the list of names for boys. Before the *WKRP in Cincinnati* character Bailey Quarters, played by Jan Smithers, appeared on television in the late 1970s, Bailey was a very rare name for girls and was used mostly in the South. Since then, the name has become increasingly fashionable for girls all over the United States.

Bairbre (see **Barbara**)

Barabal (see **Barbara**)

Barb (see **Barbara**)

Barbara Latin feminine form of Greek *barbaros*, "strange, foreign." St. Barbara was an early and possibly legendary Christian martyr whose devotion to her faith so enraged her father, Dioscurus, that he ordered her tortured. When she refused to renounce her religion despite her suffering, her father beheaded her, and he was struck by lightning and killed. St. Barbara became the patron saint invoked against thunder and lightning and the protectress of gunners and miners. The powder room on French ships was called *la Sainte Barbe.* Between 1915 and 1955, Barbara was an immensely popular name for American girls. Two of the seven women in the U.S. Senate in 1993, Mikulski of Maryland and Boxer of California, are named Barbara. Barbara's popularity has now faded, and it was only 211th on the list for girls born in 1991.

Famous names: Barbara Harris (Episcopal bishop)
Barbara Jordan (member of Congress)
Barbara Stanwyck (actress)
Barbra Streisand (singer and actress)
Barbara Walters (broadcast journalist)

Nicknames: **Babbie, Babs, Barb, Barbi, Barbie, Bobbi, Bobbie, Bobby, Bobette**

Other spelling: **Barbra**

Variations: **Babette** (French), **Bairbre** (Irish Gaelic), **Barabal** (Scots Gaelic), **Barbe** (French), **Barbel** (German), **Barbora** (Czech), **Barbro** (Swedish), **Barica** (Slovakian), **Baruska** (Czech), **Basia** (Polish), **Borbala** (Hungarian), **Varenka** (Russian), **Varu** (Estonian), **Varvara** (Russian), **Varya** (Russian)

Barbe, Barbel (see **Barbara**)

Barbi, Barbie (see **Barbara**)

Barbora (see **Barbara**)

Barbra (see **Barbara**)

Barbro (see **Barbara**)

Barica (see **Barbara**)

Baruska (see **Barbara**)

Basia (see **Barbara**)

Bathsheba Hebrew "daughter of the oath." In the Old Testament, Samuel tells the story of the courtship of Bathsheba and King David. After her husband was sent off to die in battle, she became David's wife.

Variation: **Sheba**

Bea (see **Beatrice**)

Beatrica (see **Beatrice**)

Beatrice Latin *Viatrix,* "voyager," later altered to resemble *Beatus,* "blessed." St. Beatrix, a young Christian martyr during the Roman Empire, was killed because she rescued the bodies of her slain brothers. The deaths of all three siblings can be blamed on the greed of a neighboring landowner, Lucretius, who used the excuse of their Christianity to abscond with their property. According to legend, he paid for his avarice when he died in agony from an unknown cause shortly after St. Beatrix's death. In literature, Beatrice guides Dante through Paradise in the *Divine Comedy.* The character was based on Beatrice Portinari, a young woman whom Dante met when he was nine or ten years old. Even though she died at age 24, Beatrice became Dante's symbol of the ideal woman. One of Shakespeare's most memorable female characters is the witty and energetic Beatrice in *Much Ado About Nothing.* The form **Beatrix** was used for several hundred years in England until about 1250, when it faded from popularity. In the 19th century, the name was revived when Queen Victoria named her youngest daughter Beatrice. Although the name is no longer popular, it may experience a revival now that Prince Andrew of England and the Duchess of York, the former Sarah Ferguson, have named a daughter Beatrice Elizabeth Mary.

Famous names: Beatrice Arthur (actress)
Beatrice Lillie (actress)

Nicknames: **Bea, Beattie, Bee, Trissie, Trix, Trixie, Trixy**

Variations: **Beatrica** (Bulgarian and Croatian), **Beatrisa** (Russian), **Beatrix** (German), **Beatriz** (Spanish), **Beatryks** (Polish), **Beitris** (Scots Gaelic), **Betrys** (Welsh), **Bice** (Italian), **Veatriks** (modern Greek), **Viatrix**

Beatrisa (see **Beatrice**)

Beatrix German form of **Beatrice.**

Famous names: Beatrix (queen of the Netherlands)
Beatrix Potter (writer)

Beatriz Spanish form of **Beatrice.** Although Beatrice is now only rarely given in the United States, Beatriz is still fairly common in the Hispanic-American community.

Beatryks (see **Beatrice**)

Beattie (see **Beatrice**)

Becca Form of **Rebecca**. Becca has recently been used more as an independent name, probably because of admiration for Becca Thatcher, a character on the television series *Life Goes On*, played by Kellie Martin.

Beckie (see **Becky, Rebecca**)

Becky Form of **Rebecca**. This nickname has been popular for many years. William Thackeray's heroine Rebecca Sharpe of *Vanity Fair* was known as Becky, and in the United States, Samuel Clemens, writing as Mark Twain, created the character Becky Thatcher for *Tom Sawyer*.
Other spellings: **Beckie, Bekki**

Bee (see **Beatrice**)

Beitris (see **Beatrice**)

Bekki (see **Becky, Rebecca**)

Bel (see **Belinda, Belle, Isabel**)

Belinda Origin unclear; perhaps from Old German *betlindis*, "dragonlike"; German *Berlinde* from *bero* [bear] + *linta* [linden wood shield]; or an Italian invention based on *bella*, "beautiful." Belinda's popularity began in the 17th century, partly because it was one of the pretty-sounding names that Restoration dramatists liked so much. In his famous 18th-century satire *The Rape of the Lock*, Alexander Pope probably chose the name specifically to mock the earlier plays as well as to poke fun at society's petty rules and concentration on trivial matters.
Famous names: Belinda Carlisle (singer)
                Belinda Montgomery (actress)
Nicknames: **Bel, Binnie, Linda**
Variations: **Bella, Berlinda, Velinda** (Hispanic)

Belita (see **Isabel**)

Bell (see **Belle, Isabel**)

Bella Latin and Italian *bella*, "beautiful"; also, a variation of **Isabel**.
Famous names: Bella Abzug (politician)
                Bella Davidovich (pianist)
Variations: **Belinda, Belle**

Belle French *belle,* "beautiful"; or form of **Isabel.** The name Belle got a great deal of positive publicity in 1991 when the Disney studios used it for the heroine of the animated film *Beauty and the Beast.* This may counteract its previous associations with Belle Starr, the notorious Western outlaw.

    Variations: **Bel, Bell, Bella**

Beonca, Beonka (see **Bianca**)

Berenice (see **Bernice**)

Berenika, Berenike (see **Bernice**)

Berit (see **Bridget**)

Berlinda (see **Belinda**)

Bernadette French feminine form of **Bernard,** Old German "brave as a bear." The bear was sacred in ancient Europe, and Bernard and its feminine versions, such as **Bernadine** and **Bernharda,** have been commonly used for centuries. A French version of the name, Bernadette, is currently the most popular, particularly because it was the name of a young girl who in 1858 saw visions of the Virgin Mary at a spring near Lourdes. People came there to watch her pray, and many claimed that they were cured by drinking water from the spring. Bernadette said that she was told to build a church at the site. In 1933, Bernadette Soubirois was canonized, although the church specifically recognized St. Bernadette for her faith, not her visions.

    Famous name: Bernadette Peters (actress)

    Nicknames: **Bernie, Berny**

    Variations: **Bernadine, Bernarda, Bernardette, Bernardina** (Italian), **Berneen** (Irish), **Bernetta, Bernharda** (German and Norwegian), **Bernita, Vernarda** (modern Greek)

Bernadine (see **Bernadette**)

Bernarda (see **Bernadette**)

Bernardette (see **Bernadette**)

Bernardina (see **Bernadette**)

Berneen (see **Bernadette**)

Bernetta (see **Bernadette**)

Bernharda (see **Bernadette**)

Bernice Ancient Macedonian form of Greek *Pherenike,* "bringer of victory," from *pheros* [bringer] and *nike* [victory]. This is a form of the ancient name **Berenice,** which was used widely in the Greek and Roman empires. In Egypt, many of the wives and daughters of the ruling Macedonian kings had this name. It is an uncommon name today, although it was somewhat popular in the early part of the 20th century.

Nicknames: **Bernie, Berny**

Other spelling: **Berenice**

Variations: **Berenika** (Czech), **Berenike** (German), **Bernike** (Latvian), **Veronica**

Bernie, Berny (see **Bernadette, Bernice**)

Bernike (see **Bernice**)

Bernita (see **Bernadette**)

Berta (see **Alberta, Bertha**)

Bertha Old German *berhta,* "bright." Berchta, the name of a Teutonic goddess, was the original form of this name. Her celebration day was January 6, now Epiphany, and girls born on that date traditionally were named for her. The mother of Charlemagne was named Berchta. St. Bertha has an obscure history; she built three churches, but little else is known about her. Bertha was very popular in the late 19th century, being one of many medieval names that the Victorians revived. It is very unusual today because of its association with Big Bertha, a powerful German gun used to shell France in World War I. The cannon was named in honor of industrialist Bertha Krupp, owner of the Krupp manufacturing concern where the guns were made.

Famous name: Bertha Harris (novelist)

Nicknames: **Berti, Bertie, Berty, Birdie, Birdy**

Variations: **Berta** (German, Italian, Slavic, and Spanish), **Berthe** (French), **Bertina** (German)

Berthe (see **Bertha**)

Berti, Bertie, Berty (see **Alberta, Bertha**)

Bertina (see **Bertha**)

Beryl Greek *beryllos,* a semiprecious stone. Like other jewel names, this one was popular in the late 19th century, especially in England, but it is rarely used today.
Famous name: Beryl Markham (aviatrix)

Bess (see **Elizabeth**)

Besse, Bessie, Bessy Form of **Elizabeth.**
Famous name: Bessie Smith (singer)

Bet (see **Beth, Elizabeth**)

Beta Greek; also, a variation of **Elizabeth.** This name is the second letter in the Greek alphabet.

Beth Form of **Elizabeth;** also, Hebrew *Bethia,* "daughter of the Lord." The Scots are primarily responsible for the popularity of this name, perhaps because of its connection with the Celtic word *beath,* "life." Usually it is a nickname for Elizabeth, although it is often used as a middle name.
Famous name: Beth Henley (playwright)
Variation: **Bet**

Bethany Biblical name of a village near Jerusalem that Jesus visited more than once. The meaning of the place name is disputed; "house of figs" and "house of poverty" have been suggested. Bethany was the home of Mary and Martha, the sisters in the famous biblical episode where Martha complains that she is doing all the housework while Mary listens to Jesus; Jesus tells Martha that she is "distracted by many things" and that "Mary has chosen the better part." In England, Bethany is a rare name that is mostly used by Roman Catholics in honor of Mary of Bethany. In the United States, however, Bethany has probably been most often chosen by evangelical Protestant parents. The name is now becoming generally popular in America, probably because it's similar in sound to **Brittany.** Bethany was 92nd on the list of names given American girls born in 1991 and rising.

Betrys (see **Beatrice**)

Bets (see **Betsy, Elizabeth**)

Betsey, Betsie (see **Betsy**)

Betsy Form of **Elizabeth**. This name is associated with Betsy Ross, who is said to have made the first American flag at the request of George Washington.
Other spellings: **Betsey, Betsie**
Variation: **Bets**

Betta (see **Elizabeth**)

Bette French form of **Elizabeth**. The final "e" is silent in the pronunciation of this French name, but many Americans use this form as another spelling of **Betty.**
Famous names: Bette Davis (actress)
Bette Midler (actress)

Bettina German variation of **Elizabeth** or Italian feminine form of **Benedict.**

Betty Form of **Elizabeth**. This popular nickname has often been used as a given name, particularly in the 1940s because of the fame of two American actresses, Betty Grable and Betty Hutton.
Famous name: Betty Friedan (writer)
Variation: **Bette**

Beula (see **Beulah**)

Beulah Hebrew "married." This name was used as a poetic name for the land of Israel in the Bible. Beulah came into regular use as an American name in the late 19th century after Augusta Evans Wilson published her best-selling novel *Beulah.* Since 1920, however, the name has again been very rare.
Other spelling: **Beula**

Bev (see **Beverley**)

Beverlee, Beverley (see **Beverly**)

Beverly Old English *Beferlic,* "beaver stream." This is an aristocratic English surname that was sometimes used as a masculine name in the 19th century. Its use as a feminine name in the United States dates from around 1900. Beverly was among the top 50 names for girls born in the United States between 1920 and 1955. The name's popularity has since faded.

It was adopted by soprano Beverly Sills, whose original name was Belle Silverman.

Famous names: Beverly Cleary (children's writer)
Beverly D'Angelo (actress)
Beverly Garland (actress)

Nickname: **Bev**

Other spellings: **Beverlee, Beverley**

Bianca Italian form of **Blanche.** Shakespeare named characters Bianca in both *The Taming of the Shrew* and *Othello.* Although the original meaning of this name is "white," since the 1980s, it has been particularly popular in the African-American community. Bianca was the 29th most common name given to nonwhite girls born in the United States in 1991.

Variations: **Beonca, Beonka, Bianka, Vianca**

Bianka (see **Bianca**)

Bibi Swedish form of **Vivian.**

Famous name: Bibi Andersson (actress)

Bice (see **Beatrice**)

Biddie, Biddy (see **Bridget**)

Billie Feminine form of **Billy** or form of **Wilhemina.** This name probably started out as a boy's nickname, but it is now a name for girls that is more popular in the southern part of the United States than in other parts of the country. It is often found in combinations such as Billie Jean or Billie Jo.

Famous names: Billie Holiday (singer)
Billie Jean King (tennis player)

Variation: **Billy**

Billy (see **Billie, Wilhelmina**)

Bina (see **Sabina**)

Binnie (see **Belinda**)

Birdie, Birdy (see **Alberta, Bertha**)

Birgit (see **Bridget**)

Birgitta (see **Bridget**)

Birte (see **Bridget**)

Birunji Luganda (Uganda) "pretty, perfect."

Blair Celtic "plains." Like **Ashley** and **Beverly,** this name was almost exclusively masculine until the 20th century. Today, it is an increasingly popular name for girls and is disappearing as a name for boys. Blair Warner, a character on the long-running 1980s television series *The Facts of Life* played by Lisa Whelchel, helped to give the name a "preppy" image.
Famous name: Blair Brown (actress)

Blanca (see **Blanche**)

Blanch (see **Blanche**)

Blanche Old French "white." The 12th-century French queen Blanche of Castile is the first historic reference to this name; it also appears among members of the House of Lancaster in Britain. The most famous Blanche in literature is Blanche DuBois in Tennessee Williams's *A Streetcar Named Desire.* The creators of the television sitcom *The Golden Girls* must have had her in mind when they named a character in their series Blanche Devereaux.
Famous name: Blanche Yurka (actress)
Other spelling: **Blanch**
Variations: **Bianca** (Italian), **Blanca** (Spanish), **Blanka** (Polish and Czech), **Bljanka** (Russian and Ukrainian)

Blanka (see **Blanche**)

Bliss Old English *bliths,* "supreme happiness."
Other spelling: **Blisse**

Blisse (see **Bliss**)

Blithe (see **Blythe**)

Bljanka (see **Blanche**)

Blossom Old English *blosma,* "flower of a plant." This is a very rare name, and it's too soon to tell if the popularity of the television series *Blossom,* where Mayim Bialik plays the teenage title character, will lead to increased use of this name.
Famous name: Blossom Rock (actress)

Blythe Old English "blithe, joyous, carefree." Recent use of this
name may be connected to its cheerful meaning.
Famous name: Blythe Danner (actress)
Other spelling: **Blithe**

Bobbi (see **Barbara, Bobbie, Roberta**)

Bobbie Feminine form of **Bobby**; variation of **Barbara** and **Roberta**.
This former nickname is now given fairly often as an
independent name to girls.
Famous names: Bobbie Gentry (singer)
Bobbie Ann Mason (writer)
Other spellings: **Bobbi, Bobby**

Bobby (see **Barbara, Bobbie, Roberta**)

Bobette (see **Barbara**)

Bonita Feminine form of Spanish *bonito,* "pretty." This name, an
American creation, is not found in Spanish-speaking countries.
Nickname: **Bonnie**

Bonni (see **Bonnie**)

Bonnie Use of this name probably stems from the Scottish word
bonnie, which means beautiful with a connotation of goodness.
According to an old ballad, "The child who is born on the
Sabbath day is blithe and bonnie and good and gay." Bonnie
was a popular name in the United States between 1940 and
1967, but it began to lose popularity after the film *Bonnie and
Clyde* associated it with the notorious outlaw Bonnie Parker,
who robbed a number of banks in the 1930s.
Famous names: Bonnie Blair (speed skater)
Bonnie Franklin (actress)
Bonnie Raitt (singer)
Other spellings: **Bonni, Bonny**
Variation: **Bonita** (Spanish)

Bonny (see **Bonnie**)

Borbala (see **Barbara**)

Brandi, Brandy Origin uncertain; perhaps a feminine form of
Brandon or from Dutch *brandewijn,* "burnt wine," the name of
the alcoholic beverage. Brandy was very popular in the United

States in the early 1980s, but its use is now beginning to fall off.
Famous name: Brandy Johnson (gymnast)

Breanna, Breanne (see **Briana**)

Bree (see **Bridget**)

Bregetta (see **Bridget**)

Brenda Feminine form of Old Norse *Brandr,* "sword"; also, a
feminine form of **Brendan.** This name was very popular in the
1940s. It is connected with the title character of the long-
running cartoon strip *Brenda Starr.*
Famous names: Brenda Lee (singer)
Brenda Maddox (biographer)
Brenda Vaccaro (actress)

Briana, Brianna Feminine form of Celtic **Brian,** "high, noble."
Until recently this name was quite unusual, but it is suddenly
becoming quite popular. There is disagreement at the moment
as to whether the first syllable of Brianna should rhyme with
"fry" or "free."
Variations: **Breanna, Breanne, Brianne, Bryanna**

Brianne (see **Briana**)

Brid (see **Bridget**)

Bride (see **Bridget**)

Bridget Celtic *Brigenti,* "the high one." This name was extremely
popular in Ireland for hundreds of years, although it is finally
going out of fashion there. It is the name of the goddess of
wisdom in Irish mythology and is associated with the female
patron saint of Ireland, St. Bridget, who is also called St. Brigid
and St. Bride. St. Bridget, the sixth-century daughter of a
Druid who was converted to Christianity by a nephew of St.
Patrick, lived beneath an oak tree and devoted her life to
charitable deeds. In Scandinavia, the name's popularity is
based on the fame of St. Birgitta, the patron saint of Sweden.
She was descended from the Gothic kings, according to legend,
and she and her husband, Ulpho, a Swedish prince, withdrew
from their court and devoted themselves to pious lives. In the
United States, the name is still most commonly given to girls
with Irish ancestry.
Famous name: Bridget Fonda (actress)

Nicknames: **Biddie, Biddy, Bree, Bridie, Brie** (Irish)

Other spellings: **Bridgett, Bridgette**

Variations: **Berit** (Scandinavian), **Birgit** (Scandinavian), **Birgitta** (Swedish), **Birte** (Danish), **Bregetta** (Dutch), **Brid** (Irish Gaelic), **Bride** (Irish), **Brighid** (Gaelic), **Brigid** (Irish), **Brigida** (Italian, Portuguese, Russian, and Spanish), **Brigita** (Czech, Latvian, Lithuanian, and Croatian), **Brigitta** (Estonian), **Brigitte** (French), **Brita** (Swedish), **Britt** (Swedish), **Britta, Brygida** (Polish and Ukrainian), **Gitta** (German and Hungarian), **Pirkko** (Finnish), **Vrijida** (modern Greek)

Bridgett, Bridgette (see **Bridget**)

Bridie (see **Bridget**)

Brie (see **Bridget**)

Brighid, Brigid (see **Bridget**)

Brigida (see **Bridget**)

Brigita, Brigitta (see **Bridget**)

Brigitte French form of **Bridget**.
Famous name: Brigitte Bardot (actress)

Brita (see **Bridget**)

Britanee, Britani, Britany (see **Brittany**)

Britney, Britni, Britny (see **Brittany**)

Britt Swedish form of **Bridget**. The fame of Swedish actress Britt Ekland may have helped create the fashion for **Brittany** in the United States.

Britta (see **Bridget, Brittany**)

Brittani, Brittanie (see **Brittany**)

Brittany French *Bretagne,* a region of France settled by Celtic refugees from Britain. The idea of turning this place name into a first name is purely American. It appeared rarely in the late 1960s and then exploded in popularity during the 1980s. By 1989, Brittany was in a close race with **Ashley** for the top spot on the list of names given American girls. It's possible that some parents saw Brittany as the full form of **Britt,** not realizing that Britt was a Swedish form of Bridget. The popularity of other names for girls ending in "-any" and "-anie," combined with the fashion for similar names for boys such as **Brent** and **Brett,** also helped to spur the use of this name.

Other spellings: **Britanee, Britani, Britany, Britney, Britni, Britny, Brittani, Brittanie, Brittney, Brittni, Brittnie**

Variations: **Britt, Britta, Brittin, Britton**

Brittin, Britton (see **Brittany**)

Brittney, Brittni, Brittnie (see **Brittany**)

Brook (see **Brooke**)

Brooke Old English "brook, stream." The fame of the New York socialite and philanthropist Brooke Astor (born Roberta Brooke Russell) is probably what originally turned this formerly masculine name into an increasingly popular name for girls. The name's connotations of wealth and beauty have since been greatly reinforced by the image of actress Brooke Shields.

Famous name: Brooke Adams (actress)

Variation: **Brook**

Bryanna (see **Briana**)

Brygida (see **Bridget**)

Caci (see **Casey**)

Cacilia (see **Cecilia**)

Cairistiona (see **Christina**)

Caitlin Irish Gaelic form of *Cateline,* an Old French form of
Katherine brought to Ireland by the Normans. Caitlin is really
just the Gaelic spelling of **Kathleen,** but Americans unfamiliar
with Gaelic who saw the name written out naturally began
pronouncing it as if it were a combination of Kate and Lynn.
After **Katie** became the most popular nickname for Katherine
in the 1970s, parents of Irish descent in the eastern United
States enthusiastically began to name their daughters Caitlin.
The name spread quickly and became very popular throughout
the country in the 1980s. By 1991, Caitlin was the eighth most
popular name given to American girls.
Famous name: Caitlin Thomas (writer)
Other spellings: **Caitlyn, Caitlynn, Kaitlin, Kaitlyn, Kaitlynn,
Katelin, Katelyn, Katelynn**

Caitlyn, Caitlynn (see **Caitlin**)

Caitriona (see **Katherine**)

Camila (see **Camilla**)

Camilla Possibly Etruscan through Latin *camillus,* "acolyte" or
"young ceremonial attendant." In Roman mythology, Camilla
was an attendant to the goddess Diana. In England, the name
was used during the 18th century, when the classics were
revered. The name has always been popular in Italy.

Nicknames: **Cami, Cammie, Cammy, Kami, Millie, Milly**

Variations: **Camila** (Spanish), **Camille** (French), **Kamila** (Polish and Czech), **Kamilla** (German, Hungarian, and Latvian)

Cami (see **Camilla**)

Camille French form of **Camilla**. Camille has always been much more popular in the United States than Camilla, perhaps because of Greta Garbo's role in the 1936 movie *Camille*. Its unfortunate contemporary connotation is Hurricane Camille, one of the most powerful storms to strike the United States mainland. Because of the destruction caused in 1969, Camille was officially retired from the list of hurricane names.

Cammie, Cammy (see **Camilla**)

Candace A title of the queens of ancient Ethiopia of uncertain meaning. In the 19th century, this name was often pronounced "can-DAY-suh"; but in the 20th century, "CAN-diss" has become the popular version and has led to many alternative spellings. The name has been fairly common since the 1950s and was especially popular with African-Americans in the 1980s.

Famous names: Candace Stevenson (poet)

Nicknames: **Candee, Candi, Candie, Candy, Dace, Dacey, Kandi, Kandie, Kandy**

Other spellings: **Candice, Candis, Kandace, Kandice, Kandis**

Candee, Candi, Candie (see **Candace, Candida**)

Candice Modern form of **Candace**, now as common as the original spelling.

Famous name: Candice Bergen (actress)

Candida Late Latin *canditia*, "whiteness." English teachers are likely to identify this rare name with George Bernard Shaw's play *Candida*, but other Americans are more likely to remember the song made popular by Tony Orlando and Dawn in the late 1960s.

Variations: **Candee, Candi, Candie, Candy, Kandi, Kandie, Kandida** (Norwegian), **Kandy**

Candis (see **Candace**)

Candy Form of **Candace** and **Candida;** also, Sanskrit "sugar candy."

Cara (see **Kara**)

Carel (see **Carol**)

Caren (see **Karen**)

Carey (see **Carrie**)

Cari (see **Carrie**)

Carin (see **Karen**)

Carina (see **Karina**)

Carisa (see **Carissa**)

Carissa Latin form of Greek *charis,* "grace," or Italian "dear little one." Because Carissa blends the sounds of the fashionable names **Carrie** and **Melissa,** it has recently become fairly common in the United States.
Variations: **Carisa, Charissa, Karisa, Karissa**

Carla Feminine form of **Carlo,** Italian form of **Charles;** or form of German **Karla.** This name now brings to mind Carla Tortelli, the caustic waitress played by Rhea Perlman in the long-running television sitcom *Cheers.*
Variations: **Carlene, Carline, Carly, Karla, Karlene, Karline**

Carlene (see **Carla**)

Carlee, Carley, Carlie (see **Carly**)

Carline (see **Carla, Caroline**)

Carlota (see **Charlotte**)

Carlotta (see **Charlotte**)

Carly Modern form of **Carla.** This name is steadily becoming more popular, rising from 91st to 64th on the list of names given American girls between 1989 and 1991.
Famous name: Carly Simon (singer)
Other spellings: **Carlee, Carley, Carlie, Karlee, Karlie, Karly**

Carma Sanskrit "destiny"; also, a variation of **Carmel.**

Variation: **Karma**

Carmel Hebrew "the garden." In the 12th century, the order of the Carmelite nuns was founded on Mount Carmel in Israel. In the United States, the name is usually associated with the beautiful village of Carmel on the Monterey peninsula in California.

Nicknames: **Carma, Carmie, Lita**

Variations: **Carmela** (Italian), **Carmelina, Carmelita** (Spanish), **Carmen** (Spanish), **Karmel, Karmela** (Polish), **Melina**

Carmela (see **Carmel**)

Carmelina (see **Carmel**)

Carmelita (see **Carmel**)

Carmen Spanish form of **Carmel** modified in medieval times to resemble Latin *carmen*, "song." Carmen has recently been popular not only with Hispanic-Americans but also in the African-American community. Many adults will think of the famous opera *Carmen* by Bizet when they hear this name, but children in the 1990s will associate Carmen with the computer and television geography game *Where in the World Is Carmen Sandiego?*, where the title character is the beautiful ringleader of a gang of international thieves.

Famous name: Carmen Miranda (entertainer)

Variations: **Carmencita** (Spanish), **Carmina, Carmine, Carmita**

Carmencita (see **Carmen**)

Carmie (see **Carmel**)

Carmina (see **Carmen**)

Carmine (see **Carmen**)

Carmita (see **Carmen**)

Caro (see **Caroline**)

Carol A shortened form of **Caroline**, also associated with French "song." Carol first appeared as an independent name in the late 19th century. Carol was a top ten name for American girls born in the 1930s and 1940s, but it is now falling out of fashion and was only the 320th most popular name for girls born in 1991.

Famous names: Carol Burnett (actress)
　　　　　　　Carol Kane (actress)
Other spellings: **Carel, Carole, Carroll, Caryl, Karel, Karole**
Variation: **Carola** (Latin)

Carola This feminine form of *Carolus,* the Latin form of **Charles,** has always been very rare itself, but it is the base from which **Carol, Carolina,** and **Caroline,** were created.

Carole Variation of **Carol.**
Famous name: Carole King (singer)

Carolina Italian and Spanish form of **Caroline.**
Famous name: Carolina Herrera (fashion designer)

Caroline French and English form of **Carolina,** an Italian derivative of **Carola.** This name has Italian origins, but it began appearing frequently in 18th-century England after Caroline of Anspach married George II and was crowned queen in 1727. Caroline of Brunswick married that queen's great-grandson; she was abandoned by her husband, later George IV, and founded a new order of knighthood, the Order of St. Caroline. In literature, the name was favored by George Gordon, Lord Byron, who addressed three poems to Caroline. Today, the name retains its association with royalty through Princess Caroline of Monaco.
Famous names: Caroline Herschel (astronomer)
　　　　　　　Caroline Kennedy Schlossberg (lawyer)
Nicknames: **Caro, Carol, Carrie, Carry, Lina, Line**
Variations: **Carline, Carolina** (Spanish, Portuguese, and Italian), **Carola, Carolyn, Kara, Karolina** (Polish and Russian), **Karoline** (German)

Carolyn Variation of **Caroline.**
Famous name: Carolyn Waldo (swimmer)

Carrie, Carry Form of **Caroline.** Carrie first appeared as an independent name in the 19th century and was very popular in the United States. It was one of the top 50 names between 1875 and 1900. After falling from favor, it enjoyed a revival in the 1970s and 1980s.
Famous names: Carrie Fisher (actress)
　　　　　　　Carry Nation (temperance leader)

Other spellings: **Carey, Cari, Cary**

Carroll Variation of **Carol.**

Famous name: Carroll Baker (actress)

Cary (see **Carrie**)

Caryl (see **Carol**)

Casey, Casie From Gaelic *Cathasach,* "watchful." This traditionally male name is currently becoming quite fashionable for girls in the United States. Casey was 53rd on the popularity list for American girls born in 1991.

Variations: **Caci, Kaci, Kacie, Kasey**

Cass (see **Cassandra**)

Cassandra Greek, uncertain meaning. Cassandra was the unfortunate daughter of Priam and Hecuba, the king and queen of Troy. The god Apollo was attracted to her, and she agreed to a liaison in exchange for the gift of prophecy. When she spurned him, he sought revenge by making sure that his gift would be useless; he caused her to be believed by no one. Cassandra foresaw the fall of Troy but could do nothing to prevent it. This name is more popular now than it has ever been. It was especially popular with African-Americans in the 1970s but had also been taken up by other ethnic groups by 1990.

Nicknames: **Cass, Cassie, Sandi, Sandra, Sandy**

Variations: **Cassandre** (French), **Kassandra** (Greek)

Cassandre (see **Cassandra**)

Cassie Form of **Cassandra.** Cassie is now frequently being given as an independent name in the United States.

Cat (see **Catherine**)

Catalina, Catarina (see **Katherine**)

Caterina (see **Katherine**)

Cath (see **Catherine**)

Catharina (see **Katherine**)

Catharine (see **Catherine**)

Catherine French form of **Katherine;** between 1700 and 1950, this was the most common spelling in the United States. In England, Catherine was overtaken by **Katharine** in 1985. St. Catherine of Siena was a 14th-century saint who campaigned for the pope's return to Rome from Avignon and resurgence of a devout life for all Christians. There are at least three other saints with the name: St. Catherine dei Ricci, St. Catherine of Genoa, and St. Catherine of Bologna. The name also has an impressive royal lineage in France and Russia. The wife of Henry II of France, Catherine di Medici, vigorously persecuted the Huguenots. Catherine II, empress of Russia, was the wife of Peter III. She became known as Catherine the Great and is famous both for her decadent personal life and her long and impressive reign. Today, Catherine is the name of many prominent actresses, including Catherine Bach, Catherine Deneuve, Catherine Hicks, Catherine Oxenberg, and Catherine Spaak.
Nicknames: **Cat, Cath, Cathie, Cathy, Catie**
Other spellings: **Catharine, Cathryn, Katharine, Kathryn**

Cathie (see **Catherine**)

Cathleen (see **Kathleen**)

Cathryn (see **Catherine**)

Cathy (see **Catherine**)

Catie (see **Catherine**)

Catrin (see **Katherine**)

Catrina (see **Katherine**)

Catriona (see **Katherine**)

Cecca (see **Frances**)

Cecelia (see **Cecilia**)

Cecile (see **Cecilia**)

Cecilia Feminine form of **Cecil,** Latin *caecus,* "blind." St. Cecilia was a third-century Christian who converted her husband and brother and was martyred for her faith. She's the patron saint of music and has often been celebrated in song and poetry. Chaucer tells her story in *The Canterbury Tales,* while William Wordsworth, Alexander Pope, and John Dryden wrote poems in honor of her and in celebration of music.

Nicknames: **Cele, Celie, Cissie, Cissy, Sissie, Sissy**

Other spelling: **Cecelia**

Variations: **Cacilia** (German), **Cecile** (French), **Cecilie, Cecily, Cecylia** (Polish), **Celia, Cicelle** (Hungarian), **Cicely, Kikilia** (Russian), **Sheila, Sidsel** (Danish), **Sile** (Irish), **Sileas** (Scots Gaelic), **Sissel** (Norwegian)

Cecilie, Cecily (see **Cecilia**)

Cecylia (see **Cecilia**)

Cele (see **Cecilia**)

Celena (see **Selena**)

Celesta (see **Celeste**)

Celeste Latin *caelestis,* "heavenly." This name is regularly but infrequently used and might be a good choice for parents looking for a slightly unusual name with celestial connotations.

Famous name: Celeste Holm (actress)

Variations: **Celesta, Celestina, Celestine**

Celestina (see **Celeste**)

Celestine (see **Celeste**)

Celia Latin *Caelia,* perhaps from *caelum,* "heaven"; also, a form of **Cecilia**.

Variations: **Celie, Celina** (Polish), **Celine** (French), **Zelia**

Celie (see **Cecilia, Celia**)

Celina (see **Celia, Selena**)

Celine (see **Celia**)

Chanel French *chenal,* "canal." This French surname has become a fashionable first name for girls in honor of Gabrielle "Coco" Chanel, the famous Parisian fashion designer for whom Chanel No. 5 perfume was named.

Chantal Old French *cantal,* "stone," a place name that became a first

name for girls in honor of St. Jeanne de Chantal, a widowed
baroness who founded the Visitation Order of nuns in 1610.

Famous name: Chantal (Hollywood entertainment reporter)

Variations: **Chantel, Shantal**

Chantel American variation of **Chantal.** This name seems to have
been created for the Chantels, a 1950s female rock group. The
French word *chanteur,* "singer," may have influenced their
choice of a name. Chantel has been much more successful as a
first name in the United States than Chantal. In 1991, Chantel
was the 149th most popular American name for girls.

Other spellings: **Chantell, Chantelle, Shantel, Shantell,
Shantelle, Shontel, Shontell, Shontelle**

Chantell, Chantelle (see **Chantel**)

Charissa (see **Carissa**)

Charlaine (see **Charlene**)

Charleen (see **Charlene**)

Charlene Modern feminine form of **Charles,** Old German "a man."
Most bearers of this name pronounce it with the "Sh-" sound
as in Charlotte, but some Southerners prefer the "Ch-" sound
of Charles.

Famous name: Charlene Tilton (actress)

Other spellings: **Charleen, Charline**

Variations: **Charlaine, Charli, Charlie, Charlotte, Sharleen,
Sharlene, Sharline**

Charli, Charlie (see **Charlene, Charlotte**)

Charline (see **Charlene**)

Charlot (see **Charlotte**)

Charlotta (see **Charlotte**)

Charlotte Feminine form of **Charles.** Charlotte was probably
invented in the Savoy region of the French Alps and spread
from there to the rest of Western Europe after Princess
Charlotte of Savoy wed King Louis XI of France in the 15th
century. It is likely that it preceded **Caroline,** another feminine
form of Charles, but Charlotte has not been as popular with
royalty as Caroline. Charlotte Corday was the French

revolutionary who stabbed Marat to death. She died on the guillotine.

Famous names: Charlotte Bronte (writer)
Charlotte Rampling (actress)

Nicknames: **Charli, Charlie, Lotta, Lotti, Lottie, Lotty**

Other spelling: **Charlot**

Variations: **Carlota** (Spanish, Portuguese, and Rumanian), **Carlotta** (Italian), **Charlene, Charlotta** (Finnish), **Karlotta, Searlait** (Irish Gaelic)

Charyl (see **Cheryl**)

Chelsea English place name, "landing place for chalk," now a neighborhood of greater London. The idea of using Chelsea as a name for girls seems to have begun in Australia. American use of the name may have been influenced by the character played by actress Jane Fonda in the movie *On Golden Pond*. Chelsea boomed in popularity during the late 1980s; by 1991, it was the 14th most common name given to American girls, and this was before Chelsea Clinton was known outside of Arkansas. Her parents have said that she was named after the London district, where they spent many romantic times.

Other spellings: **Chelsey, Chelsi, Chelsie**

Chelsey, Chelsi, Chelsie (see **Chelsea**)

Cher Variation of **Cherie, Cherilyn,** or **Cheryl.** The actress Cher created her name from her given name, Cherilyn.

Chere, Cheri (see **Cherie**)

Cherie French *chere,* "cherished, beloved."
Variations: **Cher, Chere, Cheri, Cheryl**

Cherilyn Modern blend of **Cheryl** and **Carolyn.**
Nickname: **Cher**

Cherry Greek *kerasion,* "cherry tree or fruit", or a nickname for Cheryl. Names from plants and flowers, such as **Blossom, Fern,** Pansy, Poppy, and **Viola,** were popular at the beginning of the 20th century, and Cherry seems to fall into this category.

Cheryl The origin of this name is obscure, but it was probably created around 1900 as a blend of **Cherry** or **Cherie** with the gem name **Beryl.** Cheryl was extremely fashionable between 1940 and 1970, but it has been steadily going out of style since and is no longer even among the top 300 names given to American girls.

Famous names: Cheryl Ladd (actress)
Cheryl Wheeler (musician)

Nicknames: **Cher, Cherie, Cherry, Sherry**

Other spellings: **Charyle, Cheryll, Sharyl, Sherryl, Sheryl, Sheryll**

Cheryll (see **Cheryl**)

Cheyanne (see **Cheyenne**)

Cheyenne Name of an American Indian nation, of unknown meaning. The Cheyenne nation originally lived in Minnesota and the Dakotas, but now is divided between reservations in Montana and Oklahoma. The initial use of Cheyenne as a first name seems to have been for the television character Cheyenne Bodie, played by Clint Walker, who was featured in a Western series called *Cheyenne* that ran from 1955 through 1963. Despite his masculine image, when those who had watched the program as children grew up, they named many more daughters than sons Cheyenne. This is probably because the name sounds like "shy Anne" and is accented on the second syllable, which for most Americans implies femininity. In the early 1990s, Cheyenne rapidly became quite fashionable, rising from 318th to 126th in popularity for girls between 1989 and 1991.

Other spellings: **Cheyanne, Shianne, Shyann, Shyanne**

Chiara (see **Clara, Kiara**)

Chinue Ibo (Nigeria) "God's own blessing."

Chloe Greek *kloe,* "green, young plant." Chloe is becoming trendy with sophisticated young parents. It rose from 307th to 175th on the American popularity list for girls between 1989 and 1991.

Famous name: Chloe Webb (actress)

Chris Form of **Christina** or **Christine.**

Famous name: Chris Evert (tennis player)

Other spellings: **Cris, Kris**

Chrissie, Chrissy (see **Christina**)

Christa Variation of **Christina**.
Famous name: Christa McAuliffe (teacher and astronaut)

Christal (see **Crystal**)

Christie Variation of **Christina**.
Famous name: Christie Brinkley (fashion model)
Other spellings: **Christy, Kristi, Kristie, Kristy**

Christin (see **Kristen**)

Christina Feminine form of **Christian**. The third-century martyr St. Christina reportedly was shot to death with arrows after angels helped her survive drowning. In literature, the first character with this name was the wife of Christian in John Bunyan's *Pilgrim's Progress*. The 18th-century Scot Robert Burns addressed poems to Cristina. The name is exceedingly popular in the United States and Europe and has spun off many variations.
Famous name: Christina Rossetti (poet)
Nicknames: **Chris, Chrissie, Chrissy, Christie, Crissie, Crissy, Kirstie** (Scottish), **Kirsty, Kris, Kristy, Tina**
Variations: **Cairistiona** (Scots Gaelic), **Christa, Christine** (French), **Chrystyna** (Ukrainian), **Cristina** (Spanish, Italian, and Portuguese), **Kerstin** (Swedish), **Kirsten** (Danish), **Kirstin** (Scottish), **Krista** (German, Czech, and Estonian), **Kristen, Kristin** (Norwegian), **Kristina** (Czech, Swedish, and Lithuanian), **Kristine** (Latvian), **Krisztina** (Hungarian), **Krystyna** (Polish), **Stina** (Swedish and Norwegian)

Christine French form of **Christina**. Christine was a favorite name with American parents between 1945 and 1975, but in the 1980s, Christina once again became the most popular feminine form of **Christian**.
Famous name: Christine Kaufmann (actress)
Nickname: **Chris**
Other spelling: **Kristine**

Christy (see **Christie**)

Chrystal (see **Crystal**)

Chrystyna (see **Christina**)

Cicelle (see **Cecilia**)

Cicely Variation of **Cecilia.**
    Famous name: Cicely Tyson (actress)

Cilla (see **Priscilla**)

Cinda (see **Cindy, Lucinda**)

Cindi, Cindie (see **Cindy, Cynthia, Lucinda**)

Cindy Form of **Cynthia** or **Lucinda;** also, French *cendre,* "ashes,"
    with reference to Cinderella.
    Famous names: Cindy Crawford (fashion model)
                Cindy Pickett (actress)
    Other spellings: **Cinda, Cindi, Cindie, Cyndi, Cyndie, Cyndy,**
              Sindy

Cinthia, Cintia, Cinzia (see **Cynthia**)

Cissie, Cissy (see **Cecilia**)

Claartje (see **Clara**)

Clair, Claire French form of **Clara.** This was the top name for girls
    born in England in the late 1970s, and it is now the most
    popular variation of Clara in the United States. However,
    despite the television character Clair Huxtable on *The Cosby
    Show,* played by Phylicia Rashad, African-American parents
    are much less likely to give this name to their daughters than
    are Americans from other ethnic backgrounds.
    Famous names: Claire Bloom (actress)
                Claire Moore (artist)
    Other spelling: **Clare**

Clara From the Latin *clarus,* "bright, clear, famous." Although it
    may have older forms, this name appears to date to the 13th-
    century saint who founded an order of nuns who emulated the
    Franciscan brothers. Clara was popular among the Victorians,
    but it has not been a popular name in the 20th century.
    Famous name: Clara Barton (founder of the American Red
               Cross)
    Variations: **Chiara** (Italian), **Claartje** (Dutch), **Clair, Claire**

(French), **Clare** (English), **Clarina** (Dutch), **Clarinda, Clarine** (German), **Clarita, Clary, Klara** (Slavic, Germanic, and Baltic), **Klare** (Danish)

Clare This original English form of **Clara** was popular in medieval times, but today is mainly thought of as an alternative spelling for **Claire.**

Famous name: Clare Boothe Luce (playwright and politician)

Claribel A blend of **Clara** and **Belle,** first featured in "Claribel," a poem by Alfred, Lord Tennyson. The name is better known to baby boomers through the clown Clarabell on the 1950s children's television show *Howdy Doody.*

Clarice French form of Latin *Claritia,* "fame."

Variations: **Clarisa** (Spanish), **Clarissa** (English)

Clarina (see **Clara**)

Clarinda Variation of **Clara** created in 1596 by English poet Edmund Spenser for a character in his poem *The Faerie Queene.* Clarinda was a popular name in Restoration comedies.

Clarine (see **Clara**)

Clarisa (see **Clarice**)

Clarissa English form of **Clarice.** Clarissa is the title character of Samuel Richardson's popular 17th-century novel. The name occurs regularly in the United States.

Other spelling: **Klarissa**

Clarita (see **Clara**)

Clary (see **Clara**)

Claudette French form of **Claudia.**

Famous name: Claudette Colbert (actress)

Claudia Feminine form of *Claudus,* Latin "lame." This is a very old name, dating in Britain to the first century. Today, it is fairly popular in the Hispanic-American community.

Famous name: Claudia Cardinale (actress)

Variations: **Claudette** (French), **Claudina** (Spanish), **Claudine** (French), **Gladys** (Welsh), **Klaudia** (German and Polish)

Claudina (see **Claudia**)

Claudine (see **Claudia**)

Clea (see **Cleo**)

Cleo Greek *kleios,* "praise, fame"; also, a form of Cleopatra.
Variations: **Clea, Clio**

Clio (see **Cleo**)

Clotilda Old German *Chlotichilda,* "famous battle maiden," from *hlut* [loud, renowned] + *hiltja* [battle].

Coleen, Colene (see **Colleen**)

Coleta (see **Colette**)

Colette Form of **Nicole;** French feminine form of **Nicholas;** Greek "victorious people."
Famous name: Colette Sidonie (novelist)
Variations: **Coleta** (Spanish), **Collette, Cosette**

Colleen Irish Gaelic *cailin,* "girl." This name was created in 1917 for the American silent film star Colleen Moore. Colleen is not used as a name in Ireland, but it has been quite popular since the 1940s with Americans and Australians of Irish descent. The character called Colleen in the popular television Western *Doctor Quinn, Medicine Woman* is misnamed, because there were no girls named Colleen in the Old West period.
Famous names: Colleen Dewhurst (actress)
                     Colleen McCullough (novelist)
Other spellings: **Coleen, Colene, Colline**

Collette (see **Colette**)

Colline (see **Colleen**)

Concepción (see **Concetta**)

Concetta Italian from Latin *conceptio,* "conception," a reference to the Immaculate Conception of the Virgin Mary. Concetta was the original name of the singers Connie Francis and Connie Stevens.
Variations: **Concepción** (Spanish), **Conchita** (Spanish), **Connie**

Conchita (see **Concetta**)

Connie Form of **Concetta, Constance,** or **Consuelo.**
Famous name: Connie Chung (broadcast journalist)
Other spelling: **Conny**

Conny (see **Connie, Constance**)

Consolata (see **Consuelo**)

Constance Latin *Constantia,* "constancy." The name **Constantia**
was used in imperial Roman families, and it spread throughout
the empire. The diminutive form **Connie** was far more popular
from 1940 through 1960 than today.
Famous names: Constance Bennett (actress)
                     Constance Towers (actress)
Nicknames: **Connie, Conny**
Variations: **Constancia** (Spanish), **Constancy, Constantia,**
Constanta (Rumanian), **Costanza** (Italian), **Konstancia**
(Russian), **Konstanze** (German)

Constancia (see **Constance**)

Constancy (see **Constance**)

Constantia (see **Constance**)

Constanta (see **Constance**)

Consuelo Spanish from Latin "consolation." This popular Spanish
name is shortened from *Nuestra Señora de Consuelo,* "Our
Lady of Consolation."
Variations: **Connie, Consolata** (Italian)

Cora Probably created by American author James Fenimore
Cooper for the heroine of his 1826 novel *The Last of the
Mohicans,* possibly from Greek *kore,* "girl." In Greek
mythology, Kore was the daughter of Demeter, the goddess of
grain. Kore was captured by the god of the underworld, and to
get her daughter back, Demeter had to promise that Kore,
renamed Persephone, would return to the underworld for half
of the year. Cora was one of the top 20 names given to
American girls born in the 1870s, but it has been out of fashion
during the 20th century.

Variations: **Coralie, Coreen, Corene, Coretta, Cori, Koren**

Coral Latin *corallium,* "coral," a gem name that began to be used as a first name for girls in the 19th century.
Variation: **Coralie**

Coralie (see **Cora, Coral**)

Corazon Spanish "heart."

Cordelia Created by William Shakespeare for the tragic heroine of his play *King Lear,* possibly by blending Latin *cordis* "of the heart" with **Cornelia.**

Coreen, Corene (see **Cora, Koren**)

Coretta Variation of **Cora.**
Famous name: Coretta Scott King (civil rights activist)
Variation: **Corette**

Corette (see **Coretta**)

Corey (see **Cori**)

Cori Female form of **Corey** or form of **Cora, Corinna,** or **Cornelia.** This former nickname is now much more common as an independent name than any of the names from which it was derived. Cori is among the 200 most popular names for American girls.
Other spellings: **Corey, Corrie, Cory, Kori**

Corina (see **Corinna**)

Corine (see **Corinna**)

Corinna Greek *Korinna,* probably a form of *kore,* "girl." This very old name is unusual today and may have been at the height of its popularity in the 17th century, when the name had several literary references. The best known is probably Robert Herrick's "Corinna's Going A-Maying," a poem that celebrates living life to its fullest.
Variations: **Cori, Corina** (Spanish), **Corine, Corinne** (French)

Corinne French form of **Corinna.** Although Corinna is extremely rare in the United States, Corinne is in regular use and was the 239th most popular name given to American girls born in 1991.

Corliss British surname, perhaps from Old English "cheerful."

Cornela (see **Cornelia**)

Cornelia Latin feminine form of *Cornelius,* a Roman clan name probably from *cornu,* "a horn." Despite its ancient lineage, Cornelia has never been a popular name. The best-known reference is the mother of two famous Romans, Tiberius and Caius Gracchus.
Famous name: Cornelia Otis Skinner (actress)
Nicknames: **Cori, Corrie, Cory, Nelie, Nelleke** (Dutch)
Variations: **Cornela, Cornelie** (French), **Cornelle**

Cornelie (see **Cornelia**)

Cornelle (see **Cornelia**)

Corrie, Cory (see **Cori, Cornelia**)

Cortney, Cortnie (see **Courtney**)

Cosette (see **Colette**)

Cosima Feminine form of Greek *Kosmas,* "order, beauty."

Costanza (see **Constance**)

Courteney (see **Courtney**)

Courtney Middle English *de Curtenay* from *Courtenay,* French place name, "short one's manor." Like **Ashley,** Courtney is an aristocratic British surname that first became a name for girls in the American South. A 1977 psychological study found that a woman named Courtney was expected to be a smart, upper-class, attractive, strong-willed, and creative leader. With that image it's not surprising that this formerly rare name has been steadily increasing in popularity. By 1990, Courtney was among the top 20 names given to American girls.
Famous name: Courteney Cox (actress)
Other spellings: **Cortney, Cortnie, Courteney, Kortney, Kortnie, Kourtney**

Cris (see **Chris**)

Crissie, Crissy (see **Christina**)

Cristina (see **Christina**)

Crystal Greek *krystalos,* "rock crystal, clear ice." Crystal was one of the most popular names of the 1980s. Its popularity was largely due to the character Krystle Carrington, played by Linda Evans, on the television series *Dynasty.* Although its use has now begun to fall off, Crystal was still the 40th most common name given to American girls born in 1991.
Famous name: Crystal Gayle (singer)
Variations: **Christal, Chrystal, Kristal, Krystle**

Cybil Variation of **Sybil.** Actress Cybill Shepherd has stated that her parents chose the unusual spelling of her name to honor her two uncles, Cy and Bill.
Other spellings: **Cybill, Cybille**

Cybill, Cybille (see **Cybil**)

Cydney, Cydnie (see **Sydney**)

Cyndi Form of **Cindy**; nickname for **Cynthia** or **Lucinda.**
Famous name: Cyndi Lauper (singer)

Cyndie, Cyndy (see **Cindy, Cynthia, Lucinda**)

Cynthia Greek *Kynthia,* a title of Artemis, the moon goddess, from Mount Kynthos, a place name. The Greek goddess Artemis had many names, including Phoebe, Diana, and Cynthia. Artemis was born on Mount Kynthos on the Aegean island of Delos, according to legend, which is apparently how the name developed. Cynthia was among the top 50 names given to American girls born between 1945 and 1975. By 1991, it had fallen to 125th place and is much more popular with Hispanic-Americans than other parents today.
Famous name: Cynthia Sikes (actress)
Nicknames: **Cindi, Cindie, Cindy, Cyndi, Cyndie, Cyndy**
Variations: **Cinthia, Cintia** (Spanish), **Cinzia** (Italian), **Cynthie** (French), **Cyntia** (Polish)

Cynthie, Cyntia (see **Cynthia**)

Dace, Dacey (see **Candace**)

Dael (see **Dale**)

Daffodil Middle English *affodile* from Latin *affodillus*, "lily." This flower name is hardly ever chosen today.
Nickname: **Daffy**

Daffy (see **Daffodil, Daphne**)

Dagmar Danish from Old Scandinavian *dag* [day] + *mar* [maid].

Daisie (see **Daisy**)

Daisy Old English *daeges-eage*, "the day's eye," because the flower looks like the sun. Several literary heroines have this name, including Henry James's Daisy Miller; Daisy Buchanan, the girl pursued by Jay Gatsby in F. Scott Fitzgerald's *The Great Gatsby;* Judith Krantz's best-selling *Princess Daisy;* and the title character of *Driving Miss Daisy,* which won the 1988 Pulitzer Prize. Daisy is slowly coming back into fashion. Although this name was invented in England in the 19th century, it is particularly popular today with Hispanic-Americans.
Famous name: Daisy Fuentes (host on MTV)
                          Daisy Lowe (founder of the Girl Scouts)
Other spelling: **Daisie**

Dakota Name of an American Indian nation. Although Dakota is now popular as a name for boys, it is rapidly becoming fashionable for girls as well. In 1991, it was among the top 300 names given to girls born in the United States.

Dale Old English "valley." This name is only rarely used for girls in the United States, even though it is the name of several famous women, including actress Dale Evans and cosmetics entrepreneur Dale Arden.
Variations: **Dael, Dayle**

Dalila (see **Delilah**)

Dana Perhaps Old English "a Dane." In Irish mythology, Dana or Danu is the mother of a race of demigods who ruled Ireland in a golden age. Although this name is used for both boys and girls in the United States, it is now much more likely female than male.
Famous name: Dana Delany (actress)

Danelle (see **Daniele**)

Danette (see **Daniele**)

Dani (see **Daniele**)

Dania Latin form of Denmark, name of a town in Florida; or a modern blend of **Daniele** and **Tanya.**
Other spelling: **Danya**

Danica Form of *Danika,* a Slavic name meaning "morning star."
Famous name: Danica McKellar (actress)

Daniela, Daniella (see **Daniele**)

Daniele, Danielle French feminine form of **Daniel,** Hebrew "God is my judge." Danielle was the most common name for girls born in France between 1944 and 1947. It became steadily more popular in England and the United States from 1950 on, at the same time that Daniel was becoming a fashionable name for boys. Although Danielle seems to have peaked in popularity in the late 1980s, it is falling off very slowly and was still among the top 25 names given American girls born in 1991.
Nicknames: **Dani, Danni, Dannie**
Variations: **Danelle, Danette, Daniela** (Spanish), **Daniella** (Estonian and Hungarian), **Danila** (Serbian, Slovakian, and Slovenian), **Danita**

Danila (see **Daniele**)

Danita (see **Daniele**)

Danni, Dannie (see **Daniele**)

Danya (see **Dania**)

Daphna (see **Daphne**)

Daphne Greek "laurel tree." In Greek mythology, the nymph Daphne had pledged herself to the goddess Artemis, and when the god Apollo pursued Daphne, she prayed to Artemis to save her. The goddess answered her request by transforming her into a laurel tree. In ancient Greece, the laurel was bestowed on the winners of athletic contests, and in England, a crown of laurels is given to the poet laureate.
Famous name: Daphne du Maurier (novelist)
Nickname: **Daffy**
Variation: **Daphna**

Darci, Darcie (see **Darcy**)

Darcy French *d'Arcy,* "from Arcy," a French place name perhaps meaning "Bear's home"; or Irish Gaelic *O Dorchaidhe,* "dark one's descendant." This was formerly a male name, but in the United States it is now given almost exclusively to girls.
Famous name: Darci Kistler (ballerina)
Other spellings: **Darci, Darcie**

Daria Feminine form of **Darius,** Persian "maintaining goodness." Daria is an extremely unusual name in English-speaking countries, but it is fairly common in Italy and Poland.
Famous name: Daria Nicoloda (actress)

Darla (see **Darlene**)

Darleen (see **Darlene**)

Darlene Probably from Old English *deorling,* "darling." This name is a 20th-century creation. It was popular from the late 1940s through the 1960s, but it is very rarely given today.
Other spellings: **Darleen, Darline**
Variations: **Darla, Darlyn**

Darline (see **Darlene**)

Darlyn (see **Darlene**)

Darta (see **Dorothy**)

Daryl Feminine form of **Darryl.**
> Famous name: Daryl Hannah (actress)

Dawn Old English *dagian,* "daybreak." Aurora was the Roman goddess of dawn, and her name was occasionally used in England during the 19th century. The English translation of the goddess's name, Dawn, came into use as a given name sometime in the late 1800s, but it wasn't until the 1960s that the name became popular in the United States. By 1970, Dawn was the 11th most popular name. Its use today appears to be undergoing a similarly spectacular decline.
> Famous names: Dawn Riley (crew member in America's Cup yacht race)
> Dawn Upshaw (opera singer)

Dayle (see **Dale**)

Dayo Yoruba (Nigeria) "joy arrives."

Deanna Modern form of **Diana** or feminine form of **Dean.** This name began to be used regularly in the 1940s because of the fame of actress Deanna Durbin, and it has been one of the top 200 names for American girls ever since. Today, it's probably best known through the character Deanna Troi, the psychological counselor played by Marina Sirtis on television's *Star Trek: The Next Generation.*

Deb (see **Deborah**)

Debbie Form of **Deborah.**
> Famous names: Debbie Allen (dancer)
> Debbie Reynolds (actress)
> Debi Thomas (figure skater)
> Other spellings: **Debby, Debi**

Debby (see **Debbie, Deborah**)

Debi (see **Debbie, Deborah**)

Debora (see **Deborah**)

Deborah Hebrew "bee." The first biblical Deborah was Rebecca's nurse; the second Deborah called for an uprising against the Canaanites. She is attributed with the Song of Deborah, one of the oldest poems in the Bible; it honors the triumph of the Israelites. The Puritans frequently used this name, and several forms of the name were popular in the 1950s and 1960s, perhaps because of actress Debbie Reynolds.

Famous names: Debrah Farentino (actress)
Deborah Kerr (actress)
Deborah Norville (broadcast journalist)
Deborah Raffin (actress)
Debra Winger (actress)

Nicknames: **Deb, Debbie, Debby, Debi**

Other spellings: **Debra, Debrah**

Variations: **Debora, Deetsje** (Dutch), **Devora, Devorah, Dvora, Dvorah** (Israeli)

Debra (see **Deborah**)

Debrah (see **Deborah**)

Dede (see **Deidra, Delia**)

Dee Welsh *du,* "dark"; Celtic "sacred river"; or a form of **Deidre, Delia,** or **Dorothy.**
Other spelling: **Deigh**

Deetsje (see **Deborah**)

Deidra, Deidre American forms of **Deirdre.**
Famous names: Diedra English (writer and publisher)
Deidre Hall (actress)
Nicknames: **Dede, Dee**

Deigh (see **Dee**)

Deirdre Irish Gaelic *Derdriu,* possibly "chatterer." The heroine of an Irish legend, Deirdre fled with her lover to England, and when he was killed on their return, she died on his grave.
Other spellings: **Deidra, Deidre**

Delia Greek "from Delos," a Mediterranean island.
Nicknames: **Dede, Dee**

Delila (see **Delilah**)

Delilah Biblical name of unknown meaning. The biblical Delilah robbed Samson of his power by cutting off his hair while he slept. With this odious connotation, it's not surprising that the name hasn't been very popular, but it is occasionally used.
Other spelling: **Delila**
Variations: **Dalila, Lila, Lilah**

Delinda A modern blend of **Delia** or **Della** with **Belinda.**

Della Nickname for **Adela.**
Famous name: Della Reese (singer)

Delores, Deloris (see **Dolores**)

Delta Greek. Delta is the fourth letter of the Greek alphabet.
Famous name: Delta Burke (actress)

Deni (see **Denise**)

Denice (see **Denise**)

Denise Feminine form of **Dennis,** French "god of wine." Dionysus was the Greek god of wine and drama and was also known as Bacchus. Denise was especially popular in the 1950s and 1960s but is now slowly going out of style.
Famous name: Denise Levertov (poet)
Nicknames: **Deni, Denni**
Other spellings: **Denice, Denyce, Denyse**
Variations: **Dione, Dionne, Dionisia** (Spanish and Italian)

Denni (see **Denise**)

Denyce, Denyse (see **Denise**)

Desiree French "desired one." Desiree is steadily becoming more popular in the United States and reached 94th on the list of names given American girls in 1991.

Destany, Destinee, Destiney (see **Destiny**)

Destiny Middle English *destinee,* "fortune, fate," from Latin *destinata,* "established." It's a mystery who first thought of turning this word into a first name for girls, but it seems to have happened in the United States around 1970. Some parents choose the name with the idea that they were destined to have a daughter; perhaps others hope that the name will ensure that their daughter is destined for great things. Whatever the motivation, Destiny is becoming a fashionable American name, rising from 189th to 128th on the popularity charts between 1989 and 1991.

Other spellings: **Destany, Destinee, Destiney**

Devan, Deven, Devin (see **Devon**)

Devon For the possible origins of this name, see **Devin** in the list of names for boys. Although the trend is for Devon to be the feminine spelling for this name and Devin the masculine, each form is regularly used for both sexes. The name's popularity for girls as well as boys is steadily increasing, and Devon was 104th on the list of names given American girls born in 1991.

Other spellings: **Devan, Deven, Devin, Devyn**

Devyn (see **Devon**)

Devora, Devorah (see **Deborah**)

Di (see **Diana**)

Diahann Variation of **Diane.**

Famous name: Diahann Carroll (actress)

Diamond Old French *diamant,* "diamond." This name was not especially popular in the 19th century when other jewel names such as **Ruby** and **Pearl** were common, but it is rapidly becoming fashionable with African-American parents, who made it one of their 100 most popular names for girls in 1991.

Diana Greek *deus,* "god, divine," through Latin *dius.* Diana was a major Roman goddess, derived from two Greek goddesses: Artemis, the goddess of the hunt and the moon, and Jana, the wife of Janus and goddess of the night. The Romans applied the myths about Artemis to Diana. She was a powerful goddess, rivaling Minerva, the goddess of wisdom, and Venus, the goddess of love and beauty. The name today has important royal connotations through Diana, the princess of Wales. Diana took a jump in popularity after Charles and Di were married in 1981 but, as their marital problems have been publicized, the name is steadily decreasing in use.

Famous names: Diana Ross (singer)
Diana Vreeland (fashion journalist)
Variations: **Deanna, Di, Diane** (French), **Dianne**

Diane, Dianne French variation of **Diana.** Diane became well
known in the 16th century because of Diane de Poitiers, the
famous mistress of Henry II of France. Diane was incredibly
popular with American parents during the 1940s and 1950s,
but by 1970 its fashion had passed. Today, it is once again
considerably less common than Diana.
Famous names: Diane Keaton (actress)
Dianne Feinstein (U.S. senator)
Diane Sawyer (journalist)
Diane Schuur (jazz singer)
Other spellings: **Diahann, Dyan, Dyanne**

Dina Form of **Dinah** or feminine form of **Dean** or **Dino.**
Famous name: Dina Merrill (actress)

Dinah Hebrew "judgment." In the Bible, Dinah was the beautiful
daughter of Jacob and Leah. The name has never been very
popular, even though it's been in existence for centuries.
Famous names: Dinah Manoff (actress)
Dinah Shore (singer)
Other spelling: **Dina**

Dione (see **Denise, Dionne**)

Dionisia (see **Denise**)

Dionne Feminine form of **Dion** or variation of **Denise.**
Famous name: Dionne Warwick (singer)
Variation: **Dione**

Dixie Latin *dixi,* "I have spoken"; or form of Dixon, "son of
Richard." This unusual name has enjoyed its greatest
popularity in the southern part of the United States, probably
because it is the affectionate name for the Old South.
Famous names: Dixie Carter (actress)
Dixie Lee Ray (governor of Washington state)
Other spelling: **Dixy**

Dixy (see **Dixie**)

Dodie, Dody (see **Dorothy**)

Doll (see **Dolly, Dorothy**)

Dolley, Dollie (see **Dolly**)

Dolly Variation of **Dorothy.** This name may have begun as a
    nickname, but it appears to have developed roots of its own. It
    is the name of several minor characters in 18th-century fiction.
    Dolley Madison, the wife of President James Madison and a
    celebrated hostess, used the "-ey" ending.

    Famous name: Dolly Parton (singer)

    Nickname: **Doll**

    Other spellings: **Dolley, Dollie**

Dolores Latin *dolere,* "pain, sorrow." Maria de Dolores is a
    Spanish name for the Virgin Mary, and this name honors her.

    Famous name: Delores Del Rio (actress)

    Variations: **Delores, Deloris, Dolorita, Doloroza** (Ukrainian and
        Hungarian), **Lola, Lolita**

Dolorita (see **Dolores**)

Doloroza (see **Dolores**)

Dominique French feminine form of **Dominic.** Dominique has been
    a very popular name in the African-American community ever
    since Diahann Carroll began playing the part of Dominique
    Deveraux on the television series *Dynasty* in 1984. Dominique
    was still among the top 20 names given African-American girls
    born in 1991.

Dona (see **Donna**)

Donella (see **Donna**)

Donna Italian form of Latin *domina,* "lady." This name sounds like
    a feminine version of **Don** or **Donald,** which may explain why it
    became such a popular name in the 1940s and 1950s.

    Famous names: Donna Mills (actress)
                  Donna Shalala (U.S. Secretary of Health and
                   Human Services)
                   Donna Summer (singer)

    Variations: **Dona** (Spanish), **Donella, Donnie**

Donnie (see **Donna**)

Dora Variation of **Dorothy** or, very rarely, **Pandora.** Although this name started out as a nickname, it was a given name in its own right by the 19th century. In literature, Dora is the wife of the title character in Charles Dickens's *David Copperfield.*
Nicknames: **Dori, Dorie, Dorrie, Dory**
Variations: **Doreen, Dorena, Dorette, Dorina**

Dorcas Greek "gazelle." If you want your baby daughter to be graceful and light on her feet, you might choose this name.

Dordi (see **Dorothy**)

Doreen Form of **Dora** or Irish Gaelic *Doireann,* "daughter of the fair hero." Doreen was a top ten name in Britain during the 1920s, but it has never been very popular in the United States.
Famous name: Doreen Tracey (actress)
Other spellings: **Dorene, Dorine**

Dorena (see **Dora**)

Dorene (see **Doreen**)

Dorete (see **Dorothy**)

Dorette (see **Dora**)

Dori, Dorie (see **Dora, Doris**)

Dorice (see **Doris**)

Dorina (see **Dora**)

Dorine (see **Doreen**)

Doris Greek "woman from Doris (central Greece)"; also, the name of a mythological sea nymph. This name was popular in the late 19th and early 20th centuries, but few parents today choose to name their daughters Doris.
Famous names: Doris Day (actress)
Doris Duke (philanthropist)
Doris Lessing (novelist)
Nicknames: **Dori, Dorie, Dorrie**
Other spellings: **Dorice, Dorris**
Variation: **Doryda** (Polish)

Dorla (see **Dorothy**)

Dorli (see **Dorothy**)

Doro (see **Dorothy**)

Dorofija (see **Dorothy**)

Dorota (see **Dorothy**)

Dorotea, Doroteya (see **Dorothy**)

Dorothea Latin and German form of **Dorothy**. St. Dorothea was an early Christian martyr who refused to worship idols. In literature, the most prominent Dorothea appears in Goethe's *Hermann und Dorothea.* Although Dorothea received some use in 19th-century America, it has always been much rarer than Dorothy, the traditional English form.

Famous names: Dorothea Dix (civil rights reformer)
Dorothea Lange (photographer)

Dorothee (see **Dorothy**)

Dorothy English feminine form of Greek *Dorotheus,* "gift of God." Dorothy was a such a popular name in Shakespeare's time that the pet name **Doll** became the name for the children's toy. The name's second period of great popularity began around 1900, just the time when L. Frank Baum chose Dorothy Gale as the name of his heroine in *The Wizard of Oz.* Dorothy started going out of fashion again around 1940; in 1991, it fell below the top 500 names given American girls for the first time in a century.

Famous names: Dorothy Hamill (figure skater)
Dorothy Parker (writer)

Nicknames: **Dee, Dodie, Dody, Doll, Dolly, Doro, Dot, Dottie, Dotty**

Variations: **Darta** (Latvian), **Dora, Dordi** (Norwegian), **Dorete** (Danish), **Dorla** (Czech), **Dorli** (Swiss), **Dorofija** (Ukrainian), **Dorota** (Polish and Czech), **Dorotea** (Italian, Spanish, Finnish, and Swedish), **Doroteya** (Russian), **Dorothea, Dorothee** (French), **Dorottya** (Hungarian), **Dorte** (Danish and Norwegian), **Dorthy, Dosia** (Polish), **Dosya** (Russian)

Dorottya (see **Dorothy**)

Dorrie (see **Dora, Doris**)

Dorris (see **Doris**)

Dorte (see **Dorothy**)

Dorthy (see **Dorothy**)

Dory (see **Dora**)

Doryda (see **Doris**)

Dosia, Dosya (see **Dorothy**)

Dot, Dottie, Dotty (see **Dorothy**)

Dru (see **Drusilla**)

Drucilla (see **Drusilla**)

Drusie (see **Drusilla**)

Drusilla Latin *Drusus,* a Roman family name. This name is associated with strength.
Nicknames: **Dru, Drusie**
Variation: **Drucilla**

Dulce, Dulci (see **Dulcie**)

Dulcie Latin *dulcis,* "sweet." Although Don Quixote's love was named Aldonza, he decided to call her Dulcinea.
Variations: **Dulce, Dulci, Dulcia, Dulcy**

Dulcia (see **Dulcie**)

Dulcy (see **Dulcie**)

Dvora, Dvorah (see **Deborah**)

Dyan Variation of **Diana.**
Famous name: Dyan Cannon (actress)

Dyanne (see **Diana**)

Eabha (see **Eva**)

Ealasaid (see **Elizabeth**)

Earline Feminine form of **Earl,** blending it with sound of **Arlene.**
Variations: **Erlene, Erlina, Erline**
Nickname: **Lina**

Eartha Old German *erde,* "earth, ground."
Famous name: Eartha Kitt (singer)
Other spelling: **Ertha**
Variation: **Erda** (German)

Easter Old English *eastre,* "spring."

Ebeny (see **Ebony**)

Ebonee, Eboni, Ebonie (see **Ebony**)

Ebony Middle English *hebeny* from Latin *ebenus,* "ebony wood."
Ebony is a hard, durable wood from trees that grow in India
and Sri Lanka. The most prized variety of this wood is a deep,
lustrous black, and so the word *ebony* has come to signify that
color. Around 1970, African-American parents began to name
their daughters Ebony. The name grew quickly in popularity;
in the middle 1980s, it was one of the top ten names given to
African-American girls. Although the vogue for Ebony has
now begun to recede, it was still the 18th most common first
name for nonwhite girls born in 1991.
Other spellings: **Ebeny, Ebonee, Eboni, Ebonie, Ebyni**

Ebun Yoruba "gift."

Ebyni (see **Ebony**)

Eda Old English *ead,* "prosperity, fortune, riches"; also, a variation of **Edith.**
Famous name: Eda LeShan (author)
Nicknames: **Eddie, Eddy**
Variation: **Edda**

Edda (see **Eda**)

Eddie, Eddy (see **Eda, Edna**)

Ede (see **Edith**)

Edie Form of **Edith.**
Famous name: Edie Adams (actress)
Variation: **Edith**

Edit (see **Edith**)

Edita (see **Edith**)

Edith Old English *Eadgyth* from *ead* [riches, prosperity] and *gyth* [war]. Two tenth-century saints were named Edith, including Edith of Wilton, a nun who was an illegitimate daughter of King Edgar of England and who was noted for her friendship with wild animals. Two Ediths were queens of England in the 11th century. The name was revived in Victorian times as part of that era's fascination with medieval chivalry, and Edith was one of the top ten names for American girls born in the 1880s. The name is now identified with the character Edith Bunker, played by Jean Stapleton, on the long-running television comedy *All in the Family.* Her memory may ensure that the lack of enthusiasm American parents have shown for this name since the 1930s will continue for another generation.
Famous names: Edith Hamilton (classicist)
               Edith Oliver (theater critic)
               Edith Piaf (chanteuse)
               Edith Sitwell (poet)
               Edith Wharton (novelist)
Nicknames: **Eda, Ede, Edie, Eydi, Eydie**
Other spellings: **Edithe, Edyth, Edythe**

Variations: **Edit** (Swedish and Hungarian), **Edita** (Spanish, Portuguese, Russian, and Rumanian), **Editha, Editta** (Italian), **Edyta** (Polish)

Editha (see **Edith**)

Edithe (see **Edith**)

Editta (see **Edith**)

Edna Hebrew *ednah*, "delight." Edna is the name of the wife of Tobit in the Book of Tobit, which is part of the Old Testament in Roman Catholic Bibles and of the Apocrypha in Protestant ones. The name became very popular in America in the 19th century because of Edna Earl, heroine of Augusta Evans Wilson's 1866 novel *St. Elmo.* The book remained a best-seller for decades. In the late 20th century, however, the name Edna is almost completely ignored.

    Famous names: Edna Buchanan (journalist and crime novelist)
                    Edna Ferber (novelist)
                    Edna St. Vincent Millay (poet)
    Nicknames: **Eddie, Eddy**

Edwina Feminine form of **Edwin,** Old English "rich friend."

Edyta (see **Edith**)

Edyth, Edythe (see **Edith**)

Effie Form of Greek *Euphemia*, "well-spoken."

Eileen Irish Gaelic *Eibhlin*, originally a form of **Evelyn,** although later also used as the Irish variation of **Helen.** This traditionally Irish name is now especially popular in the Hispanic-American community.

    Famous names: Eileen Brennan (actress)
                    Eileen Cowin (photographer)
                    Eileen Heckart (actress)
    Other spellings: **Aileen, Ilene**

Eilidh (see **Helen**)

Eilis (see **Elizabeth**)

Eirene (see **Irene**)

Eirin (see **Irene**)

Ekaterina (see **Katherine**)

Ela, Elah Hebrew "terebinth tree" or "goddess," a fairly common name in modern Israel.

Elain (see **Elaine**)

Elaine Old French form of **Helen**. Elaine was the wife of Sir Lancelot and the mother of Sir Galahad in Sir Thomas Malory's *Morte d'Arthur*. In *Idylls of the King*, poet Alfred, Lord Tennyson, introduced the name to a wide audience. Elaine was quite popular during the 1940s and 1950s in the United States, but it is now going out of fashion.
Famous names: Elaine May (film director)
Elaine Stritch (actress)
Other spellings: **Elain, Elane, Elayne**

Elane (see **Elaine**)

Elayne (see **Elaine**)

Elberta (see **Alberta**)

Eldora Spanish *el dorado*, "the golden one."

Eleanor Old Provencal *Alienor*, meaning uncertain; perhaps based on Greek *eleas*, "mercy," or Germanic *ali*, "foreign"; since medieval times, however, the name has often been used as a variation of **Helen**. Eleanor was a popular name for centuries, most likely because of its many links with royalty. Eleanor of Aquitaine, wife of Henry II, may have introduced the name to England. Eleanor was the wealthiest woman in Europe and heir to Aquitaine. Henry may have married Eleanor for her landholdings in France, but she bore him eight children, including two sons who would sit on the throne: Richard I, Coeur de Lion; and John, whose son Henry III, would begin the century-long reign of the Plantagenets. Henry III married Eleanor of Provence. In literature, the name appears infrequently, although Nathaniel Hawthorne wrote *Lady Eleanore's Mantle*. In the United States, First Lady Eleanor Roosevelt brought her own influence to the government and is considered to be one of the great humanitarians of the 20th century.

Famous name: Eleanor Powell (dancer)

Nicknames: **Ella, Ellie, Elly, Nell, Nellie, Nelly, Nora, Norah**

Other spellings: **Eleanore, Elenore, Elinor, Elinore, Ellenor**

Variations: **Elenor** (Swedish), **Elenora** (Dutch), **Eleonora** (Italian, Polish, and Russian), **Eleonore** (French and German), **Elna** (Swedish and Norwegian), **Elnora, Lenora, Lenore, Leonor** (Spanish and Portuguese), **Leonora** (Italian)

Eleanore (see **Eleanor**)

Electra Greek "amber." In Greek mythology, Electra was the daughter of Clytemnestra and Agamemnon. With her brother Orestes, she avenged the murder of their father. Eugene O'Neill used this myth as the basis for his play *Mourning Becomes Electra.*

Elen (see **Helen**)

Elena Spanish, Italian, and Russian form of **Helen.** This name is still quite common in the Hispanic-American community.

Famous names: Elena Castedo (novelist)
Elena Shoushounova (gymnast)

Eleni (see **Helen**)

Elenor, Elenora (see **Eleanor**)

Elenore (see **Eleanor**)

Eleonora, Eleonore (see **Eleanor**)

Elga (see **Helga**)

Eliisa (see **Elizabeth**)

Elin (see **Ellen, Helen**)

Elina (see **Ellen, Helen**)

Elinor Variation of **Eleanor.**

Famous name: Elinor Wylie (poet)

Elinore (see **Eleanor**)

Elisa (see **Elizabeth**)

Elisabet (see **Elizabeth**)

Elisabeth Variation of **Elizabeth.**
Famous name: Elisabeth Shue (actress)

Elisabetha (see **Elizabeth**)

Elisabetta (see **Elizabeth**)

Elise French form of **Elizabeth,** also now frequently used in Germany and the United States.
Other spelling: **Elyse**

Eliska (see **Elizabeth**)

Elissa Phoenician name of Dido, the legendary queen who founded ancient Carthage; used in modern times as a form of **Elizabeth.**
Famous names: Elissa Benedek (psychiatrist)
                Elissa Landi (actress)
Other spelling: **Elyssa**

Eliz (see **Elizabeth**)

Eliza This short form of **Elizabeth** has been used as an independent name since the 16th century. The most famous Eliza is Eliza Doolittle, the Cockney flower girl who is transformed into a lady in George Bernard Shaw's play *Pygmalion.* This story later became the basis for the popular Broadway musical *My Fair Lady.*

Elizabeta (see **Elizabeth**)

Elizabeth Hebrew *Elisheba,* traditionally interpreted as "the Lord is an oath," although many modern scholars of ancient Hebrew believe "the Lord is good fortune" is a more accurate translation. The first biblical Elisheba was the wife of Aaron and the sister-in-law of Moses. But St. Elizabeth, the mother of John the Baptist, is better known. The second St. Elizabeth was the daughter of the king of Hungary, a 12th-century woman who was married to a German prince named Ludwig. She was expelled from the palace on his death and walked the streets with the poor, performing miracles. Among royalty, the name is used in many European countries. Elizabeth Petrovna was an empress of Russia in the 18th century, and there have been several famous Isabellas in Spain and Portugal. The most famous royal Elizabeth was the daughter of King Henry VIII of England and Anne Boleyn. Queen Elizabeth I gave her name to a golden age of English literature. Queen Elizabeth II is the current British monarch. One of the most personable characters in fiction is Elizabeth Bennet of Jane Austen's novel *Pride and Prejudice.*

Famous names: Elizabeth Ashley (actress)
Elizabeth Barrett Browning (poet)
Elizabeth Dole (politician)
Elizabeth McGovern (actress)
Elizabeth Perkins (actress)
Elizabeth Taylor (actress)

Nicknames: **Bess, Bessie, Bessy, Bet, Beta, Beth, Bets, Betsy, Betta, Bette, Betty, Elsie, Libby, Liz, Liza, Lizzie, Lizzy**

Variations: **Babette** (French), **Besse** (Norwegian), **Bettina, Ealasaid** (Scots Gaelic), **Eilis** (Irish Gaelic), **Eliisa** (Finnish), **Elisa** (Italian, Spanish, and Greek), **Elisabet** (Scandinavian), **Elisabeth** (French and German), **Elisabetha** (Dutch), **Elisabetta** (Italian), **Elise** (French), **Eliska** (Czech and Slovakian), **Elissa, Eliz** (Hungarian), **Eliza, Elizabeta** (Latvian and Slovenian), **Elizaveta** (Russian and Bulgarian), **Elli** (German), **Elsa** (Danish and German), **Elsbeth** (Swiss German), **Elspeth** (Scottish), **Elza** (Bulgarian, Czech, and Hungarian), **Elzbieta** (Polish), **Erzsebet** (Hungarian), **Ilsa** (German), **Ilse** (German), **Ilze** (Latvian), **Isabel** (Spanish), **Isabella, Liese** (German), **Lillian, Lis** (Scandinavian), **Lisa** (Italian and Scandinavian), **Lisabeth, Lisbet** (Swedish), **Lisbeth, Lise** (French), **Lisette** (French), **Lissette, Lizabeth, Yelizaveta** (Russian), **Ysabel**

Elizaveta (see **Elizabeth**)

Ella Norman French form of Old German *ali,* "foreign"; also, a variation of **Eleanor, Ellen, Helen,** and **Joella.**
Famous name: Ella Fitzgerald (singer)

Ellen English variation of **Helen.** Ellen was fashionable in the 1950s and 1960s, especially in the northeastern United States, but it's now fallen below the top 200 names for American girls.
Famous names: Ellen Barkin (actress)
Ellen Burstyn (actress)
Ellen Goodman (columnist)

Nicknames: **Ellie, Elly**
Other spellings: **Ellyn, Elyn**
Variations: **Ella, Ellette, Elin** (Welsh and Swedish), **Elina**

Ellenor (see **Eleanor**)

Ellette (see **Ellen**)

Elli (see **Elizabeth**)

Ellie, Elly (see **Eleanor, Ellen**)

Ellyn (see **Ellen**)

Elna (see **Eleanor, Helen**)

Elnora (see **Eleanor**)

Eloisa (see **Eloise, Heloise**)

Eloise Modern French and English form of **Heloise.** There was a minor fashion for Eloise around 1900, but it is very rare in the United States today.
Variation: **Eloisa**

Elona (see **Ilona**)

Elsa Variation of **Elizabeth.**
Famous name: Elsa Schiaparelli (fashion designer)
Variations: **Else, Ilsa, Ilse**

Elsbeth (see **Elizabeth**)

Else (see **Elsa**)

Elsie Variation of **Elizabeth,** originally a Scottish form, but extremely popular in the United States at the end of the 19th century. Today, the name is likely to remind Americans of the cow used in dairy ads, and it is very rare despite the huge success of the similar-sounding names **Kelsey** and **Chelsea.**
Other spelling: **Elsy**

Elspeth (see **Elizabeth**)

Elsy (see **Elsie**)

Elvera (see Elvira)

Elvina (see Alvina)

Elvira Spanish form of Visigothic German *Alvera,* perhaps "noble guardian." Unlike some movie heroines, Elvira Madigan, from the popular Swedish film of the same name, failed to inspire new interest in the name. Today, the name is as unpopular with American parents as it has been throughout the 20th century.
   Variations: **Alvira, Elvera, Elvire** (French), **Vira, Virita**

Elvire (see Elvira)

Elyn (see Ellen)

Elyse American spelling of **Elise.** The popularity of the long-running television comedy *Family Ties* and the character of the mother, Elyse, played by Meredith Baxter-Birney, caused some increase in the popularity of this name.

Elyssa (see Elissa)

Elza (see Elizabeth)

Elzbieta (see Elizabeth)

Em (see Emily, Emma)

Ema (see Emma)

Emelina (see Emmeline)

Emeline (see Amelia, Emmeline)

Emelyne (see Emmeline)

Emila (see Emily)

Emilia (see Emily)

Emilie French form of **Emily.** In 1985, Emilie became the most popular name for girls born in France.

Emilija (see Emily)

Emiline (see Emmeline)

Emilka (see Emily)

Emily English feminine form of *Aemilius,* an ancient Roman family name possibly from Latin *aemulus,* "rival." Emily was a rare name in England until the 18th century when the German Hanoverian dynasty began to use it as an English version of **Amelia,** a name that actually has a different origin. Emily became very popular in the early 19th century, but its use faded considerably after 1880. Emily has staged an incredible comeback since 1970 and is now one of the 25 most popular names in England, Australia, and the United States. The popular film *The Americanization of Emily,* starring American actor James Garner and British actress Julie Andrews, may have helped to revive interest in the name.

Famous names: Emily Bronte (writer)
      Emily Dickinson (poet)
      Emily Post (etiquette arbiter)

Nicknames: **Em, Emmi, Emmie, Emmy, Millie, Milly**

Variations: **Emila** (Latvian and Ukrainian), **Emilia** (Spanish, Italian, and German), **Emilie** (French and Scandinavian), **Emilija** (Russian, Lithuanian, and Bulgarian), **Emilka** (Czech and Bulgarian), **Mila** (Serbo-Croatian and Czech), **Milka** (Slavic)

Emma Old German "whole, universal." The first Queen Emma was the Norman wife of Ethelred II. Their marriage united parts of Britain with Normandy. After Ethelred died, Emma married his successor, Canute (Cnut), becoming the only English queen to be married to two kings. Jane Austen's *Emma* is considered to be one of the finest novels in English literature. Emma Bovary is the tragic heroine of Gustave Flaubert's novel *Madame Bovary,* a classic in French literature. Emma has been fantastically popular in Britain since 1975, and was the top name for girls born in England and Wales in 1990. Although for many Americans Emma still has an elderly image, the current fashion for **Emily** and the recent celebrity of English actresses such as Emma Thompson and Emma Samms started to revive interest in the name in the United States. Emma moved up to 143rd from 172nd on the list of names given American girls between 1989 and 1991.

Famous name: Emma Lou Diemer (composer)

Nicknames: **Em, Emmi, Emmie, Emmy**

Variation: **Ema** (Spanish, Bulgarian, Czech, and Lithuanian)

Emmaline (see **Emmeline**)

Emmalyn (see **Emmeline**)

Emmanuelle French feminine form of **Emmanuel,** Hebrew "God is in us."
Famous name: Emmanuelle Seigner (actress)

Emmeline Norman French *Ameline.* Emmeline was introduced into England at the time of the Norman Conquest. Even then it was unclear whether the name was derived from **Amelia** or **Emma.** There was a minor vogue for Emmeline in the early 19th century while **Emily** was enjoying its first era of popularity, but despite today's renewed fashion for Emily, American parents have yet to rediscover Emmeline as an alternative.
Variations: **Emelina, Emeline** (French), **Emelyne, Emiline, Emmaline, Emmalyn**

Emmi, Emmie, Emmy (see **Emily, Emma**)

Emogene (see **Imogene**)

Engel (see **Angela**)

Enid Welsh, uncertain meaning, perhaps "pure." In the Arthurian romances, Enid was the saintly wife of Geraint. Although her fidelity was questioned, she passed every test of purity, and her husband came to regret his lack of faith in her virtue.
Famous name: Enid Bagnold (writer)

Enrica (see **Henrietta**)

Enrichetta (see **Henrietta**)

Enrika (see **Henrietta**)

Enriqueta (see **Henrietta**)

Erda (see **Eartha**)

Erica Feminine form of **Eric,** possibly Old Norse "ever-ruler." Erica became common in the United States around 1970, about a decade after Eric had become a popular name for boys. It's probably no accident that Erica's rise to the heights of fashion began while *All My Children*'s Erica Kane, played by actress Susan Lucci, was becoming one of the most celebrated characters ever to appear on daytime television. Erica is now especially popular in the African-American community.

Famous name: Erica Jong (writer)
Nicknames: **Ricki, Rickie, Rikki**
Other spellings: **Ericka, Erika** (Scandinavian)

Ericka, Erika (see **Erica**)

Erin Gaelic *Eireann,* perhaps "western island," a poetic name for
Ireland. This is based on *Eriu,* the name of a legendary Irish
goddess. Like **Colleen,** Erin is an example of an Irish word that
is hardly ever used as a name in Ireland itself but that has
become very popular in the United States.
Famous names: Erin Gray (actress)
Erin Quigley (costume designer)
Variations: **Erina, Eryn**

Erina (see **Erin**)

Erlene (see **Earline**)

Erlina, Erline (see **Earline**)

Erma Variation of **Irma.**
Famous name: Erma Bombeck (humorist)

Ernesta (see **Ernestine**)

Ernestina (see **Ernestine**)

Ernestine Feminine form of **Ernest,** German "serious, earnest."
Ernestine isn't a popular name today, perhaps because there's
little enthusiasm for the male name Ernest. The best-known
Ernestine may be actress Lily Tomlin's comic character who
comments from her switchboard on the ways of the world.
Variations: **Ernesta, Ernestina**

Ertha (see **Eartha**)

Erzsebet (see **Elizabeth**)

Eryn (see **Erin**)

Esfir (see **Esther**)

Esmeralda Spanish "emerald." This jewel name is rarely used.
Victor Hugo gave the name to the young woman who is adored
by the hunchback of Notre Dame.

Essi (see **Esther**)

Essie (see **Estelle, Esther**)

Estela (see **Estelle**)

Estell, Estella (see **Estelle**)

Estelle French *estoile,* "star." Although this name was popular in the first half of the 20th century, it is unusual today.

> Famous names: Estelle Getty (actress)
> Estelle Parsons (actress)
> Estelle Winwood (actress)
>
> Nickname: **Essie**
>
> Other spelling: **Estell**
>
> Variations: **Estela** (Polish, Czech, and Spanish), **Estella** (Italian), **Estrelita** (Spanish), **Estrella** (Spanish), **Estrela** (Portuguese), **Stella**

Ester (see **Esther**)

Estera (see **Esther**)

Esteri (see **Esther**)

Esterina (see **Esther**)

Esther Possibly Persian *satarah,* "star, the planet Venus." Esther is one of two feminine names used to title a book of the Bible, reflecting the great honor given to the first Esther, a young Jewish slave originally named Hadassah who was made a queen of Persia. Esther saved the Jews from the scourge of Haman, an event that is remembered in the feast of Purim.

> Famous name: Esther Williams (swimmer and actress)
>
> Nicknames: **Essie, Ettie, Etty**
>
> Variations: **Esfir** (Russian), **Essi** (Finnish), **Ester** (Spanish), **Estera** (Polish, Czech, and Rumanian), **Esteri** (Finnish), **Esterina** (Italian), **Eszter** (Hungarian), **Hester**

Estrela, Estrella (see **Estelle**)

Estrelita (see **Estelle**)

Eszter (see **Esther**)

Ethel Old English *aethel,* "noble." The Anglo-Saxon prefix "Ethel-" was used with many other names, such as *Ethelwyne* and *Etheldreda* (see **Audrey**). It wasn't until the 19th century that Ethel became an independent name.

Famous names: Ethel Barrymore (actress)
Ethel Merman (actress)
Ethel Waters (singer)

Variations: **Ethelle, Ethyl**

Ethelle (see **Ethel**)

Ethyl (see **Ethel**)

Etta Form of **Henrietta** or other names ending in "-etta."

Famous name: Etta James (singer)

Ettie, Etty (see **Esther, Henrietta**)

Eubh (see **Eva**)

Eudora Greek "good gift," a modern name created from ancient Greek elements.

Famous name: Eudora Welty (writer)

Eugenia, Eugenie English and French feminine forms of **Eugene,** Greek "well born." Despite her long reign, the wife of Napoleon III, Eugenie, empress of France, appears to have had little positive influence on the popularity of this name.

Nicknames: **Gena, Gene, Genia**

Variations: **Evgenia** (Russian), **Gina** (Italian)

Eunice Greek *Eunike,* "good victory," from *eu* [good, well] + *nike* [victory]. In the Bible, Eunice was the mother of the apostle Timothy, but this name has rarely been used.

Famous name: Eunice Kennedy Shriver (humanitarian)

Nicknames: **Eunie, Euny**

Eunie, Euny (see **Eunice**)

Eustacia Feminine form of Greek *Eustakhios,* "good grapes, fruitful." This name is very unusual today, but the short form **Stacy** has been quite popular in the United States.

Nicknames: **Stacey, Stacia, Stacie, Stacy**

Eva Latin form of Hebrew *Chava,* "life." The name of the biblical mother of the human race has enjoyed great popularity in Europe throughout history, even though it is not linked to either royalty or saints.

    Famous names: Eva Chun (fashion designer)
                     Eva Marie Saint (actress)

    Nicknames: **Evie, Evy**

    Variations: **Ava, Eabha** (Irish Gaelic), **Eubh** (Scots Gaelic), **Eve** (English and French), **Evica** (Bulgarian), **Evita** (Spanish), **Ewa** (Polish), **Ieva** (Latvian and Lithuanian), **Zoe** (Greek)

Evangeline Greek "messenger of good news."

Eve (see **Eva**)

Eveleen (see **Evelyn**)

Evica (see **Eva**)

Evelina (see **Evelyn**)

Eveline (see **Evelyn**)

Evelyn Modern English form of Norman French *Aveline,* a medieval name of unknown origin. In England, this name was formerly used for boys, but today it is usually a girl's name in all English-speaking countries. Hispanic-Americans are now fond of the name.

    Famous names: Evelyn Ashford (sprinter)
                     Evelyn Fox Keller (historian of science)

    Variations: **Aveline, Eileen** (Irish), **Eveleen, Evelina, Eveline**

Evgenia (see **Eugenia**)

Evie (see **Eva**)

Evita (see **Eva**)

Evonne (see **Yvonne**)

Evy (see **Eva**)

Ewa (see **Eva**)

Eydi, Eydie (see **Edith**)

Fae (see **Faith, Fay**)

Faith Latin *fides,* "belief in God" or "trust," through Old French
feid. The legendary St. Sophia's martyred daughters were
Faith, Hope, and Charity, named for the three virtues. It's not
surprising that the Puritans restored these names to favor
during Oliver Cromwell's reign in England when they gained
great popularity. In the Colonies, they were also very popular
Puritan names.

Famous name: Faith Baldwin (novelist)

Other spellings: **Fayth, Faythe**

Variations: **Fae, Fay, Faye**

Fallon Irish Gaelic *Fallamhan,* "leader." This Irish surname became
quite popular as a first name for American girls because of the
character Fallon Carrington on the successful television series
Dynasty.

Fanchon (see **Frances**)

Fanni, Fannie (see **Fanny**)

Fanny Form of **Frances.** This nickname for the popular name
Frances became an independent name in the 17th century.
Through his poetry, John Keats immortalized his love for
Fanny Brawne.

Famous name: Fannie Flagg (comedienne and author)

Other spellings: **Fanni, Fannie**

Fante (Ghana) "born on Friday."

Farrah Perhaps a form of Arabic *Farah,* "joy, happiness," the name of the wife of the late shah of Iran. However, the actress Farrah Fawcett has stated that her parents simply made up the name, so a blend of **Sarah** with the word *fair* may be the best explanation.

Fatima, Fatimah Arabic "weaner, abstainer," a name implying both motherly care and chastity. Fatima is a very common name in all Muslim communities because it was the name of the prophet Muhammad's favorite daughter, the mother of his only grandchildren. The name is also occasionally given by devout Roman Catholics in honor of the visions of the Virgin Mary that occurred at the village of Fatima in Portugal in 1917.
Variation: **Fatma**

Fatma (see **Fatima**)

Fawn Middle French *faon,* "young deer," from Latin *feton,* "offspring." This is an extremely rare name.
Variation: **Fawna**

Fawna (see **Fawn**)

Fay, Faye Old French *faie,* "fairy"; also, variation of **Faith.**
Famous name: Faye Dunaway (actress)
Other spelling: **Fae**

Fayola Yoruba (Nigeria) "good fortune walks with honor."

Fayth, Faythe (see **Faith**)

Fedora (see **Theodora**)

Felia (see **Felicia**)

Felicata (see **Felicity**)

Felicia Feminine form of **Felix,** Latin "lucky, happy." Felicia is now among the top 100 names given American girls.
Famous name: Felicia Farr (actress)
Variations: **Felia** (Dutch), **Felice, Felicie** (French), **Felicija** (Russian), **Feliksa** (Polish and Greek), **Felizia** (German), **Licia** (Hungarian), **Phylicia**

Felice (see **Felicia**)

Felicie (see **Felicia**)

Felicidad (see **Felicity**)

Felicija (see **Felicia**)

Felicita, Felicitas (see **Felicity**)

Felicite (see **Felicity**)

Felicity English form of Latin *felicitas,* "good fortune." The first St. Felicity was a second-century martyr who endured many tortures herself and was forced to watch her sons being tortured and killed before she was slain. The second St. Felicity was one of the victims thrown to the wild animals in the amphitheater. Felicity is more popular in Britain than the related name **Felicia,** but it is extremely rare in the United States.
> Variations: **Felicata** (Russian), **Felicidad** (Spanish), **Felicita** (Italian, Czech, and Baltic), **Felicitas** (Dutch, German, Scandinavian, and Rumanian), **Felicite** (French)

Feliksa (see **Felicia**)

Felipa (see **Philippa**)

Felizia (see **Felicia**)

Fenella Scottish form of Gaelic *Fionnguala,* "white shoulder."

Feodora (see **Theodora**)

Fern Old English *fearn,* "fern." Like many other flower names, this one appears to have enjoyed its greatest popularity in the late 19th century.
> Other spelling: **Ferne**

Fernanda Feminine form of **Fernando,** much less common among Hispanic-Americans today than the masculine form.

Ferne (see **Fern**)

Fialka (see **Violet**)

Fifi (see **Josephine**)

Filida (see Phyllis)

Filippa (see Philippa)

Filisa (see Phyllis)

Fillide (see Phyllis)

Fiona Form of Scots Gaelic *fionn,* "white, fair." This name was invented by Scottish poet James Macpherson in the 18th century. In the 20th century, it has become quite common as a first name in Scotland, England, and Australia, but it is still only rarely found in the United States. The heroine of the beloved Broadway musical *Brigadoon* is named Fiona.
Famous name: Fiona Ritchie (radio personality)

Fiora (see Flora)

Fiorella (see Flora)

Fiorenza (see Florence)

Flannery Irish Gaelic *Flannabhra,* "red eyebrows."
Famous name: Flannery O'Connor (writer)

Flavia Latin "golden yellow."
Famous name: Flavia Hodges (lexicographer)

Fleur French "flower." This name is only occasionally used in France itself. Fleur is the name of Irene's daughter in John Galsworthy's Forsyte novels, and the name developed some minor popularity in England in the 1970s after *The Forsyte Saga* was shown on British television. However, the presentation of the same series on American public television failed to arouse any interest in Fleur in the United States.

Fleurette (see Flora)

Flo (see Flora, Florence)

Floora (see Flora)

Flor (see Flora)

Flora Latin *floris,* "flower." Flora was the Roman goddess of spring. This name was especially common in Scotland because of admiration for Flora MacDonald, an 18th-century heroine of the fight to restore Prince Charles and the royal house of Stuart to the British throne.

Famous names: Flora Lewis (columnist)
Flora Robson (actress)

Nicknames: **Flo, Florrie, Florry**

Variations: **Fiora** (Italian), **Fiorella** (Italian), **Fleur** (French), **Fleurette, Floora** (Estonian and Finnish), **Flor** (Spanish), **Flore** (French), **Florella, Florette, Floria, Florica** (Rumanian), **Florinda, Florka** (Bulgarian), **Flower**

Florance (see **Florence**)

Flore (see **Flora**)

Florella Combination of **Flora**, Latin "flower," and the diminutive suffix "-ella," meaning "little flower."

Florence Latin *Florentia,* from *florens,* "flourishing, in the prime of life." This name is associated with Florence Nightingale, an English nurse who helped the wounded during the Crimean War. She was given the name Florence because she was born in the city of Florence, Italy.

Famous name: Florence Griffith Joyner (athlete)

Nicknames: **Flo, Flori, Florrie, Florry, Floss, Flossie, Floy**

Variations: **Fiorenza** (Italian), **Florance, Florencia** (Spanish, Portuguese, Hungarian, and Dutch), **Florencja** (Polish), **Florenta** (Rumanian), **Florentia** (German and Finnish), **Florenza** (Italian), **Florenze** (German and Estonian)

Florencia (see **Florence**)

Florencja (see **Florence**)

Florenta, Florentia (see **Florence**)

Florenza, Florenze (see **Florence**)

Florette (see **Flora**)

Flori (see **Florence**)

Floria (see **Flora**)

Florica (see **Flora**)

Florida Spanish "flowery," the name of the American state given to it in 1513 by Spanish explorer Ponce de Leon. This place name has been given to girls on rare occasions for more than a century.

Florinda (see **Flora**)

Florka (see **Flora**)

Florrie, Florry (see **Flora, Florence**)

Floss, Flossie (see **Florence**)

Flower (see **Flora**)

Floy (see **Florence**)

Fonda Origin unknown; perhaps a modern creation based on the word *fond,* "loving," from Middle English *fonned,* "foolish."

Fran Form of **Frances.**
Famous name: Fran Lebowitz (writer)

Frances Feminine form of **Francis,** Latin "a Frenchman." The difference in spelling between the male and female forms of this name was not set until the 17th century. Frances was among the top 50 names for American girls born between 1890 and 1950, which was a very long run of popularity. The fashion for the name can be traced to Frances Cleveland, wife of President Grover Cleveland. She was exceptionally young and beautiful and was the first presidential spouse to be featured on her husband's campaign posters. By 1991, Frances had fallen to only 319th on the list of names given baby girls in the United States.
Nicknames: **Fanny, Fran, Francie, Francy, Frankie, Franky, Frannie, Franny**
Variations: **Cecca** (Italian), **Fanchon** (French), **Francesca** (Italian), **Francine** (French), **Francisca** (Spanish), **Franciska** (Bulgarian, Danish, and Hungarian), **Franciszka** (Polish), **Francoise** (French), **Franka** (Russian and Norwegian), **Fransina** (Dutch), **Frantiska** (Czech and Greek), **Franuse** (Latvian), **Franzi** (German), **Franziska** (German), **Prane** (Lithuanian)

Francesca Italian form of **Frances.** This Italian name is now more fashionable in the Hispanic-American community than is **Francisca**, the normal Spanish form of Frances.

Francie (see **Frances**)

Francine Variation of **Frances**.

Francisca (see **Frances**)

Franciska (see **Frances**)

Franciszka (see **Frances**)

Francoise French variation of **Frances**. Francoise was the most common name for French girls born in the late 1940s, but the name is now almost completely out of fashion with French parents.

Francy (see **Frances**)

Franka (see **Frances**)

Frankie, Franky (see **Frances**)

Frannie, Franny (see **Frances**)

Fransina (see **Frances**)

Frantiska (see **Frances**)

Franuse (see **Frances**)

Franzi, Franziska (see **Frances**)

Freda Variation of **Frederika** or **Winifred**.
　　Other spellings: **Freida, Frieda**
　　Variation: **Frida** (Hungarian and Spanish)

Freddie, Freddy (see **Frederika, Winifred**)

Frederica, Fredericka (see **Frederika**)

Frederika Feminine form of **Frederick**, Old German "peace ruler."
　　Nicknames: **Freda, Freddie, Freddy, Rica, Ricky**
　　Other spellings: **Frederica, Fredericka**

Freida, Frida, Frieda (see **Freda**)

Gabby, Gabie, Gaby (see **Gabrielle**)

Gabra (see **Gabrielle**)

Gabriela Spanish and Portuguese form of **Gabrielle.** This name is very popular in Latin America and in the U.S. Hispanic community. It is now being used by other Americans as an alternative feminine form for **Gabriel.** Gabriela rose from 239th to 165th place on the list of names for girls in America from 1989 to 1991.

Famous names: Gabriela Mistral (poet)
                Gabriela Sabatini (tennis player)
                Gabriella Tucci (soprano)

Other spelling: **Gabriella**

Gabriele (see **Gabrielle**)

Gabriella (see **Gabriela, Gabrielle**)

Gabrielle French feminine form of **Gabriel,** Hebrew "man of God." This name is not very popular in France, but it is becoming fashionable in the United States as Gabriel becomes more popular for boys. The drawback to this pretty name is the nickname Gabby, which has a negative connotation of "gossipy."

Famous name: Gabrielle "Coco" Chanel (clothing and
                  perfume designer)

Nicknames: **Gabby, Gabie, Gaby**

Variations: **Gabra** (Czech), **Gabriela** (Spanish, Portuguese, and Polish), **Gabriele** (German), **Gabriella** (Italian and Swedish), **Gabysia** (Polish), **Gavraila** (Bulgarian), **Gavrina** (Rumanian)

Gabysia (see **Gabrielle**)

Gae (see **Gay**)

Gail Form of **Abigail**. Although this name started out as a nickname, it was very popular as an independent name from the 1940s through the 1960s in the United States.
Famous names: Gail Godwin (novelist)
Gail Sheehy (writer)
Gail Strickland (actress)
Other spellings: **Gale, Gayle**
Variations: **Gayla, Gayleen**

Gale Form of **Gail**, nickname for **Abigail**.
Famous name: Gale Storm (actress)

Gali Modern Hebrew "my ocean wave." In the 1980s, this was the most popular name for newborn girls in Israel.

Garnet Latin *granulum*, "granular, seedlike." This is one of the jewel names that was popular at the end of the 19th century.

Gavraila (see **Gabrielle**)

Gavrina (see **Gabrielle**)

Gay Old French *gai*, "joyful."
Other spellings: **Gae, Gaye**

Gaye (see **Gay**)

Gayla (see **Gail**)

Gayle (see **Abigail, Gail**)

Gayleen (see **Gail**)

Gaynor (see **Guinevere**)

Gazella (see **Gazelle**)

Gazelle Arabic "small antelope" or "gazelle."
Variation: **Gazella**

Geena Form of **Gena** or **Gina.**
Famous name: Geena Davis (actress)

Geertruida (see **Gertrude**)

Gemma Italian *gemma,* "jewel, gem." In England in the mid-1980s, this became one of the top ten most popular names for girls. However, it is still exceedingly rare in the United States.

Famous name: Gemma Jones (actress)

Gen (see **Genevieve**)

Gena Form of **Eugenia** or **Gina.**

Famous name: Gena Rowlands (actress)

Other spelling: **Geena**

Gene (see **Eugenia, Jean**)

Geneva French *Geneve,* possibly from Latin *janua,* "gateway"; also, a variation of **Genevieve.** This name is often chosen in direct reference to Geneva, Switzerland.

Genevie (see **Genevieve**)

Genevieve Probably a French form of *Genovefa,* Old German from *genos* [race of people] and *wefa* [woman]. This French name is slowly increasing in use in the United States. St. Genevieve is the patron saint of Paris because she saved the city from an attack by Attila the Hun.

Famous name: Genevieve Bujold (actress)

Nicknames: **Gen, Geni, Genni, Gennie, Genny, Jen, Jennie, Jenny**

Variations: **Geneva, Genevie, Genna, Genovaite** (Lithuanian), **Genovefa** (Dutch and Russian), **Genoveffa** (Italian), **Genoveva** (Spanish, Swedish, and German), **Genowefa** (Polish), **Jenovefa** (Czech and Greek)

Geni (see **Genevieve**)

Genia (see **Eugenia**)

Genna (see **Genevieve, Jenna**)

Genni, Gennie, Genny (see **Genevieve, Jennifer**)

Gennifer (see **Jennifer**)

Genovaite (see **Genevieve**)

Genovefa, Genoveffa (see **Genevieve**)

Genoveva (see **Genevieve**)

Genowefa (see **Genevieve**)

Georgeanna, Georgeanne (see **Georgiana**)

Georgette Form of **Georgiana.**
Famous name: Georgette Heyer (novelist)

Georgia Form of **Georgiana.** This is the most common feminine form of **George** in the United States.
Famous name: Georgia O'Keeffe (painter)

Georgiana Feminine form of **George,** Greek "farmer." Georgiana seems to have been the original feminine form of George in English-speaking countries, but it's hardly been used since the 18th century.
Nicknames: **Georgie, Gigi, Gina**
Variations: **Georgeanna, Georgeanne, Georgette** (French), **Georgia, Georgianna, Georgina, Georgine**

Georgianna (see **Georgiana**)

Georgie (see **Georgiana**)

Georgina Form of **Georgiana.** Although rare in America, Georgina has been the most popular feminine version of **George** in Britain for two centuries. This name is now among the top 50 names in England.

Georgine (see **Georgiana**)

Geralda (see **Geraldine**)

Geraldina (see **Geraldine**)

Geraldine Feminine form of **Gerald,** Old German "spear ruler." The pet forms of this name, **Gerri** and **Jerri,** are now more popular as official names on birth certificates than Geraldine itself.
Famous names: Geraldine Chaplin (actress)
Geraldine Ferraro (politician)
Geraldine Fitzgerald (actress)
Geraldine Page (actress)

Nicknames: **Gerri, Gerrie, Gerry, Jeri, Jerri, Jerry**

Variations: **Geralda** (Czech and Dutch), **Geraldina** (Spanish, Portuguese and Italian), **Giralda** (Italian)

Gerlinda, Gerlinde German from *geri* [spear] + *linta* [lindenwood shield].

Germaine Feminine form of Late Latin *Germanus,* "brother."

Famous name: Germaine Greer (writer)

Gerri, Gerrie, Gerry (see **Geraldine**)

Gert, Gertie (see **Gertrude**)

Gertraud (see **Gertrude**)

Gertrud (see **Gertrude**)

Gertrude Old German *Gertrud* from *ger* [spear] and *trud* [strength]. In ancient Norse mythology, Gertrude was one of the goddesses who accompanied dead heroes to Valhalla. Four saints have the name, which probably helped it become very popular during the Middle Ages. St. Gertrude of Nivelles is the patron saint of travelers, and St. Gertrude the Great was a mystic. The most famous fictional Gertrude is the mother of Hamlet in Shakespeare's play *Hamlet.*

Famous names: Gertrude Ederle (swimmer)
               Gertrude Lawrence (actress)
               Gertrude Stein (writer)

Nicknames: **Gert, Gertie, Gerty, Truda, Trudi, Trudie, Trudy**

Variations: **Geertruida** (Dutch), **Gertraud** (German), **Gertrud** (German, Scandinavian, and Hungarian), **Gertrudis** (Spanish), **Trude** (German and Norwegian)

Gertrudis (see **Gertrude**)

Gerty (see **Gertrude**)

Gianna Italian form of **Jane.** This name is just starting to rise in popularity in the United States, especially with Hispanic-Americans.

Variations: **Giannina, Jeanna**

Giannina (see **Gianna**)

Gigi Form of **Georgiana** or **Virginia.** The Lerner and Loewe musical *Gigi* was made into an Oscar-winning movie starring Leslie Caron and Maurice Chevalier.
Famous name: Gigi Mahon (writer)

Gilda Italian form of Old German *gild,* "sacrificed." In Verdi's opera, Gilda is Rigoletto's daughter.
Famous name: Gilda Radner (actress)

Gill (see **Gillian**)

Gillian Medieval English form of **Juliana.** This name was popular in the Middle Ages and enjoyed renewed popularity in Great Britain during the 1960s. It is starting to catch on in the United States, but in America **Jillian** is the preferred spelling. As a name for girls, Gillian is pronounced with a soft "g"; with a hard "g" it becomes a Scots Gaelic name for boys meaning "servant of St. John."
Nicknames: **Gill, Gillie, Gilly**
Variations: **Jill, Jillian, Jillie, Jilly**

Gillie, Gilly (see **Gillian**)

Gina Form of **Eugenia, Georgiana, Luigina,** or **Regina.**
Famous name: Gina Lollobrigida (actress)
Other spellings: **Geena, Gena**

Ginebra (see **Guinevere**)

Ginevra (see **Guinevere**)

Ginger Latin *gingiber* from Greek *zingiberis,* "ginger spice"; also, a variation of **Virginia.**
Famous name: Ginger Rogers (actress)

Ginnie (see **Ginny, Virginia**)

Ginny Variation of **Virginia.**
Other spelling: **Ginnie**

Giovanna (see **Jane**)

Giralda (see **Geraldine**)

Gisela (see **Giselle**)

Gisele (see **Giselle**)

Gisella (see **Giselle**)

Giselle French form of *Gisila,* Old German "pledge, hostage."
Giselle is one of the most often performed ballets, with music
composed by Adolphe Charles Adam. Nijinsky and Anna
Pavlova made the ballet famous through their dynamic
presentation of it. This traditionally French name is now
especially popular in the United States with parents of
Hispanic ancestry.
Famous names: Giselle Fernandez (television journalist)
Gisele MacKenzie (singer)
Variations: **Gisela** (German, Dutch, Spanish and Finnish),
Gisele (French), **Gisella** (Italian), **Gizela** (Polish)

Gitta (see **Bridget**)

Giuditta (see **Judith**)

Giulia (see **Julia**)

Giulietta Italian form of **Julia.** This is the original name of the
heroine of Shakespeare's *Romeo and Juliet.*
Famous name: Giulietta Masina (actress)

Giuseppina (see **Josephine**)

Giustina (see **Justina**)

Gizela (see **Giselle**)

Glad (see **Gladys**)

Gladdie, Gladdy (see **Gladys**)

Gladine (see **Gladys**)

Gladys English form of Welsh *Gwladus,* meaning uncertain. The
name may possibly be from an ancient Welsh word for "ruler,"
or it may simply be the Welsh form of **Claudia.** Gladys stormed
out of Wales around 1890 and was one of the top ten names for
girls in both England and the United States by 1900. However,
it was already out of fashion again by 1925. It's probable that
the fashion for Gladys was helped by the name's similarity to
the flower name *gladiolus* (Latin "lily") and the common word

glad, although there is no real etymological connection between the name and either of these words. Gladys is now extremely rare as a name for newborn girls.

Famous name: Gladys Knight (singer)

Nicknames: **Glad, Gladdie, Gladdy**

Variations: **Gladine, Gwladys**

Glenda Probably a feminine form of **Glenn,** blending it with the sound of **Linda.** In Britain it is often interpreted as Welsh *glen* [clean, pure] + *da* [good].

Famous name: Glenda Jackson (actress)

Glenn Celtic *gleann,* "wooded valley, glen." Despite the recent fame of actresses Glenn Close and Glenne Headly, this is still almost invariably a name for boys in the United States.

Other spelling: **Glenne**

Variations: **Glenna, Glynn**

Glenna Feminine form of **Glenn.**

Glenne (see **Glenn**)

Glorea (see **Gloria**)

Glori (see **Gloria**)

Gloria Latin *gloria,* "glory." This name first became widely known through actress Gloria Swanson, who began appearing in silent movies in 1915. She was one of the few silent movie stars to maintain her popularity after sound was introduced to film. Gloria was one of the top 50 names for American girls born between 1925 and 1950. Although the name is much less popular today, it is still being regularly used, especially in the Hispanic-American community.

Famous names: Gloria Estefan (singer)
Gloria Naylor (novelist)
Gloria Steinem (writer)

Variations: **Glorea, Glori, Gloriana, Glorianna, Glory**

Gloriana, Glorianna (see **Gloria**)

Glory (see **Gloria**)

Glynis Welsh "little valley."

Famous names: Glynis Johns (actress)
Glynnis O'Connor (actress)
Other spellings: **Glynnis, Glynys**

Glynn (see **Glenn**)

Glynnis (see **Glynis**)

Glynys (see **Glynis**)

Golda Yiddish and Old English "gold."
Famous name: Golda Meir (prime minister of Israel)
Variation: **Goldie**

Goldie Form of **Golda.**
Famous name: Goldie Hawn (actress)

Gosia (see **Margaret**)

Goslin (see **Jocelyn**)

Grace Latin *gratia,* "grace." In Greek mythology, the three
Graces—Aglaia, Euphrosyne, and Thaleia—are associated
with art and beauty. This name, however, appears to have been
initiated by the Puritans, who used it to mean "favor and love
of God." But Grace remained a common name after most
other Puritan virtue names died out, which probably means
that later parents once again interpreted it as "beauty of form
or movement." Grace is still among the top 200 names given to
American girls, and it seems to be gradually increasing in
popularity.
Famous names: Grace Kelly (princess of Monaco)
Grace Paley (poet)
Nicknames: **Gracie, Gracye**
Variations: **Gracia** (Spanish), **Graciela** (Spanish and
Bulgarian), **Gracja** (Polish), **Gratia** (German, Dutch, and
Scandinavian), **Gratija** (Greek and Russian), **Grazia**
(Italian), **Graziella** (Italian)

Gracia (see **Grace**)

Gracie (see **Grace**)

Graciela (see **Grace**)

Gracja (see **Grace**)

Gracye (see **Grace**)

Gratia (see **Grace**)

Gratija (see **Grace**)

Grazia, Graziella (see **Grace**)

Greer Scottish surname, form of **Gregory,** Greek "watchful." The general use of this last name as a first name for girls in the 20th century is entirely due to the fame of actress Greer Garson. Greer was her mother's maiden name.

Greet (see **Margaret**)

Greta Swedish variation of **Margaret.**
   Famous names: Greta Garbo (actress)
                 Greta Scacchi (actress)

Gretchen Form of **Margaret.** This German diminutive for the name Margaret has become an independent name in Germany as well as the United States. In *Faust,* Goethe often referred to his heroine as Gretchen.

Grete (see **Margaret**)

Gretel (see **Margaret**)

Griselda Old German *gris* [gray] + *hild* [battle]. This name is now extremely rare, but it is still used occasionally in the Hispanic-American community.
   Variations: **Grizel** (Scottish), **Zelda**

Grizel (see **Griselda**)

Guendolina (see **Gwendolyn**)

Guenevere (see **Guinevere**)

Guglielma (see **Wilhelmina**)

Guillemette (see **Wilhelmina**)

Guillerma (see **Wilhelmina**)

Guinevere Old French form of Welsh *Gwenhwyfar* from *gwen* [white, blessed] + *hwyfar* [soft, smooth]. In the Arthurian legend, Guinevere, the wife of King Arthur, falls in love with Sir Lancelot. Guinevere is very rare as a modern name, but its Cornish form, Jennifer, has been one of the most popular names for girls since the late 1960s.

Nicknames: **Gwen, Gwynne**

Variations: **Gaynor, Ginebra** (Spanish), **Ginevra** (Italian), **Guenevere, Gwenore, Jennifer** (Cornish), **Vanora** (Scottish)

Gussie (see **Augusta**)

Gusta (see **Augusta**)

Gvendolina (see **Gwendolyn**)

Gwen Form of **Guinevere** or **Gwendolyn.**

Gwenda (see **Gwendolyn**)

Gwendalina (see **Gwendolyn**)

Gwendolen (see **Gwendolyn**)

Gwendoline (see **Gwendolyn**)

Gwendolyn Welsh *Gwendolen* from *gwen* [white, fair, holy] + *dolen* [link, ring, bow]. This name was extremely popular with educated African-American parents during the 1950s and 1960s because of admiration for poet Gwendolyn Brooks. In 1950, she was the first African-American poet to win a Pulitzer Prize.

Nickname: **Gwen**

Variations: **Guendolina** (Spanish), **Gvendolina** (Czech), **Gwenda, Gwendalina** (Polish), **Gwendolen, Gwendoline** (French)

Gwenore (see **Guinevere**)

Gwladys (see **Gladys**)

Gwynne (see **Guinevere**)

Hailee, Hailey (see **Haley**)

Haley Old English *Hayley,* "hay clearing," a British place name and surname; in the 19th century, also a rare pet form of **Mahala.** Although the modern fashion for this name can be traced to the fame of actress Hayley Mills, Haley is now definitely the more popular spelling in the United States. Haley has steadily been growing more popular and was the 44th most common name given to American girls in 1991.

Other spellings: **Hailee, Hailey, Haylee, Hayley**

Halle, Hallie Form of **Harriet;** Hallie developed as a nickname for Harriet in the same way that **Hal** evolved as a nickname for **Harry.** This 19th-century name has recently begun to show signs of renewed popularity in the United States.

Famous name: Halle Berry (actress)

Hana, Hanna (see **Hannah**)

Hanka (see **Jane**)

Hannah Hebrew "the Lord has favored me." In the Bible, Hannah was the mother of the prophet Samuel. Hannah has rapidly returned to popularity in both England and the United States recently. By 1990, the name was well into the top 50 list for girls on both sides of the Atlantic, with strong indications that Hannah will be a top ten name soon.

Famous names: Hannah Arendt (historian)
Hana Mandlikova (tennis player)

Other spellings: **Hana, Hanna**

Variations: **Anna, Anne, Hanne** (Scandinavian and German), **Hannele** (German), **Hannie, Hanny, Nan**

Hanne (see **Hannah**)

Hannele (see **Hannah**)

Hannie, Hanny (see **Hannah**)

Harmony Greek *harmonia,* "framework, agreement."

Harriet Form of **Henrietta** created in 17th-century England. Harriet was a name of choice in the 18th and 19th centuries, but it is now fairly unpopular. It's difficult to tell whether the name's strong association with the 1950s television series *The Adventures of Ozzie and Harriet* had a positive or negative influence on this name. Although the author of *Frankenstein,* Mary Shelley, is usually considered to be the love of poet Percy Bysshe Shelley's life, he wrote the lovely poem "To Harriet" for his first wife.

Famous names: Harriet Doerr (writer)
Harriet Beecher Stowe (author)
Harriet Tubman (civil rights activist)
Harriet Zuckerman (scholar)

Nicknames: **Halle, Hallie, Hattie, Hatty**
Other spelling: **Harriette**
Variation: **Harrietta**

Harrietta (see **Harriet**)

Harriette (see **Harriet**)

Hattie, Hatty (see **Harriet**)

Haylee, Hayley (see **Haley**)

Hazel Old English *haesel,* "hazel tree." The cartoon series *Hazel* and its spin-off television show, in which actress Shirley Booth played an outspoken maid, ruined this name's chances for early revival. Like Abigail, which dropped from use when it became associated with a lady's maid in the 17th century, Hazel will sound like a servant's name for a long time.

Famous name: Hazel O'Leary (U.S. Secretary of Energy)
Variations: **Hazell, Hazelle**

Hazell, Hazelle (see **Hazel**)

Heather Middle English *hathir,* "heather." This flower name first became popular in England in the 1950s. In the 1970s, Heather was transplanted to the United States and became extremely fashionable. Although it has now started to go out of style, Heather was still the 29th most popular name for American girls born in 1991.

Famous names: Heather Locklear (actress)
Heather McCrae (actress)
Heather Watts (ballerina)

Hedda Scandinavian variation of **Hedwig**. Because Hedda sounds so much better to most modern Americans than Hedwig, it's not surprising that this variation is used more frequently in the United States than the original version of the name. But it is still extremely rare and may be shadowed by its association with Ibsen's dark play *Hedda Gabler.*

Famous name: Hedda Hopper (columnist)

Hedy Form of **Hedwig**.

Famous name: Hedy Lamarr (actress)

Hedwig Old German *hadu* [dispute] + *wig* [war].

Variations: **Hedda** (Scandinavian), **Hedy**

Heide (see **Heidi**)

Heidi Form of **Adelaide**. The cheerful Swiss girl in Johanna Spyri's *Heidi* always comes to mind when you hear this name.

Famous name: Heidi Landesman (set designer)

Other spelling: **Heide**

Hela (see **Helen**)

Helaine (see **Helen**)

Helen Greek *Helene,* perhaps "bright, sunbeam." The legend of the beautiful Helen of Troy has caused parents to choose this name for their daughters for thousands of years. In Homer's *Iliad,* Helen was the wife of Menelaus, the king of Greece. There are conflicting accounts about whether Helen was stolen by Paris, the son of Priam who was king of Troy, or whether she agreed to flee with him. Because Helen had been promised to Paris by the goddess Aphrodite, she may not have had much choice in the matter. But for whatever reason Helen went off with Paris, the Greeks waged war on the Trojans to get her back. She was "the face that launched a thousand ships." Helen also appears in Christopher Marlowe's *Dr. Faustus* and in Shakespeare's *A Midsummer Night's Dream* and *All's Well That Ends Well.* In 1900, Helen was second only to Mary as a popular name for American girls. Although now out of fashion in the United States, Helen has been at the height of popularity in England since 1965.

Famous names: Helen Gurley Brown (publisher)
　　　　　　　Helen Hayes (actress)
　　　　　　　Helen Keller (author and educator)
　　　　　　　Helen Thomas (journalist)

Variations: **Eileen** (Irish), **Eilidh** (Scots Gaelic), **Elaine, Eleanor, Elen** (Welsh and Norwegian), **Elena** (Italian, Spanish, Portuguese, Baltic, and Russian), **Eleni** (Greek), **Elin** (Scandinavian), **Elina** (Finnish), **Ella, Ellen, Elna, Hela** (Czech), **Helaine, Helena** (Latin), **Helene** (French, Latvian, and German), **Helenka** (Czech), **Ileana** (Rumanian), **Ilona** (Hungarian), **Jelena** (Croatian and Slovenian), **Lean** (Irish Gaelic), **Lena** (German, Dutch, and Scandinavian), **Lenka** (Slavic), **Lenuta** (Rumanian), **Lina, Nell, Nellie, Olena** (Ukrainian), **Yelena** (Russian)

Helena Latin form of **Helen** and normally the full form of the name in Germany, Scandinavia, and Poland. St. Helena was the mother of Constantine the Great, the Roman emperor who converted to Christianity.

Famous name: Helena Sukova (tennis player)

Helene (see **Helen**)

Helenka (see **Helen**)

Helga Old Norse *heilagr,* "prosperous, blessed."

Variations: **Elga** (Danish, Latvian, and Greek), **Oili** (Finnish), **Ola** (Serbian and Slovenian), **Olga** (Russian, Polish, Spanish, Portuguese, and Italian), **Ollo** (Estonian)

Helma (see **Wilhelmina**)

Helmine (see **Wilhelmina**)

Heloise Origin unclear; perhaps a French form of Old German *Helewidis* from *haila* [healthy] + *vid* [wide]; or perhaps a form of **Louise.** The letters exchanged between Heloise and Abelard, a 12th-century philosopher, are among the most beautiful expressions of love ever written. Heloise was Peter Abelard's student; they fell in love, but her family was opposed to their marriage. After they secretly wed, her uncle had Peter castrated. He entered a monastery and she became a nun, but the two lovers continued to write each other until their deaths.
    Variations: **Eloisa, Eloise**

Hendrika (see **Henrietta**)

Henna (see **Henrietta**)

Henrietta Feminine form of **Henry,** Old German "home ruler."
    Famous name: Henrietta Maria (wife of King Charles I of England)
    Nicknames: **Etta, Ettie, Etty, Hettie, Hetty**
    Variations: **Enrica** (Italian), **Enrichetta** (Italian), **Enrika** (Greek), **Enriqueta** (Spanish), **Harriet, Hendrika** (Dutch), **Henna** (Finnish), **Henriette** (French), **Henrika** (Swedish), **Yetta** (Yiddish)

Henriette (see **Henrietta**)

Henrika (see **Henrietta**)

Hera Greek "lady." In Greek mythology, Hera was the wife of Zeus and a powerful goddess in her own right.

Hermanna German feminine form of **Herman.**

Hermia Latin feminine form of Greek *Hermes,* name of the god who served as Zeus's messenger.
    Variation: **Hermione**

Hermione Variation of **Hermia.** There are two legendary Hermiones: the daughter of Mars and Venus, who was turned into a serpent, and the daughter of Helen of Troy and Menelaus.
    Famous name: Hermione Gingold (actress)

Hester Variation of Persian *Ester,* "star." Hester Prynne, the heroine of Nathaniel Hawthorne's *The Scarlet Letter* who was forced by her Puritan community to wear a badge of adultery, may give this lovely old name an unpleasant association.

Variations: **Esther, Hestera, Hettie, Hetty**

Hestera (see **Hester**)

Hestia Name of the Greek goddess of the hearth, of unknown derivation.

Variation: **Vesta** (Latin)

Hettie, Hetty (see **Henrietta, Hester**)

Hilaria (see **Hilary**)

Hilarie (see **Hilary**)

Hilary Latin *Hilaria,* form of *hilaris,* "cheerful." In medieval times, this was considered a male name, but it was revived in England around 1890 as a female form. Hilary was very popular in Britain during the 1950s and 1960s. In the United States, Hilary began to be used around 1960. The name has been slowly but steadily becoming generally popular, however, and was the 102nd most common name given to American girls in 1991. Although it remains to be seen whether Hillary Rodham Clinton's fame will have a positive or negative effect on use of the name, a negative one is more likely because most Americans since the 1950s have avoided naming children after political figures.

Other spellings: **Hillary, Hillery**

Variations: **Hilaria** (Spanish, Portuguese, Danish, and Hungarian), **Hilarie** (French), **Ilaria** (Russian and Italian)

Hilda Latin form of Germanic *hild,* "battle." This name was briefly popular around 1900, but it is very rarely given today.

Famous name: Hilda Doolittle (poet known as H.D.)

Nicknames: **Hildie, Hildy**

Variations: **Hilde** (Norwegian and German), **Ildiko** (Hungarian)

Hilde (see **Hilda**)

Hildie, Hildy Form of **Hilda.** Rosalind Russell created a flashy cinematic Hildy in *His Girl Friday,* in which she goes head to head with Cary Grant.

Hillary Form of **Hilary.** This spelling has been somewhat more common than the original in the United States for at least a decade.

Hillery (see **Hilary**)

Holley, Hollie (see **Holly**)

Holly Old English *holegn,* "holly." Holly used to be an especially popular name for girls born around Christmas, but parents now give this cheerful-sounding name to girls born at other times of the year also. American writer Truman Capote dubbed the heroine of his story *Breakfast at Tiffany's* Holly Golightly.
Famous names: Holly Hunter (actress)
                   Holly Near (singer)
Other spellings: **Holley, Hollie**

Honor Latin "honorable."
Famous name: Honor Blackman (actress)
Variations: **Honora** (Irish), **Honoria, Nora, Norah**

Honora, Honoria (see **Honor**)

Hope Old English *hopian,* "hope." The Puritans liked to give their children names that they should live up to, and as one of the three virtues, Hope was common for girls in 17th-century England and America. Although most other virtue names are not often used today, **Faith,** Hope, and Charity have remained somewhat popular. On the television series *thirtysomething,* actress Mel Harris played the character Hope Murdoch.
Famous name: Hope Lange (actress)

Hortense French feminine form of Latin *Hortensius,* a Roman family name, possibly meaning "gardener."
Variations: **Hortensia, Hortenzie** (Danish), **Ortensia** (Italian)

Hortensia (see **Hortense**)

Hortenzie (see **Hortense**)

Hyacinth Greek "blue larkspur." This flower name is very unusual.

Hypatia Greek "highest, surpassing."

Iantha, Ianthe Greek "violet."

Ida Old German *id,* "work, labor." The Normans brought this name with them to the British Isles when they invaded in 1066. But the name was very popular in the 19th century, partly because of "The Princess" by Alfred, Lord Tennyson, and especially because of Gilbert and Sullivan's operetta *Princess Ida.*
Famous names: Ida Lupino (actress)
　　　　　　　Ida B. Wells (educator)
Variations: **Idda** (German), **Ide** (French and Danish), **Idis** (German), **Iida** (Finnish)

Idalia From a title of Aphrodite, the Greek goddess of love. This is a form of *Idalion,* a town where there was an important temple of the goddess. The town's name is legendarily explained as being a contraction of Greek *eidon helios,* "I see the sun."

Idda (see **Ida**)

Ide (see **Ida**)

Idis (see **Ida**)

Iesha American form of **Aisha**. This name has quickly become incredibly popular in the African-American community. In 1991, Iesha was the fifth most popular name given to nonwhite girls born in the United States.

Ieva (see **Eva**)

Ifetayo Yoruba (Nigeria) "love brings happiness."

Iida (see **Ida**)

Ilaria (see **Hilary**)

Ildiko (see **Hilda**)

Ileana Rumanian form of **Helen,** now regularly used in the
   Hispanic-American community. Ileana Ros-Lehtinen of Miami
   was the first Cuban-American elected to the U.S. Congress.

Ilene (see **Eileen**)

Ilka Variation of **Ilona.**
   Famous name: Ilka Chase (actress and columnist)

Ilona Hungarian form of **Helen.**
   Variations: **Elona, Ilka, Ilonka**

Ilonka (see **Ilona**)

Ilsa, Ilse German forms of **Elizabeth** or **Elsa.**

Ilze (see **Elizabeth**)

Iman, Imani Arabic and Swahili "faith."

Imelda Italian and Spanish form of Germanic *Irmhild* from *irmen*
   [whole, entire] + *hild* [battle]. This name will probably be
   associated with Imelda Marcos, wife of the Philippine dictator
   who was removed from power by a popular uprising against his
   government in the 1980s.

Imogen From Celtic *Innogen,* perhaps from *inghean,* "maiden."
   This unusual name first appears in Shakespeare's play
   Cymbeline. Most experts believe that Shakespeare simply
   misread "Innogen" as "Imogen" when he consulted the written
   sources on which he based this play. The name has never
   appealed to many parents.
   Famous name: Imogen Cunningham (photographer)
   Variation: **Imogene**

Imogene Modern form of **Imogen,** blending it with the sound of
   Jean.
   Famous name: Imogene Coca (comedienne)
   Variations: **Emogene, Imogine, Imojean**

Imogine, Imojean (see **Imogene**)

Ina The origin of this name is disputed, but it is probably just a nickname for any name for girls ending in "-ina," such as **Christina, Georgina, Wilhelmina,** and so forth. Because this name is normally pronounced to rhyme with "China," it probably originated in Scotland. Scots commonly use "-ina" with this pronunciation as a feminine suffix to change a masculine name to a feminine one, as in Robertina or Jamesina.

Famous names: Ina Balin (actress)
Ina Claire (comedienne)

India Sanskrit *sindhuh,* "river," name of the country. India is now a fairly popular name for girls of African-American parents.

Indira Hindi *Indra,* "India."

Famous name: Indira Gandhi (prime minister of India)

Ines (see **Agnes, Inez**)

Inez Spanish form of **Agnes.** When Inez de Castro married Don Pedro, her father-in-law, King Alfonso I of Portugal, was so displeased that he had her killed. The distraught bridegroom never forgave his father, and when he became king, he crowned his dead wife queen. This romantic tale has made the name Inez consistently popular in Europe and the Americas. In his epic poem *Childe Harold's Pilgrimage,* George Gordon, Lord Byron, used the name Inez of Cadiz for his heroine.

Other spelling: **Ines**

Inga, Inge (see **Ingrid**)

Inger (see **Ingrid**)

Ingrid Old Norse *Ingfrid* from *Inge* [a Norse god] + *frid* [pretty]. Inge was the powerful god of the harvest in Norse mythology. The name Ingrid honored the god and also blessed the child to whom the name was given.

Famous name: Ingrid Bergman (actress)

Variations: **Inga** (Swedish), **Inge** (Danish and German), **Inger** (Swedish)

Iola Greek "cloud at dawn."

Iolanda, Iolande (see **Yolanda**)

Iolanthe From the Greek words *iole,* "violet," and *anthos,* "flower," evidently created in 1882 by Gilbert and Sullivan for the title character of their operetta *Iolanthe.*
Variation: Violet

Iona Latin form of Old Norse *ey,* "island," the name of a famous island off the coast of Scotland where St. Columba founded a monastery; or a form of **Ione.**

Ione Origin unclear; perhaps Greek "violet" or "one from Ionia," which is the ancient name for the western part of Asia Minor bordering the Aegean Sea.
Variations: **Iona, Ionia**

Ionia (see **Ione**)

Ira (see **Irene**)

Irena (see **Irene**)

Irene Greek *Eirene,* "peace." Eirene was the Greek goddess of peace, and Greek queens took this name at their coronations, as did some of the Russian empresses. In England, this name used to be pronounced with three syllables, as in the name of the beautiful heroine Irene of John Galsworthy's Forsyte novels.
Famous names: Irene Cara (actress)
                Irene Dunne (actress)
                Irene Worth (actress)
Nicknames: **Rena, Rene, Renie, Rina**
Variations: **Eirene** (Greek), **Eirin** (Norwegian), **Ira** (Serbo-Croatian), **Irena** (Polish), **Irina** (Russian and Rumanian)

Irida (see **Iris**)

Irina Variation of **Irene.**
Famous name: Irina Ratushinskaya (poet)

Iris Greek "rainbow." This flower name is now regularly being given to Hispanic-American girls.
Famous name: Iris Murdoch (writer)
Variations: **Irida** (Bulgarian and Croatian), **Irisa** (Rumanian)

Irisa (see **Iris**)

Irma Old German *irmen,* "whole, universal." Shirley MacLaine's high-stepping portrayal of Irma la Douce in the movie of the same name may have brought the actress much praise, but the character's occupation may have tainted this name in the minds of many parents.

Variations: **Erma, Irmina** (Polish, Lithuanian, and Italian)

Irmina (see **Irma**)

Isa (see **Isabel**)

Isabeau (see **Isabel**)

Isabel Spanish variation of **Elizabeth.** Isabel was exported through royal marriages from Spain to both France and England during the Middle Ages.

Famous names: Isabel Allende (writer)
　　　　　　　Isabel Bishop (artist)

Other spellings: **Isabele, Isabell**

Variations: **Bel, Belita, Bell, Bella, Belle, Isa** (Danish and German), **Isabeau** (French), **Isabelita, Isabella** (Italian and Swedish), **Isabelle** (French), **Isbel** (Scottish), **Iseabail** (Scots Gaelic), **Ishbel** (Scottish), **Isibeal** (Irish Gaelic), **Isobel** (Scottish), **Issie, Issy, Izabela** (Polish and Bulgarian), **Izabella** (Czech and Russian), **Izzie, Izzy, Ysabel** (Spanish)

Isabele, Isabell (see **Isabel**)

Isabelita (see **Isabel**)

Isabella Variation of **Elizabeth** and **Isabel.** Isabella I, queen of Castile, was so sure that Christopher Columbus knew the quickest route to India that she sold her jewelry to help pay for his voyage. In Boston, another generous and public-minded woman of this name, Isabella Stewart Gardner, turned her home, a reconstructed Venetian palace, into a museum for her magnificent art collection.

Isabelle French form of **Isabel.**

Famous name: Isabelle Adjani (actress)

Isadora, Isidora Greek "gift of Isis" from *Isis* [goddess of the Nile] + *dorus* [gift]. If you want your baby girl to grow up to be a dancer, you might name her after the famous 20th-century dancer and free spirit Isadora Duncan.

Isbel (see Isabel)

Iseabail (see Isabel)

Ishbel (see Isabel)

Isibeal (see Isabel)

Isobel (see Isabel)

Isolda (see Isolde)

Isolde Perhaps Celtic "beautiful" or Old German "ice rule." Isolde is the heroine of an often-told tale of tragic love that was incorporated into the Arthurian legend by Sir Thomas Malory. Sir Tristram was sent to Ireland to bring Isolde the Fair to Cornwall, where she was to marry his uncle, King Mark. Unwittingly, she and Tristram swallowed a love potion and fell in love. After many secret meetings, the lovers became estranged, and Tristram married another Isolde. But on his deathbed, Tristram called for his true love. She came to him but arrived too late and found that Tristram had died in despair, believing that Isolde was not coming back to him. Isolde then died of grief beside Tristram. Wagner wrote the opera, and Matthew Arnold, Algernon Swinburne, and many other modern writers have also retold the sad story of Isolde.
Variations: **Isolda, Isotta** (Italian), **Yseult, Ysonde**

Isotta (see Isolde)

Issie, Issy (see Isabel)

Ivana (see Jane)

Ivie (see Ivy)

Ivonne (see Yvonne)

Ivy Old English *ifig*, "ivy." This plant was sacred to Bacchus and played a part in the religious ceremonies of the Druids. In England, it used to be hung as a tavern sign.
Famous name: Ivy Compton-Burnett (novelist)
Other spelling: **Ivie**

Izabela, Izabella (see Isabel)

Izzie, Izzy (see Isabel)

Jacalyn (see **Jaclyn**)

Jacinta Spanish "hyacinth."
Variation: **Jacinthe** (French)

Jacinthe (see **Jacinta**)

Jackeline (see **Jaclyn**)

Jackelyn (see **Jaclyn**)

Jacki (see **Jackie, Jacqueline**)

Jackie Form of **Jacqueline**. This nickname became a popular independent name in the 1960s.
Famous names: Jackie Collins (novelist)
Jackie Joyner-Kersee (athlete)
Other spellings: **Jacki, Jacky, Jacquie**

Jacklyn, Jacklynn (see **Jaclyn**)

Jacky (see **Jackie, Jacqueline**)

Jaclyn Modern variation of **Jacqueline**. This name may have been deliberately created to provide a feminine form for the masculine name **Jack**. Jaclyn has been a popular alternative to Jacqueline after actress Jaclyn Smith became famous in the 1970s.
Other spellings: **Jacalyn, Jackeline, Jackelyn, Jacklyn, Jacklynn**

Jacoba (see **Jacobina**)

Jacobina Feminine form of **Jacob,** especially common in Scotland.
Variations: **Jacoba** (Spanish and Dutch), **Jacqueline** (French),
Jakobina (Swedish and Hungarian), **Jakobine** (German)

Jacquelin (see **Jacqueline**)

Jacqueline Feminine form of **Jacques,** the French form of **Jacob** or
James. Jacqueline was one of the first French derivatives of a
traditionally masculine name to become a popular name for
girls in the United States and was widely used in the 1930s.
When Jacqueline Bouvier Kennedy became first lady in the
early 1960s, the name again became popular, especially with
African-Americans. Ace pilot Jacqueline Auriol was the first
woman to break the sound barrier.
Nicknames: **Jacki, Jackie, Jacky, Jacquie**
Other spellings: **Jacquelin, Jacquelyn, Jaqueline**
Variations: **Jaclyn, Jacobina, Jacquetta, Zakelina** (Czech)

Jacquelyn (see **Jacqueline**)

Jacquetta (see **Jacqueline**)

Jacquie (see **Jackie, Jacqueline**)

Jade Italian *giada,* "jade," from Spanish *piedra de ijada,* "stone of
the bowels," because in medieval times jade was thought to
protect its wearers from intestinal diseases. This name was
always very rare until Mick and Bianca Jagger named their
daughter Jade in the late 1970s. It then began to climb in
popularity and was among the top 30 names given to English
girls by 1990. Although Jade has yet to be as successful in the
United States, it's now among the top 200 American names
for girls.

Jaime (see **Jamie**)

Jaimie (see **Jamie**)

Jakobina, Jakobine (see **Jacobina**)

Jaleesa, Jalisa An African-American creation blending "Ja-" from
names such as **Jamila** or **Janelle** with **Lisa.** This formerly rare
name exploded in popularity in 1988 when the character
Jaleesa Vinson, played by actress Dawnn Lewis, was
introduced on the television comedy *A Different World.* By
1991, Jaleesa was the 41st most popular name for African-

American girls but had hardly any impact on the naming choices of parents from other ethnic backgrounds.

Jamaica Arawak "island of springs," the Caribbean nation.
Famous name: Jamaica Kincaid (author)

Jamee, Jami (see **Jamie**)

Jamie Feminine form of **James.** Although many currently popular names for girls are versions of masculine names, Jamesina is rarely used. But Jamie, in all its various spellings, has been very popular since Lindsay Wagner played Jaime Sommers in the 1970s television series *The Bionic Woman.*
Famous names: Jami Gertz (actress)
Jamie Lee Curtis (actress)
Other spellings: **Jaime, Jaimie, Jamee, Jami, Jayme, Jaymee, Jaymie**

Jamila Arabic and Swahili "beautiful." This name is now regularly used in the African-American community.

Jan Modern form of **Jane, Janet,** or **Janice.**
Famous name: Jan Morris (writer)

Jana (see **Jane**)

Janae (see **Janet**)

Jane Feminine form of **John,** Hebrew "the Lord is gracious." Until the 16th century, the older form **Joan** was used much more frequently in England than Jane. After Henry VIII married his third wife, Jane Seymour, and she bore his only son, the name began to appear more often. Following the brief reign of Henry's son, Lady Jane Grey was appointed his successor, but the court rallied to Henry's first daughter, Mary, and Lady Jane was beheaded. In the 19th century, the remarkable writer Jane Austen brought literary fame to the name. *Jane Eyre* by Charlotte Bronte began a line of fictional Janes that extends to Jane Marple, Agatha Christie's detective whose observations of village life help her solve vicious crimes. Jane is also a popular name for actresses, including Jane Alexander, Jane Curtin, Jane Fonda, Jane Seymour, and Jane Wyman.
Famous names: Jane Goodall (primatologist)
Jane Pauley (television journalist)
Nicknames: **Janey, Janie, Jany**

Other spelling: **Jayne**

Variations: **Gianna, Giovanna** (Italian), **Hanka** (Frisian), **Ivana** (Czech and Russian), **Jan, Jana** (Czech), **Janelle, Janet, Janice, Janina** (Polish and Latvian), **Janine, Janka** (Hungarian), **Janna** (Dutch), **Janne** (Norwegian), **Jannike** (Norwegian), **Jean, Jeanne** (French), **Jenni, Jennie, Jenny** (Scottish), **Jensine** (Danish), **Jinny, Joan, Joana** (Portuguese and Lithuanian), **Joann, Joanna, Joanne, Johana** (Czech and Slovakian), **Johanna** (German), **Johanne** (Norwegian), **Johnette, Johnna, Jonna** (Danish), **Jonnie, Jony, Jovanka** (Serbian), **Juana** (Spanish), **Juanita** (Spanish), **Sheena** (Scottish), **Sian** (Welsh), **Sine** (Gaelic), **Vanya** (Russian), **Zanna** (Polish)

Janel, Janell (see **Janelle**)

Janella (see **Janelle**)

Janelle This modern form of **Jane** has been in use since the 1940s and is now among the top 200 names for girls in America.

Variations: **Janel, Janell, Janella**

Janet Variation of **Jane**. Janet used to be particularly popular in Scotland, but it was extremely fashionable in all English-speaking countries during the 1940s and 1950s.

Famous names: Janet Gaynor (actress)
Janet Leigh (actress)
Janet Lynn (figure skater)
Janet Maslin (film critic)

Nickname: **Jan**

Variations: **Janae, Janette, Jannette, Jennet, Jessie, Seonaid** (Scots Gaelic), **Sinead** (Irish Gaelic)

Janette (see **Janet**)

Janey (see **Jane**)

Janice Variation of **Jane**. This name was created in 1899 for *Janice Meredith,* a novel by Paul Leicester Ford. He probably blended the sounds of **Janet** and **Alice** to come up with Janice. The novel was a best-seller in 1900, but the name didn't hit its peak of popularity until the 1960s.

Famous name: Janice Merrill (track athlete)

Nickname: **Jan**

Other spellings: **Janis, Janise**

Janie (see **Jane**)

Janina (see **Jane**)

Janine Form of **Jane**.
Famous name: Janine Turner (actress)

Janis Variation of **Janice**.
Famous name: Janis Joplin (singer)

Janise (see **Janice**)

Janka (see **Jane**)

Janna, Janne (see **Jane**)

Jannette (see **Janet**)

Jannike (see **Jane**)

Jany (see **Jane**)

Jaqueline (see **Jacqueline**)

Jasmin (see **Jasmine**)

Jasmine Persian *yasemin,* a flower name. Jasmine is often
associated with passionate love. Jasmine was fairly uncommon
until it skyrocketed into first place as a name for nonwhite
American girls by 1991. Part of Jasmine's success can be
attributed to the fame of actress Jasmine Guy, who began
appearing in the television series *A Different World* in 1987.
Several of the alternative spellings for the name also show that
many parents relate Jasmine to jazz music, although there is no
historical connection between the two words. Jasmine is also
popular with Hispanic-Americans and Asian-Americans. The
name is just beginning to be discovered by white parents, and
now that Disney's *Aladdin* with its character Princess Jasmine
has become a highly popular animated film, Jasmine will
probably grow rapidly in use all over the English-speaking
world.
Other spellings: **Jasmin, Jasmyn, Jazmin, Jazmine, Jazmyn,
Jazzmin, Jazzmine, Jazzmyn**
Variations: **Jessamine, Jessamyn, Yasmin, Yasmine**

Jasmyn (see **Jasmine**)

Jayme, Jaymee, Jaymie (see **Jamie**)

Jayne Variation of **Jane**.
      Famous names: Jayne Meadows (actress)
                      Jayne Anne Phillips (writer)

Jazmin, Jazmine, Jazmyn (see **Jasmine**)

Jazzmin, Jazzmine, Jazzmyn (see **Jasmine**)

Jean English and Scottish variation of **Jane**. Jean is probably derived from the old French *Jehane,* not the male name Jean. The name is a favorite in Scotland, and the best-loved Scottish poet Robert Burns wrote a charming poem in Scots dialect to his wife called "I Love My Jean." Maggie Smith portrayed another Scottish woman named Jean in her stunning performance as the title character in the movie *The Prime of Miss Jean Brodie,* based on a novel by Muriel Sparks.
      Famous names: Jean Harlow (actress)
                      Jean Peters (actress)
                      Jean Simmons (actress)
      Other spellings: **Gene, Jeane, Jeanne**
      Variations: **Jeanette, Jeanie, Jeannie**

Jeane Variation of **Jean**.
      Famous name: Jeane Kirkpatrick (ambassador)

Jeanette Variation of **Jean** or **Jeannette**.
      Famous name: Jeanette MacDonald (actress)

Jeanie Variation of **Jean**. "I dream of Jeanie with the light brown hair" from the song by Stephen Foster endeared this name to people in the 19th century. A charming genie named Jeannie, played by Barbara Eden in the television series *I Dream of Jeannie,* kept the name popular in the 1960s and 1970s.
      Other spelling: **Jeannie**

Jeanna (see **Gianna**)

Jeanne French variation of **Jane**. Although the name Joan of Arc is better known to English speakers, the French call the Maid of Orleans Jeanne d'Arc.

Famous name: Jeanne Moreau (actress)

Variations: **Jean, Jeannette, Jeannine**

Jeannette French diminutive form of **Jeanne.**

Variations: **Jeanette, Jennetta, Jennette, Zaneta** (Czech)

Jeannie (see **Jean, Jeanie**)

Jeannine (see **Jeanne**)

Jelena (see **Helen**)

Jemima Hebrew "dove." In the Old Testament, Jemima was the first daughter born to Job after his affliction; this was not an auspicious beginning for a name. Many Puritans baptized their daughters with this name, but it is no longer used. The name is well known through the pancake brand name and two fictional characters, Beatrix Potter's Jemima Puddle-Duck and Antonia Fraser's Jemima Shore, the liberated London broadcast journalist who doubles as a sleuth. Although Jemima is still regularly used in Britain, modern American parents almost never give the name to their daughters.

Variations: **Jemimah, Jemmie**

Jemimah (see **Jemima**)

Jemmie (see **Jemima**)

Jen (see **Genevieve, Jennifer**)

Jenefer, Jenifer (see **Jennifer**)

Jenna Form of **Jennifer.** This was the name of the character Priscilla Presley played on television's long-running soap opera *Dallas.*

Other spelling: **Genna**

Jennefer (see **Jennifer**)

Jennet Form of **Janet.** Christopher Fry gave the name Jennet to the lovely witch in his play *The Lady's Not for Burning.*

Jennetta (see **Jeannette**)

Jennette (see **Jeannette**)

Jenni, Jennie (see **Genevieve, Jane, Jennifer**)

Jennifer Cornish form of **Guinevere.** Jennifer developed in
Cornwall and then became popular throughout England in the
mid-20th century. Educated American parents began to use the
name around 1950, and it slowly grew in popularity
throughout the 1960s. Then the best-selling author Erich Segal
used the name for the heroine of *Love Story,* a bittersweet love
tale that was wildly popular in the 1970s. The hit movie based
on the book starred Ali MacGraw. As a result, Jennifer became
the top name for girls in the United States in 1971, a position it
held through 1984. This was a very long run at the top for a
name for girls. Although Jennifer has now begun to fall off,
it was still 16th on the list of names given American girls born
in 1991.

    Famous names: Jennifer Grey (actress)
                  Jennifer Jones (actress)
                  Jennifer O'Neill (actress)

    Nicknames: **Genni, Gennie, Genny, Jen, Jenni, Jennie, Jenny**
    Other spellings: **Gennifer, Jenefer, Jenifer, Jennefer**
    Variations: **Jenna**

Jenny Form of **Genevieve, Jane,** and **Jennifer.** Jenny Lind, the
Swedish Nightingale, took the United States by storm in the
middle of the 19th century, when P. T. Barnum persuaded her
to tour America singing arias from famous operas. Wherever
she sang, audiences adored her and parents named their babies
Jenny.

Jenovefa (see **Genevieve**)

Jensine (see **Jane**)

Jeri, Jerri, Jerry (see **Geraldine**)

Jesica (see **Jessica**)

Jess (see **Jessica**)

Jessamine, Jessamyn (see **Jasmine**)

Jessie Form of **Jessica** or **Janet.** As a name for girls, Jessie
originated in Scotland, where it was a pet name for Janet. It
was very popular as an independent name in the United States
in the late 19th century. Jessie has once again become popular,
although now it's become a pet form of Jessica.

Jesseca (see **Jessica**)

Jessica Feminine form of **Jesse**, Hebrew "God exists." Shakespeare, who probably invented the name, called Shylock's lovely daughter Jessica in *The Merchant of Venice*. Until the 1970s, Jessica was a very unusual name, but it suddenly rose to prominence; since 1981, it has been one of the top three names for American girls. By 1992, Jessica was also in the English top ten and was the very top name for girls born in Australia.

    Famous names: Jessica Lange (actress)
                       Jessica Tandy (actress)
                       Jessica Walter (actress)

    Nicknames: **Jess, Jessie, Jessy**

    Other spellings: **Jesica, Jesseca**

Jessy (see **Jessica**)

Jewel Old French *jouel,* "jewel." Although less specific than **Pearl** or **Crystal,** this is one of the jewel names that were popular at the beginning of the 20th century.

    Other spellings: **Jewell, Jewelle**

Jewell, Jewelle Form of **Jewel.**

    Famous name: Jewelle Gomez (poet)

Jill Variation of **Gillian.** In Shakespeare's *A Midsummer Night's Dream,* the name Jill is paired with Jack. "Jack shall have Jill; Nought shall go ill."

    Famous names: Jill Clayburgh (actress)
                       Jill Eikenberry (actress)
                       Jill St. John (actress)

    Variations: **Jillie, Jilly**

Jillian Variation of **Gillian.** Until recently, the short form **Jill** was much more popular in the United States than Jillian, but the situation has now reversed. By 1991, over three times as many American girls were being named Jillian than were being named Jill.

    Variations: **Juliana, Julianna**

Jillie, Jilly (see **Gillian, Jill**)

Jina Swahili "name."

Jinny (see **Jane**)

Jitka (see **Judith**)

Jo Variation of **Joan, Joanna, Joanne, Joella,** or **Josephine.** Jo is the strong-willed sister in Louisa May Alcott's *Little Women.* She is the character that represents the author, and later novels follow her as a grown-up. In the movie, Katharine Hepburn played Jo.

Famous name: JoBeth Williams (actress)

Joan Feminine form of **John,** Hebrew "the Lord is gracious." The name Joan dates back to at least the 12th century, when it is recorded as the name of a daughter of Henry II of England. Jeanne d'Arc, who became know as Joan primarily through George Bernard Shaw's play *Saint Joan,* is the patron saint of France. She was a poor peasant girl, but after hearing the voices of saints, she donned armor and inspired the French forces in battle. After several initial successes in battle, she was captured and turned over to the English. They caused her to be burned at the stake as a witch in 1431.

Famous names: Joan Benoit (Olympic marathoner)
　　　　　　　Joan Crawford (actress)
　　　　　　　Joan Sutherland (soprano)

Nicknames: **Jo, Joanie, Joni, Jonie, Jonnie, Jony**

Variations: **Jane, Joana, Joann, Joanna, Joanne, Jodie, Jody, Siobhan** (Irish Gaelic), **Siubhan** (Scots Gaelic), **Siwan** (Welsh)

Joana (see **Jane, Joan, Joanna**)

Joanie (see **Joan**)

Jo Ann (see **Joanne**)

Joann (see **Jane, Joan, Joanna, Joanne**)

Joanna Variation of **Jane** or **Joan.** Joanna was the name of the wife of Henry V of England.

Famous names: Joanna Cassidy (actress)
　　　　　　　Joanna Pacula (actress)
　　　　　　　Joanna Pettet (actress)

Variations: **Jo, Joana, Joann, Joanne, Jodie, Jody, Joeanna**

Joanne Variations of **Jane, Joan** or **Joanna.**
Famous name: Joanne Woodward (actress)
Variations: **Jo, Jo Ann, Joann, Joanna, Joeanne**

Jocelyn Norman French form of Old German *gautelen,* probably "of the Goths." This lovely old name is becoming more popular in the United States. Jocelyn is now quite fashionable with Hispanic-American parents, who evidently interpret it as a modern feminine form for **Jose.**
Other spellings: **Joscelin, Josceline, Joselyn**
Variations: **Goslin, Joslyn, Josselyn**

Jodie, Jody Variation of **Joan, Joanna, Josephine,** and **Judith.** This name was particularly popular in the 1970s.
Famous name: Jodie Foster (actress)

Jodoca (see **Joyce**)

Joeanna (see **Joanna**)

Joeanne (see **Joanne**)

Joella Feminine form of **Joel,** Hebrew "the lord is God."
Variations: **Ella, Jo, Joely**

Joely (see **Joella**)

Johana (see **Jane**)

Johanna (see **Jane**)

Johanne (see **Jane**)

Johnette, Johnna (see **Jane**)

Joice (see **Joyce**)

Joleen, Jolene (see **Joline**)

Joline Blend of **Jo** and the feminine suffix "-line."
Other spellings: **Joleen, Jolene**

Joni, Jonie Form of **Joan.**
Famous name: Joni Mitchell (songwriter)
Variations: **Jonnie, Jony**

Jonna (see **Jane**)

Jonnie, Jony (see **Jane, Joan, Joni**)

Jordan Hebrew *Yarden,* "descender," the name of the Palestinian
river. Although Jordan was used for both boys and girls in
medieval times, it disappeared as a woman's name for several
centuries until its 20th-century revival. In 1925, F. Scott
Fitzgerald chose Jordan as the name of a female character in
his novel *The Great Gatsby.* In the 1980s, Jordan quickly
became fashionable for both sexes in the United States. By
1991, it was the 58th most common name for newborn girls. At
that point considerably more boys than girls were receiving the
name, but if the past history of similar names is a guide, Jordan
may well become predominantly female soon.
Variations: **Jordana, Jordanka** (Czech), **Jordanne**

Jordana, Jordanka, Jordanne (see **Jordan**)

Joscelin, Josceline (see **Jocelyn**)

Josee (see **Josephine**)

Josefa (see **Josephine**)

Josefina (see **Josephine**)

Joselyn (see **Jocelyn**)

Josepha (see **Josephine**)

Josephina (see **Josephine**)

Josephine Feminine form of **Joseph,** Hebrew "the Lord added."
The most famous royal woman to bear this name is Josephine
Beauharnais, who became the wife of Napoleon and empress of
France. Her first husband was beheaded, but she was saved
from execution and later met General Bonaparte. Empress
Josephine's contribution to history is the Empire dress. She
also introduced the practice of wearing court dresses with
trains.
Famous name: Josephine Jacobsen (poet)
Nicknames: **Jo, Jodie, Jody, Josee, Josie**
Variations: **Fifi** (French), **Giuseppina** (Italian), **Josefa**
(Spanish), **Josefina** (Spanish), **Josepha** (German),

Josephina (Portuguese), Josette (French), Josypa (Ukrainian), Jozefa (Polish), Pepita (Spanish), Seosaimhin (Irish Gaelic)

Josette (see **Josephine**)

Josie Form of **Josephine,** now often used as an independent name.

Joslyn (see **Jocelyn**)

Josselyn (see **Jocelyn**)

Josypa (see **Josephine**)

Jovanka (see **Jane**)

Joy Old French *joie,* "joy."
Variation: **Joya**

Joya (see **Joy**)

Joyce Norman French *Josce,* form of Breton *Iodoc,* "lord." In the Middle Ages, this was a male name, but since the 17th century it has been used for girls, probably because of its similarity in sound to **Joy.**
Famous name: Joyce Carol Oates (novelist)
Variations: **Jodoca** (Dutch), **Joice**

Jozefa (see **Josephine**)

Juana (see **Jane**)

Juanita Spanish form of **Jane.**
Variation: **Nita**

Jude (see **Judith**)

Judie (see **Judith**)

Judit (see **Judith**)

Judith Hebrew "a Jewish woman." Judith of Brittany married Richard II, duke of Normandy, and became the grandmother of William the Conqueror.
Famous names: Dame Judith Anderson (actress)
Judith Rossner (novelist)

Nicknames: **Jodie, Jody, Jude, Judie, Judy**

Variations: **Giuditta** (Italian), **Jitka** (Czech), **Judit** (Spanish and Swedish), **Jutta** (German and Finnish), **Yehudit** (Israeli)

Judy Variation of **Judith.** This popular diminutive of Judith was the stage name of one of the 20th century's greatest performers, Judy Garland.

Famous names: Judy Collins (singer)
Judy Holliday (actress)

Juli (see **Julia**)

Julia Feminine form of **Julius,** a Latin family name. Julia was a popular name during the Renaissance in Italy. Since then, parents in Europe and the United States have often used the name.

Famous names: Julia Child (food expert)
Julia Duffy (actress)
Julia Ward Howe (poet and reformer)
Julia Roberts (actress)

Nicknames: **Juli, Julie**

Variations: **Giulia** (Italian), **Giulietta** (Italian), **Juliet, Julieta** (Spanish), **Julietta, Juliette** (French)

Juliana, Julianna Feminine form of **Julian.** St. Juliana got into trouble by rejecting the advances of a nobleman. According to legend, more than 500 people were converted after she was thrown into a furnace and the fire went out.

Variations: **Gillian, Jillian, Julianne, Julina, Juline, Liana** (Italian)

Julianne (see **Juliana**)

Julie French form of **Julia.** Between 1955 and 1985, Julie was a very popular name in its own right, ranking among the 50 most popular names in the United States. It is now falling rapidly, and Julia was once again the more popular American form of the name by 1991.

Famous names: Julie Andrews (singer and actress)
Julie Kavner (actress)

Juliet Form of **Julia.** William Shakespeare coined this name from the Italian name Giulietta for the famous tragic heroine of *Romeo and Juliet.*

Famous names: Juliet Mills (actress)
　　　　　　　　Juliet Prowse (dancer)
Other spelling: **Juliette**

Julieta, Julietta (see **Julia**)

Juliette French form of **Julia.**

Julina (see **Juliana**)

Juline (see **Juliana**)

June Latin *mensis Junius,* name of the month. *Junius* was a Roman clan name, probably derived from the goddess Juno. In the early 20th century, this was the most popular month name, but today it has been surpassed by April.
Famous name: June Allyson (actress)
Variations: **Junette, Junia, Junie, Junine**

Junette (see **June**)

Junia (see **June**)

Junie (see **June**)

Junine (see **June**)

Justina Feminine form of **Justin,** Latin "the just." St. Justina shared horrible tortures with St. Cyprian, although it was said that neither saint suffered. She is the patron saint of Padua, Italy.
Variations: **Giustina** (Italian), **Justine** (French), **Justyna** (Polish, Czech, and Ukrainian), **Jusztina** (Hungarian)

Justine French form of **Justina.** Justine is now more than twice as common as an American name for girls than is Justina. However, neither feminine form is anywhere near as popular as the very fashionable male form, **Justin.**
Famous name: Justine Bateman (actress)

Justyna (see **Justine**)

Jusztina (see **Justine**)

Jutta (see **Judith**)

Kaci, Kacie (see **Casey**)

Kaeleigh (see **Kaylee**)

Kaia (see **Katherine**)

Kaila (see **Kayla**)

Kailee, Kaileigh, Kaily (see **Kaylee**)

Kaitlin, Kaitlyn, Kaitlynn (see **Caitlin**)

Kala (see **Kayla**)

Kaleigh, Kaley (see **Kaylee**)

Kali Sanskrit "dark goddess." Kali is the Hindu goddess of destruction, often pictured wearing a necklace of severed human heads. Nevertheless, her name is now being regularly given to American girls. It's probable that although Kali is properly pronounced "KAH-lee," many parents are using it as a spelling variation of **Kaylee.**

Kalie (see **Kaylee**)

Kalila Feminine form of Arabic *Khalil,* "close friend."

Kamaria Swahili "like the moon."

Kami (see **Camilla**)

Kamilah Feminine form of Arabic *Kamil,* "perfect."

Kamila, Kamilla (see **Camilla**)

Kandace, Kandice, Kandis (see **Candace**)

Kandi, Kandie, Kandy (see **Candace, Candida**)

Kandida (see **Candida**)

Kanisha African-American creation, "Ka-" + "-n-" + "-isha." This new name, invented to rhyme with **Tanisha,** has recently soared in popularity; by 1991, it was the 31st most common name given to nonwhite American girls. It is often respelled as **Kenisha** and considered a modern feminine form for **Kenneth.**

Kara Form of Latin *cara,* feminine of *carus,* "dear"; or a form of **Caroline** or **Katherine.** Kara has been a fairly popular name for American girls since the late 1970s.
Famous name: Kara Young (fashion model)
Other spelling: **Cara**

Karel (see **Carol**)

Karen Danish form of **Katherine.** Karen began its rise to prominence around 1930 and was a top ten name for American girls throughout the 1950s and 1960s. Its popularity has been receding since then; by 1991, it had fallen to 142nd on the list of names for girls in the United States.
Famous names: Karen Allen (actress)
　　　　　　　Karen Black (actress)
　　　　　　　Karen Horney (psychoanalyst)
　　　　　　　Karen Valentine (actress)
Other spellings: **Caren, Carin, Karyn**
Variations: **Kari** (Norwegian), **Karin** (Swedish), **Karina**

Karena (see **Karina**)

Kari (see **Karen, Katherine**)

Karin (see **Karen, Katherine**)

Karina Latin feminine form of Greek *karinos,* "witty"; form of *carina,* Italian "dear one"; or a 19th-century Swedish expansion of **Karen.** Recently this name has been especially popular in the Hispanic-American community.
Other spellings: **Carina, Karena**

Karisa, Karissa (see **Carissa**)

Karla German feminine form of **Karl**. **Carla** used to be the more popular spelling of this name in the United States, but Karla is now slightly ahead.

Famous name: Karla Bonoff (singer)

Karlee, Karlie (see Carly)

Karlene, Karline (see Carla)

Karlotta (see Charlotte)

Karly (see Carly)

Karma (see Carma)

Karmel, Karmela (see Carmel)

Karole (see Carol)

Karolina (see Carolina)

Karoline (see Caroline)

Karyn (see Karen)

Kasey (see Casey)

Kasia (see Katherine)

Kassandra (see Cassandra)

Kat, Kata (see Katherine)

Katalin (see Katherine)

Katarina German and Scandinavian variation of **Katherine**. The most famous Katarina today is professional figure skater Katarina Witt, who as an amateur won a gold medal for the former East Germany at the 1988 Winter Olympics.

Katarzyna (see Katherine)

Kate Variation of **Katherine**. William Shakespeare used this diminutive for his Katharina in *The Taming of the Shrew,* and the famous lines, "Come on, and kiss me, Kate," inspired Cole Porter to write the Broadway musical *Kiss Me Kate*. Today, the name is no longer considered to be just a nickname, as evidenced by the many actresses who call themselves Kate.

Famous names: Kate Capshaw (actress)
Kate Jackson (actress)
Kate Mulgrew (actress)
Kate Nelligan (actress)

Nicknames: **Katie, Katy**

Katelin, Katelyn, Katelynn (see **Caitlin**)

Katerina (see **Katherine**)

Katharina (see **Katherine**)

Katharine Form of **Katherine**. Because this spelling is the closest to the Greek word *katharos,* it has the best claim to a meaning of "purity." Katharine is also now the most common form in England; in the United States, however, it is still a distant fourth choice after **Katherine, Catherine,** and **Kathryn,** despite the fame of actresses such as Katharine Cornell, Katharine Ross, Katharine Schlesinger, and Katharine Hepburn.

Famous name: Katharine Graham (newspaper publisher)

Kathe German variation of **Katherine**.

Famous name: Kathe Kollwitz (artist)

Katherine Greek *Aikaterine,* meaning unknown, possibly originally from an African language. The largely legendary third-century St. Katherine of Alexandria was the first of many saints with this name. St. Katherine's opposition to the worship of idols caused her to be tortured on a spiked wheel. When the wheel shattered, 200 soldiers who had witnessed the scene immediately converted to Christianity. The Roman emperor Maxentius was so infuriated that he ordered them all beheaded. When the cult of St. Katherine became popular in Western Europe, Roman Catholic writers wrongly assumed that her name was from Greek *katharos,* "pure." This is how the original spelling of the name was altered to drop the first syllable and change "-ter-" to "-thar-." The Romans also made the usual substitution of Latin "C" for Greek "K." No matter how it is spelled, this name has been extremely popular since the Middle Ages because of its associations with purity, beauty, and grace. Except for a brief period around 1890, it has consistently appeared among the top 50 most popular names for girls in the United States since colonial times. In England, the best-known Katherines are three of the wives of Henry

VIII. Katherine of Aragon was Henry's first wife, the widow of his brother. His divorce from her led to the founding of the Church of England. The unfortunate Katherine Howard was beheaded because of her adultery. Katherine Parr, his sixth wife, outlived Henry, although she narrowly escaped the fate of some of her predecessors. Literary Katherines are also strong-willed women, from Shakespeare's *Love's Labour's Lost* to Ernest Hemingway's *A Farewell to Arms.*

Famous names: Katherine Helmond (actress)
       Katherine Mansfield (writer)
       Katherine Anne Porter (writer)

Nicknames: **Kat, Kate, Kathie, Kathy, Katie, Katy, Kay, Kitty**

Other spellings: **Catherine, Katharine, Katheryn, Kathryn**

Variations: **Caitlin** (Irish Gaelic), **Caitriona** (Irish Gaelic), **Catalina** (Spanish), **Catarina** (Portuguese), **Caterina** (Italian), **Catharina** (Dutch), **Catherine** (French), **Catrin** (Welsh), **Catrina** (Rumanian), **Catriona** (Scottish), **Ekaterina** (Bulgarian and Russian), **Kaia** (Estonian), **Kara, Karen** (Danish), **Kari** (Norwegian), **Karin** (Swedish), **Kasia** (Polish), **Kata** (Croatian and Hungarian), **Katalin** (Hungarian), **Katarina** (German and Scandinavian), **Katarzyna** (Polish), **Katerina** (Czech, Russian, and Bulgarian), **Katharina** (German and Estonian), **Kathe** (German), **Kathleen** (Irish), **Katina** (modern Greek and Bulgarian), **Katinka** (Russian), **Katri** (Finnish), **Katrien** (Dutch), **Katrina** (Latvian, German, Czech, and Scottish), **Katrine** (Norwegian and Danish), **Katrya** (Ukrainian), **Katuska** (Czech), **Katya** (Russian), **Ketterle** (German), **Kotryna** (Lithuanian), **Krin** (German), **Rina** (Norwegian and Italian), **Trine** (Danish), **Yekaterina** (Russian)

Katheryn (see **Katherine**)

Kathie (see **Katherine**)

Kathleen Irish Gaelic *Caitlin,* variation of **Katherine.**

Famous names: Kathleen Battle (operatic soprano)
       Kathleen Turner (actress)

Other spelling: **Cathleen**

Kathryn Variation of **Catherine, Katharine,** or **Katherine** first created around 1895.

Famous name: Kathryn Grayson (actress and singer)

Kathy (see **Katherine**)

Katie, Katy (see **Kate, Katherine**)

Katina, Katinka (see **Katharine**)

Katri (see **Katherine**)

Katrien, Katrine (see **Katherine**)

Katrina Variation of **Katherine,** fairly common in the 1980s.
Nickname: **Trina**

Katrya (see **Katherine**)

Katuska (see **Katharine**)

Katya (see **Katharine**)

Kay Form of **Katherine.**
Famous names: Kay Mills (historian)
Kay Yow (basketball coach)
Other spelling: **Kaye**

Kaye Variation of **Kay.**
Famous name: Kaye Ballard (singer)

Kayla Modern American creation based on **Kay;** short form of
Michaela; or Yiddish form of *Kelila,* a Hebrew name meaning
"crown of laurel." Many Jewish immigrant women who came
to the United States from Eastern Europe between 1880 and
1920 were called Kayla. However, Kayla first began to become
popular with other Americans around 1970 in rural Western
states such as Montana, so it's unlikely that the Yiddish name
was being copied. Although Kayla could be a nickname for
Michaela, it's most likely a newly invented name. The similar
creations **Gayla** and **Shayla** have been in use at least since the
1940s. Kayla was already slowly increasing in use in the
western United States in 1982 when the character Kayla Brady
was introduced on the daytime television serial *Days of Our
Lives,* causing the name to skyrocket in use. Kayla's similarity
in sound to previous 1980s fads such as **Kelly, Caitlin,** and
Casey contributed to its swift rise. By 1991, Kayla was the
ninth most popular name given to newborn American girls.
Other spellings: **Kaila, Kala, Kaylah**

Kaylah (see **Kayla**)

Kaylan (see **Kaylyn**)

Kaylee Modern blend of **Kay** and **Lee;** form of *Cayley,* English
surname from *Cailly,* French place name; or form of **Kayley,**
Irish or Manx surname from Celtic words meaning "slender."
Kaylee is the perfect example of a name that becomes popular
solely because it is made up of fashionable sounds. This is
shown by the wide variety of spellings being used; although
Kaylee is the most common spelling in the United States, it
accounts for only about 15 percent of all girls with this name.
In England, where the name has also become popular since the
mid-1980s, **Kayleigh** is the most popular spelling. Others
frequently found include **Kaeleigh, Kailee, Kaileigh, Kaily,
Kaleigh, Kaley, Kalie, Kali, Kayley, Kayli,** and **Kaylie.**
Counting all the different spellings together, Kaylee was the
60th most common name given American girls in 1991. With
the contemporary popularity of similar-sounding names such
as **Kayla, Haley, Casey, Bailey,** and so forth, Kaylee's boom is
likely to continue.

Kayleigh, Kayley (see **Kaylee**)

Kayli, Kaylie (see **Kaylee**)

Kaylyn Modern blend of **Kay** and **Lynn;** or Irish Gaelic *Caelainn,*
"slender lady." Kaylyn is still another name that has become
popular recently because it starts with the fashionable "Kay"
sound of **Kayla, Caitlin, Katie,** and so forth. It is now among
the top 150 names given American girls.
Other spellings: **Kaylan, Kaylynn, Kaylynne**

Kaylynn, Kaylynne (see **Kaylyn**)

Keisha Origin unknown. Although it's often claimed that Keisha is
from an African language, it's not mentioned in existing works
on native African names and is probably an American
invention. Keisha was first used by African-American parents
around 1970 and became very popular in the late 1970s and
early 1980s. By 1990, it had started to go out of fashion in the
African-American community but was starting to become
fashionable with whites.
Other spelling: **Keshia**

Kelci, Kelcie, Kelcy (see **Kelsey**)

Kelley, Kellie (see **Kelly**)

Kelly Irish Gaelic *Ceallagh,* uncertain meaning, perhaps "church-goer," "bright-headed," or "strife"; also, rarely, Cornish *celli,* "wood." Kelly suddenly became extremely fashionable for American girls in the late 1960s and was a top ten name during the 1970s. It's now slowly going out of style, but it was still the 35th most popular name given to girls born in 1991.

Famous name: Kelly McGillis (actress)

Other spellings: **Kelley, Kellie**

Kelsey Probably Old English *ceol* [ship] + *sige* [victory]. Kelsey was an uncommon name and used predominantly for boys until the late 1970s. Since then, it has swiftly risen out of obscurity to become one of the most fashionable names for girls. As there do not seem to be any famous women with this name, Kelsey's success is probably simply explained by its combination of the sounds of **Kelly** and **Chelsea,** two names that were already in vogue. It's a good example of a name becoming popular almost overnight because it seems to be the "different but not *too* different" name that many parents seek. By 1991, Kelsey was the 22nd most popular name given to newborn American girls, and it was still on the upswing.

Other spellings: **Kelci, Kelcie, Kelcy, Kelsi, Kelsie, Kelsy**

Kelsi, Kelsie, Kelsy (see **Kelsey**)

Kendra Probably originally a feminine form of *Kendrick,* perhaps Welsh "exalted summit," although now often given as a feminine form of **Kenneth.** Kendra has been in regular use in the United States since the 1940s. Kendra was especially popular with African-American parents during the 1970s and early 1980s.

Kenisha (see **Kanisha**)

Kenya Kikuyu *kere-nyanga,* "mountains of whiteness," name of a country in East Africa. Kenya has been used as a name for American girls since the 1970s. Some parents interpret it as being a feminine form of **Kenneth.**

Keri, Kerri (see **Kerry**)

Kerry "*Ciar's* people," Irish place name. *Ciar* itself meant "black." This name was especially popular around 1980.

Other spellings: **Keri, Kerri**

Kerstin (see **Christina**)

Keshia Variation of **Keisha.**

Famous name: Keshia Knight Pulliam (actress)

Ketterle (see **Katherine**)

Kiara Origin unclear, but probably a respelling of **Chiara,** a modern Italian form of **Clara.** Kiara has recently become extremely voguish in the African-American community. It was the 26th most popular name given to nonwhite American girls in 1991.

Variations: **Chiara, Kierra**

Kierra Probably a blend of the sounds of **Kiara** and **Sierra.**

Kikilia (see **Cecilia**)

Kiley (see **Kylie**)

Kim Probably the same derivation as the boy's name **Kim,** first used for a girl in Edna Ferber's 1926 novel *Show Boat.* Although Kim is thought of as a nickname for **Kimberly** today, it actually was in regular use for girls before Kimberly became popular.

Famous names: Kim Basinger (actress)
                         Kim Novak (actress)

Kimberley (see **Kimberly**)

Kimberly Old English *Cyneburh-leah,* "Cyneburgh's meadow." Cyneburgh was a woman's name meaning "royal fort." Kimberly was a top ten American name for girls during the 1960s and 1970s, but today its popularity is rapidly diminishing.

Nicknames: **Kim, Kimmie**

Other spelling: **Kimberley**

Variation: **Kimbra**

Kimbra (see **Kimberly**)

Kimmie (see **Kimberly**)

Kinsey Old English *Cynesige,* "royal victory." This name is becoming well known because of the success of Sue Grafton's best-selling mysteries about the adventures of Kinsey Millhone, a private investigator who lives and works in California.

Kirsten Danish variation of **Christina** or form of **Kirstin.**

Kirsti (see **Kirstin**)

Kirstie Form of **Christina** or **Kirstin.**
Famous name: Kirstie Alley (actress)

Kirstin Scottish form of **Christina.**
Variations: **Kirsten, Kirsti, Kirstie, Kirsty**

Kirsty (see **Christina, Kirstin**)

Kitty Form of **Katherine.** Although this name obviously began as a diminutive, it is now an independent name. In the 1930s, Christopher Morley wrote a popular novel *Kitty Foyle,* which was made into a movie starring Ginger Rogers.
Famous name: Kitty Wells (singer)

Klara, Klare (see **Clara**)

Klarissa (see **Clarissa**)

Klaudia (see **Claudia**)

Konstancia (see **Constance**)

Konstanze (see **Constance**)

Koren Probably a form of **Cora,** Greek "young girl."
Variation: **Korin**

Kori (see **Cori**)

Korin (see **Koren**)

Kortney, Kortnie, Kourtney (see **Courtney**)

Kotryna (see **Katherine**)

Krin (see **Katherine**)

Kris (see **Chris, Christina, Kristen**)

Krista (see **Christina**)

Kristal (see **Crystal**)

Kristen, Kristin Norwegian forms of **Christian** and **Christina**. In Norway, Kristen is a male name and Kristin the female form; in the United States, both spellings are used for girls. The name was exceedingly popular during the 1980s, partly because of the character Kristin, played by Mary Crosby, on the television series *Dallas,* and it was still 28th on the list of names given American girls born in 1991.
Nicknames: **Kris, Kristi, Kristie, Kristy**
Other spellings: **Christin, Krysten, Krystin, Krystyn**

Kristi, Kristie (see **Christie, Kristen, Kristy**)

Kristina (see **Christina**)

Kristine (see **Christina, Christine**)

Kristy Variation of **Christina** and **Kristen**.
Famous name: Kristy McNichol (actress)
Other spellings: **Christie, Kristi, Kristie**

Krisztina (see **Christina**)

Krysten, Krystin (see **Kristen**)

Krystle Variation of **Crystal**. This spelling of one of the jewel names was chosen by the writers of the television soap opera *Dynasty* for the character played by actress Linda Evans.

Krystyn (see **Kristen**)

Krystyna (see **Christina**)

Kylee, Kyley (see **Kylie**)

Kylie Probably a feminine form of **Kyle,** although in Australia, where the name was the third most popular for girls born in the mid-1970s, it is said to be an aboriginal Australian word for "boomerang." The alternative spellings **Kiley** and **Kyley** are also Irish surnames from Gaelic *cadhla,* "graceful." Since Kyle has become a very fashionable name for American boys, Kylie has also increased in use in the United States.
Other spellings: **Kiley, Kylee, Kyley**

Lacey Norman French surname from *Lassy,* French place name, "Lascius's estate." Until recently, Lacey was primarily a male name popular in the South. Now it is rapidly becoming very fashionable for girls all over the United States. This may be partly due to the fame of country singer Lacy J. Dalton.

Other spellings: **Laci, Lacie, Lacy**

Laci, Lacie, Lacy (see **Lacey**)

Laetitia (see **Letitia**)

Lakeisha African-American creation, derived by adding "La-" to the name **Keisha.** Lakeisha is now the most popular "La-" name, but other fashionable names formed in the same way include **Latasha, Latoya,** Laquisha, Lashay, **Latisha,** Latrice, Laporsha, Lashonda, and Latonya. "La-" names were particularly popular during the 1970s and 1980s; by 1990, however, "Sha-" had become a more fashionable prefix for newly created African-American names.

Lalia Feminine form of Latin *Laelius,* "fair speech."

Lana Variation of **Alana, Alanna.**

Famous names: Lana Turner (actress)
Lana Wood (actress)

Other spelling: **Lanna**

Lanna (see **Alana, Alanna, Lana**)

Lara Form of **Larissa.** This has long been a popular name for girls in Russia. Actress Julie Christie played Lara in the movie version of Boris Pasternak's *Dr. Zhivago*. The popular song from the movie, "Lara's Theme," brought this name to the attention of parents in the United States.

Laraine Form of **Lorraine.**
>Famous names: Laraine Day (actress)
>Laraine Newman (comedienne)

Larissa Russian form of Latin *hilaris,* "laughing, cheerful."
>Famous name: Larissa Fontaine (gymnast)
>Variation: **Lara**

Larsina (see **Lauren**)

Latasha Modern creation, "La-" + **Tasha.** Unlike most of the other recently created "La-" names, Latasha is regularly given to white as well as African-American girls, especially in Texas.

Latisha Form of **Letitia,** respelled to conform to the pattern of "La-" names popular in the African-American community.

LaToya In her autobiography, singer LaToya Jackson says that her mother simply made up this name. It was possibly formed by adding "La-" to **Toya,** a Mexican pet form of **Victoria.** The singer's fame made LaToya the third most popular name for African-American girls born in the early 1980s, but its use has now faded.

Laura Feminine form of Latin *Laurus,* "laurel tree." The Romans believed that a laurel wreath could protect them from lightning. They also used it as a symbol of victory. Laura was a familiar name in England by the 12th century and inspired many variations, most of which are unused today, including Laurinda and Laureola. In 1327, Petrarch caught sight of Laure de Noves in a church in Avignon. He maintained that seeing her made him a poet, and the famous sonnets Petrarch wrote for his beloved Laura immortalized the name. In the movie *Laura,* Dana Andrews is mesmerized by the portrait of Gene Tierney. Laura is also the name of Amanda's daughter in Tennessee Williams's *The Glass Menagerie.*
>Famous names: Laura Branigan (singer)
>Laura Dern (actress)
>Laura Ingalls Wilder (writer)
>Nicknames: **Laurie, Lori, Lorie, Lorrie, Lorry**

Variations: **Laure** (French), **Lauretta, Laurette** (French), **Laurice, Lavra** (Czech and Greek), **Lora** (German), **Loretta, Lorette, Lorita**

Laure (see **Laura**)

Laureen (see **Lauren**)

Laurel English form of Old French *lorer,* "bay tree, laurel." The ancient Greeks crowned the winners of certain games, as well as some office holders, with laurel wreaths.

Famous name: Laurel Thatcher Ulrich (historian)

Variations: **Laurella, Laurelle**

Laurella (see **Laurel**)

Laurelle (see **Laurel**)

Lauren Modern feminine form of **Lawrence.** This name became very popular along the East Coast around 1980. Lauren's popularity has steadily spread westward, and it was 18th on the national list of names for newborn girls in the United States by 1991.

Famous names: Lauren Bacall (actress)
                   Lauren Hutton (actress)

Variations: **Larsina** (Norwegian), **Laureen, Laurence** (French), **Laurentia** (Latin), **Laurina, Loren, Lorena, Lorene, Lorenza** (Spanish and Italian), **Lorine, Lourenca** (Portuguese)

Laurence (see **Lauren**)

Laurentia (see **Lauren**)

Lauretta (see **Laura**)

Laurette Variation of **Laura.**

Famous name: Laurette Taylor (actress)

Laurice (see **Laura**)

Laurie Form of **Laura.**

Famous name: Laurie Anderson (performance artist)

Laurina Form of **Lauren** or **Lorena.**

La Verne (see **Laverne**)

Laverne French place name and surname from a Gaulish word meaning "alder grove." It's still a mystery who first thought of turning this obscure French surname into an American first name, but Laverne was regularly being given to both boys and girls in the United States by 1880. It was never a highly popular name and has now been almost killed off by the image of the character Laverne De Fazio, played by actress Penny Marshall, in the long-running television comedy *Laverne and Shirley*.

Variation: **La Verne**

Lavina (see **Lavinia**)

Lavine (see **Lavinia**)

Lavinia Lavinia is the wife of the Trojan hero Aeneas in Virgil's *Aeneid.* The town of Lavinium was said to be named in her honor. In literature, George Bernard Shaw made Lavinia his heroine in *Androcles and the Lion,* and Lavinia Mannon is the heroine of playwright Eugene O'Neill's tragedy *Mourning Becomes Electra.*

Famous name: Lavinia Fontana (artist)

Nicknames: **Vinnie, Vinny**

Variations: **Lavina, Lavine**

Lavra (see **Laura**)

Layla (see **Leila**)

Lea Form of either **Lee** or **Leah.** Parents might be wise to avoid this spelling, as it causes confusion about whether the name should be pronounced in one or two syllables.

Famous name: Lea Thompson (actress)

Leah Origin unclear; perhaps Hebrew "languid" or "wild cow" or Assyrian "ruler." In the Bible, Leah is the sister of Rachel and the first wife of Jacob. This pleasant-sounding name has consistently held a place in the lower half of the top 100 names given American girls for many years. It's therefore a good choice for parents looking for a well-known but not overused name.

Other spellings: **Lea, Leia, Lia**

Lean (see **Helen**)

Leana (see **Lena, Leanna, Liana**)

Leandra Feminine form of *Leandros,* Greek *leon* [lion] + *andros* [man]. This is a fairly rare name.

Leann (see **Leanne**)

Leanna English form of **Liana,** reinterpreted as a blend of **Lee** and **Anna.** This is now the most common spelling of this name in the United States.
Other spellings: **Leana, Leeanna, Leighanna**

Leanne Combination of **Leah** or **Lee** and **Anne** or an English respelling of **Liane.** Leanne has been one of the top 50 names for girls born in England and Wales since 1980. The name hasn't been as popular in the United States, but it's in steady regular use.
Other spellings: **Leann, Leeanne, Leighanne**

Leda Greek, meaning unknown. In Greek mythology, Leda is the mother of four famous children: Helen of Troy, Castor, Pollux, and Clytemnestra. Helen was the child of Leda and Zeus, who seduced her by appearing to her as a swan. Irish poet William Butler Yeats wrote the stunning poem "Leda and the Swan" about this mythological event.

Lee Old English *leah,* "glade, clearing, pasture." Lee can also be used as a nickname for any name ending with "-ley."
Famous names: Lee Grant (actress and director)
Lee Remick (actress)
Lee Radziwill Ross (celebrity)
Other spellings: **Lea, Leigh**

Leeanna, Leeanne (see **Leanna, Leanne**)

Leesa (see **Lisa**)

Leia Form of **Leah.** Actress Carrie Fisher played Princess Leia in the *Star Wars* trilogy.

Leigh Variation of **Lee.** This is now the more common spelling of this first name for girls, although Lee is still very common as a middle name for girls.
Famous name: Leigh Taylor-Young (actress)

Leighanna, Leighanne (see **Leanna, Leanne**)

Leila Arabic *Layla,* perhaps "dark night" or "intoxicating wine." This is a very popular name in Middle Eastern countries, most likely because of its roots in Arabian romance literature. The English poet George Gordon, Lord Byron, chose it for two of his works, *Don Juan* and *The Giaour.*
Famous name: Leila Hyams (actress)
Variations: **Layla, Leilah, Lela, Lelah, Lelia, Lila**

Leilah (see **Leila**)

Leilani Hawaiian "heavenly garland." This name was among the top 50 names for girls born in Hawaii in the early 1980s. The name was spread to the mainland United States and Puerto Rico by the song "Sweet Leilani." Introduced in the movie *Waikiki Wedding* (1937), the song won an Academy Award. A recording of it by Bing Crosby sold over a million copies.

Lela, Lelah (see **Leila**)

Lelia (see **Leila**)

Lena Usually a variation of **Helen,** but also a form of **Adeline, Arlene,** or **Magdalena.**
Famous names: Lena Horne (singer)
Lena Olin (actress)
Other spellings: **Leana, Lina**

Lenka (see **Helen**)

Lenora (see **Eleanor, Leonora**)

Lenore Variation of **Eleanor** and **Leonora.** Edgar Allan Poe used this name in his often-memorized poem "The Raven."
Famous names: Lenore Cox (writer)
Lenore Kandel (poet)

Lenuta (see **Helen**)

Leona Feminine form of **Leo** or **Leon,** Latin "lion." This beautiful name has had its image tarnished recently by the publicity given Leona Helmsley.
Variations: **Leone** (Lithuanian), **Leonella** (Italian), **Leonelle, Leonia** (Russian and Ukrainian), **Leonie** (French), **Leonne** (French)

Leone (see **Leona**)

Leonella, Leonelle (see **Leona**)

Leonia, Leonie (see **Leona**)

Leonne (see **Leona**)

Leonor (see **Eleanor, Leonora**)

Leonora Form of **Eleanor.** In Beethoven's opera *Fidelio,* Leonora
assumes the name Fidelio. Beethoven wrote four different
overtures for this opera, and three are entitled Leonora. The
third Leonora Overture is the best known.
Famous name: Leonora Carrington (writer)
Variations: **Lenora, Lenore, Leonor, Leonore**

Leonore (see **Leonora**)

Leontine French feminine form of Latin *Leontius,* "lionlike,"
Other spelling: **Leontyne**

Leontyne Variation of **Leontine.**
Famous name: Leontyne Price (opera singer)

Lesley British feminine form of **Leslie,** Scottish place name and
surname, perhaps from Gaelic *leas celyn,* "court of hollies."
Robert Burns wrote a poem about a bonny Scottish lass named
Lesley, but this name was not regularly used for girls in
England and the United States until the 20th century.
Variations: **Lesli, Leslie, Lesly, Lezlie**

Lesli (see **Lesley**)

Leslie Variation of **Lesley.** This is considered a masculine spelling in
England, but in the United States it has also been the most
common spelling of the feminine name since the 1940s.
Famous name: Leslie Caron (actress)

Lesly (see **Lesley**)

Leta Latin *laetus,* "glad." Leta Stetter Hollingworth was an early
20th century psychologist whose research refuted the idea that
men's brains are superior to women's.

Leticia (see **Letitia**)

Letitia Latin *laetitia,* "gladness." Although this version of Laetitia is only a few centuries old, an earlier version, **Lettice,** belonged to a woman who caused a scandal in Elizabethan England. Lord Robert Dudley, later the earl of Leicester, had long been the favorite of Queen Elizabeth I. When she discovered that Robin, as she called him, had secretly taken a second wife, Lettice Knollys, it nearly broke her heart, and he nearly lost his head. Letitia is now well used among Hispanic-Americans.
Famous name: Letitia Baldrige (hostess)
Nicknames: **Lettie, Letty, Ticia, Tish, Tisha, Titia**
Variations: **Laetitia, Latisha, Leticia** (Spanish), **Letizia** (Italian), **Lettice, Letycja** (Polish)

Letizia (see **Letitia**)

Lettice (see **Letitia**)

Lettie (see **Letitia, Letty**)

Letty Variation of **Letitia.**
Famous name: Letty Cottin Pogrebin (writer)
Other spelling: **Lettie**

Letycja (see **Letitia**)

Lexi, Lexie (see **Alexandra**)

Lexine (see **Alexandra**)

Lezlie (see **Lesley**)

Lia (see **Leah**)

Liana Short form of **Juliana** or **Liliana,** or Rumanian form of **Lillian.** In the United States, this is a very unusual spelling, although filmmaker John Sayles used it for the title character of his movie *Liana.*
Other spellings: **Leana, Leanna, Lianna**

Liane French short form of *Eliane,* feminine form of Latin *Elianus* from Greek *helios,* "sun."
Other spellings: **Leanne, Lianne**

Lianna (see **Liana**)

Lianne (see **Liane**)

Libby Variation of **Elizabeth.**
 Famous name: Libby Holman (actress)

Licia (see **Alicia, Felicia**)

Liddy (see **Lydia**)

Lidia, Lidija (see **Lydia**)

Lidmila (see **Ludmila**)

Liese (see **Elizabeth**)

Lil (see **Lillian, Lillie**)

Lila Form of **Delilah** or **Leila.**
 Famous name: Lila Kedrova (actress)
 Other spelling: **Lilah**

Lilah (see **Delilah, Lila**)

Lili, Lilia (see **Lillian**)

Lilian (see **Lillian**)

Liliana (see **Liana, Lillian**)

Liliane (see **Lillian**)

Lilias (see **Lillian**)

Lilie, Lilli (see **Lillian**)

Lilith Hebrew "night monster" or "screech owl." In medieval
 Jewish folklore, Lilith was the first woman. Most people today
 will associate the name with the character Lilith Sternin on the
 television series *Cheers,* played by Bebe Neuwirth.

Lillian Origin unclear, but probably a medieval English and
 German variation of **Elizabeth.** Lillian seems to be an older
 name in Britain than **Lily.** But this name has long been
 associated with the lily, which is a symbol for purity in
 Christian art. Lillian used to be a fairly popular name, going
 back to at least the 16th century, but today it's not very
 common.
 Famous names: Lillian Gish (actress)
           Lillian Hellman (playwright)
           Lillian Vernon (entrepreneur)

Nicknames: **Lil, Lilie, Lillie, Lilly, Lily**

Other spelling: **Lilian**

Variations: **Liana** (Rumanian), **Lili** (German), **Lilia, Liliana** (Italian, Spanish, and Slavic), **Liliane** (French), **Lilias** (Scottish), **Lilli** (German), **Lilyan**

Lillie, Lilly Form of **Lillian** or **Lily**. This name was very popular in the late 19th century in the United States.

Famous name: Lillie Langtry (actress)

Nickname: **Lil**

Lily Greek *leirion,* Latin *lilium,* and Old English *lilie,* "lily"; or a variation of **Lillian.**

Famous names: Lily Pons (opera star)
Lily Tomlin (actress and comedienne)

Other spellings: **Lillie, Lilly**

Lilyan (see **Lillian**)

Lin (see **Linda, Lynn**)

Lina Form of **Arlene, Caroline, Earline, Helen, Lena,** or **Paulina.**

Famous name: Lina Wertmuller (movie director)

Linda Spanish "beautiful"; German *linde,* "weak, mild" or "linden-wood"; or a variation of **Belinda** or **Melinda.** This name was probably first derived from one of the many Germanic names ending in "-linde" or from one of the popular poetic names created in 17th-century England using the feminine suffix "-inda," such as Melinda. But when it became widely popular around 1940, it was often assumed to be from the Spanish adjective "linda." The name Linda, however, was not used in Spanish-speaking countries until after it became popular in England and the United States. Whatever its origins, Linda became an amazingly popular American name in the 20th century. In the late 1940s and the 1950s, Linda was the most popular name for girls. By 1991, however, Linda had fallen to 205th place in the United States.

Famous names: Linda Evans (actress)
Linda Gray (actress)
Linda Hamilton (actress)
Linda Hunt (actress)
Linda Ronstadt (singer)

Other spelling: **Lynda**
Variations: **Lin, Lindy**

Lindsay Old English place name "Lincoln's island" from *linn* [lake] + *coln* [Roman colony] + *eg* [island]. This formerly masculine name became very popular for girls after **Linda** started to go out of fashion. Lindsay has been one of the top 30 names given to American girls since 1980.
Famous names: Lindsay Crouse (actress)
               Lindsay Wagner (actress)
Other spellings: **Lindsey, Lindsie, Lindsy**
Variation: **Linsey**

Lindsey, Lindsie, Lindsy (see **Lindsay**)

Lindy (see **Linda, Melinda**)

Line (see **Caroline**)

Linet (see **Lynette**)

Linetta (see **Lynette**)

Linette (see **Lynette**)

Linn (see **Lynn**)

Linnea Feminine form of *Linne,* Germanic "lime tree."
Other spelling: **Lynnea**

Linsey (see **Lindsay**)

Lis (see **Elizabeth**)

Lisa Variation of **Elizabeth**. Lisa became popular during the 1960s and was a top ten name in the United States throughout the 1970s. Lisa's fashion is now rapidly receding, and it was only 90th on the list of names given American girls born in 1991.
Famous names: Lisa Bonet (actress)
               Lisa Eichhorn (actress)
               Lisa Hartman (actress)
Other spelling: **Leesa**

Lisabeth (see **Elizabeth**)

Lisbet, Lisbeth (see **Elizabeth**)

Lise (see **Elizabeth**)

Lisette, Lissette French form of **Elizabeth**. This name is now very fashionable in the Hispanic-American community.

Lisha (see **Alicia**)

Lissa (see **Melissa**)

Lita (see **Carmel**)

Liusaidh (see **Lucy**)

Liv Old Norse *hlif,* "defense."
Famous name: Liv Ullmann (actress)

Livia Possibly Latin *lividus,* "bluish." Livia was the first empress of Rome. In modern times, this name is also used as a variation of **Olivia.**

Livvie, Livy (see **Olivia**)

Liz (see **Elizabeth**)

Liza Variation of **Elizabeth.**
Famous names: Liza Cody (writer)
　　　　　　　　Liza Minnelli (actress)

Lizabeth (see **Elizabeth**)

Lizzie, Lizzy (see **Elizabeth**)

Lois Possibly Greek "the better." This name became popular in the early part of the 20th century.
Famous name: Lois Chiles (actress)

Lola Form of **Dolores**. Marlene Dietrich sings a bawdy cabaret tune called "Lola, Lola" in the movie *The Blue Angel.*
Famous names: Lola Falana (singer)
　　　　　　　　Lola Montes (actress)

Lolita Form of **Dolores**. This unusual name is associated with Vladimir Nabakov's novel, which was made into a controversial movie.

Lora (see **Laura**)

Lorain, Loraine (see **Lorraine**)

Loren (see **Lauren**)

Lorena Variation of **Lauren.**
Other spelling: **Laurina**

Lorene (see **Lauren**)

Lorenza (see **Lauren**)

Loretta Variation of **Laura;** also, a feminine form of *Loreto,*
"laurels," name of an Italian town to which angels supposedly
brought the Virgin Mary's house in the 13th century.
Famous names: Loretta Lynn (singer)
Loretta Young (actress)

Lorette (see **Laura**)

Lori Variation of **Laura** and **Lorraine.**
Famous names: Lori McNeil (tennis player)
Lori Singer (actress)

Lorie (see **Laura**)

Lorine (see **Lauren**)

Lorita (see **Laura**)

Lorna This name was invented for the heroine of the very popular
19th-century novel *Lorna Doone* by R. D. Blackmore.

Lorraine French place name, derived from **Lothair,** Old German
"loud army."
Famous name: Lorraine Hansberry (playwright)
Variations: **Laraine, Lorain, Loraine, Lori, Lorrayne, Lorrie,**
Lorry

Lorrayne (see **Lorraine**)

Lorrie, Lorry (see **Laura, Lorraine**)

Lotta (see **Charlotte, Lottie**)

Lotte German form of **Lottie.**
Famous names: Lotte Lehmann (opera singer)
Lotte Lenya (singer)

Lottey (see **Lottie**)

Lotti, Lotty (see **Charlotte, Lottie**)

Lottie Form of **Charlotte.** In the 19th century, this nickname was so
popular that it became an independent name, but few parents
choose it today.
Other spellings: **Lottey, Lotti, Lotty**
Variations: **Lotta, Lotte** (German)

Lou (see **Louisa, Louise**)

Louella (see **Louisa**)

Louisa Feminine form of **Louis,** Old German "famous warrior."
This name has a lengthy history as a favorite name of royal
women in Europe but was seldom used in England until the
17th century. Louisa of Lorraine was the wife of Henry III of
France, and Louisa of Mecklenburg-Strelitz, the wife of
Frederick William, was the queen of Prussia in the 18th
century. Americans are most familiar with the name of Louisa
May Alcott, the author of *Little Women.*
Variations: **Lou, Louella, Louise** (French), **Lovisa** (Swedish),
Ludovica (Danish and Rumanian), **Ludwika** (Polish),
Luigina (Italian), **Luisa** (Italian and Spanish), **Luise**
(German)

Louise French form of **Louisa.** Louise was a quite fashionable first
name in the United States between 1900 and 1930. It is almost
never given as an American first name today, but it retains
some popularity as a middle name. In England, however,
Louise only started to become popular after 1960 and was at its
peak around 1978 when Louise Brown, the world's first "test-
tube baby," was born. Although now fading, Louise was still
among the top 50 names for girls born in England and Wales
during the early 1990s.
Famous names: Louise Erdrich (writer)
              Louise Fletcher (actress)
              Louise Nevelson (sculptor)
              Louise Rainer (actress)
              Louise Ritter (athlete)
Variations: **Lou, Louisette, Luise, Lulu**

Louisette (see **Louise**)

Lourenca (see **Lauren**)

Lovisa (see **Louisa**)

Luca (see **Lucy**)

Luce (see **Lucy**)

Lucetta, Lucette (see **Lucy**)

Lucia (see **Lucy**)

Luciana Feminine form of **Lucian,** Latin "bringing light."
   Variations: **Lucienne** (French), **Lucina**

Lucie (see **Lucy**)

Lucienne (see **Luciana**)

Lucile (see **Lucilla, Lucille**)

Lucilla Latin diminutive of **Lucy.**
   Variations: **Lucile, Lucille** (French)

Lucille French form of **Lucilla.** This name was fairly common in the
   United States during the early 20th century, especially in the
   South, but it is out of fashion today.
   Famous name: Lucille Ball (actress)
   Other spelling: **Lucile**
   Variation: **Lucy**

Lucina (see **Luciana**)

Lucinda Variation of **Lucy,** created in the 17th century by Spanish
   author Miguel Cervantes for a character in his famous novel
   Don Quixote.
   Nicknames: **Cinda, Cindi, Cindie, Cindy, Cyndi, Cyndie, Cyndy**

Lucita (see **Lucy**)

Lucja (see **Lucy**)

Lucrece (see **Lucretia**)

Lucrecia (see **Lucretia**)

Lucretia Feminine form of *Lucretius,* ancient Roman family name
of unknown derivation. In the 15th century, Lucrezia di Borgia
was a powerful member of the Borgia family of Italy. She was
accused of poisoning her enemies.
Famous name: Lucrezia Bori (opera singer)
Variations: **Lucrece** (French), **Lucrecia** (Spanish), **Lucrezia**
(Italian)

Lucrezia (see **Lucretia**)

Lucy Latin feminine form of **Lucius,** a Roman family name,
probably meaning "light." Although it seems that Lucy ought
to be a derivative of **Lucille,** it's actually the other way around.
The name goes back to a Roman name, Lucia, the name of
three saints.
Famous name: Lucy Stone (suffragist)
Variations: **Liusaidh** (Scots Gaelic), **Luca** (Hungarian), **Luce**
(French), **Lucetta, Lucette, Lucia** (Spanish, Italian,
Portuguese, and Scandinavian), **Lucie** (Dutch, French,
Czech, and German), **Lucilla, Lucinda, Lucita** (Spanish),
Lucja (Polish), **Lukija** (Greek and Ukrainian), **Luzia**
(Portuguese)

Ludmila, Ludmilla Russian from Old Slavonic *lud* [people,
nation] + *mil* [grace, favor].
Famous name: Ludmilla Tcherina (ballerina)
Variation: **Lidmila** (Czech)

Ludovica (see **Louisa**)

Ludwika (see **Louisa**)

Luigina Italian form of **Louisa.**
Nickname: **Gina**

Luisa (see **Louisa**)

Luise (see **Louisa, Louise**)

Lukija (see **Lucy**)

Lula (see **Lulu**)

Lulita (see **Lulu**)

Lulu Swahili "pearl"; also, a form of **Louise.**
   Variations: **Lula, Lulita**

Luzia (see **Lucy**)

Lyda (see **Lydia**)

Lydia Greek place name *Lydios,* an ancient country in Asia Minor, which was once ruled by Croesus, a king who was noted for his great wealth. In the New Testament, Lydia is the name of a businesswoman convert to Christianity who entertained the apostle Paul in her home.
   Variations: **Liddy, Lidia** (Spanish, Polish, and Italian), **Lidija** (Russian), **Lyda, Lydie** (French)

Lydie (see **Lydia**)

Lyn (see **Lynn**)

Lynda (see **Linda**)

Lynelle (see **Lynn**)

Lynette Old French form of Welsh *Eluned,* meaning uncertain. Lynette is often thought of as a modern variation of **Lynn,** but it's actually a much older name. Tennyson featured the name in his poem "Gareth and Lynette."
   Other spellings: **Linette, Lynnette**
   Variations: **Linet, Linetta**

Lynn, Lynne Old English *hlynn,* "stream." Lynn was considered a masculine name until the 20th century. It probably changed sexes after **Linda** became a popular name for girls and it was reinterpreted as a short form of that name. Lynn was fairly popular as a first name in the 1950s and 1960s. It is rare as a first name today but remains one of the top middle names for American girls.
   Famous names: Lynne Cohen (photographer)
                      Lynn Redgrave (actress)
   Other spellings: **Lin, Linn, Lyn**
   Variation: **Lynelle**

Lynnea (see **Linnea**)

Lynnette (see **Lynette**)

Maara (see Mary)

Maarva (see Martha)

Mabel Latin *amabilis,* "lovable, amiable." Mabel is a very old variation of **Amabel,** dating to at least the 13th century. It was a popular name among the Victorians but is considered old-fashioned today.

Famous name: Mabel Mercer (singer)

Variations: **Amabel, Mabelle, Mable, Maible** (Irish), **Maybelle**

Mabelle (see Mabel)

Mable (see Mabel)

Mackenzie Scots Gaelic "son of Kenneth." This name was almost never used for girls before the 1970s when actress Mackenzie Phillips began appearing on the television series *One Day at a Time.* The name is steadily growing more popular and was 105th on the list of names given American girls in 1991.

Other spellings: **Makenzie, McKenzie**

Mada (see Madeline)

Madailein (see Madeline)

Madalena (see Madeline)

Madalene (see Madeline)

Madaline (see Madeline)

Maddalena (see Madeline)

Maddie Variation of **Madeline.** On the popular television show *Moonlighting,* Cybill Shepherd played Maddie, a model turned investigator whose personal life often posed more problems than the crimes she was hired to solve.

Maddy (see Madeline)

Madel (see Madeline)

Madelaine (see Madeline)

Madeleine (see Madeline)

Madelena (see Madeline)

Madelina (see Madeline)

Madeline English form of *Magdalene,* "woman of Magdala"; or Greek form of Hebrew place-name *migdal,* "high tower." This became a popular name in medieval times in honor of St. Mary Magdalene. Madeline is the name of the heroine of John Keats's poem "The Eve of St. Agnes" and also of the most famous cookie in literature. Eating a madelaine inspired Marcel Proust to write *Remembrance of Things Past.*
Famous names: Madelaine Carroll (actress)
                     Madeline Kahn (actress)
                     Madeleine Kunin (governor)
Nicknames: **Mada, Maddie, Maddy**
Other spellings: **Madaline, Madelaine**
Variations: **Alena** (Czech), **Madailein** (Irish Gaelic), **Madalena** (Portuguese), **Madalene, Maddalena** (Italian), **Madel** (Norwegian), **Madeleine** (French), **Madelena** (Dutch), **Madelina** (Dutch), **Madelon** (French), **Madge, Madi** (German), **Madlen** (German), **Madzia** (Polish), **Magdalen, Magdalena** (Spanish), **Magdalene** (German), **Magdalina** (Russian), **Magdalini** (Greek), **Magdolna** (Hungarian), **Magli** (Danish), **Makalonca** (Slovenian), **Malena** (German), **Malene** (Danish), **Malin** (Swedish), **Malina** (Swedish), **Maudlin**

Madelon (see Madeline)

Madge (see Magdeline, Margaret)

Madi (see **Madeline**)

Madison Middle English *Madyson,* either "son of Matthew" or "son of Maud." Madison was exclusively a name for boys until 1984 when the Disney Studios used it for the mermaid character played by actress Daryl Hannah in the movie *Splash.* Even though the name was presented as a joke in the movie— the character, asked her name, looks at a New York City street sign and names herself after Madison Avenue—parents immediately began to give the name to their daughters. It seems that American parents are enamored with mermaids in Disney films, because a few years later **Ariel** became popular through *The Little Mermaid.* Madison may have been readily accepted as a name for girls despite its "-son" ending because **Maddie** and **Madeline** were given a boost by *Moonlighting* just a few months after the film came out. By 1991, Madison was the 111th most popular name given newborn American girls, putting it just behind its sound-alike Madeline, which was 110th that year.

Madlen (see **Madeline**)

Madzia (see **Madeline**)

Mae Variation of **May.**
Famous name: Mae West (actress)

Maegan Modern American variation of **Megan,** blending it with the sound of **Mae.**

Mag (see **Magnolia, Margaret**)

Magda Variation of **Magdalena.** This was formerly a very popular name in German-speaking countries.

Magdalen (see **Madeline**)

Magdalena Form of **Madeline.** This is the main form of this name in Spain, Portugal, Germany, the Netherlands, and Poland.
Nicknames: **Lena, Magda, Maggie**

Magdalene (see **Madeline**)

Magdalina (see **Madeline**)

Magdalini (see **Madeline**)

Magdolna (see **Madeline**)

Maggie Form of **Magdalena, Magnolia,** or **Margaret.** This
nickname has become an independent name. Stephen Crane's
Maggie: A Girl of the Streets tells the story of an urban
prostitute. The novel was very controversial when it was
published and may have tainted the name. In Tennessee
Williams's play *Cat on a Hot Tin Roof,* Maggie the Cat is a
young wife stifled by her Southern in-laws. Rod Stewart
popularized the song "Maggie May." Television today features
Maggies on both *The Simpsons* and *Northern Exposure.*
Famous name: Maggie Smith (actress)
Other spelling: **Maggy**

Maggy (see **Maggie, Magnolia, Margaret**)

Magli (see **Madeline**)

Magnolia New Latin "magnolia flower and tree" from Pierre
Magnol, a French botanist. This name is best known as that of
a character in the famous Broadway musical *Show Boat,* which
was based on the novel of the same name by Edna Ferber.
Variations: **Mag, Maggie, Maggy, Nola, Nolie**

Mahala Form of *Mahalath,* an Old Testament Hebrew name
perhaps meaning "harp."
Famous name: Mahalia Jackson (singer)
Variations: **Haley, Mahalah, Mahalia, Mahalie**

Mahalah (see **Mahala**)

Mahalia (see **Mahala**)

Mahalie (see **Mahala**)

Mai (see **May**)

Maible (see **Mabel**)

Mair (see **Mary**)

Maire, Mairi (see **Mary, Moira**)

Mairead (see **Margaret**)

Maisie Scottish variation of **Margaret.** Henry James used the name
for the child heroine in *What Maisie Knew.*

Maitilde (see Mathilda)

Maj (see Margaret)

Makalonca (see Madeline)

Makenzie (see Mackenzie)

Malena (see Madeline)

Malene (see Madeline)

Malerie (see Mallory)

Malgorzata (see Margaret)

Malin (see Madeline)

Malina (see Madeline)

Malinda (see Melinda)

Malkin (see Mary)

Mallori, Mallorie (see Mallory)

Mallory Old French *malheure,* "unlucky, unhappy." This formerly masculine name has become a common name for girls in the United States. It was the name of the oldest daughter on the popular television comedy *Family Ties;* Justine Bateman played the part. In 1991, Mallory was the 121st most popular name given American girls.
Other spellings: **Malerie, Mallori, Mallorie, Malorie, Malory**

Malorie, Malory (see Mallory)

Malvina Created by Scottish poet James Macpherson in the 1700s, possibly from Gaelic *mala mhin,* "smooth brow."
Famous name: Malvina Hoffman (sculptor)

Mame, Mamie Forms of **Mary.** In a movie version of the novel, a Broadway musical, and a movie of the musical, actresses Rosalind Russell, Angela Lansbury, and Lucille Ball all played Auntie Mame. In James W. Blake's song "The Sidewalks of New York," Mamie O'Rourke was the girl with whom he tripped the light fantastic.
Famous name: Mamie Eisenhower (first lady)

Manda (see **Amanda**)

Mandi, Mandie (see **Amanda, Mandy**)

Mandita (see **Amanda**)

Mandy Form of **Amanda.**
Other spellings: **Mandi, Mandie**

Manette (see **Mary**)

Manica (see **Mary**)

Manon (see **Mary**)

Manuela Spanish feminine form of **Emmanuel,** Hebrew "God is with us."

Mar (see **Mary**)

Mara Hebrew "bitter." The name appears in the biblical Book of Ruth, when Naomi refers to herself as Mara to express her grief and bitterness over the death of her husband and sons.

Maraline (see **Mary**)

Marca (see **Marcia**)

Marcelena (see **Marcella**)

Marcelia (see **Marcella**)

Marcella Feminine form of *Marcellus,* Latin "little **Marcus.**" In *Don Quixote,* Marcella is a shepherdess who is described as "the most beautiful creature ever sent into the world." All the young men are in love with her.
Nicknames: **Marcie, Marcey**
Variations: **Marcelena, Marcelia, Marcelline**

Marcelline (see **Marcella**)

March (see **Marcia**)

Marcheta (see **Marcia**)

Marchita (see **Marcia**)

Marcia Feminine form of *Marcius,* Latin family name derived from Mars, the god of war.

Nicknames: **Marcie, Marcy**

Variations: **Marca, March, Marcheta, Marchita, Marcile, Markita, Marquita, Marsha, Marsi** (Estonian), **Marzia** (Italian)

Marcie (see **Marcella, Marcia**)

Marcile (see **Marcella, Marcia**)

Marcy (see **Marcella, Marcia**)

Mare (see **Mary**)

Marella (see **Mary**)

Marelle (see **Mary**)

Maren (see **Marina**)

Maressa (see **Marisa**)

Maret (see **Margaret**)

Marete (see **Margaret**)

Maretta (see **Mary**)

Marette (see **Mary**)

Marfa (see **Martha**)

Marga (see **Margaret**)

Margalo (see **Margaret**)

Margaret Greek *Margarites,* form of *margaron,* "pearl." There are many saints named Margaret, but only St. Margaret, the maid of Antioch, is represented wearing pearls. Margaret is a name that often occurs among English royalty. There is Margaret, the daughter of Henry III; Margaret of Anjou, the queen of Henry VI; Margaret Beaufort, the mother of Henry VII; Margaret, the countess of Richmond and the mother of Henry VIII; and many princesses, including Princess Margaret, the sister of Queen Elizabeth II. Like other long-popular names, Margaret has given rise to many variations.

Famous names: Margaret Atwood (writer)
                  Margaret Mead (anthropologist)
                  Margaret Mitchell (novelist)
                  Margaret Chase Smith (member of Congress)
                  Margaret Thatcher (prime minister of Great Britain)
                  Margaret Truman (writer)

Nicknames: **Madge, Maggie, Maggy, Marge, Margie, Meg, Midge, Peg, Peggie, Peggy**

Variations: **Gosia** (Polish), **Greet** (Dutch), **Greta** (Swedish), **Gretchen** (German), **Grete** (Danish and German), **Gretel** (German), **Mag, Mairead** (Irish and Scots Gaelic), **Maisie** (Scottish), **Maj** (Swedish), **Malgorzata** (Polish), **Maret** (Danish), **Marete** (Norwegian), **Marga, Margalo, Margareta** (Swedish), **Margarete** (Danish and German), **Margaretha** (Dutch), **Margarethe** (German), **Margaretta, Margarette, Margarida** (Portuguese), **Margarita** (Lithuanian and Spanish), **Margherita** (Italian), **Margit** (Hungarian and Norwegian), **Margola, Margot** (French), **Margret, Margrethe** (Danish), **Margriet** (Dutch), **Marguerite** (French), **Marguerta, Mariquita** (Spanish), **Marjarita** (Slavic), **Marjeta** (Slavic), **Marjorie** (Scottish), **Marketa** (Czech), **Marketta** (Finnish), **May, Megan** (Welsh), **Meggi, Merete** (Danish), **Meta** (Norwegian), **Rita, Ryta**

Margareta (see **Margaret**)

Margarete (see **Margaret**)

Margaretha (see **Margaret**)

Margarethe (see **Margaret**)

Margaretta (see **Margaret**)

Margarette (see **Margaret**)

Margarida (see **Margaret**)

Margarita (see **Margaret**)

Margaux (see **Margot**)

Marge (see **Margaret, Marjorie**)

Margery (see **Marjorie**)

Margherita (see **Margaret**)

Margie (see **Margaret, Marjorie**)

Margit (see **Margaret**)

Margo Variation of **Margot.** As Margo Channing in the movie *All About Eve,* Bette Davis played an actress who is insecure about her appearance, her career, and her personal life because she feels that she is getting old.

Margola (see **Margaret**)

Margory (see **Marjorie**)

Margot French variation of **Margaret** or **Marguerite.**
Famous name: Dame Margot Fonteyn (ballerina)
Other spellings: **Margaux, Margo**

Margret (see **Margaret**)

Margrethe (see **Margaret**)

Margriet (see **Margaret**)

Marguerite French variation of **Margaret.** In France, there was Marguerite of Navarre, the mother of Henry IV, who married Marguerite of Valois. The French word *marguerite* means daisy.
Famous name: Marguerite Chapman (actress)
Nickname: **Margot**

Marguerta (see **Margaret**)

Margy (see **Marjorie**)

Mari Variation of **Marina** or **Mary.**
Famous name: Mari Evans (poet)

Maria Latin form of **Mary.** Maria is also the normal form of Mary in Italian, Spanish, Portuguese, and most Germanic and Slavic languages. Maria Christina of Spain was the wife of Ferdinand VII, while Maria II de Gloria was a queen of Portugal. Maria Theresa of Spain was the wife of Louis XIV of France. In Leonard Bernstein's *West Side Story,* a Broadway musical that recreates the story of Romeo and Juliet, Maria is a young Puerto Rican girl who falls in love with an American boy.

Famous names: Maria Montessori (educator)
Maria Tallchief (ballerina)

Variations: **Mariah, Mia** (Swedish)

Mariah This modern form of **Maria** is used to indicate that the name should be pronounced "ma-RYE-uh," which was the normal way non-Hispanic-Americans said Maria itself before the 20th century. Mariah was a rare name until 1989 when singer Mariah Carey became famous. The name has enjoyed a sudden boom in popularity and was the 63rd most common name given American girls by 1991; this made it more common than Maria, which was in 76th place that year.

Mariam (see **Mary**)

Marian Modern form of **Marion**. Despite appearances, this name originally had no connection with **Mary Ann**.

Famous names: Marian Anderson (opera singer)
Marian Thurm (writer)

Mariana (see **Marianne**)

Mariane Variation of **Marianne**. Shakespeare used this version of the name for his play *All's Well That Ends Well.*

Marianna (see **Marianne**)

Marianne French blend of **Marie** and **Anne**. In France, the figure Marianne represents the spirit of the French Republic in much the same way that Uncle Sam and John Bull signify the United States and England.

Famous name: Marianne Moore (poet)

Variations: **Mariana** (Spanish and Russian), **Mariane**, **Marianna** (Polish, Latvian, Hungarian, and Italian), **Maryann** (English)

Marica (see **Mary**)

Marie French variation of **Mary**. This French variation of Mary has a long history, including the 16th-century Marie de Medicis, the queen regent of France, and Marie Antoinette, the ill-fated queen beheaded in the French Revolution.

Famous names: Marie Curie (chemist)
　　　　　　　Marie Dressler (actress)

Mariel Variation of **Mary.**

Famous name: Mariel Hemingway (actress)

Mariella (see **Mary**)

Marietta Variation of **Mary.**

Famous name: Marietta Tree (urban planner)

Mariette Variation of **Mary.**

Famous name: Mariette Hartley (actress)

Marika (see **Mary**)

Marilin (see **Marilyn**)

Marilyn Combination of **Mary** and **Lynn.** In the first part of the
20th century, this name was made popular by actress Marilyn
Miller, a star of Broadway musicals. By the 1950s, Marilyn was
going out of fashion despite the popularity of Marilyn Monroe,
whose original name was Norma Jean Baker.

Famous names: Marilyn French (writer)
　　　　　　　Marilyn Horne (mezzo-soprano)

Variations: **Marilin, Marylin**

Marina Perhaps a feminine form of Latin *marinus,* "of the sea."
Shakespeare used this name, which is slowly becoming more
popular in the United States. British actress Marina Sirtis plays
Counselor Deanna Troi on *Star Trek: The Next Generation.*

Variations: **Mari, Maren** (Danish), **Marna, Marni, Marnie,
Marny**

Marinka (see **Mary**)

Marion Norman French variation of **Mary.** Maid Marion is the
Queen of the May in traditional English May Day games.
Maid Marion is also the beloved of Robin Hood. Marion was
the normal spelling of this name for girls until the surname
Marion began to be given to boys as a first name around 1800.
Then some parents began spelling the name for girls as **Marian**
to differentiate it from the masculine form.

Other spelling: **Marian**

Mariquita (see **Margaret, Mary**)

Marisa Italian and Spanish blend of **Maria** with **Lisa** or **Isabel**. Although this name is usually pronounced to rhyme with Lisa, Oscar-winning actress Marisa Tomei evidently pronounces her name as if it were spelled **Marissa.**
Famous names: Marisa Berenson (actress)
　　　　　　　Marisa Pavan (actress)
Variations: **Maressa, Marissa**

Mariska (see **Mary**)

Marissa Modern American blend of the sounds of **Marisa** and **Melissa.** This name has recently become fairly popular and now is among the top 100 names given American girls.

Marita (see **Mary**)

Marite (see **Mary**)

Marja (see **Mary**)

Marjarita (see **Margaret**)

Marje (see **Marjorie**)

Marjeta (see **Margaret**)

Marjie (see **Marjorie**)

Marjorie Variation of **Margaret.** Now an independent name, Marjorie stems from either the Old French or the Scottish variation. The novel and the movie *Marjorie Morningstar* were both very popular in the 1950s when the name was at the height of its popularity in the United States.
Famous names: Marjorie Lord (actress)
　　　　　　　Marjorie Rawlings (writer)
Variations: **Marge, Margery, Margie, Margory, Margy, Marje, Marjie, Marjory, Marjy, Marsaili** (Scots Gaelic)

Marjory (see **Marjorie**)

Marjy (see **Marjorie**)

Marketa (see **Margaret**)

Marketta (see **Margaret**)

Markita (see **Marcia**)

Marla (see **Marlene**)

Marleen (see **Marlene**)

Marlena (see **Marlene**)

Marlene Form of *Marielene,* a German blend of **Maria** with either **Helene** or **Magdalena.** During World War I, Marlene Dietrich popularized a German song about a soldier going off to war called "Lili Marlene."
Variations: **Marla, Marleen, Marlena, Marline, Marlyn**

Marline (see **Marlene**)

Marlyn (see **Marlene**)

Marna (see **Marina, Marnie**)

Marne (see **Marnie**)

Marni, Marny (see **Marina, Marnie**)

Marnie Form of **Marina** or of *Marnina,* modern Hebrew "joyful."
Variations: **Marna, Marne, Marni, Marny**

Marquita Variation of **Marcia.** This was a very popular name in the early 1980s with African-American parents.

Marsaili (see **Marjorie**)

Marsha Variation of **Marcia.**
Famous name: Marsha Mason (actress)

Marsi (see **Marcia**)

Mart (see **Martha**)

Marta (see **Martha, Martina**)

Martella (see **Martha**)

Martha Aramaic feminine form of *mar,* "a lord." In the Bible, Martha, the sister of Lazarus and Mary, is admonished by Jesus for her sharp words about others. Martha Washington was the original first lady. In literature, Martha was one of Sir

Walter Scott's favorite names, while in Edward Albee's play
Who's Afraid of Virginia Woolf?, Martha is the foul-mouthed,
unhappy wife of a professor.
Famous names: Martha Graham (dancer)
                 Martha Raye (comedienne)
Nicknames: **Mart, Martie, Marty, Mat, Mattie, Matty**
Variations: **Maarva** (Estonian), **Marfa** (Russian), **Marta**
      (Hungarian, Italian, Norwegian, and Swedish), **Martella,**
      Marthe (French and German), **Marthena, Marthine,**
      Marthini, Martita, Martta (Finnish), **Mata**

Marthe (see **Martha**)

Marthena (see **Martha**)

Marthine (see **Martha**)

Marthini (see **Martha**)

Martie (see **Martha, Martina**)

Martina Feminine form of **Martin,** Latin "of Mars."
      Famous name: Martina Navratilova (tennis player)
      Variations: **Marta, Martie, Martine, Tina**

Martine (see **Martina**)

Martita (see **Martha**)

Martta (see **Martha**)

Marty (see **Martha**)

Marva Old French *Merveille,* "miraculous," or feminine form of
      Marvin.
      Famous name: Marva Collins (educator)
      Variations: **Marvel, Marvela, Marvella, Marvelle**

Marvel (see **Marva**)

Marvela, Marvella (see **Marva**)

Marvelle (see **Marva**)

Mary English form of Hebrew **Miriam,** meaning unknown,
      although "seeress" or "child we wished for" are possibilities.

Mary is without doubt the most popular name for girls in European history, particularly because it is revered as the name of the mother of Jesus, the Virgin Mary. In the British Isles, the name has been used by royalty for centuries. Mary Tudor, also known as Bloody Mary, was the first daughter of Henry VIII. Her cousin, Mary Stuart, was the queen of Scotland who was executed in England after her followers tried to put her on the throne. It is through her son James that the Stuarts sat on the English throne after the death of Elizabeth I. Mary Shelley, wife of poet Percy Bysshe Shelley, created the most popular monster in the history of literature in her novel *Frankenstein*. A magical English nanny named Mary Poppins, played in the popular movie by Julie Andrews, has become a standard in children's literature. By 1991, Mary had fallen to 46th place on the list of names given newborn girls in the United States. Even at that level, however, the name is still considerably more popular in the United States than it is in England and Wales, where Mary hasn't been among the top 100 names since 1970.

Famous names: Mary Gordon (writer)
Mary Martin (actress)
Mary Tyler Moore (actress)
Mary Stuart Masterson (actress)
Mary Pickford (actress and movie executive)
Mary Roberts Rinehart (writer)
Mary Wollstonecraft (political philosopher)

Nicknames: **Mame, Mamie, Mar, Mare, Mayme, Moll, Mollie, Molly, Poll, Polly**

Other spelling: **Mari**

Variations: **Maara** (Finnish), **Mair** (Welsh), **Maire** (Irish Gaelic), **Mairi** (Scots Gaelic), **Malkin, Manette** (French), **Manica** (Slovenian), **Manon** (French), **Maraline, Marella, Marelle, Maretta, Marette, Maria** (Italian, Latin and Spanish), **Mariam, Marica, Marie** (French), **Mariel, Mariella** (Italian), **Marietta, Mariette, Marika, Marilyn, Marinka, Marion, Mariquita** (Spanish), **Mariska, Marita** (Spanish), **Marite, Marja, Marya, Maryal, Maryse** (French), **Masha** (Russian), **Maura** (Irish), **Maureen** (Irish), **Maurene, May, Mears** (Irish), **Min, Minnie** (Scottish), **Miren** (Basque), **Miriam, Moira** (Irish), **Moire** (Scots Gaelic), **Moya** (Irish), **Muire** (Gaelic)

Marya (see **Mary**)

Maryal (see **Mary**)

Mary Ann Combination of **Mary** and **Ann.**
> Famous names: Mary Ann Childers (journalist)
> Mary Ann Mobley (actress)

Maryann (see **Marianne**)

Mary Jane Combination of **Mary** and **Jane.** This name is not only
used for girls; it's a kind of sugar candy and a style of shoe.

Marylin (see **Marilyn**)

Mary Lou Combination of **Mary** and **Lou.**
> Famous name: Mary Lou Retton (Olympic gymnast)

Maryse (see **Mary**)

Marzia (see **Marcia**)

Masha (see **Mary**)

Mat (see **Martha**)

Mata (see **Martha**)

Matelda (see **Mathilda**)

Matelle (see **Mathilda**)

Mathilda Old German *maht* [might] + *hild* [battle]. The earliest
form of this name was probably Mathilda, but by the time of
the Norman Conquest of England, it was **Matilda,** the name of
the wife of William the Conqueror who became the queen of
England. The name has gone in and out of fashion since then
and has produced several variations. The popular Australian
song "Waltzing Matilda" refers not to a woman but to a
tramp's pack.
> Other spelling: **Matilda**
> Variations: **Maitilde** (Irish), **Matelda** (Italian), **Matelle,**
> **Mathilde** (French and German), **Matilde** (Spanish),
> **Maud, Maude**

Mathilde (see **Mathilda**)

Matilda (see **Mathilda**)

Matilde (see **Mathilda**)

Mattie, Matty (see **Martha**)

Maud, Maude Variations of **Mathilda.** A granddaughter of William the Conqueror, **Matilda,** was known as Maud, but the name became an independent name many centuries ago. Although Maud is not fashionable today, it appears fairly frequently in popular culture as a name that connotes a rebellious woman, one who doesn't fit into the culturally accepted feminine mold. For example, actress Francoise Fabian is the intellectual freethinker in Eric Rohmer's movie *My Night at Maud's,* while a similar but older Maud was created by actress Ruth Gordon in *Harold and Maude.* In the popular television comedy *Maude,* actress Bea Arthur played an independent woman who went against the conventions of the time.
Famous name: Maud Adams (actress)

Maudlin (see **Madeline**)

Maura (see **Mary, Maureen**)

Maureen Irish variation of **Mary.**
Famous names: Maureen O'Hara (actress)
          Maureen Stapleton (actress)
Variations: **Maura, Maurene, Mora, Moreen, Moria**

Maurene (see **Mary, Maureen**)

Max (see **Maxine**)

Maxie (see **Maxine**)

Maxime (see **Maxine**)

Maxine Feminine form of **Max** or **Maximilian.**
Famous names: Maxine Elliott (actress)
          Maxine Kumin (poet)
Variations: **Max, Maxie, Maxime**

May Latin *maius,* the month; also, a variation of **Margaret** or **Mary.** This month name is no longer very popular.
Famous names: May Robson (actress)
          May Sarton (writer)
          May Swenson (poet)
Variations: **Mae** (Portuguese), **Mai, Maye**

Maya Probably a modern form of *Maia,* Greek "wet-nurse" or Latin "great, major." In Greek and Roman mythology, Maia was the mother of Hermes, or Mercury, the winged messenger god. Architect Maya Ying Lin designed the wall of names at the Vietnam Veterans Memorial in Washington, D.C.

Famous name: Maya Angelou (writer)

Maybelle (see **Mabel**)

Maye (see **May**)

Mayme (see **Mary**)

McKenzie (see **Mackenzie**)

Meagan (see **Megan**)

Meaghan (see **Megan**)

Mears (see **Mary**)

Meg (see **Margaret**)

Megan Welsh variation of **Margaret.** Galsworthy used this name for the heroine of his story *The Apple Tree.* Megan became extremely popular during the 1980s and was the sixth most popular name given to newborn American girls in 1991. The many respellings of this name are American attempts to make the name look Irish, but it is not an Irish name and has almost never been used in Ireland. The idea that it's Irish may have come from confusing it with the Irish surname *Meighan,* with which it has no connection.

Famous name: Megan Gallagher (actress)

Variations: **Maegan, Meagan, Meaghan, Meghan**

Meggi (see **Margaret**)

Meghan (see **Megan**)

Mehetabel (see **Mehitabel**)

Mehitabel Hebrew "favored of God." Even though this name is mentioned twice in the Bible, it has never been a popular name in the United States.

Variation: **Mehetabel**

Mel Variation of **Melanie.**
Famous name: Mel Harris (actress)

Melain, Melaine (see **Melanie**)

Melaina (see **Melanie**)

Melani (see **Melanie**)

Melania (see **Melanie**)

Melanie French form of *melaina,* Greek "dark, black." Melanie is the long-suffering wife of Ashley Wilkes in Margaret Mitchell's *Gone with the Wind.*
Famous names: Melanie Griffith (actress)
Melanie Safka (singer)
Nicknames: **Mel, Mellie, Melly**
Other spellings: **Melani, Melani, Melany, Melony**
Variations: **Melain, Melaina, Melaine, Melania** (Greek and Polish), **Melina**

Melany (see **Melanie**)

Melessa (see **Melissa**)

Melicent (see **Millicent**)

Melina Perhaps a form of **Carmel, Melanie,** or **Melissa.**
Famous name: Melina Mercouri (actress)

Melinda Created by 18th-century English poets, probably by blending **Belinda** and **Melissa.**
Famous name: Melinda Dillon (actress)
Variations: **Linda, Lindy, Malinda, Mindy**

Melisa (see **Melissa**)

Melisande (see **Millicent**)

Melise (see **Melissa**)

Melisenda (see **Millicent**)

Melissa Greek *melissa,* "honey bee." Melissa became extremely popular in the United States during the 1970s and was one of the top ten names for American girls born during the early

1980s. It has now started to fall out of fashion and was only the 33rd most common name given to girls born in 1991.
Famous names: Melissa Etheridge (singer)
Melissa Gilbert (actress)
Nicknames: **Lissa, Mellie, Melly, Missie, Missy**
Variations: **Melessa, Melina, Melisa** (Spanish and Polish), **Melise, Melisse** (French), **Melita, Melitta, Melleta**

Melisse (see **Melissa**)

Melita, Melitta (see **Melissa**)

Melleta (see **Melissa**)

Mellicent (see **Millicent**)

Mellie, Melly (see **Amelia, Melanie, Melissa**)

Melodie (see **Melody**)

Melody Greek *meloidia,* "choral singing."
Famous name: Melody Anderson (actress)
Other spelling: **Melodie**

Melony (see **Melanie**)

Mercedes Spanish "mercy, mercies" from Maria de Mercedes, "Mary of Mercies." This is a popular Spanish name for girls. The Mercedes Benz is named after Mercedes Jellinek, daughter of a financier of the German car company.
Famous names: Mercedes McCambridge (actress)
Mercedes Ruehle (actress)
Variation: **Mercedez**

Mercedez (see **Mercedes**)

Meredee (see **Meredith**)

Meredith Welsh *Maredudd,* "magnificent lord." Meredith is a male name in Wales, but it has been used primarily for girls in both England and the United States since the 1950s.
Famous name: Meredith Baxter-Birney (actress)
Other spelling: **Meridith**
Variations: **Meredee, Merri, Merrie, Merry**

Merete (see **Margaret**)

Merial (see **Muriel**)

Meridith (see **Meredith**)

Meriel (see **Muriel**)

Merilla (see **Muriel**)

Merl (see **Merle**)

Merla (see **Merle**)

Merle From the Latin *merula*, "blackbird." Actress Merle Oberon was born Estelle Merle O'Brian Thompson.
Other spelling: **Merl**
Variations: **Merla, Merlina, Merline, Myrle, Myrlene**

Merlina (see **Merle**)

Merline (see **Merle**)

Merna (see **Myrna**)

Merri, Merrie (see **Meredith, Merry**)

Merril (see **Muriel**)

Merrill Form of **Muriel** or an English place name meaning "merry hill." Merrill can also be used as a name for boys.
Famous name: Merrill Ashley (ballerina)
Other spelling: **Meryl**

Merry Old English *myrige*, "pleasant, merry"; also, a variation of **Meredith**.
Famous name: Merry Anders (actress)
Other spellings: **Merri, Merrie**

Mertice (see **Myrtle**)

Mertle (see **Myrtle**)

Meryl Form of **Merrill**. Actress Meryl Streep was born Mary Louise Streep, but her mother has called her Meryl since she was a small child.

Meta (see **Margaret**)

Mia Swedish form of **Maria;** also, Italian "mine." This name has only been used in the United States since the 1950s.

Famous names: Mia Dillon (actress)
Mia Farrow (actress)

Micaela (see **Michaela**)

Michael (see **Michaela**)

Michaela Feminine form of **Michael,** Hebrew "who is the Lord?" For unknown reasons, this name has been extremely common in Nebraska since around 1980 but rare in the rest of the United States. There are signs that parents in other states are starting to discover it, however.

Nicknames: **Micki, Mickie, Micky**

Variations: **Micaela, Michael, Michaele** (Italian), **Michaelina, Michaeline** (German), **Michaella** (Italian), **Michel, Michele, Michelina, Micheline, Michelle** (French), **Miguela** (Spanish), **Miguelita** (Spanish), **Mikaela, Mikelina** (Russian), **Mychal**

Michaele (see **Michaela**)

Michaelina (see **Michaela, Michele**)

Michaeline (see **Michaela**)

Michaella (see **Michaela**)

Michel (see **Michaela**)

Michele, Michelle French feminine form of **Michael,** Hebrew "who is the Lord?" Michelle was the number one name for American girls for a few years in the late 1960s. This probably had something to do with the Beatles song "Michelle," which was popular at that time. By 1991, Michelle had fallen to 34th place on the list of names given newborn girls in the United States.

Famous names: Michele Greene (actress)
Michelle Lee (actress)
Michelle Pfeiffer (actress)

Nicknames: **Micki, Mickie, Micky, Shelley, Shelli, Shellie, Shelly**

Variations: **Michaela, Michaelina, Miguela**

Michelina (see **Michaela**)

Micheline (see **Michaela**)

Micki, Mickie, Micky (see **Michaela, Michele**)

Midge (see **Margaret**)

Mignon French "sweet, cute, dainty." Mignon is not used as a given name in France, but was turned into a first name by the German poet Johann von Goethe in 1796.

Famous name: Mignon Eberhart (writer)

Variation: **Mignonette**

Mignonette (see **Mignon**)

Miguela (see **Michaela, Michele**)

Miguelita (see **Michaela**)

Mikaela (see **Michaela**)

Mikelina (see **Michaela**)

Mil (see **Mildred**)

Mila (see **Emily**)

Mildred Old English *mild* [gentle] + *thryth* [strength]. This is a very old Anglo-Saxon name, which was especially popular around 1900. In W. Somerset Maugham's novel *Of Human Bondage,* Mildred is the name of the waitress with whom the book's hero, Philip Carey, falls in love. In the movie *Mildred Pierce,* Joan Crawford played a mother obsessed with her daughter.

Famous names: Mildred Dunnock (actress)
Mildred MacAfee (World War II chief of WAVE)
Mildred Schmertz (editor)

Nicknames: **Mil, Millie, Milly**

Other spelling: **Mildrid**

Mildrid (see **Mildred**)

Milicent (see **Millicent**)

Milissent (see **Millicent**)

Milka (see **Emily**)

Milla Slavic *mil,* "grace, favor."
Famous name: Milla Jovovich (actress)

Millicent Old German *amal* [work] + *swintha* [strength].
Famous names: Millicent Fenwick (member of Congress)
Millicent Martin (singer)
Nicknames: **Millie, Milly, Missie, Missy**
Variations: **Melicent, Melisande** (French), **Melisenda** (Spanish),
Mellicent, Milicent, Milissent, Millisent, Milzie

Millie Form of **Amelia, Camilla, Emily, Mildred,** or **Millicent.**
Famous name: Millie Perkins (actress)
Other spelling: **Milly**

Millisent (see **Millicent**)

Milly (see **Amelia, Camilla, Emily, Mildred, Millicent, Millie**)

Milzie (see **Millicent**)

Mimi Form of **Miriam.** Mimi is the heroine of Puccini's opera *La Boheme.*
Famous names: Mimi Kramer (theater critic)
Mimi Rogers (actress)

Min (see **Mary, Minerva**)

Mina (see **Wilhelmina**)

Mindy (see **Melinda**)

Minerva Latin "wisdom." In Roman mythology, Minerva was the goddess of wisdom; she is the counterpart of the Greek goddess Athena.
Nicknames: **Min, Minnie, Minny**

Minna (see **Wilhelmina**)

Minnie Variation of **Minerva** or **Wilhelmina;** also, a Scottish variation of **Mary.** The best-known Minnie in history is Walt

Disney's cartoon mouse. Minnie is also the heroine of Puccini's opera *The Girl of the Golden West.*
Famous name: Minnie Maddern Fiske (actress)
Other spelling: **Minny**

Minny (see **Minnie, Minerva, Wilhelmina**)

Mira (see **Miranda, Myra**)

Miranda Latin "admirable." Miranda is Prospero's daughter in Shakespeare's *The Tempest.* This name is growing more popular in the United States, rising from 106th to 69th on the list of names given newborn American girls in just the years between 1989 and 1991.
Famous names: Miranda Richardson (actress)
　　　　　　　Miranda Spivack (writer)
Nicknames: **Randa, Randee, Randi, Randie, Randy**
Variations: **Mira, Mirella, Mirelle, Mirra, Myra, Myrilla**

Mirella (see **Miranda**)

Mirelle (see **Miranda**)

Miren (see **Mary**)

Miriam Hebrew form of **Mary.** This name is the original form of the name Mary. In the Old Testament, Miriam is a prophetess and the sister of Aaron.
Famous name: Miriam Makeba (singer)
Variations: **Mimi** (French), **Mitzi** (German)

Mirna (see **Myrna**)

Mirra (see **Miranda**)

Mirtle (see **Myrtle**)

Missie (see **Melissa, Millicent, Missy**)

Missy Form of **Melissa** or **Millicent.**
Other spelling: **Missie**

Mitzi Variation of **Miriam.**
Famous name: Mitzi Gaynor (actress)

Moina (see **Myrna**)

Moira English spelling of **Maire,** an Irish Gaelic form of **Mary.** This Irish form of Mary has become a popular name in Scotland.
Other spelling: **Moyra**

Moire (see **Mary**)

Moll (see **Mary**)

Mollie, Molly Form of **Mary.** During the Revolutionary War battle of Monmouth, Mary MacCauley carried water to exhausted and wounded colonial soldiers. In appreciation of her kindness, they renamed her Molly Pitcher. In literature, Molly Bloom is the heroine of James Joyce's *Ulysses.*
Famous name: Molly Ringwald (actress)

Mona Form of **Monica;** also, from Irish Gaelic *Muadhnait,* "noble." Some parents who name their daughters Mona believe that they are naming her for the "Mona Lisa" of Leonardo da Vinci's famous painting, but in that case, Mona is not a first name but an honorary title, a contraction of the Italian *ma donna,* "my lady."
Famous name: Mona Maris (actress)
Other spelling: **Monna**

Monca (see **Monica**)

Monica Origin uncertain; possibly from Greek *monos,* "alone," Latin "advise," or may be of North African origin. St. Monica was the mother of St. Augustine.
Famous name: Monica Vitti (actress)
Variations: **Mona, Monca** (Irish), **Monika** (German and Polish), **Monique** (French)

Monika (see **Monica**)

Monique French form of **Monica.**
Famous name: Monique Van Vooren (entertainer)

Monna (see **Mona**)

Mora (see **Maureen**)

Moreen (see **Maureen**)

Morgan Welsh, either *mor* [sea] or *mawr* [great] + *can* [bright]. In the Arthurian romances, Morgan le Fay, the queen of the

Incubi, is the half-sister of King Arthur. Their incestuous relationship led to the birth of a child, Mordred.
Famous name: Morgan Fairchild (actress)
Variation: **Morgana**

Morgana (see **Morgan**)

Moria (see **Maureen**)

Morna (see **Myrna**)

Moya (see **Mary**)

Moyra (see **Moira**)

Muire (see **Mary**)

Muireall (see **Muriel**)

Muirgheal (see **Muriel**)

Murial (see **Muriel**)

Muriel Old Celtic "sea-bright." During the 1850s, a popular novel by Dinah M. M. Craik, *John Halifax, Gentleman,* made this name very popular. Its use has declined steadily since then.
Famous names: Muriel Rukeyser (poet)
              Muriel Sparks (novelist)
Other spelling: **Murial**
Variations: **Merial, Meriel, Merilla, Merril, Merrill, Muireall** (Scottish), **Muirgheal** (Irish), **Murielle**

Murielle (see **Muriel**)

Muteteli Rwanda "dainty."

Mychal (see **Michaela**)

Myra Invented by English poet Fulke Greville in the 16th century, possibly as a variation of **Miranda.**
Famous name: Dame Myra Hess (pianist)
Other spelling: **Mira**

Myrilla (see **Miranda**)

Myrle (see **Merle**)

Myrlene (see **Merle**)

Myrna Irish Gaelic *Muirne,* "the loved one."
    Famous name: Myrna Loy (actress)
    Other spellings: **Merna, Mirna**
    Variations: **Moina, Morna**

Myrt (see **Myrtle**)

Myrta (see **Myrtle**)

Myrtia (see **Myrtle**)

Myrtice (see **Myrtle**)

Myrtis (see **Myrtle**)

Myrtle Latin *myrtilla,* "myrtle tree."
    Other spelling: **Mirtle**
    Variations: **Mertle, Mertice, Myrt, Myrta, Myrtia, Myrtice, Myrtis**

Nada (see **Nadia**)

Nadia Ukrainian form of Russian *nadezhda,* "hope."
    Famous name: Nadia Comaneci (Olympic gymnast)
    Variations: **Nada, Nadine** (French)

Nadine French variation of **Nadia.**
    Famous name: Nadine Gordimer (winner of the Nobel Prize
        for literature)

Nan Variation of **Ann, Anne, Hannah,** or **Nancy.**
    Famous name: Nan Goldin (photographer)

Nana Variation of **Anne.** In literature, Emile Zola's *Nana* is
considered a classic.
    Famous name: Nana Visitor (actress)

Nance (see **Nancy**)

Nancie, Nansie (see **Nancy**)

Nancy Variation of **Agnes, Ann,** or **Anne.** It is not exactly clear how
this name derived from Anne, but it has long been a popular
form of the name. In the 20th century, Nancy became
increasingly popular, although it now appears to be fading.
    Famous names: Nancy Kwan (actress)
               Nancy Lopez (golfer)
               Nancy Marchand (actress)
               Nancy Mitford (biographer)
               Nancy Reagan (first lady)
               Nancy Wilson (singer)

Nicknames: **Nan, Nance, Nanni, Nannie, Nanny**
Other spellings: **Nancie, Nansie**
Variation: **Nanette**

Nanette Variation of **Anne** and **Nancy.**
Famous name: Nanette Fabray (comedienne)

Nani (see **Anne**)

Nanni, Nannie, Nanny (see **Anne, Nancy**)

Naoma (see **Naomi**)

Naomi Hebrew "pleasantness." In the Bible, Naomi is the mother of Boaz and the mother-in-law of Ruth. The Puritans made this a popular name in the 17th century.
Variations: **Naoma, Noami, Noemi** (Spanish)

Nastasia (see **Anastasia**)

Nastassia (see **Anastasia**)

Nastassja (see **Anastasia**)

Nastka, Nastya (see **Anastasia**)

Nat (see **Natalie**)

Natala (see **Natalie**)

Natalia Variation of **Natalie.**
Famous name: Natalia Goncharova (painter)

Natalie French form of Latin *natale,* "birthday." This name was traditionally given to girls born on Christmas Day, but while that tradition has faded, the name continues to be popular.
Famous name: Natalie Wood (actress)
Nicknames: **Nat, Natty, Nettie**
Variations: **Natala, Natalia** (Polish, Portuguese, and Spanish), **Natalina, Nataline, Natalya, Natasha** (Russian), **Nathalia, Nathalie** (French), **Natividad** (Spanish), **Noelle** (French), **Talia**

Natalina (see **Natalie**)

Nataline (see **Natalie**)

Natalya (see **Natalie**)

Natasha Russian variation of **Natalie.** In the enduring television cartoon series *Rocky and His Friends,* Natasha is the colleague of spy Boris Badenov.
Nickname: **Tasha**

Nathalia (see **Natalie**)

Nathalie (see **Natalie**)

Natividad (see **Natalie**)

Natty (see **Natalie**)

Neda Slavic *Nedjelja,* "born on Sunday"; also, a feminine form of **Edward,** Old English "wealthy guardian."
Other spelling: **Nedda**
Variation: **Nedi**

Nedda (see **Neda**)

Nedi (see **Neda**)

Neema Swahili "born into prosperous times."

Nela (see **Nellie**)

Nelie (see **Cornelia**)

Nelina (see **Nellie**)

Nelita (see **Nellie**)

Nell Variation of **Eleanor** or **Helen.** Scottish poet Robert Burns wrote a poem to "Handsome Nell," and Charles Dickens breaks our hearts with his enduring character Little Nell in *The Old Curiosity Shop.*
Famous name: Nell Carter (singer)
Nickname: **Nellie**

Nella (see **Nellie**)

Nelle (see **Nellie**)

Nelleke (see **Cornelia**)

Nellie Variation of **Eleanor, Helen,** or **Nell.** On stage and screen,

Nellie Forbush was the popular heroine of the musical *South Pacific.* In culinary history, opera star Nellie Melba, who took her last name from Melbourne, Australia, the city where she was born, gave her name to melba toast after she was inadvertently served dry toasted bread and discovered that she enjoyed its crunchiness.

Famous names: Dame Nellie Melba (soprano)
Nellie Taylor Ross (first woman governor of a U.S. state)

Other spelling: **Nelly**

Variations: **Nela, Nelina, Nelita, Nell, Nella, Nelle**

Nelly (see **Eleanor, Nellie**)

Nessa (see **Agnes**)

Nessi, Nessie (see **Agnes**)

Nessy (see **Agnes**)

Nesta (see **Agnes**)

Nettie (see **Annette, Antoinette, Natalie**)

Netty (see **Antoinette**)

Nezka (see **Agnes**)

Nichola (see **Nicole**)

Nickie, Nicky (see **Nicole**)

Nicol (see **Nicole**)

Nicola Feminine form of **Nicholas,** Greek "victory of the people."
Variation: **Nicole**

Nicole French feminine form of **Nicholas,** Greek "victory of the people." Nicole was among the top ten names given to American girls during the 1970s and 1980s. It has now just begun to decline in popularity, slipping from eighth place to 18th on the list between 1989 and 1991.
Nicknames: **Nickie, Nicky, Nikki**
Variations: **Colette** (French), **Nichola, Nicol, Nicola** (British), **Nicolette** (French), **Nicolina** (Greek), **Nicoline**

Nicolette (see Nicole)

Nicolina (see Nicole)

Nicoline (see Nicole)

Nikki (see Nicole)

Nina Form of **Anne** or **Antonia.**
Variations: **Ninetta, Ninette** (French)

Ninetta (see **Nina**)

Ninette (see **Anne, Nina**)

Ninon (see **Anne**)

Nita (see **Anita, Juanita**)

Noami (see **Naomi**)

Noelle (see **Natalie**)

Noemi (see **Naomi**)

Nola (see **Magnolia**)

Nolie (see **Magnolia**)

Nollie (see **Olivia**)

Nora, Norah Form of **Eleanor** or **Honor.**
Famous name: Nora Ephron (writer)
Variations: **Noreen** (Irish), **Norina, Norine, Norita**

Noreen (see **Nora**)

Norina (see **Nora**)

Norine (see **Nora**)

Norita (see **Nora**)

Norma Latin *norma,* "standard" or "pattern"; or feminine form of **Norman.**

Octavia Latin "eighth." Octavia was the wife of Mark Antony, but she is not nearly as well known as his mistress, Cleopatra.
Nicknames: **Tavi, Tavy**
Variations: **Octavie** (French), **Ottavia** (Italian)

Octavie (see Octavia)

Ofelia (see Ophelia)

Oili (see Helga)

Ola (see Helga, Olga, Olivia)

Olena (see Helen)

Olenka (see Olga)

Olga Russian form of **Helga.** This is a very old Russian name, brought to Russia and the Ukraine by Scandinavian settlers in the ninth century. Olga has been much more successful than Helga outside its homeland. It has been popular in Germany, Italy, and Latin America and even has been reexported to Scandinavia where it competes in fashion with Helga, the original name.
Famous name: Olga Korbut (Olympic gymnast)
Variations: **Ola, Olenka, Ollo**

Olimpia (see Olympia)

Oliva (see Olivama, Olivia)

Olivama Spanish form of *Oholibamah,* Hebrew "my tent is in them"; in the Old Testament, one of the wives of Esau, Jacob's older brother whom Jacob tricked out of his birthright. This very rare name was used in the early 20th century within the small community of Hispanic-American Protestants.

Nicknames: **Oliva, Olive**

Olive (see **Olivama, Olivia**)

Olivette (see **Olivia**)

Olivia Italian form of Latin *oliva,* "olive tree." Shakespeare used Olivia in his play *Twelfth Night,* in which Olivia is a rich and beautiful countess. Olivia is suddenly becoming fashionable, rising from 130th to 66th on the list of names given American girls between 1989 and 1991. The character Olivia on *The Cosby Show,* played by Raven Symone, may have helped to create this new vogue for the name.

Famous names: Olivia de Havilland (actress)
　　　　　　　Olivia Hussey (actress)
　　　　　　　Olivia Newton-John (singer)

Nicknames: **Livia, Livvie, Livy, Nollie, Ollie, Olly**

Variations: **Ola, Oliva, Olive, Olivette, Olivka** (Czech)

Olivka (see **Olivia**)

Ollie, Olly (see **Olivia**)

Ollo (see **Helga, Olga**)

Olympe (see **Olympia**)

Olympia Greek "heavenly" from Mount Olympus. Olympus was the mountain home of the gods and goddess of Greek mythology. In Offenbach's popular opera *Tales from Hoffman,* Olympia is one of the heroines.

Famous names: Olympia Dukakis (actress)
　　　　　　　Olympia Snowe (politician)

Variations: **Olimpia** (Italian and Portuguese), **Olympe** (French), **Olympie** (Czech)

Olympie (see **Olympia**)

Ona (see **Anne**)

Ondine (see **Undine**)

Oona (see **Una**)

Opal Sanskrit *upala,* "gem stone." This jewel name is not often used today.

Variation: **Opaline**

Opaline (see **Opal**)

Ophelia Probably a feminine form of Greek *Ophelos,* "help." This is the name of the mad, tragic character in Shakespeare's *Hamlet.*

Variations: **Ofelia, Ophelie** (French)

Ophelie (see **Ophelia**)

Oprah This name was unknown until the 1980s when the success of actress and talk show hostess Oprah Winfrey made it a household word. She says that her parents intended to give her the biblical name **Orpah,** but when the clerk who filled out her birth certificate made a typographical error, they decided they liked the mistake better than their original choice. A few African-American parents have named their daughters Oprah since she became famous, but it is not yet a common name.

Oralie (see **Aurelia**)

Orelia (see **Aurelia**)

Oriana Perhaps a form of Latin *aurum,* "gold." The name Oriana was used by poets in verses celebrating both Queen Elizabeth I and Queen Anne of England.

Variation: **Oriane** (French)

Oriane (see **Oriana**)

Orpah Old Testament name of uncertain meaning. In the Book of Ruth, Orpah is Ruth's sister-in-law who remains in Moab when Ruth follows her mother-in-law Naomi back to Israel.

Variation: **Oprah**

Orsel (see **Ursula**)

Orsola (see **Ursula**)

Ortensia (see **Hortense**)

Ottavia (see **Octavia**)

Page, Paige Greek *pais,* "child," through Italian *paggio,* "young servant." This name became increasingly popular in the 1980s. It originally referred to a knight's attendant at court.

Paloma Spanish "dove."
Famous name: Paloma Picasso (jewelry designer)

Pam Form of **Pamela.**
Famous name: Pam Dawber (actress)

Pamela Possibly Greek *pan-meli,* "all honey." In the 18th century, Samuel Richardson's novel *Pamela or Virtue Rewarded* boosted the popularity of this name, which probably dates to at least the 16th century when Philip Sidney used the name in his novel *Arcadia.* The name was enormously popular in the 1950s. Actress Victoria Principal played the character **Pamela** Ewing on the television soap opera *Dallas.*
Famous names: Pamela Mason (actress)
                Pamela Tiffin (actress)
                Pamela Zoline (writer)
Nicknames: **Pam, Pammie, Pammy**
Variations: **Pamelia, Pamella**

Pamelia (see **Pamela**)

Pamella (see **Pamela**)

Pammie, Pammy (see **Pamela**)

Pandora Greek "all gifted" from *pan* [all, universal] + *dorus* [gift].
In Greek mythology, Pandora was the equivalent of the curious
cat. She was warned not to open a box given to her husband by
the gods, but she couldn't resist. All the troubles of the world
escaped when she opened it, although she managed to shut the
lid in time to retain the virtue hope.

Variations: **Dora, Pandoura**

Pandoura (see **Pandora**)

Paola (see **Paula**)

Paolina (see **Paula**)

Pat (see **Patricia**)

Patience Latin "patience." Like Charity and **Hope,** this is a virtue
name, which was popular in Puritan times. Sir Thomas Carew,
speaker of the British House of Commons in the 17th century,
named his four daughters Patience, Temperance, Silence, and
Prudence.

Patrice (see **Patricia**)

Patricia Feminine form of **Patrick,** Latin "member of the nobility."
Between 1925 and 1965, Patricia was one of the top ten names
for girls born in the United States, which was quite a long run
of popularity for a female name. It has been falling out of
fashion since the 1960s but is doing so rather slowly, still being
116th on the list for American girls born in 1991.

Famous names: Patricia Neal (actress)
Patricia Wettig (actress)

Nicknames: **Pat, Patsy, Patti, Pattie, Patty, Tricia, Trish,
Trisha**

Variations: **Patrice** (French), **Patrizia** (Italian)

Patrizia (see **Patricia**)

Patsy Variation of **Patricia.**
Famous name: Patsy Cline (singer)

Patti Form of **Patricia.**
Famous name: Patti LuPone (actress)

Pattie, Patty (see **Patricia**)

Paula Feminine form of **Paul,** Latin "small."
Famous names: Paula Prentiss (actress)
Paula Reingold (poet)
Nicknames: **Pauly, Polly**
Variations: **Paola** (Italian), **Paolina** (Italian), **Paule** (French), **Paulette** (French), **Paulina, Pauline** (French), **Pavla** (Russian, Czech, and Bulgarian), **Pola** (Slavic)

Paule (see **Paula**)

Paulette French variation of **Paula.**
Famous name: Paulette Goddard (actress)

Paulina Variation of **Paula.**
Famous name: Paulina Porizkova (model)
Nickname: **Lina**

Pauline French variation of **Paula.**
Famous name: Pauline Kael (movie critic)

Pauly (see **Paula**)

Pavla (see **Paula**)

Pearl Latin *perna,* "sea mussel"; Middle English *perle,* "pearl." This used to be the most popular jewel name, but it is only rarely given today.
Famous names: Pearl Bailey (singer)
Pearl S. Buck (writer)
Variations: **Pearla, Pearle, Pearline, Perla** (Spanish)

Pearla (see **Pearl**)

Pearle (see **Pearl**)

Pearline (see **Pearl**)

Peg Form of **Margaret.**
Famous name: Peg Bracken (writer)

Peggie (see **Margaret, Peggy**)

Peggy Form of **Margaret.**

> Famous names: Peggy Ashcroft (actress)
>
>   Peggy Fleming (Olympic figure skater)
>
> Other spelling: **Peggie**

Pen (see **Penelope**)

Penelopa (see **Penelope**)

Penelope Greek *penelops*, "duck." In Homer's *Odyssey*, Penelope was the wife of Odysseus, or Ulysses. A wealthy woman, she was pursued by a horde of suitors after Odysseus went off to the Trojan War, where he was believed to have been killed. To keep her suitors at bay, she promised to wed after she finished weaving a tapestry. To prevent the project from ever being completed, Penelope unraveled all her work of the day each night. Her husband finally returned from his travels after 20 years.

> Famous names: Penelope Lively (novelist)
>
>   Penelope Spheeris (movie director)
>
>   Penelope Ann Miller (actress)
>
> Nicknames: **Pen, Penny**
>
> Variation: **Penelopa** (Slavic)

Penny Variation of **Penelope.** Harry Haenigsen's comic-strip heroine Penny attempted to illuminate the problems of teenagers growing up in the middle of the 20th century.

> Famous name: Penny Marshall (movie director)

Pepita (see **Josephine**)

Perla (see **Pearl**)

Perri Female form of **Perry,** Old English "pear tree."

> Famous name: Perri Klass (writer)

Phaedra, Phaidra Greek "bright one." In Greek mythology, Phaidra, or Phaedra, was the wife of Theseus. She fell in love with her stepson and great tragedy resulted. Euripides used the story for his play *Hippolytus.*

Phebe (see **Phoebe**)

Philippa Feminine form of **Philip,** Greek "lover of horses." Philippa of Hainault was the wife of Edward III of England.

> Variations: **Felipa** (Spanish), **Filippa** (Italian), **Philippine** (French)

Philippine Variation of **Philippa.**

> Famous name: Philippine Leroy-Beaulieu (actress)

Philis, Phillis (see **Phyllis**)

Phoebe Greek *Phoibe,* "the bright one." Like Artemis, **Diana,** and **Cynthia,** Phoebe is another name associated with the moon. In Greek mythology, she was the daughter of Hyperion and Theia and the twin of Phoebus, or Apollo. Phoebe was once a very popular Christian name, although it is unusual today.

> Famous names: Phoebe Mills (gymnast)
>
> Phoebe Snow (singer)
>
> Variation: **Phebe**

Phylicia Variation of **Felicia** or **Phyllis.**

> Famous name: Phylicia Rashad (actress)

Phylida (see **Phyllis**)

Phylis (see **Phyllis**)

Phyllis Greek *phullis,* "foliage, leafy." Phyllis, the daughter of the king of Thrace, is the mythological source of the almond tree, or *philla.* She committed suicide after her lover did not return to her, and a tree grew over her grave. When he finally returned, the tree bloomed. The name has been continuously popular in England and was used in many minor novels and poems.

> Famous names: Phyllis Diller (comedienne)
>
> Phyllis Rose (writer)
>
> Phyllis Whitney (novelist)
>
> Other spellings: **Philis, Phillis, Phylis, Phyllys**
>
> Variations: **Filida** (Bulgarian and Polish), **Filisa** (Russian), **Fillide** (Italian), **Phylicia, Phylida**

Phyllys (see **Phyllis**)

Pier Perhaps a feminine form of **Peter,** Greek "rock."

> Famous name: Pier Angeli (actress)

Piper Old English "pipe player."
Famous name: Piper Laurie (actress)

Pirkko (see **Bridget**)

Piroska (see **Priscilla**)

Pola (see **Paula**)

Poll (see **Mary**)

Polly Variation of **Mary** or **Paula.** "Polly Put the Kettle On" is an
enduring children's song.
Famous names: Polly Bergen (actress)
Polly Draper (actress)

Pollyanna Combination of **Polly** and **Anne.** The heroine of Eleanor
Porter's novel *Pollyanna* was the epitome of naivete. Today,
the name is ascribed to anyone who is foolishly naive.

Porsche, Porsha (see **Portia**)

Portia Latin family name *Porcius,* "pig farmers." In Shakespeare's
The Merchant of Venice, Portia saves Antonio's life by cleverly
outwitting Shylock. Portia is becoming popular in the African-
American community, although it is now usually spelled as
Porsha or as **Porsche**, like the expensive German automobile.

Prane (see **Frances**)

Pris (see **Priscilla**)

Priscilla Latin *Priscus,* "ancient," a family name. In literature,
Henry Wadsworth Longfellow immortalized the name in "The
Courtship of Miles Standish."
Famous name: Priscilla Presley (actress)
Nicknames: **Cilla, Pris, Prissie**
Variation: **Piroska** (Hungarian)

Prissie (see **Priscilla**)

Pru (see **Prudence**)

Prudence Latin *prudentia,* "foresight, intelligence." Like other
virtue names, Prudence was popular with the Puritans.
Nicknames: **Pru, Prudy, Prue**

Prudy (see **Prudence**)

Prue (see **Prudence**)

Psyche Greek "soul." In Greek mythology, Eros, the son of the goddess of love, Aphrodite, fell in love with a mortal woman named Psyche. Aphrodite did not approve of the match, but after several failed attempts to end the relationship, she capitulated because Eros had found his true love.

Quaneesha (see **Quanisha**)

Quanesha, Quaneshia (see **Quanisha**)

Quanisha African-American creation, "Qua-" + "-nisha" from **Tanisha.** Just as **Kanisha** has become popular recently, this newly created name is also growing in use. Quanisha is now among the top 150 names given to nonwhite American girls.
Other spellings: **Quaneesha, Quanesha, Quaneshia, Quinesha**

Queen (see **Queena**)

Queena Old English *Cwen,* "a queen."
Variations: **Queen, Queenie**

Queenie (see **Queena**)

Quenta (see **Quintina**)

Quentina (see **Quintina**)

Querida Spanish "beloved."

Quinesha (see **Quanisha**)

Quinta (see **Quintina**)

Quintana Spanish "country home," Mexican place name.

Quintina Latin "fifth."
Variations: **Quenta, Quentina, Quinta**

Rachel Hebrew "ewe." In the Bible, Rachel was the wife of Jacob and the mother of many sons, including Joseph. As with many biblical names that had faded from use, this name was revived in 17th-century England by the Puritans. The name was a favorite of Sir Walter Scott, who used it in both *Waverly* and *Peveril of the Peak*. Actress Joanne Woodward played a repressed schoolteacher in the movie *Rachel, Rachel*. The name is enjoying tremendous popularity in both England and the United States today and was 13th for American girls born in 1991.

> Famous names: Rachel Carson (biologist)
> Rachel Field (author)
> Rachel Ward (actress)

> Nicknames: **Rachie, Rae, Ray**

> Variations: **Rachele** (Italian), **Rachelle**, **Rahel** (Hungarian and German), **Raquel** (Spanish)

Rachele (see **Rachel**)

Rachelle Many people assume this is the French form of **Rachel**, but it is actually an American creation blending Rachel with **Rochelle**. The actual French form of Rachel is Rachel. Rachelle was a fairly popular name between 1940 and 1970. It was still among the top 250 American names for girls in 1991.

> Nicknames: **Shelley, Shelli, Shellie, Shelly**

Rachie (see **Rachel**)

Rae Variation of **Rachel**.

> Famous name: Rae Dawn Chong (actress)

Rahel (see **Rachel**)

Raimonda (see **Ramona**)

Raina (see **Regina**)

Raine (see **Regina**)

Rajmunda (see **Ramona**)

Ramona Feminine form of **Ramon,** a Spanish form of **Raymond.**
    Variations: **Raimonda** (Italian), **Rajmunda** (Polish and
        Hungarian), **Raymonde** (French)

Ranae (see **Renee**)

Randa (see **Miranda**)

Randee (see **Miranda**)

Randi Feminine form of **Randall** or **Randolph,** Old English "shield-
    wolf"; also, a form of **Miranda.**
    Other spellings: **Randie, Randy**

Randie, Randy (see **Miranda, Randi**)

Ranee (see **Rani**)

Rani Hindu "queen."
    Variation: **Ranee**

Raquel Spanish form of **Rachel.**
    Famous name: Raquel Welch (actress)

Rasheeda Arabic "mature, rightly guided." This name is now
    regularly given by African-American parents.
    Other spelling: **Rashida**

Rashida (see **Rasheda**)

Raven Old English *hraefn,* "raven." Until recently, Raven was a
    very rare name for boys. But after **Robin** became a popular
    name for girls, some parents were inspired to give the names of
    other birds, such as Lark and Wren, to their daughters. In the
    early 1980s, the television soap opera *The Edge of Night*
    featured a character called Raven Alexander, and this

prompted the birth of a few Ravens. But the name literally exploded in popularity in the African-American community after the child actress Raven Symone began appearing as Olivia on *The Cosby Show* in the fall of 1989. Raven shot up from obscurity to become the 27th most common name given to nonwhite American girls born in 1991. A factor in the name's success with African-American parents has undoubtedly been that ravens are beautiful *black* birds.

Ray (see **Rachel**)

Raymonde (see **Ramona**)

Rea (see **Rhea**)

Reba Variation of **Rebecca**. Reeba was the mail lady on *Pee-wee's Playhouse,* a Saturday morning live-action TV show for children.

Famous name: Reba McEntire (singer)

Other spelling: **Reeba**

Rebeca, Rebecah (see **Rebecca**)

Rebecca Hebrew *Ribqah,* uncertain meaning, perhaps "heifer" or "yoke." In the Bible, Rebecca was the wife of Isaac and the mother of Jacob and Esau. Like the name **Rachel,** Rebecca became very popular among the Puritans. Rebecca is a central character in Sir Walter Scott's *Ivanhoe,* William Makepeace Thackeray's *Vanity Fair,* and Kate Douglas Wiggin's *Rebecca of Sunnybrook Farm.* In Daphne du Maurier's *Rebecca,* the haunting Rebecca is already dead when the novel begins. Rebecca was the top name being given to newborn girls in England and Wales in the early 1990s. Rebecca has also been quite popular in the United States since the 1950s and was 21st for American girls born in 1991.

Famous names: Rebecca DeMornay (actress)
                         Dame Rebecca West (novelist)

Nicknames: **Becca, Beckie, Becky, Bekki, Reba, Reeba**

Other spellings: **Rebecah, Rebeka, Rebekah**

Variations: **Rebeca** (Spanish), **Rebecka** (Swedish), **Rebekka** (German), **Revekka** (Russian), **Rivka** (modern Hebrew)

Rebecka (see **Rebecca**)

Rebeka, Rebekah, Rebekka (see **Rebecca**)

Reeba (see **Reba, Rebecca**)

Regina Latin "queen." In the 19th century, this name was
synonymous with the queen of England, referred to as Victoria
Regina. More recently, the name is associated with Regina
Giddons, the greedy wife who allows her husband to die in
Lillian Hellman's play *The Little Foxes*.

Famous name: Regina Taylor (actress)

Nickname: **Gina**

Variations: **Raina** (Belorusan), **Raine, Regine** (French), **Reina**
(Spanish), **Reine** (French), **Reinette, Reyna, Riona** (Irish
Gaelic)

Regine (see **Regina**)

Rehema Swahili "compassion."

Famous name: Rehema Stephens (basketball player)

Reina (see **Regina**)

Reine (see **Regina**)

Reinette (see **Regina**)

Rena (see **Irene, Rowena**)

Renae (see **Renee**)

Renata Latin "born again."

Famous names: Renata Adler (writer)
Renata Tebaldi (soprano)

Nicknames: **Rene, Renie, Rennie, Renny**

Variations: **Renate** (German), **Renee** (French)

Renate (see **Renata**)

Rene (see **Irene, Renata, Renee**)

Renee French form of **Renata**. Renee was a popular first name in
the United States during the 1960s. Its fashion as a first name
has now passed, but its pleasant rhythm has made Renee one
of the most common middle names for American girls.

Famous name: Renee Taylor (actress and writer)

Other spellings: **Ranae, Renae, Rene**

Renie (see Irene, Renata)

Rennie, Renny (see Renata)

Resi (see Theresa)

Revekka (see Rebecca)

Reyna (see Regina)

Rhea Greek, perhaps "earth." Rhea was one of the ancient Greek goddesses and the mother of Zeus. The name is unusual today.
Famous name: Rhea Perlman (actress)
Other spelling: **Rea**

Rho (see Rhoda)

Rhoda Greek *rhodon,* "rose." In the Bible, there is mention of a Rhoda helping St. Peter escape from prison, but the best-known Rhoda today is Rhoda Morgenstern, the character played by actress Valerie Harper in the popular comedy *The Mary Tyler Moore Show* and later on the spin-off series *Rhoda.*
Variations: **Rho, Rhodia, Rhody**

Rhodia (see Rhoda)

Rhody (see Rhoda)

Rhona (see Rona)

Rhonda Welsh, perhaps from *rhon* [lance] + *da* [good].
Famous name: Rhonda Fleming (actress)

Rica (see Frederika)

Rickey (see Ricki)

Ricki, Rickie Feminine form of **Ricky,** a short form of any name containing the Germanic syllable "ric," meaning "rule, power," such as **Erica.**
Famous names: Rickie Lee Jones (singer)
Ricki Lake (actress and talk show hostess)
Other spellings: **Rickey, Ricky, Rikki**

Ricky (see Frederika, Ricki)

Rikki (see **Erica, Ricki**)

Rina Variation of **Irene** or **Katherine;** also, Hebrew "song."

Riona (see **Regina**)

Rise Origin unknown.
Famous name: Rise Stevens (opera singer)

Rita Form of **Margarita,** Spanish form of **Margaret.**
Famous names: Rita Mae Brown (writer)
Rita Dove (poet laureate of the United States)
Rita Hayworth (actress)
Rita Moreno (actress)
Rita Tushingham (actress)

Rivka (see **Rebecca**)

Robbie, Robby (see **Roberta**)

Roberta Feminine form of **Robert,** Old English "shining in fame."
The popular tune "Smoke Gets in Your Eyes" is from Jerome
Kern's musical *Roberta.*
Famous names: Roberta Flack (singer)
Roberta Maxwell (actress)
Roberta Peters (opera singer)
Nicknames: **Bobbi, Bobbie, Bobby, Robbie, Robby**
Variations: **Roberte** (French), **Robertina** (Dutch and
Hungarian), **Robin, Robina, Robine** (French), **Robinett,
Robinette, Robinia, Ruperta** (German)

Roberte (see **Roberta**)

Robertina (see **Roberta**)

Robin Variation of **Robert** or **Roberta.** Robin was especially popular
as a name for girls in the 1960s. There are now many more
women than men named Robin, but, unlike most formerly
male names that become common for girls, Robin has never
completely died out as a name for boys.
Famous names: Robin Duke (comedienne)
Robin Morgan (poet)
Other spelling: **Robyn**

Robina (see **Roberta**)

Robine (see **Roberta**)

Robinett, Robinette (see **Roberta**)

Robinia (see **Roberta**)

Robyn Form of **Robin**. This spelling is almost always feminine.
Famous name: Robyn Lively (actress)

Rochella (see **Rochelle**)

Rochelle French "little rock."
Nicknames: **Shelley, Shelli, Shellie, Shelly**
Variations: **Rochella, Rochette**

Rochette (see **Rochelle**)

Romaine French feminine form of **Roman.**
Famous name: Romaine Brooks (painter)

Rona Feminine form of **Ronald;** or from Rona, the name of one of the islands in the Hebrides off Scotland.
Famous name: Rona Barrett (columnist)
Other spelling: **Rhona**

Ronnie Feminine form of **Ronald** or form of **Veronica.**
Other spelling: **Ronny**

Ronny (see **Ronnie, Veronica**)

Rora (see **Aurora**)

Ros (see **Rosalind**)

Rosa Latin form of **Rose**. Rosa Parks is considered the mother of the civil rights movement in the United States. Her refusal to move to the back of a bus initiated a bus strike in Montgomery, Alabama, that eventually led to far-reaching social change.
Famous names: Rosa Bonheur (painter)
Rosa Mota (marathoner)

Rosabel, Rosebelle (see **Rose**)

Rosabella (see **Rose**)

Rosaleen (see **Rosalind, Rose**)

Rosalia Variation of **Rose**; also, Latin "festival of roses."
> Variations: **Rosalie** (French), **Roselie, Rozalie, Rozele** (Lithuanian)

Rosalie (see **Rosalia**)

Rosalind Old German *hros* [horse] and *lind* [tender, soft]; reinterpreted in medieval times as Latin *rosa linda,* "pretty rose." The English poet Edmund Spenser revived this name, and Shakespeare made it popular with his play *As You Like It.*
> Famous names: Rosalind Cartwright (psychologist, dream expert)
> Rosalind Russell (actress)
> Rosalind Solomon (photographer)
> Variations: **Ros, Rosaleen, Rosalinda, Rosaline, Rosalyn, Roselin, Roslyn, Roslynd, Roz, Rozalin**

Rosalinda (see **Rosalind**)

Rosaline (see **Rosalind, Rosalyn, Rose**)

Rosalyn Variation of **Rosalind** or **Rose**.
> Famous name: Rosalyn Yallow (physicist)
> Other spelling: **Rosaline**

Rosamund Old Germanic *hros* [horse] + *mund* [protection].

Rosana, Rosanna Forms of **Rosanne**.
> Famous name: Rosanna Arquette (actress)

Rosanne Combination of **Rose** and **Anne**. This name is well known today, thanks to comedienne and actress Roseanne Arnold and to singer Rosanne Cash, not to mention the character Rosanne Rosannadanna that Gilda Radner created on the television show *Saturday Night Live.*
> Variations: **Rosana, Rosanna, Roseann, Roseanne**

Rose English form of *rosa,* Latin "rose"; or Old German *Hrodohaidis,* "famous kind." The Germanic form was probably the original version of this name, but its similarity to the word *rose,* often considered the most beautiful flower in the world, greatly increased its popularity. Rose was the first flower name

used in Europe and probably inspired the many others that
came later. St. Rose of Lima was the first person born in the
New World to be canonized by the Roman Catholic church.
Rose was very popular around 1900, but it's not often chosen
today.

Famous names: Rose Kennedy (mother of John F. Kennedy,
                   35th president of the United States)
                   Rose Mofford (governor)

Nicknames: **Rosi, Rosie, Rosy**

Variations: **Rosa** (Dutch, Italian, Latin, Spanish, and Swedish),
    Rosabel, Rosabella, Rosabelle, Rosaleen (Irish), **Rosalia**
    (Italian), **Rosaline, Rosalyn, Rosel** (Swiss), **Rosella,**
    Roselle, Rosena, Rosetta (Italian), **Rosette, Rosina**
    (Italian), **Rosine, Rosita** (Spanish), **Rozina, Rozy**

Roseann, Roseanne (see **Rosanne**)

Rosel (see **Rose**)

Roselie (see **Rosalia**)

Roselin (see **Rosalind**)

Rosella (see **Rose**)

Roselle (see **Rose**)

Rosemarie Combination of **Rose** and **Marie.**

Rosemary Combination of **Rose** and **Mary.** The herb rosemary is
the symbol of remembrance, but today the name is
unfortunately associated with the horror movie *Rosemary's
Baby,* in which Rosemary, played by actress Mia Farrow, gives
birth to a child of the devil.

Famous names: Rosemary Clooney (singer)
                   Rosemary Harris (actress)

Rosemin Combination of **Rose** and **Mina.**

Rosena (see **Rose**)

Rosetta, Rosette (see **Rose**)

Rosi, Rosie (see **Rose**)

Rosina (see **Rose**)

Rosine (see **Rose**)

Rosita (see **Rose**)

Roslyn, Roslynd (see **Rosalind**)

Rosy (see **Rose**)

Rowe (see **Rowena**)

Rowena Perhaps Old English *hrod* [fame] + *wynn* [joy]. Sir Walter Scott immortalized this name in *Ivanhoe*.
  Famous name: Rowena Morrill (painter and illustrator)
  Nickname: **Rowe**
  Variation: **Rena**

Rox (see **Roxanne**)

Roxana, Roxanna (see **Roxanne**)

Roxane, Roxann (see **Roxanne**)

Roxanne Persian *Raokhshna*, "dawn" or "brilliant." Roxana was the Persian wife of Alexander the Great. Roxanne is the heroine of *Cyrano de Bergerac* by Edmond Rostand, and she got top billing in a movie based on the story. Comedian Steve Martin played a modern-day Cyrano, a firefighter with an extremely long nose, who fell in love with actress Daryl Hannah in the movie *Roxanne*.
  Famous name: Roxanne Kuter Williamson (architectural historian)
  Nicknames: **Rox, Roxie, Roxy**
  Other spellings: **Roxane, Roxann**
  Variations: **Roxana, Roxanna, Roxene, Roxine**

Roxene (see **Roxanne**)

Roxie, Roxy (see **Roxanne**)

Roxine (see **Roxanne**)

Roz Variation of **Rosalind.**
  Famous name: Roz Kelly (actress)

Rozalie (see **Rosalia**)

Rozalin (see **Rosalind**)

Rozele (see **Rosalia**)

Rozina (see **Rose**)

Rozy (see **Rose**)

Rubia (see **Ruby**)

Ruby Latin *rubinus lapis,* "red stone."
    Famous names: Ruby Dee (actress)
                    Ruby Keeler (actress and dancer)
    Variations: **Rubia, Rubye**

Rubye (see **Ruby**)

Rue Name of a flowering herb (see **Ruta**) or a form of **Ruth.**
    Famous name: Rue McClanahan (actress)

Ruperta (see **Roberta**)

Rut (see **Ruth**)

Ruta Lithuanian *ruta,* "rue," a medicinal herb with yellow blossoms
    that is considered the national flower of Lithuania.
    Famous name: Ruta Lee (actress)
    Variation: **Rue**

Ruth Hebrew, perhaps "companion." In the Bible, Ruth is the
    daughter-in-law of Naomi, and their story is the ideal of
    devotion. Ruth adopts the religion and customs of her
    husband's family, and after his death, she follows her mother-
    in-law to Naomi's home country.
    Famous names: Ruth Benedict (anthropologist)
                    Ruth Fainlight (poet)
                    Ruth Gordon (actress)
                    Ruth Rendell (mystery writer)
    Nicknames: **Rue, Ruthie**
    Variation: **Rut** (Spanish, Polish, and Scandinavian)

Ruthie (see **Ruth**)

Ryta (see **Margaret**)

Saara (see Sarah)

Saartje (see Sarah)

Sabina Latin "of the Sabines." St. Sabina was a first-century
Christian martyr. The name is unusual today.
Famous name: Sabina Spielrein (psychoanalyst)
Nickname: **Bina**
Variations: **Sabine** (French and German), **Saidhbhin** (Irish
Gaelic), **Savina, Savyna** (Ukrainian)

Sabine (see Sabina)

Sabrina Name of the legendary goddess of the Severn River in
England. In the movie *Sabrina,* actress Audrey Hepburn is a
chauffeur's daughter who is romanced by Humphrey Bogart, a
middle-aged tycoon, and by William Holden, Bogart's playboy
brother. The movie is based on a popular play *Sabrina Fair* by
Samuel Taylor.
Famous name: Sabrina LeBeauf (actress)
Variation: **Zabrina**

Sada (see Sadie)

Sadie Form of **Sarah.**
Variations: **Sada, Sadye**

Sadye (see Sarah, Sadie)

Saidhbhin (see Sabina)

Sal (see Sarah)

Salima (see **Salome**)

Sallie (see **Sally, Sarah**)

Sally Form of **Sarah.** No fictional Sally is as memorable as Sally Bowles, the creation of Christopher Isherwood in *The Berlin Stories.* She became well known when the book was made into a movie, *I Am a Camera,* with Julie Harris; a long-running Broadway musical, *Cabaret;* and then the film of the musical in which Liza Minnelli gained fame as the delightfully decadent Sally.

Famous names: Sally Field (actress)
Sally Kellerman (actress)
Sally Kirkland (singer)
Sally Mann (photographer)
Sally Ride (astronaut)

Other spelling: **Sallie**

Salma Swahili "safe."

Saloma (see **Salome**)

Salome Hebrew *shalom,* "peace." In the New Testament, Salome was the daughter of Herodias and the stepdaughter of Herod Antipas. Before she would dance for her stepfather's guests, she demanded the head of John the Baptist. Not surprisingly, this name has never enjoyed vast popularity.

Famous name: Salome Jens (actress)

Variations: **Salima** (Arabic), **Saloma, Salomea** (Polish), **Salomi, Selima** (Turkish), **Selma** (German and Scandinavian)

Salomea, Salomi (see **Salome**)

Sam (see **Samantha**)

Samantha A colonial American creation, probably combining **Sam** with "-antha," the feminine form of Greek *anthos,* "flower." This was an unusual name until actress Elizabeth Montgomery played the witch-who-would-be-a-housewife on the television comedy *Bewitched.* Plagued by her mother, Endora, for not exercising her magic, Samantha also has to contend with her husband's distaste for her ability to twitch her nose and right all wrongs. In 1991, Samantha was the seventh most popular name given to American girls.

Famous name: Samantha Eggar (actress)
Nicknames: **Sam, Samanthy, Sami, Sammi**

Samanthy (see **Samantha**)

Sami, Sammi (see **Samantha**)

Sandi, Sandie (see **Alexandra, Cassandra, Sandy**)

Sandra Form of **Alexandra** or **Cassandra**. This variation is now an independent name and was very popular in the 1950s and 1960s.
Famous names: Sandra Day O'Connor (U.S. Supreme Court justice)
Sandra Dee (actress)
Nickname: **Sandy**

Sandy Form of **Alexandra, Cassandra**, or **Sandra.**
Famous names: Sandy Dennis (actress)
Sandy Duncan (actress)
Other spellings: **Sandi, Sandie**

Sanna (see **Susan**)

Sanura Swahili "civet cat."

Sara Form of **Sarah.**
Famous names: Sara Paretsky (novelist)
Sara Teasdale (poet)

Sarah Hebrew "princess." In the Old Testament, Sarah was the wife of Abraham and the mother of Isaac. Her name is one of the first examples of a name change commanded by God. She had been called Sarai. Sarah was a very popular English name by the 17th century when the name almost became associated with nobility. Sarah Jennings married John Churchill, later duke of Marlborough. She was a close friend of Anne Stewart, who became Queen Anne. The court was so jealous of the duchess of Marlborough and her influence on the queen that "Queen Sarah" became a common slur used against her. Queen Anne later became disillusioned with the Churchills, and they were banished from the court. In the 19th century, actress Sarah Bernhardt reigned on the stage, as had the English tragic actress Sarah Kemble Siddons before her. The name is very popular today.

Famous names: Sarah Brightman (soprano)
  Sarah Miles (actress)
Variations: **Saara** (Finnish and Estonian), **Saartje** (Dutch),
  Sadie, Sadye, Sal, Sallie, Sally, Sara, Sari (Hungarian),
  Sarina (Dutch), **Sarita** (Spanish), **Sarra** (Russian), **Sassa**
  (Swedish), **Shari, Zadee, Zara, Zarah**

Sari (see Sarah)

Sarina (see Sarah)

Sarita (see Sarah)

Sarra (see Sarah)

Sasha Form of **Alexandra.** This is a popular nickname in Russia.

Sassa (see Sarah)

Savana, Savanna (see Savannah)

Savannah From Taino (Caribbean Native American) *zabana,*
  "meadow," later given as a name to the river and city in
  Georgia. Savannah has been steadily increasing in popularity
  as a name for girls in the United States, probably because its
  sound is similar to other more popular names such as
  Samantha and **Hannah.**
  Variations: **Savana, Savanna, Vanna**

Savina (see Sabina)

Savyna (see Sabina)

Scarlett English "deep red." Before Scarlett O'Hara, the heroine of
  Margaret Mitchell's novel *Gone With the Wind,* no girls were
  named Scarlett, but now the name appears occasionally.

Schura (see Susan)

Sean Variation of **John,** Hebrew "the Lord is favored." Sean is a
  very common name for boys in the United States, but it's also
  been used as a name for girls on rare occasions since the 1940s.
  Famous name: Sean Young (actress)
  Variation: **Shawn**

Searlait (see Charlotte)

Secunda Latin "the second." This is a traditional name for a second daughter.

Sela (see **Selena**)

Selena Greek "the moon."
>Variations: **Celena, Celina, Sela, Selene, Selie, Selina, Selinda, Sena**

Selene (see **Selena**)

Selie (see **Selena**)

Selima (see **Salome**)

Selina (see **Selena**)

Selinda (see **Selena**)

Selma Possibly a form of Norse *Anselm,* "divine helmut," or a German and Scandinavian form of **Salome.**
>Variation: **Zelma**

Sena (see **Selena**)

Seonaid (see **Janet**)

Seosaimhin (see **Josephine**)

Septima Latin "the seventh."
>Famous name: Septima Poinsette Clark (civil rights activist)

Serafina (see **Seraphina**)

Seraphina Latin form of Hebrew *seraphim,* "burning ones." In the celestial hierarchy, seraphs, or seraphim, are the highest ranked of the nine types of angels. St. Seraphina was a 15th-century saint. The name is extremely unusual today.
>Variations: **Serafina, Seraphine**

Seraphine (see **Seraphina**)

Shaina Yiddish "beautiful."
>Famous name: Shana Alexander (writer)
>Variations: **Shana, Shanna, Shayna**

Shana (see **Shaina, Shanna, Shannon**)

Shanae African-American creation, blend of the fashionable prefix "Sha-" with the sound of **Renee.** Shanae has been rapidly increasing in use; in 1991, it was the 69th most common name given to nonwhite American girls, which made it exactly 250th on the overall American popularity chart.
Other spellings: **Shanay, Shanaye**

Shanay, Shanaye (see **Shanae**)

Shaneequa, Shanequa, Shanikwa (see **Shaniqua**)

Shaneice (see **Shanice**)

Shanice African-American creation, blend of "Sha-" + "-n-" + "-ice." Shanice had a very sudden burst of great popularity in the African-American community in 1989 and 1990 after singer Shanice Wilson (who now prefers to be known as just Shanice) won top prize on the television talent contest *Star Search.* However, the name is now losing some of this popularity.
Other spellings: **Shaneice, Shaniece, Shanise**

Shaniece (see **Shanice**)

Shaniqua African-American creation, "Sha-" + "-n-" + "-iqua." "Sha-" has now replaced "La-" as the most popular prefix for newly created African-American names for girls, and Shaniqua is the one such creation that is enjoying the biggest boom in use. In 1991, Shaniqua was the 25th most common name given to newborn nonwhite girls in the United States. Other fashionable "Sha-" names include **Shanae, Shanice,** Shanika, Shameka, and Shatara.
Other spellings: **Shaneequa, Shanequa, Shanikwa**

Shanise (see **Shanice**)

Shanna Variation of **Shaina** or **Shannon.**
Other spellings: **Shana, Shannah**

Shannah (see **Shanna**)

Shannon Name of an Irish river, Celtic "the ancient god." Shannon was a popular American name during the 1970s and 1980s.
Famous names: Shannon Garst (author)
                  Shannon Miller (Olympic gymnast)
Variations: **Shana, Shanna**

Shantal (see **Chantal**)

Shantel, Shantell, Shantelle (see **Chantel**)

Shara (see **Sharon**)

Shari Form of **Sharon** or **Sherry**; also, an Americanized spelling of *Sari,* Hungarian variation of **Sarah.**
Famous names: Shari Belafonte (actress)
Shari Lewis (puppeteer)

Sharleen, Sharlene (see **Charlene**)

Sharline (see **Charlene**)

Sharon Hebrew "a plain," usually a place name. Sharon is a plain in western Palestine that was famous for its fertility. In his novel *The Grapes of Wrath,* John Steinbeck ironically named an abandoned pregnant girl Rose of Sharon in reference to a verse from the Song of Solomon describing the plain. Although Sharon was a very popular name between 1940 and 1950, it is now fading away very quickly.
Famous names: Sharon Gless (actress)
Sharon Olds (writer)
Sharon Stone (actress)
Nicknames: **Shari, Sherri, Sherrie, Sherry**
Variations: **Shara, Sharona**

Sharona (see **Sharon**)

Sharyl (see **Cheryl**)

Shauna (see **Shawna**)

Shawn (see **Sean**)

Shawna Feminine form of **Sean** or **Shawn.**
Other spelling: **Shauna**

Shayla (see **Sheila**)

Shayna (see **Shaina**)

Sheba (see **Bathsheba**)

Sheela (see **Sheila**)

Sheelagh (see **Sheila**)

Sheelah (see Sheila)

Sheena Scottish form of **Jane.**
Famous name: Sheena Easton (singer)
Variations: **Sheenagh, Shena, Sine** (Gaelic)

Sheenagh (see Sheena)

Sheila Irish Gaelic form of **Cecilia.**
Famous name: Sheila Graham (writer)
Other spellings: **Sheela, Sheelagh, Sheilah, Shela, Shelagh**
Variations: **Shayla, Sheelah, Sile** (Gaelic)

Sheilah (see Sheila)

Shela (see Sheila)

Shelagh (see Sheila)

Shelbey, Shelbi, Shelbie (see Shelby)

Shelby English place name, perhaps meaning "village on a ledge"
or "willow village." This British surname has long been used
as a first name for boys in the American South and has
sometimes been given to Southern girls at least since 1930.
But only after Julia Roberts played a character called Shelby
in the film *Steel Magnolias* did the name become popular all
over the country. Its similarity in sound to **Shelley, Chelsea,**
and **Kelsey** probably recommended it to parents looking for
the proverbial "different but not *too* different" name. Shelby
soared from 182nd place to 30th place on the list of names
given newborn American girls between 1989 and 1991, and it
has a good chance of making the top ten list soon.
Other spellings: **Shelbey, Shelbi, Shelbie**

Shelley Old English *Selleg,* "clearing on a ledge," a place name;
also, a variation of **Michele, Rachelle,** or **Rochelle.** Because the
name of the poet Percy Bysshe Shelley is so well known, this
name is always associated with him to some degree.
Famous names: Shelley Duvall (actress)
Shelley Hack (actress)
Shelley Long (actress)
Shelley Winters (actress)
Other spellings: **Shelli, Shellie, Shelly**

Shelli, Shellie, Shelly (see **Michele, Rachelle, Rochelle, Shelley**)

Shena (see **Sheena**)

Sher (see **Sherry**)

Sheree, Sheri (see **Sherry**)

Sherie (see **Sherry**)

Sheril (see **Sheryl**)

Sherilyn Modern blend of **Sherry** and **Marilyn.**
   Famous name: Sherilyn Fenn (actress)

Sherri, Sherrie (see **Sharon, Sherry**)

Sherrill (see **Sheryl**)

Sherry Variation of **Cheryl** and **Sharon.** The wine takes its name
   from the town of Xeres, Spain, which was named for Caesar,
   but this name for girls is probably influenced not by the sweet
   wine as much as by the well-known French love word, *cherie.*
   Famous names: Sherry Lansing (movie executive)
                         Sheree North (actress)
   Other spellings: **Shari, Sher, Sheree, Sheri, Sherie, Sherri,
                         Sherrie, Sherye**

Sherryl (see **Cheryl**)

Sherye (see **Sherry**)

Sheryl Form of **Cheryl.**
   Other spellings: **Sheril, Sherrill, Sheryll**

Sheryll (see **Sheryl**)

Shianne (see **Cheyenne**)

Shirl (see **Shirley**)

Shirlee (see **Shirley**)

Shirleen, Shirlene (see **Shirley**)

Shirley Old English *Scirleah,* "bright forest clearing," a place name. Charlotte Bronte first used this name for a girl in her novel *Shirley,* but the name was already a common surname. Because of the fame of Shirley Temple, this name was fantastically popular during the 1930s and 1940s, but it's not often given today.

Famous names: Shirley Booth (actress)
Shirley Chisholm (member of Congress)
Shirley Knight (actress)
Shirley MacLaine (actress)

Other spellings: **Shirlee, Shirlie**
Variations: **Shirl, Shirleen, Shirlene**

Shirlie (see **Shirley**)

Shontel, Shontell, Shontelle (see **Chantel**)

Shoshana (see **Susan**)

Shoshi (see **Susan**)

Shyann, Shyanne (see **Cheyenne**)

Sian (see **Jane**)

Sibelle (see **Sybil**)

Sibil (see **Sybil**)

Sibilla, Sibille (see **Sybil**)

Sibyl, Sibyll (see **Sybil**)

Sibylla (see **Sybil**)

Sibylle (see **Sybil**)

Sidsel (see **Cecilia**)

Sierra Spanish "saw-toothed mountain range." Sierra has been used as a first name in the United States since about 1970. It is now most popular in the African-American community, probably because its sound fits in with other popular African-American names such as **Kierra** and **Tierra.** Sierra's popularity may also be linked to Sierra Esteban, a character on the long-running daytime soap opera *As the World Turns.* Although this character was presented as having roots in Central America, Sierra is not used as a given name in Spanish-speaking countries.

Signe Old Norse *sigr* [victory] + *ny* [new].
> Famous name: Signe Wilkinson (cartoonist)
> Variation: **Signy**

Signy (see **Signe**)

Sigourney Origin unknown, but perhaps related to French surname *Seigneury,* "senior tenant." Actress Sigourney Weaver changed her first name from Susan as a teenager after finding a male character named Sigourney while reading F. Scott Fitzgerald's *The Great Gatsby.* Fitzgerald was probably thinking of the 19th-century religious poet Lydia Huntley Sigourney when he named the character.

Sile (see **Cecilia, Sheila**)

Sileas (see **Cecilia**)

Silva (see **Sylvia**)

Silvia (see **Sylvia**)

Simona (see **Simone**)

Simone French feminine form of **Simon,** Hebrew "he heard."
> Famous names: Simone de Beauvier (writer)
> Simone Signoret (actress)
> Variations: **Simona, Simonette, Simonia, Ximena** (Spanish)

Simonette (see **Simone**)

Simonia (see **Simone**)

Sindy (see **Cindy**)

Sine (see **Jane, Sheena**)

Sinead (see **Janet**)

Siobhan Irish Gaelic form of **Joan.**
> Famous name: Siobhan McKenna (actress)

Sisi Fante "born on Sunday."

Sissel (see **Cecilia**)

Sissie (see **Cecilia, Sissy**)

Sissy Form of **Cecilia** or a nickname from "sister."
Famous name: Sissy Spacek (actress)
Other spelling: **Sissie**

Siubhan (see **Joan**)

Siusaidh, Siusan (see **Susan**)

Siwan (see **Joan**)

Sochil (see **Xochitl**)

Sofia (see **Sophia**)

Sofie (see **Sophia, Sophie**)

Soleil French "sun, sunshine."

Sommer (see **Summer**)

Sondra Form of **Alexandra**.
Famous name: Sondra Locke (actress)

Sonia Russian form of **Sophia**. Sonya is the heroine of Fyodor
Dostoyevsky's novel *Crime and Punishment*.
Famous names: Sonia Braga (actress)
Sonja Frissell (opera director)
Sonia Johnson (feminist activist)
Sonia Rykiel (fashion designer)
Other spellings: **Sonja, Sonya**

Sonja, Sonya (see **Sonia, Sophia**)

Sophia Greek "wisdom." St. Sophia was a third-century Christian
saint remembered for her three martyred daughters: Faith,
Hope, and Charity. The mosque at Constantinople, built by
Constantine the Great in 325, is dedicated to St. Sophia. The
name was widely used among Ottoman royalty and appears to
have traveled to Europe first through Austria. In the 17th
century, when the house of Hanover inherited the English

throne, the name became popular in England. Sophia Western is the heroine of Henry Fielding's novel *Tom Jones,* and Sophia Primrose is the heroine of Oliver Goldsmith's *The Vicar of Wakefield.*

Famous name: Sophia Loren (actress)

Nicknames: **Sophie, Sophy**

Variations: **Sofia** (Swedish), **Sofie** (Danish, Dutch, and German), **Sonia, Sonja** (Danish and Slavic), **Sonya** (Russian), **Sophie** (French), **Zofia** (Polish), **Zosia** (Polish)

Sophie Variation of **Sophia.** Actress Bette Midler got her start in show business borrowing Sophie Tucker's jokes and voice, so it's no surprise that she honored her mentor by naming her daughter Sophie.

Other spellings: **Sofie, Sophy**

Sophy (see **Sophia, Sophie**)

Sosana (see **Susan**)

Stacey Form of **Anastasia** or **Eustacia.** Stacey was an extremely fashionable name between about 1965 and 1985. It has now started to rapidly decline. In 1991, it fell below the top 100 names for girls born in the United States for the first time in over two decades.

Other spellings: **Stacie, Stacy**

Stacia (see **Eustacia**)

Stacie, Stacy (see **Anastasia, Eustacia, Stacey**)

Stefania (see **Stephanie**)

Stefanida (see **Stephanie**)

Stefanie, Stefanny (see **Stephanie**)

Steffi, Steffie, Steffy (see **Stephanie**)

Stella Latin "star," variation of **Estelle.** This name has plummeted in popularity because of its theatrical associations. In the movie *Stella Dallas,* the heroine was the epitome of the lower-class social climber, while in Tennessee Williams's *A Streetcar Named Desire,* the character Stella Kowalski, who is married to the lout Stanley, symbolizes how the romance and beauty of

the past can be overwhelmed by a crude but vital modern man.
Famous names: Stella Adler (dancer)
Stella Stevens (actress)

Stepana (see **Stephanie**)

Stephania (see **Stephanie**)

Stephanie French feminine form of **Stephen,** Greek "crown." This
name has been extremely popular since the 1970s and was a top
ten name for American girls throughout the 1980s.
Famous names: Stephanie Powers (actress)
Stephanie Zimbalist (actress)
Nicknames: **Steffi, Steffie, Steffy, Stevie**
Variations: **Stefania** (Polish, Swedish, and Italian), **Stefanida**
(Russian), **Stefanie, Stefanny** (Danish and Norwegian),
Stepana (Czech), **Stephania, Stevanka** (Serbian), **Stevena,
Tiennette** (French)

Stevanka (see **Stephanie**)

Stevena (see **Stephanie**)

Stevie Variation of **Stephanie.**
Famous name: Stevie Smith (poet)

Stina (see **Christina**)

Sue Variation of **Susan.**
Famous name: Sue Grafton (writer)

Sukey, Suki, Sukie (see **Susan**)

Sula (see **Ursula**)

Summer Old English *sumar,* "summer." The name of this season
has been steadily growing as a name for girls, but as yet the
number of Summers blooming in the United States is only
about half of the harvest of American girls named **Autumn.**
Famous name: Summer Sanders (Olympic swimmer)
Other spelling: **Sommer**

Susa (see **Susan**)

Susan English form of Hebrew *shushannah,* "lily." Although the story of Susanna and the Elders is a part of the Apocrypha and excluded from the Protestant Bible, it remains a popular Christian story. Susanna was falsely accused of infidelity and was saved by Daniel, who demonstrated that her accusers had given conflicting testimonies. Feminists sometimes choose this name to honor Susan B. Anthony, the women's rights advocate.

Famous names: Susan Hayward (actress)
Susan Isaacs (novelist)
Susan Sarandon (actress)
Susan Sontag (writer)

Nicknames: **Sue, Sukey, Suki, Sukie, Susie, Suzie, Suzy**

Variations: **Sanna** (Finnish), **Schura** (Russian), **Shoshana** (Hebrew), **Shoshi** (Israeli), **Siusaidh** (Scots Gaelic), **Siusan** (Scots Gaelic), **Sosana** (Rumanian), **Susa** (Italian and German), **Susana** (Spanish and Portuguese), **Susanna** (Italian and Russian), **Susannah, Susanne** (German), **Suse** (German), **Susetta** (Italian), **Suzana** (Rumanian, Bulgarian, and Croatian), **Suzanna, Suzannah, Suzanne** (French), **Suzette** (French), **Suzon** (French), **Zosel** (German), **Zsa Zsa** (Hungarian), **Zuzana** (Czech), **Zuzanna** (Polish), **Zuzi** (Swiss), **Zuzu**

Susana (see **Susan**)

Susanna Biblical form of **Susan.**
Other spelling: **Susannah**

Susannah (see **Susan, Susanna**)

Susanne (see **Susan**)

Suse (see **Susan**)

Susetta (see **Susan**)

Susie (see **Susan**)

Suzana (see **Susan**)

Suzanna, Suzannah (see **Susan**)

Suzanne Variation of **Susan.**
Famous names: Suzanne Pleshette (actress)
Suzanne Vega (singer)

Suzette (see **Susan**)

Suzie (see **Susan**)

Suzon (see **Susan**)

Suzy (see **Susan**)

Sybil Greek *Sybilla,* "a woman prophet."
　　Famous name: Dame Sybil Thorndike (actress)
　　Other spellings: **Cybil, Sibil, Sibille, Sibyl, Sibyll**
　　Variations: **Sibelle, Sibilla** (Italian), **Sibylla** (Dutch and
　　　　Swedish), **Sibylle** (German), **Sybilla** (Polish), **Sybille**
　　　　(French)

Sybilla (see **Sybil**)

Sybille Variation of **Sybil**.
　　Famous name: Sybille Pearson (playwright)

Sydney Feminine form of **Sidney,** Old English *sidenieg,* "wide, well-
　　watered land." Although Sydney has on rare occasions been
　　given to girls for a couple of centuries, only within the last few
　　years has it become fashionable. The name rose from 193rd to
　　101st on the list of names given American girls between 1989
　　and 1991.
　　Other spellings: **Cydney, Cydnie**

Sylva (see **Sylvia**)

Sylvia Perhaps Latin *silva,* "wood." In Roman mythology, Rhea
　　Silvia was the mother of Romulus and Remus, the founders of
　　Rome.
　　Famous name: Sylvia Plath (poet)
　　Other spelling: **Silvia**
　　Variations: **Silva** (Bulgarian), **Sylva, Sylvie** (French), **Sylwia**
　　　　(Polish), **Zilvia**

Sylvie (see **Sylvia**)

Sylwia (see **Sylvia**)

Tabbi, Tabbie, Tabby (see **Tabitha**)

Tabita (see **Tabitha**)

Tabitha Greek "gazelle." In the Book of Acts in the New Testament, Tabitha, who was also known as Dorcas, is mentioned. Both names mean gazelle. More recently, Tabitha was the daughter of Samantha on the popular television comedy *Bewitched.*
Famous name: Tabitha King (novelist)
Variations: **Tabita** (Spanish and Polish)**, Tabbi, Tabbie, Tabby**

Tahnee Actress Tahnee Welch claims that her name is from a Lakota (Native American) word for "desirable." Although this is still a rare name, her fans are starting to name their daughters Tahnee.

Talia Usually a form of **Natalia;** also, Spanish form of Greek *Thalia,* "plentiful," and modern Israeli name from Hebrew *tal,* "dew."
Famous name: Talia Shire (actress)

Tam (see **Tamara**)

Tamar Hebrew "palm tree." There are three women named Tamar in the Old Testament.
Variation: **Tamara** (Russian)

Tamara Russian form of **Tamar,** much more popular in English-speaking countries than the original biblical form. Tamara was among the top 200 names given American girls in 1991.

Famous name: Tamara Asseyev (movie producer)
Nicknames: **Tam, Tammie, Tammy**

Tameika, Tameka, Tamica (see **Tamika**)

Tamika African-American form of *Tamiko,* Japanese *tami* [people]
+ *-ko* [feminine suffix]. This name was probably introduced to
the United States by the 1962 film *A Girl Named Tamiko.* It
was a very common name with African-American parents
during the 1970s and 1980s, but its popularity has now begun
to fade.
Variations: **Tameika, Tameka, Tamica, Tamiko, Tomika**

Tamiko (see **Tamika**)

Tammie (see **Tamara, Tammy**)

Tammy Form of **Tamara** or *Tamsin,* British feminine form of
Thomas. This name became popular in the 1950s because of the
movie *Tammy and the Bachelor,* in which actress Debbie
Reynolds played a country woman in love with an urban man.
Famous names: Tammy Amerson (actress)
Tammy Grimes (actress)
Other spelling: **Tammie**

Taneisha (see **Tanisha**)

Tanesha, Taneshia (see **Tanisha**)

Tania (see **Tanya**)

Taniesha (see **Tanisha**)

Tanisha Origin unknown, but possibly an African-American form
of *Tani,* a Hausa (northern Nigeria) name meaning "born on
Monday." Tanisha has been very popular with African-
American parents since the actress Ta-Tanisha appeared on the
television series *Room 222* during the early 1970s.
Other spellings: **Taneisha, Tanesha, Taneshia, Taniesha,
Tanishia, Tenecia, Teneisha, Tenesha, Teniesha, Tenisha,
Tinisha**

Tanishia (see **Tanisha**)

Tanja (see **Tanya**)

524 / Girls

Tanya Russian short form of **Tatiana.** Tanya is one of several Russian names, such as **Alisa, Olga,** and **Sasha,** that have emigrated to the United States. It was the name that Patty Hearst took during her captivity by the Symbionese Liberation Army.

Famous names: Tanya Berezin (movie director)
Tanya Roberts (actress)
Tanya Tucker (singer)

Other spellings: **Tania, Tanja** (German), **Tonya**

Tara Gaelic "crag, high prominent rock"; or form of Latin *terra,* "earth." Tara was among the top 50 names for American girls in the late 1970s and early 1980s, but its fashion is now fading.

Famous name: Tara O'Connor (musician)

Other spellings: **Tarah, Tera, Terra**

Tarah (see **Tara**)

Tasha (see **Natasha**)

Tatiana Feminine form of *Tatius,* Latin name of unknown meaning. Tatiana is popular in Greece, Russia, and Latin America.

Variation: **Tanya**

Tavi, Tavy (see **Octavia**)

Taylor Old French *tailleur,* "tailor." When Janet Miriam Taylor Caldwell wrote her first novel in 1938, she used Taylor Caldwell as her pen name because she thought her book would be more successful if people thought it had been written by a man. Ironically, she soon became so celebrated as an author of best-sellers that she no longer needed to hide her sex, and the American public came to think of Taylor as being an appropriate name for a woman. Since 1985, this name has rapidly increased in fashion for both boys and girls and along with **Jordan** has become a popular "unisex" name for the 1990s. Taylor was the 36th most popular name given to girls born in the United States by 1991, and about six girls were being named Taylor to every five boys who were receiving the name.

Teddi, Teddie, Teddy (see **Theodora**)

Teena, Teenie (see **Tina**)

Tenecia (see **Tanisha**)

Teneisha, Tenesha (see **Tanisha**)

Teniesha, Tenisha (see **Tanisha**)

Teodora (see **Theodora**)

Tera (see **Tara, Theresa**)

Teresa Variation of **Theresa.**
Famous name: Teresa Wright (actress)

Terese (see **Theresa**)

Teresia (see **Theresa**)

Teresina (see **Theresa**)

Teresita (see **Theresa**)

Teressa (see **Theresa**)

Terez, Tereza (see **Theresa**)

Terezia, Terezie (see **Theresa**)

Teri (see **Terri**)

Terka (see **Theresa**)

Terra (see **Tara**)

Terri Feminine form of the male name **Terry** or a variation of
Theresa.
Other spellings: **Teri, Terrie, Terry**

Terrie, Terry (see **Terri, Theresa**)

Tess Form of **Tessa** or **Theresa.** Thomas Hardy's *Tess of the
D'Urbervilles* presents one of the saddest heroines in literature,
so it's not surprising that this name isn't widely imitated.
Famous name: Tess Harper (actress)

Tessa Form of **Theresa** or of Italian *contessa,* "countess."
Variations: **Tess, Tessi, Tessie, Tessy**

Tessi, Tessie, Tessy (see **Tessa, Theresa**)

Thandiwe Xhosa (South Africa) "a loving person."

Thea Greek "goddess."
Famous name: Thea Astley (author)

Theda Form of German *theod,* "people, race"; or form of Greek *Theodosia,* "divinely given." No one knows whether silent-screen star Theda Bara, born Theodosia Goodman, was aware that her name was an anagram for "Arab death."

Thelma Possibly Greek *thelema,* "wish, will." This name sounds so old that it seems as if it should date to at least the Middle Ages, but it doesn't. Thelma is the 19th-century literary invention of Marie Corelli for *Thelma, a Norwegian Princess.*
Famous names: Thelma Houston (singer)
Thelma Ritter (actress)

Thena (see **Athena**)

Theodora Feminine form of **Theodore,** Greek "gift of God." The sixth-century Byzantine empress Theodora was the wife of Justinian the Great. Theodora has always been a rare name in English-speaking countries.
Nicknames: **Teddi, Teddie, Teddy**
Variations: **Fedora** (Czech, Slovakian, and Ukrainian), **Feodora** (Russian), **Teodora** (Italian and Spanish), **Todora** (Bulgarian)

Theresa Origin unknown, possibly "woman from Therasia," ancient name for two small Mediterranean islands. This name's Spanish heritage dates to at least the sixth century, but its popular use in other countries dates to the 16th-century Carmelite nun St. Theresa of Avila, the first woman to be declared an official theologian of the Roman Catholic church. This name was especially popular in the United States during the 1960s.
Famous names: Theresa Russell (actress)
Theresa Saldana (journalist)
Nicknames: **Terri, Terrie, Terry**
Other spelling: **Teresa**
Variations: **Resi** (German), **Tera, Terese** (Lithuanian), **Teresia** (Swedish), **Teresina** (Italian), **Teresita** (Spanish), **Teressa,**

Terez (Hungarian), Tereza (Rumanian and Portuguese), Terezia (Hungarian), Terezie (Czech), Terka (Bulgarian and Hungarian), Tess, Tessa, Tessi, Tessie, Tessy, Therese (French), Theresia (German), Toireasa (Irish Gaelic), Tracy, Trexa (Basque)

Therese (see **Theresa**)

Theresia (see **Theresa**)

Tiara Latin "headdress, jeweled coronet" from Greek word for "turban." Tiara has become quite common as a name for African-American girls since 1980. It's an interesting example of a modern jewel name, where the reference is to a kind of jewelry rather than to an individual gemstone as in **Diamond, Amber,** or **Ruby.**
Variations: **Tiarra, Tierra**

Tiarra (see **Tiara**)

Ticia (see **Letitia**)

Tiennette (see **Stephanie**)

Tierra Spanish "earth" or "land." This name, which has recently gained popularity in the African-American community, probably developed as a blend of the sounds of **Tiara** and **Sierra.**

Tifany (see **Tiffany**)

Tiff (see **Tiffany**)

Tiffany Greek *Theophania,* "God appears." Tiffany was common in the Middle Ages, when it was often given to children born on Epiphany, January 6. The 1961 film *Breakfast at Tiffany's* reintroduced the name to American parents and associated it with the famous jewelry store in New York City. By 1980, Tiffany was a popular name with all Americans and was the top name for African-American girls. It then began an inevitable decline in fashion, but Tiffany was still the 27th most common name for American girls born in 1991.
Famous names: Tiffany Darwish (singer)
　　　　　　　　Tiffany Chin (Olympic skater)
Nicknames: **Tiff, Tiffie, Tiffy**
Other spellings: **Tifany, Tiffeny, Tyffany**

Tiffeny (see **Tiffany**)

Tiffie, Tiffy (see **Tiffany**)

Timmie, Timmy (see **Timothea**)

Timothea Feminine form of **Timothy,** Greek "honor God."
Nicknames: **Timmie, Timmy**

Tina Form of names ending in "-tina," including **Christina** and
Martina.
Famous names: Tina La Blanc (dancer)
Tina Louise (actress)
Variations: **Teena, Teenie, Tiny**

Tinisha (see **Tanisha**)

Tiny (see **Tina**)

Tish (see **Letitia**)

Tisha, Titia (see **Letitia**)

Todora (see **Theodora**)

Toireasa (see **Theresa**)

Tomika (see **Tamika**)

Toni Variation of **Antoinette** and **Antonia.** African-American
novelist Toni Morrison won the Nobel Prize for literature
in 1993.
Other spellings: **Tonie, Tony**

Tonia (see **Antonia**)

Tonie, Tony (see **Antoinette, Antonia, Toni**)

Tonya (see **Antonia, Tanya**)

Tori (see **Victoria**)

Tovah Hebrew "good," a common name for girls in modern Israel.
Famous name: Tovah Feldshuh (actress)

Toya (see **Victoria**)

Tracey, Traci, Tracie (see **Tracy**)

Tracy Variation of **Theresa**. Tracy Samantha Lord was played by Katharine Hepburn in the movie *The Philadelphia Story* and by Grace Kelly in the musical version *High Society*. Tracy was the fifth most popular name for girls born in 1970, but America's infatuation with the name quickly evaporated during the 1980s. Tracy was no longer among the top 150 names for girls in 1991.
Famous names: Tracy Austin (tennis player)
Tracy Chapman (singer)
Other spellings: **Tracey, Traci, Tracie**

Trexa (see **Theresa**)

Tricia (see **Patricia**)

Trina (see **Katrina**)

Trine (see **Katherine**)

Trish Variation of **Patricia**.
Famous name: Trish Van DeVere (actress)

Trisha (see **Patricia**)

Trissie (see **Beatrice**)

Trix (see **Beatrice**)

Trixie Variation of **Beatrice**.
Other spelling: **Trixy**

Trixy (see **Beatrice, Trixie**)

Truda, Trude (see **Gertrude**)

Trudi, Trudie (see **Gertrude, Trudy**)

Trudy Variation of **Gertrude**.
Other spellings: **Trudi, Trudie**

Twyla Origin unknown, but perhaps originally a Louisiana Cajun name from the French word *etoile*, "star."
Famous name: Twyla Tharp (choreographer)

Tyffany (see **Tiffany**)

Tyne Celtic *Tina*, "flowing," the name of an English river.
Famous name: Tyne Daly (actress)

Uilani Hawaiian "youthful heavenly child." The syllable "lani" in native Hawaiian names means "heaven" or "heavenly" and also had connotations of royalty. Many names for girls still commonly used by native Hawaiian parents today end in this syllable. Other examples include **Leilani,** Kanoelani ("the heavenly mist"), and Pualani ("heavenly flower").

Ulla (see **Ursula**)

Uma Sanskrit "flax" or "turmeric." In the Upanishads, Uma is a goddess who mediates between the high god, Brahma, and the lesser gods. She is considered the personification of speech.
   Famous name: Uma Thurman (actress)

Umayma Swahili "young mother."

Una Latin "one"; also, possibly Irish Gaelic *uan,* "lamb." This name was very common in medieval Ireland. In the first book of Spenser's *The Faerie Queene,* the heroine Una symbolizes truth.
   Famous names: Oona O'Neill Chaplin (actress)
                 Una Merkel (actress)
   Other spelling: **Oona**

Undine English form of *undina,* "water sprite," from Latin *unda,* "wave." This word was coined in 1658 by the Swiss alchemist Paracelsus while he was writing in Latin about the magical female water spirits featured in Germanic myths. In German, these beautiful but dangerous creatures are called *Nixen.*
   Variation: **Ondine** (French)

Urbi Benin (Nigeria) "princess."

Ursa (see Ursula)

Ursel (see Ursula)

Ursie (see Ursula)

Urska (see Ursula)

Ursley (see Ursula)

Ursula Latin *ursa,* "female bear." The legend of St. Ursula was responsible for this name traditionally being the most popular European name for girls beginning with "U." Ursula was the daughter of a British noble who put a high price on her hand in marriage: a three-year pilgrimage accompanied by anywhere from 11 to 11,000 virgins (the number varies depending on the source) and enough ships to carry the group. It is said that a suitor complied and that Ursula and the virgins made their way toward Rome, but they met with Huns at Cologne and were slaughtered after refusing to submit. The story of St. Ursula may be disputed, but a church in Cologne has a stone inscribed to the saint, who is considered the patron of young women. Ursula was a fairly popular name in 17th-century England, but it has been rare in all English-speaking countries since 1750.
Famous name: Ursula Andress (actress)
Ursula LeGuin (writer)
Nicknames: **Sula, Ursa, Ursie, Ursy**
Variations: **Orsel** (Dutch), **Orsola** (Italian), **Ulla** (German), **Ursel** (Dutch and German), **Urska** (Croatian and Slovenian), **Ursley, Ursulina** (Spanish), **Uschi** (German)

Ursulina (see Ursula)

Ursy (see Ursula)

Uschi (see Ursula)

Uzuri An ancient Basque name, perhaps a form of *Uzu,* "valiant, indomitable."

Val (see **Valentina, Valerie**)

Valaree (see **Valerie**)

Valarie (see **Valerie**)

Valencia Spanish place name based on *Valens,* a Roman given name from Latin *valere,* "to be strong." Valencia is regularly used as a first name in the southeastern United States.

Valentia (see **Valentina**)

Valentina Feminine form of **Valentine,** Latin "healthy, strong." In June 1963, cosmonaut Valentina V. Tereshkova of the former Soviet Union became the first woman in space.
Variations: **Val, Valentia, Valentine** (French and Norwegian), **Valja** (Estonian), **Vallatina** (Dutch)

Valentine (see **Valentina**)

Valera (see **Valerie**)

Valeria (see **Valerie**)

Valerie French feminine form of *Valerius,* Roman family name probably from Latin *valere,* "to be strong." This French name became very popular in England around 1930. In the 1940s, Valerie crossed the Atlantic and became a popular American name during the 1950s and 1960s. Its fashion is slowly fading today, but it was still among the top 200 American names for girls in 1991.
Famous names: Valerie Bertinelli (actress)
                Valerie Harper (actress)
                Valerie Perrine (actress)

Nickname: **Val**

Other spellings: **Valaree, Valarie, Valery, Valoree, Valorie**

Variations: **Valera** (Bulgarian), **Valeria** (Italian, Spanish, Portuguese, and Hungarian), **Valora, Walli** (German)

Valery (see **Valerie**)

Valja (see **Valentina**)

Vallatina (see **Valentina**)

Valora (see **Valerie**)

Valoree, Valorie (see **Valerie**)

Van (see **Vanessa**)

Vanda (see **Wanda**)

Vanesa (see **Vanessa**)

Vanessa This name was invented in 1713 by Irish author Jonathan Swift for one of the title characters in his long poem *Cadenus and Vanessa*. The name honors his friend Esther Vanhomrigh. The "Van-" comes from her surname, and "Essa" is a nickname for Esther. A century later, a genus of butterflies was named after the character in the poem. Samuel Barber, who claimed he got the name from a book of babies' names, won a Pulitzer Prize for his opera *Vanessa*. Vanessa has been a fairly popular name in the United States since the 1970s and has been especially popular with Hispanic-Americans, being one of the top ten names for girls in that community since about 1980. This is because of a Spanish-language television series called *Vanessa* that starred Lucia Mendez, one of Mexico's favorite actresses, in the title role.

Famous names: Vanessa Bell (painter)
Vanessa Redgrave (actress)

Nicknames: **Van, Vanna, Vanny**

Other spellings: **Vanesa, Venessa**

Vanna Possibly a form of **Savannah** or **Vanessa**.

Famous name: Vanna White (TV game show hostess)

Vanny (see **Vanessa**)

Vanora (see **Guinevere**)

Vanya (see **Jane**)

Varenka (see **Barbara**)

Varina Meaning unknown. Varina was the name of the Virginia plantation where British settler John Rolfe lived with his Native American bride, Pocahontas, after their wedding in 1614. In the early 18th century, romantic Southerners began naming their daughters Varina. The wife of Jefferson Davis, Varina Davis, was the first lady of the Confederate States of America.

Varu (see **Barbara**)

Varvara, Varya (see **Barbara**)

Vashti Persian "beautiful one."

Veatriks (see **Beatrice**)

Veda Sanskrit "knowledge."

Velinda (see **Belinda**)

Velma Probably an American form of **Wilhelmina.** Velma Banky was Rudolph Valentino's leading lady in many silent-screen romances.

Velvet Middle English from Latin *velvetum,* "a soft fabric." The 1945 movie *National Velvet,* based on Enid Bagnold's sentimental novel about a young horsewoman, starred Elizabeth Taylor.

Venessa (see **Vanessa**)

Vera Russian "faith," or Latin *verus,* "true"; also, a form of **Verena.** Famous name: Vera Frankle (reporter)

Vere (see **Verena**)

Verena Name of a third-century Swiss saint, uncertain meaning, but perhaps from Latin *vereri,* "fearful, shy."
Variations: **Vera, Vere, Verene** (French), **Verina, Verine**

Verene (see **Verena**)

Verina (see **Verena**)

Verine (see **Verena**)

Verity English form of Latin *veritas,* "truth." Verity became a name for girls during Puritan times. It is still used in England but is now almost nonexistent in the United States.

Vernarda (see **Bernadette**)

Veronica Variation of **Bernice,** Greek "bringer of victory"; probably modified in ancient times to resemble Latin *vera icon,* "true image." According to legend, St. Veronica wiped the brow of Jesus as he carried his cross to Calvary. The imprint of his face was miraculously imprinted on the cloth.
Famous names: Veronica Hamel (actress)
Veronica Lake (actress)
Nicknames: **Ronnie, Ronny, Vonnie, Vonny**
Variations: **Veronika, Veronike** (German), **Veronique** (French)

Veronika (see **Veronica**)

Veronike (see **Veronica**)

Veronique (see **Veronica**)

Vesta Latin form of **Hestia.** Vesta was the Roman goddess of the hearth in whose temple a perpetual flame was kept burning by priestesses known as Vestal Virgins.
Famous names: Vesta (blues singer)
Vesta Tilley (vaudevillian)

Vi (see **Violet**)

Vianca (see **Bianca**)

Viatrix (see **Beatrice**)

Vic (see **Victoria**)

Vicki Form of **Victoria.**
Famous name: Vicki Lawrence (actress)

Vickie, Vicky (see **Victoria**)

Victoire (see **Victoria**)

Victoria Feminine form of **Victor,** Latin "conqueror." St. Victoria was a third-century martyr, and the name became very popular in Italy in the form of **Vittoria.** But not until Alexandrina Victoria, daughter of Edward, duke of Kent, and Princess Victoire of Saxe-Coburg-Saalfeld, was crowned queen of England that the name became known in the British Isles. Like Queen Elizabeth I, Queen Victoria's name is given to a historic period because of the long duration of her reign during a time when Great Britain was very powerful. Although she held the title of empress of India, Queen Victoria did not enjoy the sovereignty of Elizabeth I because most of the power of the government had already passed to Parliament. But Victoria was honored throughout the British Empire with the names of many places, including Lake Victoria in Africa and a state in Australia. In the late 1980s, Victoria began to become more popular in the United States and was among the top 50 names given American girls by 1991.

Famous names: Victoria de los Angeles (soprano)
Victoria Jackson (comedienne)
Victoria Principal (actress)

Nicknames: **Vic, Vicki, Vickie, Vicky, Vik, Vikkie, Vikky, Vita**

Variations: **Tori, Toya** (Mexican), **Victoire** (French), **Victorine** (French), **Vikte** (Lithuanian), **Viktoria** (German and Swedish), **Vitoria** (Portuguese), **Vittoria** (Italian)

Victorine (see **Victoria**)

Vida Feminine form of **David,** Hebrew "beloved."

Vijole (see **Violet**)

Vik (see **Victoria**)

Vikkie, Vikky (see **Victoria**)

Vikte (see **Victoria**)

Viktoria (see **Victoria**)

Vilhelmina (see **Wilhelmina**)

Vilma (see **Wilhelmina, Wilma**)

Vinnie, Vinny (see **Lavinia**)

Viola Variation of **Violet.** Viola is the heroine of Shakespeare's *Twelfth Night.*
Famous name: Viola Dana (actress)

Violante (see **Violet**)

Violet Latin *viola,* "violet." Although not as popular as **Rose,** this flower name has enjoyed considerable popularity, particularly in the late 19th century when names of flowers and jewels were favored.
Famous names: Violet Kemble Cooper (actress)
　　　　　　　Violet Heming (actress)
　　　　　　　Violet Weingarten (screenwriter)
Nickname: **Vi**
Variations: **Fialka** (Czech), **Iolanthe, Vijole** (Lithuanian), **Viola, Violante** (Spanish), **Violeta** (Spanish), **Violete, Violetta** (Italian), **Violette** (French), **Viorica** (Rumanian), **Wioletta** (Polish), **Yolanda**

Violeta, Violetta (see **Violet**)

Violete, Violette (see **Violet**)

Viorica (see **Violet**)

Vira (see **Elvira**)

Virga (see **Virginia**)

Virginia Feminine form of *Verginius,* name of a Roman family of unknown meaning, but reinterpreted in ancient times as meaning "virginlike." In North America, the colony Virginia was named by Sir Walter Raleigh in honor of Elizabeth I, the Virgin Queen. The first British child born in America was named Virginia Dare in the queen's honor. Virginia was quite popular in the United States from 1870 through 1950, but was hardly used in Britain until the 1960s.
Famous names: Virginia Mayo (actress)
　　　　　　　Virginia Wade (tennis player)
　　　　　　　Virginia Woolf (novelist)
Nicknames: **Gigi** (French), **Ginger, Ginnie, Ginny**
Variations: **Virga** (Estonian), **Virginie** (Dutch and French)

Virginie French form of **Virginia.** In the early 1980s, Virginie was one of the top ten names given newborn girls in France.

Virita (see **Elvira**)

Vita Latin *vita,* "life," or form of **Victoria.**

Vitoria, Vittoria (see **Victoria**)

Viv (see **Vivian**)

Viveca Swedish form of Germanic *Wigburg,* "war-fortress."
Famous name: Viveca Lindfors (actress)
Other spelling: **Viveka, Vivica**

Viveka (see **Viveca**)

Vivian From the Latin *vivus,* "alive." Vivian is the relatively new
spelling of the ancient name **Viviana.** In the Arthurian legend,
she was the enchantress who lured Merlin.
Famous names: Vivien Leigh (actress)
　　　　　　　Vivian Vance (comedienne)
Nicknames: **Viv, Vivie**
Other spellings: **Viviane, Vivien, Vyvian**
Variations: **Bibi** (Swedish), **Viviana** (Italian), **Vivienne** (French)

Viviana (see **Vivian**)

Viviane (see **Vivian**)

Vivica (see **Viveca**)

Vivie (see **Vivian**)

Vivien, Vivienne (see **Vivian**)

Vonnie, Vonny (see **Veronica, Yvonne**)

Vrijida (see **Bridget**)

Vyvian (see **Vivian**)

Walli (see **Valerie**)

Wallie, Wally (see **Wallis**)

Wallis Old English "person from Wales."
Famous name: Wallis Simpson (duchess of Windsor)
Nicknames: **Wallie, Wally**

Wanda Slavic name of uncertain meaning, perhaps a Polish form of
Wend, name of a Slavic people living in eastern Germany.
Famous names: Wanda Hendrix (actress)
Wanda Landowska (harpsichordist)
Variations: **Vanda, Wandy, Wenda**

Wandy (see **Wanda**)

Wenda (see **Wanda, Wendy**)

Wendi, Wendie (see **Wendy**)

Wendy Created by Sir James Barrie from the baby-talk word
"friendy-wendy" for a character in his play *Peter Pan.* The
fictional Wendy Darling was probably the first girl to have this
name. Wendy was a fairly popular name in the United States
between 1950 and 1975, but it had fallen below the top 300
names for newborn American girls by 1991.
Famous names: Dame Wendy Hiller (actress)
Wendy Turnbull (tennis player)
Wendy Wasserstein (playwright)
Wendy Waldman (singer/songwriter)
Variations: **Wenda, Wendi, Wendie**

Wenonah (see **Winona**)

Whitney Old English "white island." This name, which had been a surname and then a masculine name, had a sudden boom in popularity as a name for girls of all ethnic groups during the 1980s after singer Whitney Houston became famous. By 1991, however, use of the name Whitney seemed to be falling off almost as quickly as it had risen a few years before.

Famous name: Whitney Blake (actress)

Other spellings: **Whitni, Whitnie, Whittany**

Whitni, Whitnie, Whittany (see **Whitney**)

Whoopi Form of English *Whoopee!*, a shout of joy, ultimately from Old English *hwopan,* "to threaten." Caryn Johnson chose to rename herself Whoopi Goldberg when she became a stand-up comic. Because the name was obviously picked to create a bizarre comic image, it's not surprising that parents have avoided giving it to their daughters.

Wilhelma (see **Wilhelmina**)

Wilhelmina Feminine form of **William,** Old German *wil helm.* Although formerly popular in Germany, Wilhelmina has always been an unusual name in England and the United States.

Nicknames: **Billie, Billy, Minnie, Minny, Willa, Willie, Willy**

Variations: **Guglielma** (Italian), **Guillemette** (French), **Guillerma** (Spanish), **Helma, Helmine** (German), **Mina** (German), **Minna** (German), **Velma, Vilhelmina** (Swedish), **Vilma** (Estonian), **Wilhelma, Wilhelmine** (German), **Willamena, Willamina, Willemine** (Dutch), **Willetta, Willette, Wilma, Wilmette**

Wilhelmine (see **Wilhelmina**)

Willa Form of **Wilhelmina.**

Famous name: Willa Cather (writer)

Willamena, Willamina (see **Wilhelmina**)

Willemine (see **Wilhelmina**)

Willetta, Willette (see **Wilhelmina**)

Willie Form of **Wilhelmina.**
   Famous name: Willie Mae Ford Smith (singer)
   Other spelling: **Willy**

Willy (see **Wilhelmina, Willie**)

Wilma Form of **Wilhelmina.**
   Famous name: Wilma Rudolph (athlete)
   Variation: **Vilma** (Czech and Hungarian)

Wilmette (see **Wilhelmina**)

Win (see **Winifred**)

Winifred Welsh *Gwenfrewi,* probably "blessed reconciliation," but
   altered through confusion with the Old English male name
   Winfred from *wine* [friend] or *wynn* [joy] and *frith* [peace]. St.
   Winifred was a seventh-century Welsh woman who was
   martyred because she refused to marry a prince.
   Famous names: Winifred Lenihan (actress)
                  Winifred Shaw (singer and actress)
   Nicknames: **Freda, Freddie, Freddy, Win, Winnie, Winny,**
      Wynne
   Other spelling: **Winnifred**

Winnie, Winny Form of **Winifred.**
   Famous name: Winnie Mandela (civil rights activist)

Winnifred (see **Winifred**)

Winona Siouan "first-born daughter." This Native American name
   was popularized in the United States during the 19th century
   by several poets, especially Henry Wadsworth Longfellow, who
   used the variation **Wenonah** as the name of Hiawatha's mother
   in his famous 1855 poem *The Song of Hiawatha.*
   Famous name: Winona Ryder (actress)
   Variations: **Wenonah, Wynonna**

Wioletta (see **Violet**)

Wynne (see **Winifred**)

Wynonna Form of **Winona.**
   Famous name: Wynonna Judd (country singer)

Xanthe Feminine form of Greek *xanthus,* "yellow, bright."

Xenia Greek "hospitality."
Variation: **Zenia**

Ximena Medieval Spanish form of **Simone.** In Corneille's *Le Cid,* the woman who marries the Cid is named Ximena.

Xochil (see **Xochitl**)

Xochitl Nahuatl (Aztec) *xochitl,* "flower," a Native American word that has become a well-used name in Mexico and is sometimes found in Mexican-American families. The Aztec word was pronounced "show-cheat'l," but modern Spanish uses "so-cheel."
Other spellings: **Sochil, Xochil, Zochil**

Yasmin Arabic form of **Jasmine.** In the early 1990s, this name was somewhat popular with African-American and Hispanic-American parents.

Other spelling: **Yasmine**

Yasmine Form of **Jasmine** or **Yasmin.** This is the name of the daughter of Rita Hayworth and the Aga Khan.

Yehudit (see **Judith**)

Yekaterina Russian form of **Katherine.** Yekaterina Gordeyeva won a gold medal in pairs figure skating at the 1988 Winter Olympics.

Yelena (see **Helen**)

Yelizaveta (see **Elizabeth**)

Yesenia Origin unknown. This name became extremely popular in the 1980s in the Hispanic-American community due to its being the name of a Cinderella-like character on a popular Spanish-language television serial. It does not occur in any of the available Spanish-language dictionaries of first names, but it was in use in Peru by 1965 and may have a Latin American literary origin.

Other spelling: **Yessenia**

Yessenia (see **Yesenia**)

Yetta (see **Henrietta**)

Ynes, Ynez (see **Agnes**)

Yoko Japanese *yo* [positive] + *-ko* [female].
Famous name: Yoko Ono (musician and artist)

Yolanda English form of a medieval French name of unknown origin, perhaps an obscure Germanic name blended with a Greek form of **Violet.** Yolanda was extremely popular with African-American parents during the 1970s because of the publicity given Yolanda King, eldest daughter of Martin Luther King, Jr., and Coretta Scott King. Interestingly, neither Martin nor Coretta became popular names for African-American children, but their child inspired thousands of namesakes.
Variations: **Iolanda, Iolande, Yolande** (French), **Yolanta, Yolanthe**

Yolande (see **Yolanda**)

Yolanta, Yolanthe (see **Yolanda**)

Ysabel (see **Elizabeth, Isabel**)

Yseult (see **Isolde**)

Ysonde (see **Isolde**)

Yvette Form of **Yvonne.**
Famous name: Yvette Mimieux (actress)

Yvonne Feminine form of **Yvon,** French form of Germanic *iv,* "yew."
Famous name: Yvonne De Carlo (actress)
Other spelling: **Evonne**
Variations: **Ivonne** (French), **Vonnie, Vonny, Yvette**

Zabrina (see **Sabrina**)

Zadee (see **Sarah**)

Zakelina (see **Jacqueline**)

Zandra (see **Alexandra**)

Zaneta (see **Jeannette**)

Zanna (see **Jane**)

Zara, Zarah (see **Sarah**)

Zelda Form of **Griselda.**
   Famous name: Zelda Fitzgerald (writer)

Zelia Origin unknown; perhaps a form of **Celia** or a modern
   creation based on the word *zeal.*
   Famous name: Zelia Nuttall (archaeologist)

Zelma Variation of **Selma.** This unusual name might be better
   known if actress Kathryn Grayson had kept the name her
   parents gave her, Zelma Hedrick.

Zenia (see **Xenia**)

Zillah Hebrew *zillah,* "shadow." In the Bible, Zillah is the mother
   of Tubal-Cain, the blacksmith.

Zilvia (see **Sylvia**)

Zina Swahili "beauty," occasionally chosen by African-American

parents; also, form of *Zinaida,* Russian feminine form of Greek *Zenais,* "follower of Zeus," the name of two first-century martyrs revered by the Orthodox church.
Famous name: Zina Garrison (tennis player)

Zochil (see **Xochitl**)

Zoe Greek "life." This name was used in Alexandria, Egypt, to translate the Biblical name Eve. Zoe has been one of the top 40 names for girls born in England and Wales since 1975, and it may finally be about to become fashionable in the United States, where it jumped from 498th to 288th on the list of names given American girls between 1990 and 1991.
Famous names: Zoe Akins (playwright)
Zoe Caldwell (actress)

Zofia (see **Sophia**)

Zora (see **Aurora**)

Zosel (see **Susan**)

Zosia (see **Sophia**)

Zsa Zsa Hungarian form of **Susan.**
Famous name: Zsa Zsa Gabor (actress)

Zula (see **Zuleika**)

Zuleika Variation of Arabic *Zulaikha,* "amazingly beautiful." A novel by Max Beerbohm, *Zuleika Dobson,* made this name familiar in England, but Byron had also used the name in *The Bride of Abydos.*
Variation: **Zula**

Zuwena Swahili "small and beautiful."

Zuzana (see **Susan**)

Zuzanna (see **Susan**)

Zuzi, Zuzu (see **Susan**)